Lookin
can be taxing or ough...

So let us take care of
the finance for you.

As a busy member of the clergy you have enough to
do without having to worry about your tax affairs.

TMC is here to help. We were established to provide a tax
management service to the clergy and are now one of the
largest such specialist advisers in the UK. Our team travels
around the country to our regional venues so that we can
discuss, face-to-face, your individual needs with:

General tax advice | **Completion of tax returns**
Tax credits | **Payroll administration** | **Property accounts**
Student advice | **Annual Diocesan return**

tax management
for clergy

Call us on 01476 539000

Email: enquiries@clergytaxuk.com Visit: www.clergytaxuk.com

PO BOX 6621 Grantham Lincolnshire NG32 3SX

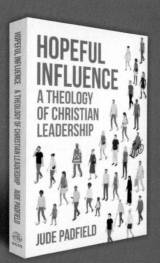

Connecting Sunday worship with everyday faith

Varied resources for worship to encourage faithful living in the week ahead

Help children and young people to connect the Bible with their everyday lives

Brand new resources each week to inspire leaders and nurture faith at home

Find out more at
www.rootsontheweb.com/discover

The ROOTS partnership The **Methodist** Church   The United Reformed Church **CHRISTIAN** *education* churches together

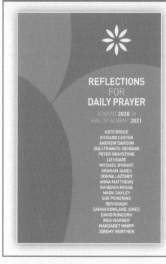

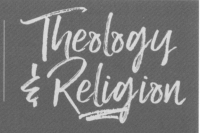

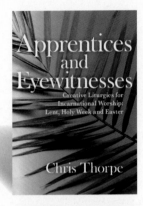
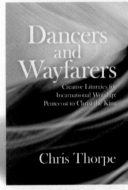
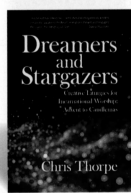

Could you be their Chaplain?

As an RAF chaplain you'll be involved in the lives of our personnel, regardless of their rank or religious background. Your personal sacrifice may be considerable as you'll serve with our people wherever they go, providing vital spiritual, pastoral and ethical support in places of conflict, including on the front-line. Your home-based duties will be equally important, in support of personnel and their families.

A whole new congregation awaits you.

Contact the Branch Recruiting Officer now:
philip.wilson126@mod.gov.uk

The Royal Air Force values every individual's unique contribution, irrespective of race, ethnic origin, religion, gender, sexual orientation or social background.

The
Canterbury Preacher's
Companion 2021

Sermons for Sundays, Holy Days,
Festivals and Special Occasions
Year B

Edited by Roger Spiller

CANTERBURY
PRESS
Norwich

© The Contributors, 2020

First published in 2020 by the Canterbury Press Norwich
Editorial office
3rd Floor, Invicta House
108–114 Golden Lane
London EC1Y 0TG, UK

www.canterburypress.co.uk

Canterbury Press is an imprint of Hymns Ancient & Modern Ltd
(a registered charity)

Hymns Ancient & Modern® is a registered trademark of
Hymns Ancient & Modern Ltd
13A Hellesdon Park Road, Norwich,
Norfolk NR6 5DR, UK

Scripture quotations are from the New Revised
Standard Version of the Bible, Anglicized Edition,
copyright © 1989, 1995 by the Division of Christian Education of the
National Council of the Churches of Christ in the USA.
Used by permission. All rights reserved.

The Authors have asserted their right under the Copyright,
Designs and Patents Act, 1988,
to be identified as the Authors of this Work

British Library Cataloguing in Publication data

A catalogue record for this book is available
from the British Library

978 1 78622 253 4

Typeset by Regent Typesetting
Printed and bound by CPI Group (UK) Ltd

Contents

Preface   xvii

Collaborative Preaching   xviii

Contributors   xxviii

SUNDAYS AND MAJOR FESTIVALS

Unless otherwise stated, the readings and the verse numbers of the psalms are taken from *Common Worship: Services and Prayers for the Church of England* (Church House Publishing, 2000), with revisions, and are for Year B.

2020

29 Nov.   **First Sunday of Advent**
         Principal Service: Isa. 64.1–9 Expectations
            Reset in the Potter's Workshop   2
         Second Service: Isa. 1.1–20
            Repent (Turn to God) and Do Justice   4

6 Dec.   **Second Sunday of Advent**
         Principal Service: Mark 1.1–8 The Advent Hope   7
         Second Service: 1 Kings 22.1–28
            The Lord has Judged   9

13 Dec.   **Third Sunday of Advent**
         Principal Service: John 1.6–8, 19–28
            Sign-posting the Messiah   11
         Second Service: Mal. 3.1–4; 4
            Ready to be Judged   14

20 Dec.   **Fourth Sunday of Advent**
Principal Service: Rom. 16.25–end
    Living the Gospel   16
Second Service: Zech. 2.10–end
    Prophecies that Fuel Hope   18

25 Dec.   **Christmas Day**
Set I: Luke 2.1–14 [5–20] May You Unwrap
    Hope this Christmas   21
Set II: Luke 2.[1–7] 8–20 Making Space at
    Christmas   23
Set III: John 1.1–14 Stories   25
Second Service: Isa. 65.17–25
    We're Coming Home!   27

27 Dec.   **First Sunday of Christmas**
Principal Service: Luke 2.15–21
    Growing Up with Jesus   30
Second Service: Col. 1.9–20 The Cosmic Christ   32

2021

3 Jan.   **Second Sunday of Christmas**
Principal Service: Eph. 1.3–14 Who is to Blame?   34
Second Service: Rom. 12.1–8 Worship:
    A Living Sacrifice   37

10 Jan.   **Baptism of Christ (First Sunday of Epiphany)**
Principal Service: Mark 1.4–11 Jesus' Baptism   39
Second Service: Isa. 42.1–9 The Servant of
    the Lord   42

17 Jan.   **Second Sunday of Epiphany**
Principal Service: John 1.43–end Seeing Christ   44
Second Service: Isa. 60.9–end
    The Future is Bright   46

24 Jan.   **Third Sunday of Epiphany**
Principal Service: John 2.1–11
    Backstairs to Glory   49
Second Service: Jer. 3.21—4.2
    Return, Return to God   51

31 Jan.   **Fourth Sunday of Epiphany** (*or* Candlemas)
Principal Service: Mark 1.21–28
    The Authority of Jesus   53
Second Service: 1 Sam. 3.1–20
    The Light was Still Burning   56

7 Feb.   **Second Sunday before Lent**
Principal Service: John 1.1–14
    The Centrality of Jesus   58
Second Service: Gen. 2.4b–end 'Only Human'?   60

14 Feb.   **Sunday next before Lent**
Principal Service: Mark 9.2–9
    Clouds of Glory in the Fog   62
Second Service: 1 Kings 19.1–16 God's Fugitive   65

17 Feb.   **Ash Wednesday**
Principal Service: Matt. 6.1–6, 16–21
    The Second Pancake   69

21 Feb.   **First Sunday of Lent**
Principal Service: Mark 1.9–15
    Into the Wilderness   71
Second Service: Gen. 2.15–17; 3.1–7
    Does the Snake Speak with a Forked Tongue?   73

28 Feb.   **Second Sunday of Lent**
Principal Service: Mark 8.31–end
    Suffering to End Suffering?   76
Second Service: Gen. 12.1–9 When God Says Go   78

7 Mar.   **Third Sunday of Lent**
Principal Service: John 2.13–22
    Church Cleansing   81
Second Service: Phil. 3.4b–14 Confidence and
Credentials   83

14 Mar.   **Fourth Sunday of Lent** (Mothering Sunday)
Principal Service: John 3.14–21 'God so loved
    the world …'   85
Mothering Sunday: Luke 2.33–35 Soul-piercing   88

21 Mar.   **Fifth Sunday of Lent** (Passiontide)
           Principal Service: John 12.20–33 Seeing Jesus   90
           Second Service: Ex. 7.8–24 Departures   93

28 Mar.   **Palm Sunday**
           Principal Service: Mark 11.1–11
             A Challenge to the Nation   96
           Second Service: Isa. 5.1–7 A Sinister Song in
             a Vineyard   99

29–31   **First Three Days of Holy Week**
  Mar.   *John 12.1–11 Two Kinds of Love*   101

1 Apr.   **Maundy Thursday**
           John 13.1–17, 31b–35 Learn How to Receive   103

2 Apr.   **Good Friday**
           John 18.1 — 19.end Sorrow and Love Flow
             Mingling Down   106

3–4 Apr.   **Easter Vigil**
           Mark 16.1–8 The World Turned Upside-down   108

4 Apr.   **Easter Day**
           Principal Service: Mark 16.1–8 Complete
             the Story   110
           Second Service: Ezek. 37.1–14 You Shall Live!   113

11 Apr.   **Second Sunday of Easter**
           Principal Service: John 20.19–end
             Doubting Thomas?   115
           Second Service: Luke 24.1–12
             The Thin Black Line of the Horizon   117

18 Apr.   **Third Sunday of Easter**
           Principal Service: Luke 24.36b–48
             Wounded Resurrection   120
           Second Service: Deut. 7.7–13
             Love from of Old   122

25 Apr.   **Fourth Sunday of Easter**
          Principal Service: Acts 4.5–12 Living Vocation   125
          Second Service: John 6.30–40
              Living Just for Today   127

2 May   **Fifth Sunday of Easter**
          Principal Service: John 15.1–8 New Branches   129
          Second Service: Isa. 60.1–14 A Worshipful
              Company   131

9 May   **Sixth Sunday of Easter**
          Principal Service: John 15.9–17 Fullness of Life 134
          Second Service: Ps. 45 The Royal Wedding   136

13 May   **Ascension Day**
          Principal Service: Luke 24.44–end
              When Going is Also a Coming   139
          Second Service: Matt. 28.16–end Now it's
              Our Commissioning!   142

16 May   **Seventh Sunday of Easter**
          (Sunday after Ascension Day)
          Principal Service: John 17.6–19 Knowing Jesus   144
          Second Service: Isa. 61 The Social Gospel
              of Christianity   147

23 May   **Day of Pentecost** (Whit Sunday)
          Principal Service: Acts 2.1–21; John 15.26–27;
              16.4b–15 A Bunch of Amateurs   149
          Second Service: Ezek. 36.22–28 Whole in Spirit   151

30 May   **Trinity Sunday**
          Principal Service: John 3.1–17
              Living the Trinity   154
          Second Service: Ezek. 1.4–10, 22–28a
              Heaven's Above   156

6 June   **First Sunday after Trinity** (Proper 5)
          Principal Service: Mark 3.20–end God's
              Family Values   159
          Second Service: Jer. 6.16–21 Ask for the
              Ancient Paths   161

13 June   **Second Sunday after Trinity** (Proper 6)
Principal Service: Mark 4.26–34
     Speaking in Parables   164
Second Service: Jer. 7.1–16 Inconvenient Truths   167

20 June   **Third Sunday after Trinity** (Proper 7)
Principal Service: Mark 4.35–end
     The Fear of Fear   169
Second Service: Rom. 11.25–end
     When Theology and Experience Clash   172

27 June   **Fourth Sunday after Trinity** (Proper 8)
Principal Service: Mark 5.21–end
     Healing and Wholeness   175
Second Service: Rom. 13.1–10
     Good Citizens: Good Neighbours   177

4 July   **Fifth Sunday after Trinity** (Proper 9)
Principal Service: Mark 6.1–13 Jesus on His
     Terms, Not Ours   180
Second Service: Jer. 20.1–11a Between a Rock
     and a Hard Place   182

11 July   **Sixth Sunday after Trinity** (Proper 10)
Principal Service: Mark 6.14–29 When People
     Get in Our Way   185
Second Service: Rom. 15.14–29 Boasting
     in Christ   187

18 July   **Seventh Sunday after Trinity** (Proper 11)
Principal Service: Mark 6.30–34, 53–end
     Restoring the Future   189
Second Service: Heb. 2.5–end
     Shaking the Foundations   191

25 July   **Eighth Sunday after Trinity** (Proper 12)
Principal Service: John 6.1–21 Feed the Hungry   194
Second Service: Job 19.1–27a Job's Search for
     Vindication   196

1 Aug.   **Ninth Sunday after Trinity** (Proper 13)
          Principal Service: John 6.24–35 With God
          it's Always Bread Week   199
          Second Service: Job 28 Wisdom   201

8 Aug.   **Tenth Sunday after Trinity** (Proper 14)
          Principal Service: John 6.35, 41–51
          The Bread of Life   203
          Second Service: Job 39.1 – 40.4
          The Big Picture   206

15 Aug.   **Eleventh Sunday after Trinity** (Proper 15)
          Principal Service: John 6.51–58
          Living for Ever   208
          Second Service: Ex. 2.23 – 3.10
          The Fear of God   210

22 Aug.   **Twelfth Sunday after Trinity** (Proper 16)
          Principal Service: John 6.56–69 'Those who
          eat my flesh …'   213
          Second Service: Ex. 4.27 – 5.1 Moses and
          Aaron: The Plan is Set in Motion   215

29 Aug.   **Thirteenth Sunday after Trinity** (Proper 17)
          Principal Service: Mark 7.1–8, 14–15, 21–23
          Living Inside Out   217
          Second Service: Matt. 4.23 – 5.20 Blessed
          Reconciliation   219

5 Sept.   **Fourteenth Sunday after Trinity** (Proper 18)
          Principal Service: Mark 7.24–end 'Be Opened!'   222
          Second Service: Ex. 14.5–end Looking Back
          and Looking Forward   224

12 Sept. **Fifteenth Sunday after Trinity** (Proper 19)
          Principal Service: Mark 8.27–end
          Declaring Your Identity   226
          Second Service: Ex. 18.13–26
          The Management of Love   228

xi

19 Sept.   **Sixteenth Sunday after Trinity** (Proper 20)
           Principal Service: Mark 9.30–37 A Little Child   231
           Second Service: Matt. 8.23–end
           Jesus the Storm-bringer   233

26 Sept.   **Seventeenth Sunday after Trinity** (Proper 21)
           Principal Service: Mark 9.38–end The Practice
           of Community Discipleship   235
           Second Service: Ex. 24 All the Words that
           the Lord has Spoken We Will Do   238

3 Oct.   **Eighteenth Sunday after Trinity** (Proper 22)
           Principal Service: Mark 10.2–16 The Key to
           Mark's Gospel   241
           Second Service: Josh. 3.7–end Moving Closer
           to God   243

10 Oct.   **Nineteenth Sunday after Trinity** (Proper 23)
           Principal Service: Mark 10.17–31
           Salesman or Lover?   246
           Second Service: Josh. 5.13 — 6.20 God's
           Faithfulness and Historical Evidence   248

17 Oct.   **Twentieth Sunday after Trinity** (Proper 24)
           Principal Service: Mark 10.35–45
           Why Did Jesus Die?   251
           Second Service: Matt. 12.1–21
           The Purposes of the Heart   253

24 Oct.   **Last Sunday after Trinity** (Proper 25)
           Principal Service: Mark 10.46–end
           What Do You Want Me to do for You?   255
           Second Service: Eccles. 11 and 12
           Before the Days of Trouble   258

24 Oct.   **Bible Sunday**
           John 5.36b–end Route Map and Signpost
           to Jesus   260

31 Oct.   Fourth Sunday before Advent
           Principal Service: Mark 12.28–34
               Love for God   262
           Second Service: Isa. 40.27–end
               Trust Our Heaviness   265

7 Nov.   Third Sunday before Advent
           Principal Service: Jonah 3.1–5, 10
               Out of the Depths   267
           Second Service: John 14.1–29 [or 23–29]
               St Jude's Question   270

14 Nov.   Second Sunday before Advent
           (Remembrance Sunday)
           Principal Service: Mark 13.1–8
               Hope for the World   272
           Remembrance Sunday: Mark 15.33–39
               The Centurion's Confession   274

21 Nov.   Christ the King (Sunday next before Advent)
           Principal Service: John 18.33–37
               The King Who is No King   277
           Second Service: Ps. 29 The Voice of the Lord   279

SERMONS FOR SAINTS' DAYS AND SPECIAL
OCCASIONS

2020

26 Dec.   St Stephen, Deacon, First Martyr
           Acts 7.51–end Costly Discipleship   282

27 Dec.   St John, Apostle and Evangelist
           John 21.19b–25 The Beloved Disciple   284

28 Dec.   The Holy Innocents
           Matt. 2.13–18 Who Do You Want to Murder?   287

2021

1 Jan.   Naming and Circumcision of Jesus
           Luke 2.15–21 The Power of Names   289

xiii

6 Jan.	Epiphany	
	Matt. 2.1–12 'Another King, One Jesus'?	292
18–25 Jan.	Week of Prayer for Christian Unity	
	John 17 The Unity for Which Jesus Prays	294
25 Jan.	Conversion of St Paul	
	Gal. 1.11–16a Good News	297
2 Feb.	Presentation of Christ in the Temple (Candlemas)	
	Luke 2.22–40 Marking the Meaning	299
19 Mar.	St Joseph of Nazareth	
	Matt. 1.18–end Who's Cradling Jesus?	301
25 Mar.	The Annunciation of Our Lord to the Blessed Virgin Mary	
	Luke 1.26–38 The Blessed? Virgin Mary	304
26 Apr.	St Mark the Evangelist	
	Mark 13.5–13 Where to Invest Ultimate Trust?	306
1 May	SS Philip and James, Apostles	
	John 14.1–14 Seeing the Father	309
14 May	St Matthias the Apostle	
	John 15.9–17 Someone Else's Shoes	311
31 May	Visit of the Blessed Virgin Mary to Elizabeth	
	Luke 1.39–49 [50–56] Behold – Look Again	313
3 June	Day of Thanksgiving for the Institution of Holy Communion (Corpus Christi)	
	1 Cor. 11.23–26 What Christians Do	316
11 June	St Barnabas the Apostle	
	Gal. 2.1–10 The Right Man at the Right Time	318
24 June	Birth of John the Baptist	
	Luke 1.57–66, 80 Does History Have a Meaning?	320

29 June	SS Peter and Paul, Apostles *Gal. 1.13–24 Peter and Paul's Agenda*	323
3 July	St Thomas the Apostle *John 20.24–29 Blessed Are Those Who Have Not Seen*	326
22 July	St Mary Magdalene *John 20.1–2, 11–18 Apostle to the Apostles*	328
25 July	St James the Apostle *Matt. 20.20–28 Securing the Best Seats*	331
6. Aug.	The Transfiguration of Our Lord *Luke 9.28–36 The Face of Love*	333
15 Aug.	The Blessed Virgin Mary *Luke 1.46–55 Mary's Witness to God's Upheavals*	335
24 Aug.	Bartholomew the Apostle *Luke 22.24–30 Legends of Saints*	338
14 Sept.	Holy Cross Day *John 3.13–17 God So Loved the World*	340
21 Sept.	St Matthew, Apostle and Evangelist *Matt. 9.9–13 A Memorable Meal*	342
29 Sept.	St Michael and All Angels *Rev. 12.7–12 Revealing the Angels*	344
18 Oct.	St Luke the Evangelist *Luke 10.1–9 Carriers of Hope*	347
28 Oct.	SS Simon and Jude, Apostles *John 15.17–end Jesus Provokes Key Questions*	349
1 Nov.	All Saints' Day *Rev. 21.1–6a Strengthening Our Community with the Dead*	351

2 Nov.   **All Souls' Day**
Wisd. 3.1–9 *Symbols of Hope*   354

30 Nov.   **St Andrew the Apostle**
Matt. 4.18–22 *Grace to Follow without Delay* 356

Harvest Festival
Matt. 6.25–33 *Don't Worry!*   358

All-Age Services
Crib Service: Comfort and Calm Continuing   361
Christingle: Sharing and Shining   363
Mothering Sunday   365

Notes   368
Acknowledgement of Sources   371
Index of Names and Subjects   373

Preface

With this Companion I will have edited sermons for all of the three-year cycle and, both for the sake of my own sanity and for the benefit of introducing fresh thinking, I have concluded that it is right to pass the baton on to someone else.

It has been immensely enriching to have edited the book and especially to have set myself the task to work with a lot of texts that I had not preached on before, as well as other familiar texts which gave me the opportunity to reconsider. I always appreciated that engaging in a much deeper and broader study than was absolutely necessary for my regular preaching ministry in a parish context provided a discipline that contributed hugely to it, and I commend the practice. Now, in what is misclassified as 'retirement', I have submitted to that same discipline once more. If the products are challenging, it is because I am convinced that the preaching ministry is in dire need of renewal if it is to convince the world that the gospel is God's way of bringing salvation to his disfigured world.

On a lighter note, this experience has been a surprising initiation into the mysteries of the lectionary compilers. My admiration for them is increased but so is my incomprehension for some of their selection of lections!

In previous articles I have tried to cover, first, the relationship between gospel and Bible, and how we set about discerning good news. Second, I tried to show why the form or structure of our sermons is as important as their content. Now I spotlight the place of the hearers of the sermons and draw together some of the ways in which we might equip them to be not merely consumers but collaborators with us in the preaching event.

Roger Spiller

Collaborative Preaching

> Every sermon ought to be a dialogue. A monologue is where you have no consideration for the audience or congregation ... A dialogue is where you are, in your imagination, in dialogue with the people.
> (Bishop James Jones[1])

Stage 1: Preparing collaborative preaching

Why collaborative preaching?

After a service a member of my congratulation thanked me for my sermon and said emphatically, 'Now I know what I must do; I must divorce my husband!' I wasn't as shocked by the decision as by the fact that she attributed it to the sermon. The reality was that I had said nothing about marriage, divorce, relationships or anything that gave licence for her decision. It confirmed the adage that it's not what we *say* but what is *heard* that counts. There will always be space in handling the rich texts of Scripture for hearers to interpret messages that are different from the one intended by the preacher. We recognize, too, that God can also address us through our cracked human speech. Preaching is much more than reducing the scope for misunderstanding; it has to be a collaborative endeavour, a dialogue, in fact, between the preacher, the text and the hearer. The preacher is expected to be an exponent of the text, but not its custodian. The text is addressed to all believers and must move freely between speaker and hearer. In some circumstances it may even be possible to arrange for other voices to participate physically in the preaching process, either at the preparation stage or in the delivery of the sermon. But the proposal here is that by intentionally listening to the voices of the congregation, representing them before the text and addressing them in the preaching, they can be not merely engaged in the preaching but be active co-creators of it.

We can't leave it to chance that our hearers will get the message we want to deliver, because although the preacher has power – standing four feet above contradiction – the hearers have the decisive power of reception, the choice of whether and what to hear. Collaboration, however, is more than winning the consent of the congregation. As preachers we guide and resource our hearers, but our hearers will select, shape and complete the sermons that they apply to themselves. We should, therefore, imagine our congregation sitting, as it were, on our shoulders, as we mull over the text and map out our preaching. They, indeed, speak to us before we speak to them. And there are few more beneficial things we can do if we find ourselves struggling with a sermon than to go and visit a member of the congregation.

Reading the congregation

All preachers recognize the need to 'read' or exegete the biblical text when we preach. If the preacher thinks their task is to teach the Bible and expound the text, they may not recognize also the need to spend time exegeting the congregation. But if the sermon is to be 'good news', it has to be good news today, for these people in this context and at this time. In the ministry of Jesus the opening theme or 'text' was often given to him by other people or by the circumstances of the hour. The multitude are hungry and the disciples forget to take bread with them in the boat, cue for Jesus to speak about the bread of life; there's a Jewish festival of water, Sukkot, a cue for a discourse on living water; there's been a loss of life through a collapsed tower, cue Jesus taking this up in his teaching. St Paul's letters are similarly always contextual. The Acts of the Apostles gives us a good number of sermons with a similar content but which show how each of them is adapted to a different audience. People give us our sermons when we make time to listen.

Where is the congregation?

What questions might the preacher ask themselves of the congregation and the varied contexts of their lives? It's been suggested, not entirely in jest, that we might ask what side the Church was on in the Civil War! The proposition that faith usually develops during the lifespan of an individual through distinct stages was the work of James Fowler and has proved a useful diagnostic tool. It can also be applied to congregations. There will be many different perspectives but we can expect there to be a predominant character and stage in each congregation. We might then ask what best reflects our congregation's theology: a literal, clear-cut, black and white stage; a more critical stage where metaphor and story, literary truth as well as historical truth sit well; the stage where paradox and tension, living with uncertainty and believing more about less is typical. It wasn't Fowler's intention to ascribe value judgements to different 'stages' but simply to recognize that faith often unravels and reforms through the lifespan. Again we might, for example, ask how far the congregation embraces the unconditional grace of God; how secure they are in their relationship to God, what authority the Bible has for them. This is all too obvious but it can get overlooked in our preoccupation with studying the text.

Preaching to *Scripture* from *events and issues*

Sometimes attentiveness to the context of the congregation requires us to address 'events' or issues in the light of the overall witness of Scripture, rather than starting with the biblical text. If God continues to speak to us through events, should we not, occasionally, take an election or other national or local event as the starting point and subject of our preaching? If the all-consuming preoccupation of our hearers is on some significant news, communal or national, is the preacher who 'carries on regardless' not marginalizing the preaching and the God who speaks through the exigencies of human life?

Once I dropped in on a church service, which was to be followed by an annual meeting. The vicar gave a pertinent address on the way guilt, despondency and above all a subliminal strain of punitiveness can infuse our relationships as a result of our corporate angst and loss at the decline in the institutional church, which was reflected in the church's reports. His masterfully judged sermon was an all-too-rare engagement with the underlying dis-ease that a congregation can feel, which is seldom acknowledged or addressed from the pulpit.

A few years ago a heavy fall of snow brought much of our area to a standstill and provided the only topic on people's minds. Buoyed by a brilliant 'Thought for the Day' on snow, I preached on snow. I soon realized that it was a pregnant image that shed light on many aspects of the gospel salvation history and left me with sufficient material for a sermon series had I wished to pursue it. Suggestions of playfulness, finding our inner child and enforced restfulness, as well as the more direct reference to our healing, cut through to more crusty members of the congregation and brought a new vitality and freedom within our relationships.

What is happening in the other extending contexts in which our hearers live and have their being? What events in the 'secular' calendar might we be interpreting, celebrating or marking? When have you last heard a sermon on science and faith? One cathedral was sufficiently alert and imaginative to organize a service to celebrate the discovery of the electron, and drew a packed congregation of invited science teachers and researchers from schools and universities across the city. How in the preaching can we give theological resources and inspiration to people in their working lives? Having an understanding of the currents of a community's life, its ways of relating to itself and to the world, its values and the images of its fears and hopes, enables the minister to interpret the listeners to themselves and hold their lives under the judgement and blessing of the gospel.[2] A routine reading of the congregation and the different contexts in which it is set at an early stage in the sermon preparation, with some daring and ingenuity on the part of the preacher, can win a new hearing for the gospel.

Posing the hearers' problems with and to the text

If the preaching is to be collaborative, setting up a dialogue between the text and the congregation, the preacher will practise reading the text through the ears and eyes of the congregation as they hear the biblical text. 'You are for ever hearing what people are hearing and you're thinking, "as I say this, what will people be saying?" And so your next paragraph has to deal with their "Yes, but".'[3] One homiletic expert, Fred Craddock, suggests we ask: 'What is the trouble (shock, surprise) in the text?' Or again, Ernst Lange suggests that preaching is a way of 'advocating the problems of the hearers before the text'. 'I make the situation of the hearers valid over against the text ... to trace and to name the resistance, the blocks and obstacles.'[4]

One hearer I knew well surprised me with their difficulty with the beatitude, 'Blessed are the poor in spirit'. She felt this indicated approval of mean-spiritedness! But what, for example, do congregations make of sayings attributed to Jesus in John's Gospel, such as 'I am come not to judge the world', and also, 'I am come to judge the world'; St Paul's 'now before faith came' (Gal. 3.23), or John's claim that believers 'do not sin' (1 John 3.6–9) and 'will never die' (John 11.26)? This becomes even more significant when we are confronted with what have been branded Old Testament 'texts of terror' that suggest God authorizes genocide, discrimination, sexism and so on. Preachers who know their congregations will be able to anticipate and begin to defuse the blockages that stand in the way of a more informed and productive engagement with the biblical material.

Ground rules for dialogue

Preachers who wish to represent their hearers in interpreting the meaning of texts have to reckon with a nexus of contentious issues. These might be summarized thus: how can we and our hearers exercise our freedom to interpret our Scriptures if we remain dependent upon the shifting results of historical and literary scholarship? How can the independent and challenging voice of Scripture be safeguarded against the Church's attempts to domesticate and distort it for its own purposes without the custody secured by scholarship? Is the Bible simply what we ourselves make of it or does it have a meaning of its own that can be discerned? If scholarship can enable us to uncover and express the meaning of texts, what scope is there for fresh ways of voicing the gospel for our day? What freedom do we have, who are given the Spirit of truth, to interpret Scripture if we are captive to a biblical scholarship that operates according to the prevailing rationality? How can we commend the Bible to a sceptical generation without confidence in the essential veracity of Scripture that intense biblical studies have brought to it?[5]

The Bible is a rich, dense, polyphonic text that permits a wide, but not unlimited, range of meanings. As such it is analogous to the text of a play or the score of an orchestral piece. No theatre director or musical conductor would advance their own interpretation of their source without deep attention to the text and to the performance traditions that developed from it. It is through the interface between the scholarly tradition and the creative freedom of the present that an interpretation emerges that is faithful to its original creators and subsequent interpretative tradition. 'The Bible comes alive where authentic religious experience coincides with texts which are themselves testimony to an authentic religious experience: the past strikes a spark off the present or the present off the past, and both are illuminated.'[6] This sets the ground rules for a dialogue between text and congregation, enacted on their behalf by the preacher. The dialogue is like a swing or pendulum, a movement between text and hearers, until a new interpretation comes to realization and the good news springs to life. Preachers will often wait for the 'spark' and testify to it as the conception of their sermon.

Imagination set free

We are best able to engage the congregation through the neglected faculty of the imagination.[7] It's been estimated that 85 per cent or more of Scripture is in the form of narrative, story or imagery. Imagination is the only faculty we have to access and dwell in the 'world' of the gospel while we remain in a world that is at odds with it. The Bible is a strange, alien world that offers us an alternative construal of reality, where the first are last, outsiders are insiders, and insiders are cast out, where to live we have to die, and where to secure our future we have to give it no thought. The kingdom is hidden, eschatological and can only be accessed through the imagination. Doctrines, too, such as the incarnation can only be expressed as story. Story is irreplaceable. It is the vehicle for the gospel, which cannot adequately be expressed in any other way.

We live our lives as narrative, we are the stories we follow, the images we live by. But 'we live our stories best when we understand them in relation to the larger human story, the stories of our faith tradition and the story of God'.[8] We don't hear God's story at the expense of our human stories. Since God has come down to earth, our human stories can interweave with the divine story. We both find ourselves in God's story and look for God in our story. One brief example of the way Walter Wink suggested we might connect with the story of the woman who anointed Jesus with ointment reads as follows:

> This woman [is] an inner aspect of yourself. We're not talking about the woman two thousand years ago ... Ask her to tell you about yourself, about how you have treated her, but also about the new life that she has found through Jesus. Talk to the woman in you, the woman whom this story has, as it were, put inside you.[9]

In handling the figurative speech, imagery, parables and stories of Scripture, the preacher passes control to the congregation. They are set free to fill out, ruminate on and create their own storied sermons that address their own lives. Through imaginative story and speech, the congregation has space to develop their own preaching. But this also creates space for God. Imaginative speech undermines our world and makes us vulnerable to God.

> I am to bring people before the living God, not to protect people from God. I am to leave them to wander, to explore the space between us and the throne. I am to frustrate their desires to relax the tension between our ways and God's ways.[10]

So far, we have suggested how our hearers can be represented in the first preparatory stage. We now conclude by exploring the way the congregation might be activated in the delivery of the preaching.

Stage 2: Delivering the sermon – beginning, middle and end

Arresting the congregation

The preacher's time in which to capture the attention of the congregation is shrinking as fast as the ozone layer. Like the opening sentences of a book, the first few words of the preacher are usually all that is available to them before our hearers decide whether or not to listen. I find it helpful to work on the assumption that the congregation will have a low attention span and not be excited by the prospect of listening to a preacher unless I put up a fight for attention. As one guide to preachers graphically put it: 'Presume they would rather feed their children to crocodiles than listen to you.'[11]

The first utterances of the preacher can be crucial. Craddock recommended that preachers build a porch in front of their sermon. He is referring to the need to create a bridge across the gap between text and congregation. Not, he insists, to eliminate the gap, which is the strange, alternative world of the gospel that is being offered, but to narrow it so that hearers can begin to connect with its alien world. Let us briefly review some of the more frequently used sermon starters.

Long explanatory introductions can have the effect of explaining a joke before the audience has the chance to hear it. If explanation is needed, it might be best once the attention of the hearers has been secured. It's usually preferable simply to allow the experience to explain itself rather than to over-explain it. Stories and jokes entertain and relax our hearers, but unless they are integral to the rest of the sermon they can set up false expectations and feel contrived. If on the other hand the preacher develops their sermon seamlessly from their attention-grabbing opening story, they have to be wary of letting the tail wag the dog. Sermons are often skewed by the choice of a good story, and in some of them Jesus is scaled down to the level of a well-meaning youth worker. Some preachers follow Barth in scrupulously avoiding any personal references in their sermons, but occasional, judicious disclosures from the preacher can make identification with, and give authenticity to, the preacher. Care needs to be taken lest the personal story becomes intrusive rather than helpful. If, for example, the preacher tells the congregation that they are preaching on their favourite Bible passage, they can unwittingly create the impression that selective reading of the Bible is acceptable. And the preaching becomes personalized. It may be valuable to follow Craddock and lead the congregation in the inductive journey that the preacher took in order to arrive at her sermon, but it is seldom edifying to hear the preacher sharing her struggles to decide what to say, and is likely to leave the congregation wishing she hadn't bothered in the first place.

Starting directly from a biblical text can also be arresting when, as mentioned above, the preacher poses the problems of the congregation before the text. Setting preaching in a narrative framework that poses problems that keep hearers attentively waiting for a resolution can be as effective as an opening story.

Retaining congregational participation

The congregation is more likely to retain interest if they are being accompanied on an unpredictable, narrative-like journey with a trustworthy guide. The preacher will provide a clear melodic line, carrying the essential theme of the preaching. But the preacher may also provide an accompanying contrapuntal harmonic voice without confusing the primary theme, for those who wish to go a bit deeper in their own thinking.

A variety of sermon forms, chosen to suit different genres, prevent sermons from becoming too predictable and monochrome. They also contribute to delivering the shock and surprise of the gospel.[12]

Keeping the congregation in participative mode requires us to take account of learning and personality styles. Sermons, it's been suggested, should give hearers 'something to think, feel, decide and do'.[13]

Few texts leave preachers without choices that they must take. Would it be viable to let the congregation in to any significant choices that the text under consideration may be raising and set the choice before them? They may already have had to adjust to the way different texts have been handled. Do the discrepancies, as for example in the resurrection stories, create problems that need at least some referencing? Are our hearers concerned with what happened or only with meaning?

Language is the stock in trade of the preacher. It is, after all, as the Word that Jesus comes among us. Language that is visual, percussive, playful is more engaging than generic, abstract speech with an excess of nouns and adjectives. Above all, our language best reflects the gospel and is more likely to bear fruit when it is invitational rather than prescriptive.

Extending the life of the sermon in the wider world

The conclusion of the sermon is usually the time for the 'application' of the sermon to be forged. However, this has often been contrived and sometimes appeared banal as preachers have struggled to find concrete suggestions that could be applied to all worshippers. It is usually preferable that the whole course of the preaching creates opportunities for connections to be made rather than a discrete and forced 'application' at the end. Tony Thistleton cites Han-Georg Gadamer as offering a better way: 'Understanding the text is always already applying it.'[14] If I understand it correctly, he suggests that the task of the preacher is to help the congregation to understand the text and inhabit the gospel. The trouble is not that people don't know what to do with the gospel once they understand, but that they struggle to understand and accept it in the first place. Prescribing actions risks confirming the long-seated view that the Christian faith is a religion of duty, commands, instructions and moral self-achievement, rather than unconditional grace. As one writer expresses it:

Preaching is an echo, the rebound of God's voice into every corner of our lives. It's not that we create the connections in our sermons, but that we uncover them, so that everyone can see them – and hopefully, having seen the connections we have uncovered, they will go home ready to do some uncovering of their own.[15]

xxvi

Connections made in the preaching offer a paradigm for our own practices in the contexts in which we live and work.

It is tempting for the preacher to bring the sermon to a clear conclusion or resolution. It's been said that, instead, the preacher should let the hearers find their own way home, figuratively speaking. That may be good advice for some but there obviously needs to be some encouraging reiteration of the gospel at the conclusion of the preaching. But it should not tie up all lose ends. Life is not like that and the attempt to do so is both misleading and places a moratorium on the opportunities to prolong the impact and wrestling with the sermon. So neat endings are best avoided if the sermon is to continue its work with the hearers long after the dying sounds of the last hymn are over. The Methodist bishop William Willimon said, 'Only God can properly end a sermon.'[16] It's more than an issue of leaving some questions hanging for the congregation to wrestle with and discuss. It's that our faith has a future orientation. There is, then, no closure while we wait for the coming of the kingdom.

I cannot claim that the sermons that follow are all models of participation. But I am convinced that as preachers we will want to keep in mind those to and with whom we regularly preach throughout the course of our preparation as well as our delivery. After all, preachers speak to us before we speak to them, and if we're attentive to them, they can even give us our sermons.

Contributors

The Revd Dr Kate Bruce is an RAF Chaplain and Visiting Fellow of St John's College, Durham. She is the author of *Igniting the Heart* (SCM Press), on preaching and imagination.

The Revd Canon Christopher Burdon is a retired priest living in Wiltshire. After 18 years in parish ministry he moved into theological education: first in lay adult education, then as Principal of the Northern Ordination Course, and later as Canon Theologian of St Edmundsbury, with responsibility for continuing ministerial development.

The Revd Canon Dr Christopher Burkett is Director of Ministry for Chester. A sociologist, Christopher is also editor of *The Preacher* and a tutor of the College of Preachers.

The Revd Mary Cotes is a Baptist minister. Following pastorates in Devonshire and South Wales, she served as ecumenical moderator in Milton Keynes and now exercises an itinerant ministry in Britain and further afield. She is currently chair of the Milton Keynes Christian Foundation. She writes for the French website Servir Ensemble.

The Revd Dr Megan Daffern is Diocesan Director of Ordinands for Ely Diocese, former Chaplain of Jesus College, Oxford, and lecturer and tutor in the university Theology Faculty. She has published *Songs of the Spirit* (IVP).

The Revd Philip Dyer-Perry is Parish Priest of Our Lady of the Rosary Church in Staines in a relatively diverse Catholic community, situated in a medium-sized town close to Heathrow Airport.

Carolyn Edwards is the Children and Youth Adviser for the Diocese of York and the author of *Slugs and Snails and Puppy Dogs' Tails: Helping Boys Connect with God* (IVP), and *Re-Thinking Children's Work in Churches* with Sally Nash and Sian Hancock. She is currently undertaking doctoral studies on children and holiness.

Nick Harding has spent 30 years in children's and family ministry and education, working across denominations, and has written numerous resource books and songs to support churches. He is now a consultant, writer and speaker. He is a licenced lay minster, a member of General Synod, and a magistrate.

The Rt Revd Dr Christopher Herbert, former Bishop of St Albans, and currently a Trustee of the Royal Hospital for Neuro-disability, Putney, is a lecturer for the Arts Society and Visiting Professor of Christian Ethics in the University of Surrey.

The Revd Michael Hopkins is a minister of the United Reformed Church, serving a group of Methodist and United Reformed Churches in and around Farnham, Surrey. He also serves as honorary Clerk of the United Reformed Church General Assembly.

The Revd Dr Victoria Johnson is Precentor at York Minster and a Tutor for the College of Preachers. She studied Homiletics at Yale Divinity School. She teaches preaching for those training for ministry.

The Revd Dr Wendy Kilworth-Mason is a Methodist presbyter and a former Theological Tutor and Mission Partner with an interest in preaching the Old Testament.

The Rt Revd Dr Gordon Mursell is a former Dean of Birmingham, and was Bishop of Stafford until he retired. He is the author of *English Spirituality* (SPCK) and other books.

The Revd Barry Overend was born in Dorset and studied theology at King's College, London. He was Vicar of St Chad's, Far Headingley, for over 20 years before retiring in 2010. He was also a member of the College of Preachers executive for several years.

The Rt Revd Dr John Perumbalath is Suffragan Bishop of Bradwell. John hails from the ancient Syrian Christian community in Kerala,

India, and has a doctorate in hermeneutics. He chaired the Committee for Minority Ethnic Anglican Concerns and sat on the Appointment Committee of the Church of England and the Mission and Public Affairs Council.

The Revd Carey Saleh is a parish priest in the Worcester Diocese. She is drawn to Celtic spirituality and has written some liturgy for the publishers Wild Goose. She is interested in the power of metaphor and story in how we understand God and is currently writing some meditations on the voices of the women of the Hebrew Bible. She is also a published fiction writer, including a play looking at dementia and memory.

Revd Canon Roger Spiller is Chair of Trustees of the College of Preachers. He was Director of Ministry for Coventry Diocese and Chair of the Church of England CME Panel. He is Chair of the UK Bossy (Ecumenical Institute), Geneva.

Dame Mary Tanner served as the General Secretary of the Church of England's Council for Christian Unity, having taught Old Testament at Hull and Bristol Universities and Westcott House in Cambridge. She was a member of the Second Anglican–Roman Catholic International Commission and Moderator of the World Council of Churches Faith and Order Commission. From 2007 to 2013 she served as President for Europe of the WCC. In retirement she often preaches in her local parish.

The Revd Brett Ward is a parish priest of Eltham in the Anglican Diocese of Southwark, holds an MTh in preaching from the College of Preachers and has been a sermon commissioner for *The Preacher*.

The Revd Catherine Williams is an Anglican priest formerly working as a National Adviser for Selection for the Ministry Division of the Archbishops' Council. She is licensed to the Bishop of Gloucester as a Public Preacher.

The Revd Dr Stephen Wright is Vice-Principal and Academic Director of Spurgeon's College, London, the former Director of the College of Preachers and author of a number of books on preaching.

Year B, the Year of Mark

*(Year B begins on Advent Sunday
in 2020, 2023, 2026, etc.)*

Advent

First Sunday of Advent   29 November
Principal Service   Expectations Reset in the Potter's Workshop
Isa. 64.1–9; Ps. 80.1–8, 18–20 [*or* 80.1–8]; 1 Cor. 1.3–9; Mark 13.24–end

I was standing in the vestry of a fashionable Cambridge church anxiously clutching the text of the sermon I was soon to deliver as an ordinand in training. Suddenly the stillness was shattered. In rushed the verger, his face ashen, as he blurted out, 'The Lord is here'. Hearing that, the vicar suddenly sprang to life and made a hasty exit, leaving me to hope that maybe, if the Lord is here, I'd be rescued from the burden of preaching. It was, indeed *a* lord but not *the* Lord. Lord Thorneycroft, former Tory Chancellor of the Exchequer, was in the city to visit his electronics factory and joined us for evening worship.

Expectations

Do we expect and cry out for some such dramatic visitation, some powerful action from God that can match our mood of anguish, despair and powerlessness? Advent is the season of longing and waiting for the activity and return of God, but in what form are we instructed to expect him? 'O that you would tear open the heavens and come down ... to make your name known to your adversaries, so that the nations might tremble at your presence!'

The prophet who voiced those words was angry with God, because God wasn't defending himself, vindicating his name. Why did the poet think that God could act and show his power in the first place? Because Israel's God had already done so in calling down fire and floods and delivering his people from their adversaries and placing them in their own land.

Expectations confounded

But not now, no more. At the time Isaiah was preaching, the people were facing catastrophe. Judah was routed, occupied, her leading people frogmarched off to Babylon; the Temple, God's own dwelling, was destroyed, and the line of Davidic kings had ended. The apparent inaction of God, then as now, precipitated a crisis of faith. 'Because you hid yourself, we transgressed.' It's God we blame, his invisibility resulted in the collapse of faith that led to the collapse of Judah. And Isaiah laments that 'No one calls on your name or attempts to take hold of you'. Why? 'For you have hidden your face from us.' For several hundred years, the voice of God through the prophets dried up. God seemed silent, as if leaving his people to get on without him.

But they were once more in for a surprise. God hadn't finished with his people, and the prophet's cry that God may yet 'come down' was heard and answered. It was Isaiah especially, together with the Psalms, on which the young man from Nazareth, Jesus, drew to inform his own vocation.

Expectations reset

Isaiah's words will be uttered in countless carol and Christmas services around the world. He preached grace, healing, forgiveness, restoration. And his lyrical, iridescent language enables us to identify God's promised One who came to save his broken, suffering world. The one from the Father's own heart, who forsook his kingly throne, 'emptied himself of all but love' and came and dwelt among us, reigning as King not from a throne but from the tree of Calvary, and inaugurating God's kingdom 'on earth, as it is in heaven'.

Our reading – in fact the whole Advent season – challenges the way we expect God to work in the world. It challenges those who want a quick fix, a dramatic display of power politics. We have to question the expectations we have of the way God works, the way in which he comes to us. If we don't, we can miss him, and miss out on the life that he brings. Our prophet comes to our rescue. You got fixated on God as a mighty deliverer, but now it's different: 'You are our Father: we are the clay and you are our potter.' And as Father and potter he comes to us in Jesus, to shape and refashion us as his people.

Expectations in train

It's usual to think of Advent as a time of waiting for a return of Jesus, a public and unambiguous appearance accompanied by effects like a Hollywood drama. In our Gospel reading, clouds descend, the sun darkens, the moon ceases to give light, and stars fall from heaven. But the image can mislead us into hoping for another world instead of the renewal of this world. Mark's is incendiary, underground messaging, written in code on pain of death. It is most likely to have been discretely circulated a year or two before the Roman sacking of Jerusalem. But it tells us of the alternative rule of God that he has already set in train. Jesus comes to transform earth, not to replace it.

Waiting for a second coming proved difficult in the period of the early Church, and it's harder after a gap of two thousand years. But it affirms that God will have the last word. Christ rose from the dead to show us how the story will end. All the unrealized hopes and unmet desires and dashed longings will be restored. Everything we long for will be exceeded in the presence of God.

Advent is a new start, the beginning of a new year for the Christian Church, a time to allow ourselves to be shaped by the divine potter. What changes do we have yet to allow him to make as a result of his first coming? Do we prefer the darkness, or the light of his coming?

Roger Spiller

Suggested hymns

O come, o come, Emmanuel; Into the darkness of this world; There is a longing in our hearts, O Lord; Lo, he comes with clouds descending.

First Sunday of Advent   29 November
Second Service   **Repent (Turn to God) and Do Justice**
Ps. 25 [*or* 25.1–9]; **Isa. 1.1–20**; Matt. 21.1–13

Back in my schooldays, as we prepared to read a new book, we would diligently make notes about the author, learning about their life story and their geographical and historical context. Sometimes I found that far more interesting than the work we had then to read!

So, who is Isaiah, and when, where and to whom did he speak?

Whose words are these?

The passage begins by telling us that the book of Isaiah is made up of the messages revealed to Isaiah, son of Amoz. We also learn that they were from the time of four successive kings of Judah, Uzziah, Jotham, Ahaz and Hezekiah. Isaiah's prophecies were targeted at Judah and Jerusalem.

All that information comes from the very first verse, a verse that may well have been added by disciples who edited the work of the named prophet. Apart from that helpful verse, our knowledge of Isaiah (and of his context) is gleaned from the content of the book that bears his name. There may be a clue to his character (or to the expectations that are placed upon him) in the fact that his name means 'Yahweh saves'. However, it would be wrong to assume that his message will, therefore, be entirely one of hope and comfort. Remember that as a prophet Isaiah is a seer of visions, a herald who proclaims God's words. The messages he speaks are not his own but Yahweh's.

The context

Prophesying during the reigns of the four kings of Judah named in the first verse of our reading, Isaiah came to the fore at a time of crisis. To the north of Judah, Israel could be a troublesome neighbour; further afield, Assyria was gaining in strength and threatening to extend its empire at the expense of its weaker southern neighbours. Judah had been both militarily strong and prosperous during the reign of Uzziah, but it then fell into decline. In 734–733 BC, Israel allied with Syria against Judah. In 701, Assyria invaded, razing to the ground 46 of Judah's fortified cities; Jerusalem alone, though besieged, survived.

It is debatable as to which experience of defeat and destruction Isaiah is describing in our passage. Suffice it to say that the sad situation he depicts forms the context for the message Isaiah delivers. He speaks against the backdrop of international upheaval. That same context was also the situation into which his southern counterpart Micah spoke, while, to the north, Amos and Hosea were speaking out in Israel.

The message

The words of all four prophets have a similar theme: (divine) justice. Despite the predicament in which Judah finds herself, Isaiah

5

says that the nation should not rely upon alliances. The real root cause of her problems, which must be addressed, is the lack of faith in God of her kings and leaders. The true threat to her well-being is her sin and disobedience. Jerusalem is wicked, like the notorious cities of Sodom and Gomorrah. Yahweh is holy.

Isaiah says that the people have deserted Yahweh: perhaps they have been worshipping the Baalim. So, through their neglect, desertion and disobedience, they have brought their punishment upon themselves. Strangers (the Syrians or Assyrians?) have plundered the land.

However, in Jerusalem they have continued to carry out the rituals of worship. They've maintained the sacrifices in the Temple. Yahweh proclaims that he is tired of their religious observances. He's not going to listen to their prayers.

Why is God unimpressed? Their hands are covered in blood. However ardent their worship, it counts for nothing unless they repent and turn from doing evil to doing good. They are to do justice by helping the vulnerable: the oppressed, the orphans and the widows. If they will obey, God will wash away the stains of their sin and will permit them to eat the produce of the land.

The message for today

'Fake news' or a real prophecy for today? As we look around the world today, do we not see destruction on a still larger scale than that which Isaiah witnessed? We argue about global warming.

In our churches we continue to craft our rituals and perfect our liturgies. What does God think of our preoccupations?

Is justice and the support for the vulnerable in our societies our priority?

Perhaps we need an Isaiah to recall us, our peoples, nations and churches, to true faithfulness.

Wendy Kilworth-Mason

Suggested hymns

Come, thou long expected Jesus; The kingdom of God is justice and joy; Heaven shall not wait; Come, light of the world, light up our lives.

Second Sunday of Advent 6 December
Principal Service **The Advent Hope**
Isa. 40.1–11; Ps. 85.1–2, 8–end [*or* 85.8–end]; 2 Peter 3.8–15a;
Mark 1.1–8

There's a story told about an elderly woman in the west of Scotland who was at home when the air-raid sirens went during the Second World War. The fire warden came looking for her when she failed to appear in the cellar, and found her urgently searching for something. 'I'm looking for my false teeth,' she said. 'For pity's sake, hen,' the warden replied, 'it's bombs that are falling, not pies!'

That woman had got her priorities wrong. And getting your priorities right is the subject, or one of the subjects, of today's Gospel reading: the very beginning of Mark's Gospel. It's the earliest and shortest of the four. It doesn't begin with the Christmas story (as do Matthew and Luke) or with a lofty prologue (as does John). It starts straight off: 'The beginning of the good news of Jesus Christ, the Son of God.' The Greek word *euangelion*, from *eu* (good) and *angelos* (messenger), means (the announcement of) good news, and the word was used by the Romans to describe a general's triumph or the birthday of an emperor. So, as Rowan Williams has pointed out, the very opening verse tells us that this is going to be a book about regime change.[17] This is why, in Mark's Gospel, the *only* person to recognize the whole truth about Jesus Christ as 'the Son of God' (which is how Jesus is described in Mark's opening verse) is not a disciple but a Roman centurion, who says as Christ dies, 'Truly this man was God's Son!' So Mark is saying: if a hardened Roman NCO can see that Jesus is greater than his boss, the Emperor, so can you and I. This is a new regime, with a new kind of ruler.

But what does that mean in practice? What should be our priorities? Today's reading suggests three things: seeking forgiveness; leaving home; and looking forward.

Seeking forgiveness

In today's Gospel the new regime is introduced by John the Baptist preparing the way for Jesus by offering a baptism of repentance for the forgiveness of sins. The message is clear: if we want to be ready to greet this Messiah when he comes, at Christmas and in final judgement, we have to be willing to be changed. And that's not easy. We are invited to ask ourselves: what do I need to repent

7

of? What bad habit, or thing I've been putting off, or grudge I was holding on to, do I need to acknowledge and let go of? And what about forgiving someone? Forgiveness is one of the very few – possibly the *only* – power in life capable of bringing about real change, because it breaks the chain of tit-for-tat reactions. It's very often not our fault when something bad happens to us. But how we choose to respond to that is up to us. Only the one who suffers for our sins has the power to forgive us. *But do we want to be forgiven?*

Leaving home

Mark tells us that people from all over the place 'were going out' to hear John the Baptist This Messiah requires a life-changing 'going out', a willingness to leave your home and your comfort zone, and make a new beginning – perhaps by being baptized, or renewing your baptismal vows. Leaving home, stepping out from behind the false security of bad habits, is not easy. But leaving home is what God did at Christmas: 'thou didst leave thy home and thy kingly crown, when thou camest to earth for me', as the old hymn puts it. And if we really want to experience the fullness of what he has to give us, we have to step out in faith too.

Looking forward

Seeking forgiveness and leaving home are just the start of what's involved in being changed by Jesus. Today's reading ends with John the Baptist making that clear: I'm just the warm-up act, he says. You ain't seen nothing yet! Mark's Gospel shows us how, again and again, people who had nothing to look forward to in this life find new hope by following Jesus. Advent is a good time to ask yourself: what do I most hope for in my life? The woman looking for her false teeth in the air raid could be you and me. We get in a terrible tizz about trivia when the equivalent of the air-raid siren goes off and a crisis looms. It's not too late to be changed. We just have to want to be. And if we do, we can welcome the new regime of Jesus Christ the Son of God with open arms and hearts, certain that, once we do so, nothing can separate us from his love.

Gordon Mursell

On Jordan's bank, the Baptist's cry; Long ago, prophets knew; Wait for the Lord, whose day is near; Thou didst leave thy throne and thy kingly crown.

Second Sunday of Advent   6 December
Second Service   **The Lord has Judged**
Ps. 40 [*or* 40.12–end]; **1 Kings 22.1–28**; *Gospel at Holy Communion*: Rom. 15.4–13; Matt. 11.2–11

Many of the names in the Old Testament can be translated into English, and mean something. Jehoshaphat, a king of the southern kingdom of Judah, is no exception. His name means 'The LORD has judged'. 'Jeho-' is like God's proper name 'Jehovah' or 'Yahweh', which in turn means 'I am who I am' or 'I will be who I will be' (the Bible represents this as LORD, because God's revealed name is so holy). Then '-shaphat' means 'he has judged'. To judge is a common act of God in the Hebrew Bible. For a king to have the name 'The LORD has judged' is a reminder of God's acts of justice and judgement. And it is a reminder of God's ongoing relationship with his people – after all, there is a whole book of the Old Testament dedicated to the chieftains who led God's people before the monarchy – people who were called 'Judges'.

Two as one

By this time in the history of the 12 tribes of Israel, the kingdoms were divided – southern kingdom Judah and northern kingdom Israel. Only three kings had ruled all 12 tribes – Saul, David and Solomon – about 1050–930 BC. Jehoshaphat was king of Judah probably around 873–848 BC. So King Jehoshaphat's answer to King Ahab's request for military reinforcements is particularly moving: 'I am as you are; my people are your people, my horses are your horses.'

In the UK, we're used to being our own United Kingdom today. We can take joy in our connections between Wales, Scotland, Northern Ireland and England (even if there are variable degrees of devolution between our governments). And while there are many things that continually threaten to divide our society – wealth, opinion, politics, local traditions, as well as geography – can we see occasions when we too can say to one another, 'I am as you are, my neighbours are your neighbours, let me share my strengths with you'?

Decision-making

How do you go about making a decision? Do you make snap decisions, or do you prefer to take time over them? Do you pray about them? Ahab's freshly sworn ally Jehoshaphat uses his new status in the relationship to challenge Ahab's decision-making: 'Inquire first for the word of the LORD.' How often do you think that you're right when you think up your way of tackling a problem? How often do you allow for a range of different approaches to a situation? To be willing to consult may mean things take a little longer, but it can also mean we make choices out of humility not self-righteousness, and we come to decisions wisely and mindful of our Christian responsibility.

Jehoshaphat draws Ahab to consult the Lord. But Ahab's massive gathering of 400 prophets speak only about 'the Lord' (note the capitalization). That is to say, while Jehoshaphat wanted Yahweh brought into the decision, Ahab's prophets refer only to 'the Lord'. Jehoshaphat is unimpressed by these 400 – he simply wants a prophet of Yahweh. That's when Micaiah comes in.

To speak God's word

Micaiah has a reputation for saying things that Ahab doesn't want to hear. That is, he speaks the truth – but Ahab doesn't necessarily want to hear the truth.

As if the 400 have got wise to Jehoshaphat's desire for a prophecy in the name of Yahweh, they now start referring to the Lord. They tell Ahab what he wants to hear: you'll win in this battle. How often do we want false reassurance from people? Sometimes there are answers we just want to hear, in our fragility: the truth can be too much to face.

But Micaiah's not just going to say what Ahab wants him to say. He declares: 'As the LORD [Yahweh] lives, whatever the LORD says to me, that I will speak.' He's not bending his words to anyone else's agenda. He's no reed shaken in the wind. He only speaks the words Yahweh gives him.

So it's surprising Micaiah first says that Ahab will be victorious. (Later, this apparent falsehood is explained – these too are Yahweh's words, because Yahweh sends lying prophets to lure Ahab to his death.) Ahab is suspicious – after all, Micaiah is usually a prophet of doom! So Ahab wheedles the truth out of Micaiah. Micaiah can now proclaim: 'I saw all Israel scattered on the mountains, like sheep that have no shepherd.'

Judgement

Advent is a time for thinking not just about preparing for Christmas but about preparing for the second coming of Christ, the day of judgement. Ahab had previously turned away from Yahweh – Jehoshaphat, who was generally seen as a devout king of Judah, probably knew about this apostasy of Ahab, and that might explain how the two interact in this story.

The Lord has judged: he has found Ahab wanting. Despite his cunning plan in battle – indeed, *through* his cunning plan in battle – Ahab will be killed (read the rest of the story!).

May this Advent be full of moments when you turn back to the Lord. When he comes, may he find you filled with his truth, and attuned to his word.

Megan I. J. Daffern

Suggested hymns

Restore, O Lord, the honour of your name; Great shepherd of thy people; Rejoice, O land, in God thy might; Wait for the Lord, whose day is near.

Third Sunday of Advent   13 December
Principal Service   **Sign-posting the Messiah**
Isa. 61.1–4, 8–end; Ps. 126, *or Canticle*: Magnificat;
1 Thess. 5.16–24; **John 1.6–8, 19–28**

The season of Advent is gathering momentum. The Scriptures are building up to undergird the enormity of what is to happen. Future focused, hope filled, pointing to one who is to come, bringing new life and salvation – the Messiah.

Restoration

Hundreds of years before the coming of Christ the Israelites returned from exile in Babylon to find their beloved Jerusalem ransacked and destroyed. Isaiah prophesied that the ruined city would be rebuilt and the devastation repaired. The Israelites were called and commissioned to restore their home to a place of safety and prosperity. The exiled Israelites were abused, oppressed and imprisoned: broken-hearted, bowed down and grieving. Before they can repair their home, they themselves have to be restored. The promise from God is that the Spirit of the Lord will anoint a messenger who will bring good news to the oppressed, bind up the broken-hearted, proclaim liberty to the captives and release to prisoners, to turn ashes into garlands and mourning into gladness. The people will become oaks of righteousness – solid and stable – and then they will be able to rebuild their lives and their community. Several hundred years later many were beginning to think that perhaps John the Baptist was this promised person – who would turn everything around and save his people. In today's Gospel the priests and Levites from the Temple in Jerusalem go to Bethany to question John. Are you Elijah? Are you a prophet? Are you the Messiah? John says he is none of these things: he is a signpost, pointing to the Messiah, preparing the way for the Messiah to come. John is turning people around so that when the Messiah is revealed they will be ready to respond. John points away from himself to Jesus. And it is Jesus who stands up in the synagogue in Luke 4 and appropriates the words from Isaiah 61, revealing himself as the Messiah: 'The Spirit of the Lord is upon me.'

Good news

Two thousand years on and we live in a time and a place where all is not well. We aren't in the same situation as the returning Israelites, but nevertheless our communities have had a tough time of it in recent years. We are affected by natural disasters, economic crises, emotional disturbance, political chaos and societal division. We have been resilient, but still we have suffered and are suffering. Like the Israelites, many in our communities need to hear good news: news that goes deeper than material things, good news that heals and restores and saves – the good news of Jesus Christ. We have that good news to share. We carry within ourselves the saving love of Jesus and take it wherever we go. But we, the Church, must be very careful not to get in the way of the message. It's very easy to point to ourselves rather than to Christ. Sometimes we are in danger of saying, 'What a great church this is' – rather than, 'What a great God we have.' Like John the Baptist we need to point away from ourselves and help people to see and believe that Christ is at work among and within them.

Rejoice and pray

St Paul, in the reading from Thessalonians, shows us how to live that good news of Jesus for others. 'Rejoice always,' says St Paul. It's very easy at this time of the year to become jaded, cynical and fed up with the fast-approaching season of Christmas. We are celebrating again the coming of Christ, so let's rejoice! 'Pray without ceasing,' says St Paul. Prayer isn't just for Sundays, or the odd emergency. Our whole lives – every second of every day – should be underpinned with our awareness of the presence of God. Next time you walk down the street, or sit in the doctors, or push your trolley around the supermarket, ask for God's blessing on every person you see. Get into the habit of doing it and you'll be amazed at the difference in yourself and in those around you. St Paul urges us to 'Give thanks in all circumstances', for God can bring good out of every situation, however desperate. The Holy Spirit is at work and we are to expect the unexpected, be prepared for surprises and open to change. Don't try to second guess what God might do, but test everything: be wise and flexible. Hold fast to what is good; abstain from every kind of evil – be an example of Christ-like living for those around you. Paul reminds us that God is faithful and he will keep us safe and sound in spirit, soul and body. We have nothing to fear. When we live like this as Christians, we make a real difference in our communities – and we point to something or someone greater and deeper than ourselves, that others find attractive and want to know more. That's how we can be signposts for our friends and neighbours and work colleagues. As we approach Christmas there may be many guests and visitors to our churches and homes. Whoever they are, God welcomes them and longs for Christ to be revealed to them. Let's pray that we can point them to Christ who promises restoration for every person, and who is longing to bring them home.

Catherine Williams

Hymn Suggestions

On Jordan's bank the Baptist's cry; Restore, O Lord; Make way, make way; Wait for the Lord (Taizé).

Third Sunday in Advent 13 December
Second Service **Ready to be Judged**
Ps. 68.1–19 [*or* 68.1–8]; **Mal. 3.1–4; 4**; Phil. 4.4–7; *Gospel at Holy Communion*: Matt. 14.1–12

Have we prepared?

Advent is a season of preparation. But we are not just preparing for the festivities by putting up the Christmas tree or decorating the house. We are not just preparing for the festivities by busily shopping for gifts and food for Christmas Day. We do this season a disservice if, in the course of our Advent preparations, we do not seriously attend to the preparation of our hearts and minds to greet the Christ child who is coming into our midst. For this season not only brings joy, it brings judgement, and therefore we might set aside time and space to reflect on who we are and how we stand before the living God. Are we ready to meet him when he comes in glory?

When Christ comes again, he will, as we repeat every week in the words of the Creed, *come in glory to judge the living and the dead* – all people, of all ages will stand in judgement before him, no one will escape his gaze. We sing in this season, 'Come, Lord Jesus!' We pray that the heavens will drop down and pour down righteousness. We petition,'Come, thou long expected Jesus!' Do we know what we are saying? Do we realize that we are asking God to come again and be our judge? What if this were the moment when Christ came again, like a thief in the night? Would our lamps be ready for the coming of the bridegroom or would our lamps be as yet unfurnished? What if Christ appeared right here, right now, descending upon the clouds? Would we be ready to greet him? Have we prepared?

Purification and promise

During Advent, the Christian stands open to judgement. Naked and exposed before the living God. Vulnerable, yearning, hopeful

14

that we may yet be held to account for our sins, our weaknesses, our horrible selves, and then be transformed by the light of Christ finding our truest selves whom God has known from the beginning.

Judgement could be considered a new beginning, a reckoning, a purifying and cleansing, a trying as silver is tried. The prophet Malachi is asking the same question: who can endure the day of his coming? Who can stand when he appears? The purpose of that judgement, of that standing before God, is to be purified, to be a righteous offering to the Lord, to say to God from our heart, 'Here I am', and trust that through his judgement we will find joy.

The judgement of Christ is a judgement that is transformative, in which the valleys of our lives will be filled, every mountain and hill made low, the crooked ways made straight and the rough ways made smooth. The prospect of divine judgement provokes us to be aware of our utter dependence upon God. For we are nothing without God, we are staring into the empty void. But fear not, we are judged by a merciful God who weeps for humanity and longs for its redemption, who knows our every weakness, who loves us to the end of the ages, who promised us he would come again.

Disclosing the purposes of the heart

There is nothing that cannot be redeemed by the purifying power of the living God. We acknowledge that when the Lord comes, he will bring to light the things now hidden in darkness and disclose the purposes of the heart. Like a searchlight, like a beam of pure light, this child for whom we prepare and for whom we wait will expose sin and hatred and injustice. Human hearts will be opened, all desires known and no secrets hidden. Like a refiner's fire, like fuller's soap, this child will cleanse and purify and re-create us in his image. We will be transformed, we will be changed, we will be made new.

As Christians, we know who this child is. We know who he will become and we know that this child knows everything about us. The purity of this child exposes us completely in the light of his presence. Are we ready for that exposure? That being laid bare in all of our weakness and confusion and obfuscation? It will put into right perspective the petty judgements we make on each other and bring us face to face with the God who loved the world so much that he gave his only son, so that those who believe in him may not perish but have eternal life.

As we await the divine judgement that we know one day will come, we repent, we turn to the Lord once again with a pure heart and humble voice, and we pray that he might bring to light the things now hidden in darkness and disclose the purposes of the heart so that at the last day, when we stand in judgement, we may indeed come to his eternal joy.

Victoria Johnson

Suggested hymns

Hark, a Herald voice is calling; The Lord will come and not be slow; When came in flesh the incarnate word; Hark, the glad sound.

Fourth Sunday of Advent   20 December
Principal Service   **Living the Gospel**
2 Sam. 7.1–11, 16; *Canticle*: Magnificat, *or* Ps. 89.1–4, 19–26 [*or* 89.1–8]; **Rom. 16.25–end**; Luke 1.26–38

One of the endearing and irritating things about Paul is that he is not over-blessed with modesty. Take today's Epistle as an example.

He's rounding off his remarkable and richly challenging letter to the young church in Rome and so needs to find a suitably upbeat ending – a kind of memorable flourish.

So, look at what he does. Certainly, he puts God first: 'Now to God who is able to strengthen you ...' That's exactly the kind of trumpet-blasting phrase we would expect Paul to use. It's filled with faith and comfort.

But now look at what he writes next: 'according to my gospel'. Note, it's not *the* gospel. No, it's *my* gospel. That's quite a claim. Remember, he was not one of the twelve disciples; he had never met Jesus in the flesh; he had not composed a Gospel like Mark or Matthew; he was a rabbi who had had a profound and life-changing encounter on the road to Damascus, as a result of which he had to wrestle with all his old ways of thinking and discover disturbingly new ones. Some of that wrestling we can see in the earlier chapters of his letter to the church in Rome, and the results are amazing. He has fought himself almost to a standstill. He is on the edge of theological and spiritual exhaustion, but through his courage and through his determination to try to discover the truth about the nature of God in Christ, he has found himself in a new and totally unexpected place. He has discovered that God suffers, that God's power is not what he once thought it was. He has come to the belief that God's plan has been working itself out from Adam through Abraham and through the Jewish people, but the deepest secrets of that plan have now been revealed in a crucified and risen Saviour. You can almost hear him clattering his pen down on to his desk as he tries to get his head around the scale and beauty of God's purposeful love.

Toil and tears

In that sense, his phrase about '*my* gospel', which at first sight looks like an immodest boast, is nothing of the sort; it is a statement of how, through toil and tears, he has made the revelation he has discovered in Christ absolutely central to his life. He has hammered away at it, hauled it around, looked at it this way and that until the new disclosure has become part of his very being. His gospel is not, as it were, a biblical text out there; it is a lived experience, one that has taken him years to comprehend and absorb into the depths of his soul.

The account of his conversion on the Damascus road has long since entered the Christian vocabulary and has become a kind of template for our own encounters with God. It has become a well-loved Christian archetype. Less well known is the account Paul gives in his letter to the church in Galatia in which he states that immediately after his Damascus road experience he did not go up to Jerusalem but instead took himself off to Arabia – whatever that might mean. Was it there that he began his profoundly demanding vocation of seeking and rediscovering God? The process probably took years. It was not instantaneous. It was not easy. It was not straightforward.

This might be a comfort to many of us: most of the time we also struggle with our faith. We have times of searing doubt, but also times when the sun breaks through; times when we think we are making progress, and times when we feel as though we are flailing around in a swamp and will never reach solid ground.

The finite and the infinite

Yet perhaps this is how it is bound to be. After all, what we are trying to do, by God's grace, is to understand God. We, the finite, are trying to comprehend the infinite; we who are mortal are trying to understand immortality; we who are imprisoned by time are trying to grasp eternity.

But if we are to try to make the gospel our own, and to do so in the way that Paul did, then we shall need similar reserves of perseverance, determination and a kind of holy patience. We may even have to enter our own Arabias, and it may take us a lifetime. But the glimpses of joy and of liberation we receive as we struggle will be our occasional advents; for the wonderful paradox is that though we rightly struggle to know God, it is God in his mercy who reveals himself to us. Waiting in faith is all. And in the end, as Paul says, we shall know even as we are known – and that will be heaven.

Christopher Herbert

Suggested hymns

Come, thou long expected Jesus; Lo, he comes with clouds descending; Let all mortal flesh keep silence; The Lord will come and not be slow.

Fourth Sunday of Advent   20 December
Second Service   **Prophecies that Fuel Hope**
Ps. 113 [or 131]; **Zech. 2.10–end**; Luke 1.39–55

During Advent, congregations are treated to a large dose of Old Testament readings, and especially at our carol services. They're mostly taken from the prophetic writings, but some readings direct us back to the imagined creation itself, the Garden of Eden, and then to Abraham. You may well ask yourselves why we read these ancient texts every year. The obvious response is that we read them because we still wait for their promised fulfilment. But that means that what was promised 400 or so years before the birth of Jesus is still to be delivered, and that's 2,400 years ago, a long time to be waiting, when prophets like Isaiah declared that his nation would be restored and all the nations would flock to it.

Prophecies delayed, unmet, superseded

Now, before you think this is becoming negative, we must acknowledge that there were at least partial fulfilments along the way. The most prominent texts we use at Advent come from the book of the prophet Isaiah. That's a composite book of prophecies delivered before, during and after the exile in 587. The exile was the greatest catastrophe in the history of the Israelites. Jerusalem fell, the Temple was destroyed and the cream of the nation was deported to Babylon. Isaiah, who wrote the central sections of the book, promised that the Jews held captive in Babylon would return imminently to their homeland, and the future of the nation would be restored. That didn't happen, and the Jews never recovered their state. But there was an unexpected intervention, when a pagan leader, Cyrus, defeated the Babylonians and allowed all the Jewish exiles to return home. He even funded the rebuilding of the Temple in Jerusalem. The secular historian Simon Segbag Montefiore comments that 'Jewish history is filled with miraculous deliverances' and the action of Cyrus 'was one of the most dramatic'.[18] But this was hardly a fulfilment of the promises made. After 60 years, most of the Jewish exiles had made a good home for themselves in their new country and only a trickle returned to their homeland. The Temple was rebuilt, but it was a pale reflection of the Temple it replaced, and the nation of Israel did not survive.

Prophecies that help recognize Jesus' identity

Instead of hope collapsing, the greatest prophets, Isaiah, Jeremiah and Ezekiel, and a lot of 'minor prophets' voiced daring visions of a glorious new future. They are always social, political, economic, this-worldly, and all depend upon the action and intervention of God. We all know some of them. The promise to 'beat their swords into ploughshares and their spears into pruning hooks'; 'Nation shall not lift up sword against nation'; 'Behold, I am creating a new heaven and a new earth'.

These aren't programmes, blueprints, detailed, dated, action plans. They're poetic, imaginative, large dreams that capture the often inchoate but deepest longings, hopes and intimations of the human spirit. They are the wistful voicing of hope for a final consummation of human life and the natural world ... but they pinned their hopes on a new leader modelled on Moses and David. And because the future is dependent upon God's action, we have promises of a woman with a child, a suffering servant, a Messiah figure, a branch of Jesse, a new Davidic warrior. Such references are likely to have had a more immediate reference to someone who existed at the time. But they voiced a more distant, eagerly awaited future, which God would bring about.

Through the stupendous life, ministry, death and resurrection of Jesus of Nazareth, it was natural that he should be matched against the sketchy hints and hope of a Messiah figure. All the desperate expectations of a future for the people of God and a Messiah figure came to converge on Jesus. And the Gospel writers, like Matthew, are at pains to show that Jesus is the fulfilment of those ancient promises.

Why do we read these ancient texts? We hear and read these hope-filled promises and prophecies at this time so that we have expectations heightened and hearts prepared for the One who comes at Christmas. They tell us the story of God's design from the beginning of the world until now. They show that the coming of Jesus was God's intention from eternity, anticipated by the prophets, prepared by John the Baptist, and recapitulating in the figures of the New Adam, the seed of Abraham, the New Moses. As the hymn had it: 'The hopes and fears of all the earth are met in thee – tonight.' Reading the books of the prophets helps us to recognize that in Jesus God has vindicated his name and fulfilled his promise.

Prophecies that transport us in hope

But still, the daring prophecies are only partially fulfilled. The reign of peace and the end to war, the waters flowing in the dessert, the coming together of the nations of the world, and the peaceable reign of God, is far from being a reality. The prophecies aren't spent. We need them to feed and fill our stunted imaginations. We need them to subvert the prevailing hope-less narrative that we are alone, cosmically alone. That we are left to ourselves to retrieve the brutal, fragmented world of nations and avert the impending ecological catastrophe. We can only reach out in hope to a future through the imagination, through the daring, lyrical, percussive language of the prophets. We read them to celebrate God's faithfulness in bringing Jesus into our fallen world. And we read them so that as we live in this expiring world we can also live in the hope and exhilaration of the coming kingdom. Let us surrender to these evocative and lyrical texts so that we live in and from the hope and conviction of God's kingdom already present and at work among us.

Roger Spiller

Suggested hymns

The people that in darkness sat; When the King shall come again; Word of God, come down to earth; Lord, bring the day to pass.

Christmas, Epiphany and Candlemas

Christmas Day   25 December

Any of the following sets of readings may be used on the evening of Christmas Eve and on Christmas Day. Set III should be used at some service during the celebration.

Set I   **May You Unwrap Hope this Christmas**

Isa. 9.2–7; Ps. 96; Titus 2.11–14; **Luke 2.1–14 [15–20]**

Christmas season. When I was a kid I always hoped for snow at Christmas. Longed for a beautiful blanket of it. Dreamt of a white Christmas. It rarely happened, but it was always my fervent hope at Christmas time. What words and images spring to your mind in response to the word 'hope'? Hope sits close to the word possibility. It is the candle in the night. It is the first light of the dawning sun. Hope.

Hope between the lines

The Gospel reading set for this Christmas Day has hope dancing between the lines. The word is never mentioned, but the passage is laden with it. Hope. Hope is oxygen to the life of faith and the spiritual path. Hope is essential to our health in every sense of the word. Hope can enable us to stand in bleak places with resilience. Hope can suddenly break forth in joy – and add layers of meaning and nuance to life. Hope is the toast of the Christmas season. Hope will carry us through the winter – through the despair of Good Friday and beyond into Easter Sunday's promise of a life beyond the horizons of all our todays. This profound hope, born in humble places, is at the heart of Christmas.

Hope profound and trivial

The backdrop to our passage is political – a census for taxation purposes ordered by the Emperor Augustus. Everyone had to head to their place of birth to be registered. Not Brexit – but Taxit. I wonder what they hope for: 'Will we get accommodation? Hope so.' 'I hope we meet the family.' 'I hope this won't lead to more taxation.' Some of our hopes are relatively small, and often self-interested. But the music of a much greater hope is building throughout the humble setting of our reading.

In the midst of all this, Joseph and Mary head to Bethlehem; she's heavily pregnant. I wonder what they are hoping for? 'Will we find a clean, warm place to give birth? Hope so. Will the baby be OK? Oh Lord, I hope so.' I wonder what Mary is thinking. 'How am I going to do this?' I wonder if Gabriel's words of hope are ringing in her ears. This is to be a son who will reign over the House of David, his kingdom will never end. These massive hopes for the future nestle near smaller hopes for a manageable labour. For it all to be OK.

Are we any different? Huge spiritual and political hopes often co-exist with smaller, more personal hopes. I hope for resolution in our political conflicts, I hope for peace. I hope for life beyond the life we know. I hope I stay healthy. I hope for roast potatoes with my Christmas dinner and lots of gravy. Hope – profound hopes, trivial hopes – they coexist.

Hope in unlikely places

Notice how profound hope is rooted in places that the powerful might overlook. God lifts up the lowly and raises up the humble. Listen as the music of hope comes to a crescendo when a group of shabby shepherds receive a visitation beyond their wildest dreams. They are amid the normal, humdrum round of shepherding. They are probably scruffy, a tad on the ripe side. Suddenly, the fabric of their normality is rent apart. The angel of the Lord, shining, stands before them and these rough fellas are terrified. Notice the angel's first words to them are the same as to Mary – 'Don't be afraid.' The angel brings good news of great joy for all the people. This is not a hope for the favoured few, for an elite cabal. This is radical hope for all. The Saviour, Messiah and Lord is to be born. Notice that this hope is communicated to outcasts and is to be found in lowly places: 'You will find a child wrapped in bands of cloth and lying in a manger.'

God plants his eternal hope in the ordinary. The sacred nestles among the profane. This is hope.

God, Emmanuel – the Christ who is with us, Jesus, is born amid the everyday – then as now.

God is to be found over the washing-up, over a cuppa, in a conversation, in a flower, in a beautiful landscape, or seascape – in a mud hut, in a council flat, on a bus. Heavenly hope is earthed in the local – available for all.

Hope surrounds us

Hope surrounds us – God is here. Whatever you face today, whatever we face as a society. Whatever the world faces. Never give up hope. God brings light to the dark places; his love pierces the veil of tears; he breaks the rod of the oppressor; he gives us hope in his son who is named: Wonderful Counsellor, Mighty God, Everlasting Father, Prince of Peace. But don't be fooled – this hope is earthed in skin and found in the vulnerability of a child.

This Christmas – somewhere between the turkey and the washing-up – may you unwrap deep hope and discover the presence of God. Look in the ordinary places. You'll be surprised.

Kate Bruce

Suggested hymns

Angels from the realms of glory; Let all mortal flesh keep silence; In the bleak mid-winter; O come, all ye faithful.

Christmas Day   25 December
Set II   **Making Space at Christmas**
Isa. 62.6–end; Ps. 97; Titus 3.4–7; **Luke 2.[1–7] 8–20**

Sometimes the old ones are the best. Mary and Joseph arrive at Bethlehem and ask the innkeeper if he has any space. 'No, I haven't,' he says. And Joseph says, 'But my wife is about to have a baby!' 'Well, that's not my fault,' says the innkeeper. 'No,' says Joseph, 'and it's not my fault either!'

Making space

You could say that the whole message of Christmas is about making space, about a God who didn't just sit safely in heaven and watch his people make a mess of things, but who had room for them in his heart. But when he came among us, his people didn't have room for him. Joseph did – he made space for a child who was not his own. Mary did too – she gave birth to a child she hadn't looked for or expected. And the shepherds did, in today's Gospel reading: they made space in their lives to go and find out what the 'good news' the angel brought them was all about. (We may notice in passing that the angel appears to them *in their workplace*, while they were out in the fields with their sheep: would we notice an angel if one appeared in ours?) But the holy people, the powerful people and the busy people didn't have room for God at all.

Space for others

What about us? We live in a world where the sound of doors closing, walls being built, foreigners being driven out, refugees turned away, drowns out everything else. And what about you and me? How good are we at making space for other people? It's not easy: to make space for anyone – a husband or wife, a child or parent, a friend, a pet, a next-door neighbour, let alone a stranger – always involves changing your plans, reordering your own emotional furniture. The life of Jesus is full of moments when he stopped and made space for people, especially the people no one else bothered with. And not just people: he noticed sparrows, lilies, salt, donkeys, and much else too. There was always room in his inn, even though as a baby he didn't find space in someone else's.

Giving up space

But then on the other hand: think of those who are giving up their Christmas in your neighbourhood to cook a meal for people who would otherwise be on their own; or those delivering food bank supplies over the Christmas period; or doctors and nurses across the world who freely choose to spend their holiday time travelling to some of the world's most dangerous places and offer their skills. And think of the people who've made space in their lives for you – your mum, for example. Will you make space for God, and the stranger, this Christmas? If the old jokes are sometimes the best, so are the old songs. Let me end with two. The first is a famous hymn:

Thou didst leave thy throne and thy kingly crown
When thou camest to earth for me ...
O come to my heart, Lord Jesus,
There is room in my heart for thee.

The other, if you're old enough to remember it, is a popular song: 'Merry Christmas, Everybody' – the number one hit from the rock band Slade in the 1970s. It still has a message for today.

Gordon Mursell

Suggested hymns

Christians awake! Salute the happy morn; In the bleak mid-winter; Thou didst leave thy throne and thy kingly crown; Hark! the herald angels sing.

Christmas Day 25 December
Set III **Stories**
Isa. 52.7–10; Ps. 98; Heb. 1.1–4 [5–12]; **John 1.1–14**

A joke?

Happy Christmas! Ready or not, the big day has arrived. It's time to stop worrying about the details, what has or hasn't happened – and start celebrating. In the Christmas story – God coming to be with us, as a human baby, Jesus – there's a coming together of two stories – God's story and humanity's story – and the results are very unexpected: puzzling, mysterious, hard to handle, even laughable, a bit of a joke perhaps. A joke works because it is the coming together of two stories that are different but with an underlying relatedness. As the stories meet so there is an unexpected outcome that surprises us – sometimes it makes us laugh, sometimes it leaves us puzzled. Often, we are impressed by the skill and subtlety of it all.

God's story

The people of God in the Older Testament were looking for someone who would be raised up for victory, who would save them; someone with the stature of a king – like David. They were looking for someone who would liberate them from their oppressors, the

25

Romans. Looking for someone to bring peace, to rebuild Jerusalem, the holy city. They were expecting God to bare his holy arm before the nations. They were expecting to see the Lord in 'plain sight' – right before their eyes. This is exactly what God did. God's story and the Israelites' story came together in a very surprising way. God bared his holy arm, but it was the bare arm of a baby, Jesus, vulnerable, poor, illegitimate – there for all to see in 'plain sight' indeed. God – right before their eyes. What could be easier to see than another human being? But the Bible tells us: 'He came to what was his own, and his own people did not accept him.' God in Jesus wasn't what people were expecting. It seemed so topsy-turvy – no wonder people didn't get the punch line. Yet despite those who didn't believe, God's story and the stories of individuals did meet, and the result was the blossoming of the Christian faith and the spreading of the message of Jesus Christ across the world and down the centuries. It's a message of peace and good will – that God can and does transform people's lives, bringing light into the darkness. Have you noticed how much of the Christmas story takes place in the dark? The stable would have been dark. The angels appear to the shepherds in the dark. The star shines in the dark for the wise men to follow. It was as the prophets foretold: the people who walked in darkness saw a great light – those who dwelt in the land of deep shadows experienced light shining on them.

Our story

God's story wasn't just for those who were around two thousand years ago. God still longs for his story and your story to meet. Maybe you long for that too and that's why you're here. You had a choice this morning. You could have had a lie-in, you could have stayed home and watched television, started cooking the lunch, opened your presents. Instead, you chose to come and celebrate again the story of Christmas, God's gift to the world – Jesus Christ. And as you come, so you bring yourself, your own story, to meet God's story. It may be that recently you have recognized that God is around for you and for his world. It may have been a difficult year. But often when things are most bleak, most dark, then the light of God can be seen most brightly. For God it's a small step from heaven to earth, from crucifixion to resurrection, from death to new life. As God's story and your story meet so the unexpected may happen. God may surprise you, puzzle you, leave you with more questions than answers. God may make you laugh, or reduce you to tears. If you are willing to let God's story into your story then life will never be the same. Mary knew that, Joseph knew that, the visitors to the crib discovered it and so have millions of people since. When light shines in dark places important things get sorted. We think in new ways, we rise to challenges and make a fresh start. Recognizing yourself to be in God's story brings responsibility and discipline as well as joy and surprises. It's not all plain sailing: life lived to the full rarely is. On this day we remember that the baby in the manger is God's way of reaching out to the whole world – bringing salvation. It's God's way of showing love for all without exception. God reaches out to you, today – and to all those you love. Invite God to join your stories together, to shine light into dark places in your life and in our world, so that all may be transformed. Happy Christmas!

Catherine Williams

Suggested hymns

O come, all ye faithful; Joy to the world; Of the Father's love begotten; Mary, did you know?

Christmas Day   25 December
Second Service   **We're Coming Home!**
Morning Ps. 110, 117; Evening Ps. 8; **Isa. 65.17–25**; Phil. 2.5–11, or Luke 2.1–20 (*if it has not been used at the Principal Service of the day*)

Love song to Jerusalem

There are highs and lows in every relationship. In the 'sweeping saga' of Israel's relationship with God comes this lovely song of hope and love. The writings of the Hebrew Bible tell a story of God's love for a small nation going through enormous change and suffering. A chosen people, set apart, called to live in a way that would reflect God's love back to the whole world. Rising on a hill in the midst of this story there is a holy city – Jerusalem – whose Temple represented the very dwelling of God in their midst.

In 587 BC, Jerusalem was captured by the Babylonian army and its people carried off into exile. The book of Lamentations depicts

27

Jerusalem as a woman in mourning, grieving for her children, her people, her beloved, her past. It was during the time in Babylon that the people began to write down their story, to remember the past, to try to express what it meant to be the people of God and the journey of trauma and transformation they had travelled.

Re-member

As years in exile passed, fewer and fewer people would remember their lives in Judah and Jerusalem. They would begin to put down roots in a foreign land. The idea of returning would have become not just a distant dream but an enormous challenge. The generation who remembered that other life would have died. Many would have felt disconnected from the place that others had called home. Though aliens in Babylon they would have had little individual memory of Jerusalem. Where was 'home' when it felt more alien than exile? Yet deep in the collective psyche was a need to reconnect, to re-member who they were as a people, the people of God.

Isaiah's words are therefore prophetic in the truest sense: speaking truth and healing into the place of past trauma and loss of identity, speaking hope and energy to those who had become lethargic and purposeless; a voice for those who had been silenced by political and national power; to remind a people who had forgotten where they came from that they belonged to the God who liberates from slavery and calls us to abundant life.

Transforming love

What a message for Christmas Day! Such a song is a reminder that God's holy mountain will extend to all the world where it will be possible for the wolf and the lamb to live in harmony; for destruction and pain to end. It is a song of transforming love.

Of course, transformation is not reached without an openness and willingness to change. Transformation does not come through fearing the future or wanting to stay where we are simply because it's what we know and what we're used to. Transformation comes through stepping out even when it is risky. It comes about through remembering who we truly are – the people of God made for relationship, called into being for the sake of the whole world. To be witnesses of what love can do.

Return

This passage in Isaiah is about the return from exile, which is the true meaning of repentance. The word repent means 'to return'; return to who we truly are; return to the love that called us into being. To remember who we are! It is about a journey home. Isaiah encourages the exiles with a song of hope. *This is what it will mean to return. This is God's heart for you. Prepare for the journey home.*

The Christmas story is all about journeys. Refugees travel across the Roman world at the command of a foreign power. Wise men travel from the splendour of Persia to a remote town in a foreign country. Angelic messengers travel to give news to mortals. The Christ travels from majesty to vulnerable human birth. From heaven to earth. And we are called to travel the way of Jesus. It is a risky thing to do – to live this way of love. We may feel settled where we are, even if it isn't perfect. We may have forgotten who we are meant to be. There may be grief or trauma that tries to hold us back. But Christmas is about the biggest change that ever happened in human history. God came to us as one of us so that we could understand what it meant to be made in God's image. To remember who we are and who travels with us. So that we can be part of transforming the whole earth into that holy mountain. Re-turn, for the kingdom of God is here. For the journey is always about returning to the home we had forgotten – the heart of God. Our true selves.

Carey Saleh

Suggested hymns

From heaven you came, helpless babe; Longing for light, we wait in darkness; You shall go out with joy; How lovely on the mountain.

First Sunday of Christmas   27 December

(For John, Apostle and Evangelist, see p. 284.)

Principal Service   **Growing Up with Jesus**

Isa. 61.10—62.3; Ps. 148 [*or* 148.7–end]; Gal. 4.4–7;
Luke 2.15–21

A one-day wonder?

There was something rather disconcerting about the Christmas crib in our diocesan office. The shepherds were there, to be sure, and even the kings arrived, prematurely. No, what concerned some of us was that the person who had custody of the crib was determined that the ceramic baby Jesus should not appear in the crib before Christmas Day. But of course, we were not going to be at the diocesan headquarters on Christmas Day, and by the time we returned, the crib would be packed away and Jesus wrapped in bubble wrap, out of sight, for one more year.

Perhaps we're feeling we've missed out on Christmas; its impact has passed us by. Even in the gospel story, things move quickly. The angels have gone and the shepherds, having told their story, are out of the picture. Life returns to normal, as it does for most of us after Christmas: a one-day wonder, a brief interlude as we resume the fast pace of modern living.

Treasuring and pondering

But there's another figure in our story, one who offers a route to a deeper engagement with the Christmas story. Luke, like all good storytellers, likes to draw contrasts: the Pharisee and publican, the prodigal son and the resentful brother. Luke tells us that shepherds 'made known what had been told them about this child'. But, says Luke, Mary 'treasured all these words and pondered them in her heart'. Shepherds may be like those Luke describes who hear the word, receive it with joy, but have no root. But Mary is one of those who 'hearing the word, hold it fast in an honest and good heart'. The shepherds made the good news known to those at Bethlehem as they were told it, and are now discharged. But Mary is not merely reiterating good news, she is on a journey in order to penetrate the deepest meaning of the events that have happened and the mysterious sign that has been given to her. She is a believer and a disciple.

The Church urges us to speak and share what we have seen and

30

heard, like the shepherds, and that is surely right. But isn't there a prior need for us to follow Mary and to treasure and ponder and weigh the Christmas story first, for ourselves? There are, after all, experiences that are too rich or raw or intimate to be shared and must await a long period of reflection, and, as we say, 'processing', before they can be brought to speech.

God comes as story

God comes to us at Christmas as story. It's a true story because he came and comes in history. And we access him today chiefly through story. We are given a story, because only by story can our imagination begin to be amazed by God's coming down to earth in Jesus.

> There was once a king who fell in love with a lowly woman. But how was a king to make his love known to a mere country girl? He considered sending one of his servants. But on hearing of the king's love for her, the woman only laughed in unbelief. How could she know the message was really from the king and not a trick to ridicule her?
>
> What could the king do to convince her of his love. One thing he could do: he could visit her himself in all his splendour, making her forget herself in adoration. That might satisfy the woman but it wouldn't satisfy the king because he loved her and desired a genuine loving response from her, rather than his own glorification. He feared she might never be able to forget that he was the king and she a lowly maiden.
>
> What more could the king do to express his love. Only one way remained. He must renounce his rights and power and become a servant. If, thought the king, he had the heart of a servant, if his truest self was expressed in his love for the woman, there would be no deception in becoming a servant. He would be expressing his true self. (Based on a parable by Søren Kierkegaard.)

Jesus grows up in us through story

All this God has done for you and me to win our love. As St Paul says, 'Though he was rich, yet for your sake he became poor so that by his poverty, you might become rich.' And if we live with the story, inhabit it, let it roam freely and frequently in our imagination, then the effects of Christmas will take root in us. But we won't leave Jesus as a baby in a crib. We'll let Jesus grow up in us as his story unfolds through the Church's year, until the living Jesus finally becomes part and parcel of our own story. It's not the story that saves us; only Jesus saves us. But through pondering and living his story and giving space to his very own Spirit, our lives are infused with wonder, gratitude, generosity and hope.

Roger Spiller

Suggested hymns

Thou didst leave thy throne and thy kingly crown; Thou who wast rich, beyond all splendour; You were a babe of mine (Wren); Joy to the world, the Lord is come!

First Sunday of Christmas   27 December
Second Service   **The Cosmic Christ**
Ps. 132; Isa. 35; **Col. 1.9–20**, *or* Luke 2.41–end

A couple of days ago we were celebrating the *fact* of Jesus' birth. But now we are ready to edge a bit closer to what his birth *means*. St John's account in the Prologue to his Gospel has been read in all the churches. But now we're hearing what St Paul says about what Jesus Christ means. And when Paul comes to describing Jesus in his letter to the Christians at Colossae, you can tell he's on a roll and breathless to express himself. He uses a fast-flowing cascade of images whose force explodes our minds and breaks open the language and thought by which we often try to confine and pin down Jesus.

Agent before and in creation

Paul says of Jesus, the Son, that he is the image of the invisible God, the icon of God, the window into the divine reality. He is 'the firstborn of all creation', that is, the one who is before all creation; that in him and through him and for him, all things were created; he is God's agent before and in creation, and, prospectively 'in him all things hold together'; and 'through him all things, on earth or heaven will be reconciled to him'. That, in a word, speaks of a cosmic Christ, God's co-creator.

I suspect that most of us think of Christ largely as being just for us, our saviour, but not the saviour of the whole world. We think of him as the one who rescues us and carries us to heaven; not as the one who has truly 'placed us in the garden of (his) delight'. We think of creation as the messy place to escape from, rather than the project to which God has committed himself. We think, then, of the natural world as the disposable stage setting for human living, as our resource to exploit and dominate, instead of nurturing it as faithful stewards of God.

A leading environmental ethicist has claimed that for years religion, and Christianity in particular, was a prime cause of the ecological crisis in which we are enveloped.

Creation cherished and redeemed

But as we discern from St Paul, Christianity affirms God's concern for the whole of creation and for its redemption because his Son was involved in the creation of the whole cosmos no less than the agent in our redemption. More even than the divine *agent* in creation, Christ is the *reason* for creation. That is what Paul means when he claims that in him *all* things hold together and *all* things will be reconciled to him. In the eighth chapter of Paul's letter to the church at Rome, he speaks of the whole creation as well as ourselves 'waiting with eager longing to be set free from its bondage to decay'. Paul speaks not only about the survival of *Homo sapiens*; he speaks for and on behalf of the whole of the created cosmos.

In a more recent book, the writer who criticized the part played by religion in the ecological crisis makes a startling confession. He writes: 'The Church may be, in fact, our last and best chance. My conjecture is this. There are no solutions for this systemic cause of the eco-crisis apart from a religious narrative.'[19]

What's being said is that it needs a narrative, a story, to deliver both challenge and hope if we're to address the greatest crisis facing the planet and the future of humankind. And Christians have this story. Our Judaeo-Christian Scriptures tell us about the whole created order and how we fit into it. They proclaim our connectedness to creation as creatures of God, redeemed by Jesus Christ. And they tell us that 'the whole creation' is waiting, and hoping for the freedom and glory that characterizes the children of God.

Creation's praise

No wonder, then, that the Psalmist and prophets assigned human characteristics to distinct parts of creation and enticed them to share in the cosmic orchestration of praise to our divine creator. 'The heavens praise your wonders, O LORD'; 'Let the sea roar, let floods clap their hands', 'fields of grain raise their heads'; 'Valleys stand so thick with corn that they shall laugh and sing'. The inter-relationship of all creation, including ourselves, was caught by St Francis when he spoke of Sister Water and Brother Moon. We don't have to talk to plants and trees or put an anthropomorphic gloss on all the components of the created world. But we might treat them differently. And in a great religious classic, *I and Thou*, the Jewish writer Martin Buber suggested that we can relate to the parts of creation, like a tree, not merely as an 'it' but as a 'thou', as over-against me, yet embodied and as something that has to do with me, and with whom to reckon. If the creation is through Christ and for Christ then his followers have a sacred duty to value, honour and delight in the myriad creation and cherish the relationships they afford. And it's a relationship through which we may encounter Jesus, our cosmic creator.

Roger Spiller

Suggested hymns

Lord, bring the day to pass; The works of the Lord are created in wisdom; Above the moon earth rises; Touch the earth lightly.

Second Sunday of Christmas 3 January
(*or* Epiphany; see p. 292)
Principal Service **Who is to Blame?**
Jer. 31.7–14, Ps. 147 13–end; *or* Ecclus. 24.1–12,
Canticle: Wisd. 10.15–end; **Eph. 1.3–14**; John 1.[1–9] 10–18

Children can have a disarming way of challenging our thinking. So ... imagine that a child you know well has been accused by his parents of fibbing. The child, who has recently developed a vivid imagination, has been caught boasting and telling absurd lies in playtime conversation with his friends. His parents heard him say that his father has massive strength given him by an invisible giant whom no one else can see. As a result, the child claims precedence in choosing what games to play; otherwise, he says, his father, using his fearsome secret power, will turn any child who disagrees into a blob of ugly and repulsive jelly. The other children don't know what to make of this, but because they are younger, they go along with the threat and allow the older child to decide what games they should take part in.

When his parents challenge him about his boasting, he replies that he was just making things up, like people do in books and on television. What's so wrong about that, he asks?

The question is: how would you handle a situation like that? Is the child to blame? Is he not just copying a powerful feature of the adult world? Or should the parents try to explain to him that there really are important differences between the 'pretend' world and the real world, and he must not muddle them up, otherwise no one will know whether to believe him or not? The parents might even resort to the age-old story about the boy who cried 'wolf' in the hope that the threat in that story might frighten the child into telling the truth.

The child looks puzzled and crestfallen ... but behind and within this episode lies a serious moral question about blame.

Shifting the blame

It's an issue with which the media constantly assail us. You will have noticed that the media like nothing better than finding someone to blame. 'They' are to blame; society is to blame; teachers are to blame; politicians are to blame; the police are to blame – the list is endless.

Of course, the shifting of blame has gone on since humankind first walked the earth. Think of the story of Adam and Eve, innocents in the Garden of Eden. Eve is tempted by the serpent; Adam is tempted by Eve ... who is to blame?

In today's Epistle, the author states that Christians were chosen before the beginning of time and space. And therefore, says the writer, Christians are to be 'holy and blameless before him in love'.

What are we to make of such a statement? If we are honest, we have to admit that there is no way in which the words 'holy' and 'blameless' can be attached to us. We know that we have a propensity to sin: we can be jealous, filled with anger, overwhelmed by rage; we can be greedy, envious, spiteful – you name the sins, we all suffer from them.

It is simply not the case that we are 'blameless'. So, was the writer carried away on a giddy flight of rhetoric? Or was there some kernel of truth in what he wrote?

Perhaps we can try thinking of this 'blame' issue in a different way, not by living with fantastical self-deception, pretending that we are blameless, but by approaching it from the standpoint of eternity.

Let us return to the truths within the Adam and Eve story: they, representing all humans, recognized their own guilt and then tried to shift the blame for what they had done on to others. In doing so they had come to have a moral sense, no matter how feeble it was initially. To try to pin blame on to others is to work on the assumption (an assumption that is frequently unexplored) that there is in fact a moral order in the world; that some things are right and others wrong, and when we blame others it is to try to claim that we are on the side of the right and those we blame are not.

That is, of course, an oversimplification but let it stand for the moment.

But if we, who like to hand out blame, are also tainted with similar failings in ourselves, how can we handle the split in our own dispositions? How can we become more self-aware? How can we lose the egotistical and childish desire to feel superior?

Christ the reconciler

Now ask yourself a question. What if the darkness of our tormented inner beings is potentially subject to a power beyond us, a power that works for our inner healing and the reconciliation of our warring inner selves?

Is it too absurd to argue that this is precisely what Christ Jesus did for us on the cross? He did not cancel out what we are truly like. But he is the Saviour who reconciles. In the self-emptying gift of himself to God, he takes us as we are and, looking on us with the love of God, brings healing to the depths of our souls. It is a divine and secret and undeserved activity of grace. It is the process by which, throughout our lives, he draws us towards himself, so that filled with blame as we actually are, we are slowly and gradually made blameless ... and maybe, even holy.

It depends of course, on our willingness to allow Christ to enter the very depths of our souls – the choice to do so or not is ours.

Christopher Herbert

36

Suggested hymns

Immortal, invisible, God only wise; In heavenly love abiding; Lead, kindly light; O worship the Lord in the beauty of holiness.

Second Sunday of Christmas   3 January
Second Service   **Worship: A Living Sacrifice**
Ps. 135 [*or* 135.1–14]; Isa. 46.3–end; **Rom. 12.1–8**; *Gospel at Holy Communion*: Matt. 2.13–end

'Our worship has ended, our service begins'; those were the words of dismissal with which a priest in our team concluded the parish Eucharist, replacing the official words laid down by the compilers. Some church members welcomed this simple clarity. It alerts the congregation to the fact that worship doesn't discharge us from Christian duty but spills over into the rest of our lives and prepares us for service in the wider world. But other church members were a little uneasy about it, although they couldn't quite explain why.

If we look at the phrase in the light of the first verse of our Epistle reading, we will see why the phrase is theologically suspect and misleading. This is no mere semantic argument. The issue challenges the way we think about worship and, indeed, the way in which we are to understand and live out our Christian discipleship.

Worship as total and ceaseless

Christian worship isn't what is practised at sacred sites, at sacred times and in sacred acts. It's the offering of our total, bodily experience in the whole of everyday life. We are God's temple, says Paul, when we are on our own as well as when we are gathered together with fellow believers. Worship, then, doesn't come to an end when the liturgy is over but is ceaseless, and extends for believers over the whole of life, through time and space. And worship, notably intercession, is itself a form of service to the world.

Worship has no 'point' beyond itself

Worship is not confined to church services; it has even to be distinguished from churchgoing. Ask yourself why you go to church. Is it to catch up with friends, to transact business, to gain solace or inspiration, or to feel good? But true worship is 'pointless', 'useless' in human terms. It's a self-dying activity in which we both lose and find our true selves in the beauty, wonder and majesty of God. It can't be justified by serving a purpose or yielding a benefit greater than worship itself. Service and the rest of mission isn't a response to worship. Worship is its own response to all that God in Christ has done. The whole of Christian life, then, is worship. To be sure, our gathering together for worship provides sustenance and instruction for living, but that is not itself the point or purpose of worship. That can only be in, to and for God.

Worship as the goal

Worship is Paul's 'therefore', the consequence of and response to 'the glorious gospel' that he has been expounding in the preceding chapters of his letter to the Romans. Worship is 'reasonable', says St Paul, that is, it is logical, because those who have shared in the grace and mercy of Christ's sacrificial death must offer themselves as a 'living sacrifice', and this cannot be less than total.

Embodied worship

Paul mentions 'bodies' first of all, but this is no cipher or accident. The Christian Church has shown itself to have an uneasy relationship with the human body, but Paul intends us to own the fact that our living worship must be publicly visible, and evident not just in the Church but across the world. Christian existence isn't, after all, a private matter. It's one that is public, and that is important for the world. God has reached out to the world and wills to have this confirmed by the earthly conduct of the community. There is no splitting between bodily and spiritual, as Christians have so often done. Rather, the way we live in the body, and how we occupy and where we put our bodies, *is* our 'spiritual worship' if it is 'holy and acceptable to God'.

Worship for non-conformists

Paul contrasts being confirmed to this world and being transformed. We live in the world and in time, but Christians are a 'new creation' and as such we live already in the new age of the resurrection where we seek to please God. What pleases God may sometimes agree with what the world considers necessary and to which we must rightfully conform. But there will be much in our society that deviates from God's will, that is displeasing to God, which we need to resist, challenge and oppose. 'Do not be conformed to this world, but be transformed.' But how do we achieve this in each of the choices and challenges of life in a fallen, broken world?

Discernment to know what pleases God

If we know anything of Paul, we must know that it's not by human effort that we can achieve anything. Instead, it's by the 'renewing' of our 'minds' through the Spirit that equips us with the power of discernment and critical judgement. The Spirit lays demands on each of us in concrete form in our particular relationships and shapes us in a new style of life. What God wills of us in any particular situation can't be established once and for all. It can only be known afresh in any given situation. We're given a remarkable level of freedom and responsibility in the Christian life to discern and decide whether and how we present ourselves as a 'living sacrifice' to God. Paul can only appeal to, and on the grounds of, the mercies of God. Weigh and celebrate God's mercies, and worship as an unending and 'living sacrifice' becomes a compelling and the only adequate response.

Roger Spiller

Suggested hymns

New every morning is the love; O worship the Lord in the beauty of holiness; May the mind of Christ my Saviour; Forth in thy name, O Lord, I go.

Baptism of Christ (First Sunday of Epiphany)
10 January
Principal Service   **Jesus' Baptism**
Gen. 1.1–5; Ps. 29; Acts 19.1–7; **Mark 1.4–11**

Dear Vicar, I was wondering if there was any possibility of my two children being christened privately and if so how much it would cost and what would the necessary arrangements be? We do not wish to have them christened with a lot of others, all at the same time, as we feel this is a private family affair.

39

That was a request sent to me in a letter by a parent long ago when I was in parish ministry. It's tempting to mock the father's sentiments, yet he is only echoing a widespread view that baptism is a family event; one which it's for the parents to interpret and decide for themselves. But that idea of baptism is blown apart by St Mark's description of baptism. That couldn't be more public, an event witnessed by 'people from the whole Judaean countryside' and involving some life-changing choices. So there was no chance of that ceremony being rounded off with a cup of tea and a slice of christening cake in the parents' home.

John the Baptizer

Baptism takes its cue from John the Baptizer, and so to understand the significance of our own baptisms we have to attend to John. He makes his appearance right at the beginning of Mark's Gospel. There's no Christmas story in Mark, just the early appearance of this awkward, enigmatic figure with his firebrand oratory. It makes a disconcerting start for the reader. His message is unsettling, warnings of imminent judgement, the beginning of the end, and the way of escape through repentance and baptism. And why baptism? Jews are never baptized; they are Jews by birthright.

John seems to be saying that birth is no longer sufficient, the Messiah is coming soon, Israel is being reconstituted. They must prepare by having a change of heart and direction, undergoing a public ritual of renunciation and making a new beginning. At least by the time Mark wrote his Gospel, Old Testament prophecies had convinced the early Church that this was always God's plan. The appearance of an Elijah-like figure would return to prepare for and signal the imminent coming of the Lord.

Jesus submits to baptism

With the scene set, we are ready to be introduced to Jesus. In about 4 BC the young man Jesus journeyed from his home in Nazareth to the River Jordan to hear a charismatic leader who was drawing huge crowds. John's message divided the whole of human history in two, and began to call people to choose, to take sides. And Jesus himself was baptized.

Why was Jesus baptized?

Jesus' baptism was an embarrassment for the early Christians and can still be an embarrassment to us too. It was an embarrassment, because the roles were reversed and John was baptizing Jesus. It was an embarrassment, too, that Jesus underwent a baptism of repentance for the forgiveness of sins. Jesus sought baptism not for his own sake but so as to identify clearly with his nation's unfaithfulness to God. He recognized his own vocation was to bear the weight of disobedience, to break its stultifying power and to open the path for the renewal of the people, the nation and the whole social order.

What did Jesus know of his vocation? In the account set out in Mark we conclude that John didn't recognize Jesus. In his Gospel there's no altercation by John, no suggestion that he should exchange roles with Jesus or that he, John, is not worthy. And though John expects the coming one, he will not be drawn on when he will appear. The voice from heaven is heard only by Jesus. The tearing open of the heavens and the descent of the Spirit was seen only by Jesus. But this marks the transition for Jesus from private obscurity to public and national recognition; from the security of family life in the north, far from the capital, to being in a place of scrutiny, hostility and ultimately of death.

Sharing the baptism of Jesus

The baptism of Jesus is the key to understanding everything about his ministry and Passion. Through it God acknowledges Jesus as his unique Son. He's the focus of the way God deals with all of humanity. Jesus' baptism is unique. Nowhere in the New Testament is it suggested that it might be taken as a model for our own baptism. But we are called to *share* in his baptism, in a daily renunciation of self. And we too can receive the self-same gift of the Holy Spirit that anointed and empowered Jesus at the outset of his ministry. The Spirit that was God's agent in creation will re-create us too and complete our adoption as his children. The words to Jesus at his baptism can then be addressed to us also.

Roger Spiller

Suggested hymns

When Jesus came to Jordan; Awake, awake, fling off the night; When Jesus comes to be baptised; Word of God, renew your people.

Baptism of Christ (First Sunday of Epiphany)

10 January

Second Service   **The Servant of the Lord**

Ps. 46, [47]; **Isa. 42.1–9**; Eph. 2.1–10; *Gospel at Holy Communion*: Matt. 2.13–end

During Advent I'm sure that we heard a number of readings from the latter part of the book of Isaiah, so it is as if this reading is a continuation on from those, which, in Christian tradition, have come to be regarded as prophecies about the coming of Jesus. However, the tone of today's lesson is somewhat different from that of those passages which spoke of a coming Messiah. Most commentaries identify it as the first (but not the best known) of the so-called Servant Songs.

Attempts to interpret these texts often ask: who is (was) the servant? Furthermore, in writing about this particular passage there are questions: what was his mission or task? What abilities or attributes would he need to fulfil his calling? How will he fulfil his calling?

Who is (was) the servant?

Is he an individual? In which case, could the prophet be referring to himself? That interpretation could enable a reading of the text but not, I think, one that would be very fruitful for our purposes.

Alternatively, there is a long-held Christian tradition of identifying the servant as Jesus, an understanding that draws upon the ways in which these particular passages from Isaiah are quoted and reinterpreted in the New Testament. However, if we state that the servant is Jesus then we are saying that the prophecy and its fulfilment are a matter of history. Is the gate of prophecy closed? Surely we must allow for other possibilities if we are to let the passage stand in its own right.

A third possibility is that the servant could be Israel, the faithful community, the nation that embodies the covenantal relationship between God and his chosen people.

Like the writers of contemporary commentaries, we could spend a lot of time exploring these various potential solutions as to the identity of the servant, but to what avail?

A good question for us to ask might be, 'Who is the servant in relation to God?' The answers to this question lie in the passage: he

42

is chosen and filled with the Spirit, in order that he may carry out his mission.

What was his mission or task?

In the first half of our reading, God is the speaker who introduces the servant and gives him his mission. The language employed is like that of a king addressing a high official (perhaps a court officer or senior civil servant), so the servant is the divine representative, not some kind of lowly menial.

Chosen and filled with the Spirit, he is to establish justice, the justice that derives only from God. Justice is evidence of the harmony that God provides, but that harmony is damaged by human sin and so has to be restored. The servant bears witness to God's justice and his task is to rebalance the universe.

How will he fulfil his calling?

The first hearers of Isaiah's prophecies, living in exile in Babylon, might have longed for a military leader, like David, who would lead them to victory over their oppressors. However, the first half of the passage states that the servant will not be using force and that there's to be no public display of strength. So the task is not to inaugurate a holy war. The servant will not be a conqueror, but a victim. He'll draw every nation to himself by embodying God's compassion. His work is grounded in the very nature of God, founded upon his justice and compassion.

Whereas at the beginning of our text God is the speaker who is introducing the servant, now he appears to be speaking directly to the servant himself. According to this second part of the passage, the servant is to become the agent through whom a covenant will be made not just with Israel but with all peoples. He is to be the bringer of light to the nations. He will open the eyes of the blind and set the prisoners free.

Of course, it may be that this section of the passage is a later addition, a gloss or commentary inserted by the disciples of the prophet or by redactors. Nevertheless, it forms part of the Bible that we have received and it is the passage as a whole to which we must respond.

How do we respond to the passage?

If the servant was commissioned to be God's messenger, to restore God's justice, embody the covenant, to be a light to the nations, to restore sight to the blind and set the prisoners free, are we not the inheritors of the mission?

A people called by God to be disciples, the Church must today be the servant. All who love God are challenged to enter into this service: however, as the servant songs reveal, this is far from being a cost-free endeavour. Some who have God's commissioning have received the palm of martyrdom.

Pause awhile as you consider whether God is calling you to be his servant too.

Wendy Kilworth-Mason

Suggested hymns

Brother, sister, let me serve you; Give to me, Lord, a thankful heart; God is love: let heaven adore him; The kingdom of God is justice and joy.

Second Sunday of Epiphany   17 January
(For the Week of Prayer for Christian Unity, see p. 294.)
Principal Service   **Seeing Christ**
1 Sam. 3.1–10 [11–20]; Ps. 139.1–5, 12–18 [*or* 139.1–9];
Rev. 5.1–10; **John 1.43–end**

What do you see?

We are still in the season of revelations when things are revealed or made manifest to us about the Son of God, the Word made flesh. We learn more about who he is and about who we are called to be in his name. The word 'epiphany' means 'a revelation or manifestation', and in everyday speech we might use the word to indicate that we have suddenly worked something out, or a mystery has been made clear to us, or we have discovered something stupendous and wonderful. It seems that Nathanael is someone who is open to the epiphany moments of life, his eyes are open to the world around him, and when he is invited by Philip to 'come and see' Jesus of

Nazareth, the one written of by Moses and the prophets, he simply gets up and follows, unwilling to let this opportunity pass by.

Nathanael is someone in whom there is no dissembling or cloaking. He is who he is, there is no side to him and he is straightforwardly open and honest like a child. He states a truth when he asks the question, 'Can anything good come out of Nazareth?', which hints once again at the scandal of God being born as a baby in a stable full of animals and growing up in a small town of no repute. This is all looking very dubious and unlikely, but Nathanael has his eyes open to the possibilities that are being revealed.

Jesus is also someone who sees the world clearly and he sees Nathanael under the fig tree for who he really is, an Israelite in whom there is no deceit. It's as if Jesus says to Nathanael, 'I see you.' Nathanael was, from the very beginning, known and loved by God and he responds to Jesus with these words, 'Rabbi, you are the Son of God, you are the king of Israel!' This is his own personal moment of epiphany when he gets down on his knees to praise God in Christ who is standing before him.

Here I am

In some ways Nathanael embodies what it means to be a follower of Christ. Initially he has questions, he is doubtful and dubious, but his uncertainties never trump the possibility of grace and truth, which is just around the corner. He responds to the call and in a sense channels the words of Samuel, who hears God speaking to him in the Temple and responds, 'Here I am.' Nathanael and Samuel stand before God without pretence, without hypocrisy, without deceit. They are naked and unadorned, they do not try to hide. They let God see them and know them and love them. Nathanael can see Jesus because Jesus has seen him first with his all-seeing eye.

To be a Christian is to be exposed to the gaze of God, to stand humbly before the throne of grace and open up our whole lives to the light of Christ. In his light we are able to see the world and ourselves within it more clearly. In his light we offer to God all that we are and all that we have, and our response to the love and grace of God in Jesus Christ is to say boldly, here I am, as Nathanael did, and recognize Jesus as the Son of God.

You will see greater things than these

When we recognize the living God in our midst, we begin to see things differently. We see that heaven and earth are intertwined, we see the angels of God ascending and descending upon the Son of Man. He has brought heaven down to earth and raised earth heavenwards, if only we had eyes to see this wondrous thing. It is in Christ that we come to realize that all things are possible and the stuff of life is made holy through him, bread and wine become his body and his blood through which we are sanctified and made one. If we are open to seeing Christ made manifest and allow ourselves to be open to his gaze, we are guaranteed daily moments of revelation. The season of Epiphany need not be confined to the first month of the year, it can be a daily reality for those who respond to the invitation to 'come and see' and proclaim in their hearts and in their lives that Jesus Christ is the Son of God.

Victoria Johnson

Suggested hymns

Open our eyes, Lord; Songs of thankfulness and praise; Just as I am; God of mercy, God of grace.

Second Sunday of Epiphany 17 January
Second Service **The Future is Bright**
Ps. 96; **Isa. 60.9–end**; Heb. 6.17—7.10; *Gospel at Holy Communion*: Matt. 8.5–13

Hope and faith are often held suspect. In a bleak world, at a dark time, those of us who cling to our trust in a loving God who is working his purposes out may be judged as delusional, unrealistic. When dark experiences challenge our faith we can be left doubting ourselves and our beliefs, which can seem all too naive in the face of the latest natural disaster, the most recent acts of violence reported in the media. But the Bible tells us time and again that our hope in something better, our trust in a more eternally powerful divine Other, is well grounded and can both lift and light us up.

Realistic hope

The poetry of Isaiah is rooted in realism. It's not just about ever-lasting light: it's about light that shines brighter because we have real experience of the darkness. Although these sound like Advent themes, they continue through the often dull and short days of January in the northern hemisphere. Our church calendar blesses us with hope that is grown out of dark times.

We see this in our first reading, thanks to the parallelisms that are a marker of Hebrew poetry. These are phrases that are carefully balanced, usually in two parts. They come in lots of different forms, sometimes apparently repeating the same idea in two different ways. For example: 'Foreigners shall build up your walls, and their kings shall minister to you.' Or they can be stark contrasts. For example: 'For in my wrath I struck you down, but in my favour I have had mercy on you.' Phrases like this are heaped up throughout today's reading from Isaiah.

That's where the realism shows up unapologetically. Isaiah is tell-ing God's words to his people, so the 'I' here is God. There were the times when it seemed God was angry, things were going so wrong, says Isaiah. Now there are the times when it seems God is being kind and forgiving, because life is a whole lot better, says Isaiah.

Our faith encompasses bad times and good. Because it is honest about the bad times, the times of desperation, so we can know it is honest about the good times too, the hope for the future, the hope in whatever our present situation is.

Hope in community

The next verse surprises again. 'Your gates shall always be open; day and night they shall not be shut, so that nations shall bring you their wealth, with their kings led in procession.' Who is addressed here? Whose are the '*your* gates'? Literally, it is only a city or great building that has gates; metaphorically, that stands for the people who live there. There's something similar a couple of verses later: 'The descendants of those who oppressed you shall come bending low to you, and all who despised you shall bow down at your feet; they shall call you the City of the LORD, the Zion of the Holy One of Israel' (spot those parallelisms again). God is speaking directly to Jerusalem, the City of God.

Do we often stop to think of our cities, towns, villages, buildings as people? Are they blobs on a map, places we go through or past on the train or bus? Are they just far away, detached places we hear about on the news, until something happens closer to home? How can we remember to think of places as people – communities of individuals, people just like us?

When we remember that those places are also families, our horizons grow. Deepening our awareness of others like us, in different towns, counties, countries or continents, helps make us people of hope – people who think about our relationships with each other, with the planet and all created things, which gives us a different perspective. If, of cities and peoples, we think, 'we're not like them!' we're probably missing something. Quite a lot, in fact.

Bright horizons

A beautiful sunrise, an amazing view from a ridge or skyscraper invites us to look beyond ourselves, to gaze in wonder at distant things, to think how much God encompasses. Isaiah keeps hinting at a nationwide perspective. 'Violence shall no more be heard in your land, devastation or destruction within your borders; you shall call your walls Salvation, and your gates Praise.' It is within the land, the borders (see that parallelism once more?), that the walls and gates have their place (yes, there's more parallelism there too). Here's another example of the reality of gruesome past experiences giving weight to gladsome future ones. Instead of violence, there is Salvation; instead of devastation or destruction, there is Praise.

Isaiah isn't saying that everything to come will all be light and joy. He's more realistic than that – which helps us to see brightness on our own horizons, to yearn daily for a heavenly perspective, to stop looking at a hurting past and look forward to a hopeful future. Isaiah's words are honest, grounded, gritty even, in their beauty. That is how we can hear and understand for ourselves: 'the LORD will be your everlasting light, and your God will be your glory.'

Megan I. J. Daffern

Suggested hymns

Arise, shine, your light has come; Bright the vision that delighted; Christ, be our light; Light's abode, celestial Salem.

Third Sunday of Epiphany   24 January
Principal Service   **Backstairs to Glory**
Gen. 14.17–20; Ps. 128; Rev. 19.6–10; **John 2.1–11**

If you'd been fortunate enough to receive an invitation to the most talked about wedding in human history, in a provincial town in Cana, you'd have had a good day but been completely unaware of the stupendous event that had taken place behind the scenes back-stairs. Sometimes it's good that you don't know what's going on. One host at a dinner party I was attending told us of the time when the food mixer went on overdrive, spraying the delicately creamed mashed potato over the walls and ceiling just as distinguished guests were arriving. There was no option but to retrieve the potato from the walls. The guests were none the wiser and no one sued on account of food poisoning.

A couple are married and the reception is carefully choreographed. 'And when the wine gave out', well, of course it's always a possi-bility if you spread out these ancient Near Eastern ceremonies for as many days as it takes for the guests to become legless. It wasn't simply, 'We've run out of wine, so let's switch to Scotch.' If wine runs out it's treated as an antisocial gesture, bringing disgrace on a young couple just as they begin a new life together in the community.

Do something

Mothers seem born with fully developed antennae that smell out a crisis faster than a bat can detect its prey. This unnamed woman, identified only as the mother of Jesus, discretely whispers a warning to Jesus, 'They have no wine', with the clear implication, 'Do some-thing'. You can sense Jesus' frustration. 'Woman, what concern is that to you and to me?' he says. Can't we just be guests for once? Why poke your nose into things that don't concern you? Why take responsibility for someone else's predicament? But more is at stake for Jesus than the interruption of his social life. The 'hour' for Jesus to reveal his glory puts him on a path that leads inexorably to suffering and to death. Is his mother unwittingly reminding Jesus of that 'hour'? The prospects are too terrifying for Jesus to embark upon that path a moment sooner than he must.

We know the ending. The bride and groom are left to think that the ceremony has gone off as planned, without a hitch. The groom is bemused to be thanked for saving the best wine until last. And the steward knows nothing of the wine running out nor of the stupendous way a new supply was procured. He's just content to accept the credit for reversing tradition and introducing the best vintage wine when the guests were expecting stomach-churning 'plonk'. The only people to know are the servants, backstage, out of sight.

The waste of a great story

It's a waste of a great story that was hidden from the guests and important people. A waste of a miracle just to spare a bride from blushes at a little village wedding. A waste of such a mighty display of power before a few inconsequential servants. A waste of fine wine on undiscerning palates in a quantity so vast as to risk inebriating all the guests and bringing village life to a standstill.

The wedding is in Cana, and the only other thing we know about Cana is that it's the home of one Nathanael, to whom Jesus said he would see greater things than he'd seen already. And now 'On the third day' after Nathanael's call, and anticipating the 'third day' of the resurrection, he has sight and taste not merely of vast quantities of fine wine but of the wine-giver himself. Jesus doesn't merely rescue an awkward situation but he transfigures it. Without the water there would be no wine, without empty vessels there would be no filling, without the intervention of Mary there would be no celebration, without the trust of servants there would be no miracle.

Wine into water

The great nineteenth-century theologian Søren Kierkegaard is quoted as saying, 'Christ turned water into wine but the Church has succeeded in doing something even more difficult: it has been turning wine into water'! Where in our churches is this lavish, reckless superfluity of grace to be encountered? Where is the generous self-giving that is the prerequisite for being 'filled up to the brim'? Where is the baptismal water that is often measured out in spoonfuls, or the wine of communion that is hedged around by restrictions that divide and scandalize? Where is the intoxicating liberation that is meant to have replaced the sin-obsessed rites and rules of purification? Where is the space to celebrate the hidden stories of transformation without them being plundered to feed our publicity-seeking, self-justifying, image-conscious Church? Where is the light and glory breaking through for those backstage, out of sight in our divided communities? Our lives, our homes, our churches will be as bland as a wedding without wine, a pub without beer, until we not only share the wine of the gospel, but surrender to the wine-giver, who is both guest and servant.

Roger Spiller

Suggested hymns

Jesus, come, for we invite you; Songs of thankfulness and praise; Christ is our light! The bright and morning star; At the Lamb's high feast we sing.

Third Sunday of Epiphany 24 January
Second Service **Return, Return to God**
Ps. 33 [*or* 33.1–12]; **Jer. 3.21—4.2**; Titus 2.1–8, 11–14;
Gospel at Holy Communion: Matt. 4.12–23

'If a man divorces his wife and she goes from him and becomes another man's wife, will he return to her?' That's the question posed at the beginning of the chapter from which our Old Testament reading is taken. Those who kept up with the serial matrimonial antics of celebrity actors like Richard Burton and Elizabeth Taylor in the 1970s will have reached their own conclusions. But it's hard to imagine how a woman who remained faithful in a marriage, endured the gruelling divorce instigated by her husband, could then bring herself to welcome him back and remarry him as her husband once again. It's not surprising, then, that Jewish law prohibited the remarrying of a previous spouse after divorce.

Returning to a divorced partner

All the same, this is not all that uncommon. A survey by Relate, the marriage counselling service, showed that one in four divorcees regrets their split. But it's one thing longing for a new start and quite another for that to occur after all the changes in a prolonged intervening period. It takes extraordinary humility, generosity and forgiveness by the spouse who kept faithful in the marriage to accept the divorced and remarried partner back, to remarry them and begin a new life together again.

It's only as we contemplate the cost of forgiveness involved that we can gain an inkling of what it meant for God to offer a second chance to his faithless people.

Returning to God, the jilted lover

God is depicted as Israel's lover who entered into a marriage-like covenant with his people. There were, of course, conditions. Faithfulness, fidelity by both partners: 'You shall have no other gods but me.' And this was to be an exclusive relationship: 'You only have I known, of all the families on earth', and you shall 'love the LORD your God with all your heart, mind, soul and strength'.

And how did this unique relationship develop? The truth is that through the entire history of the covenant there was never a time in which Israel was faithful to its divine partner. After a brief honeymoon period called its 'youth', Israel was seeking other illicit relationships, other gods, other partners. And so Israel was rejected, first by God and then by her subsequent lovers. And the disaster of the exile is the cost and consequence of her unfaithfulness. Israel is like a woman who has been shamed and dishonoured, and now abandoned without home or refuge. That's the situation now to be addressed.

There's a revolutionary change of heart in God. He will, after all, have her unfaithful people back again. 'Return,' he says, 'O faithless children, I will heal your faithlessness.'

What a surprise, that through most of the 300 years of infidelity and idolatry during the monarchy that God gives them a second chance to return to him. That is an amazing offer in the light of all Israel's offences. But with it God sets conditions for her return. She must abandon all other loyalties and cleave to God as sovereign Lord. No other relationship is acceptable. She must refashion her life around a relationship with her God, and then both she and other nations will be blessed.

Return to God

'Return' is the oft-repeated word that should be ringing in our ears from our scripture. 'Return to me,' says God. It's a word that does a similar job to the word 'repentance'. We all know what it is to return, whether it's to a college reunion encountering high-achieving peers, or perhaps a return to make amends after misunderstandings with a friend, not knowing how we will be received.

I once heard a man explaining on the radio that he felt certain that his wife was being unfaithful to him. He was convinced of her infidelity, although he could find no evidence for it. He had persuaded himself that he was not sufficiently attractive and good looking for his wife to love him. And so he left home. He made lacerations on his face and arms and became dishevelled and un-shaven. He was desperate and needed to return home, but was filled with anxiety at the reception he might receive. When he did return, his wife received him wholeheartedly, lovingly and without condi-tion. He then knew that, since she did accept him just as he was, she was always going to love him unconditionally.

Whoever we are, and whatever the circumstance, there is always God's word to us to 'return' to him; always the opportunity for a new start; always the opportunity to discover that we will be accepted as we are.

Roger Spiller

Suggested hymns

Restore, O Lord, the honour of your name; Lord, we know that we have failed you; Amazing grace, how sweet the sound; All my hope on God is founded.

Fourth Sunday of Epiphany   31 January
(*or* Candlemas; see p. 299)
Principal Service   **The Authority of Jesus**
Deut. 18.15–20; Ps. 111; Rev. 12.1–5a; **Mark 1.21–28**

How are we to think of Jesus? Not, I suggest, as a religious man in any conventional sense, since he was brought to death for threaten-ing religious faith. Nor even as a Christian at all, since he was the unwitting founder of one religion while spending all his life in another. And it's arguable that Jesus did not intend the monolithic institution we call the Christian Church that has been created in his name. But, of course, we need to know what it is about Jesus that makes him crucial for our lives.

We can look at titles given to him in the New Testament: Son of God, Son of Man, Messiah, Lamb of God. But Jesus was diffident about the titles people gave him. We're better, instead, to discover him in the stories about him in the Gospels, such as the one Mark gives us of Jesus in today's Gospel. Quite simply, Jesus was recognized as a man with authority.

What kind of authority?

But what kind of authority? His authority contrasted with the Pharisees. So what was the authority of Pharisees? Pharisees were knowledgeable in their Scriptures; they spoke from authorities, but were not in themselves authoritative. We speak of people being an authority on something or other, but that does not necessarily give them personal authority when they are outside their specialist areas.

Authority may come through being ascribed a role. The Pharisees were professional clergy, and that conferred a kind of authority. Industrial bureaucracies and their notions of professionalism have long operated on the basis that a person's role can be separated from their person, as if they can discharge a role with the minimum intrusion of the person's personal agenda or emotions.

Self-authenticating

Now contrast Jesus with all those we meet in the Gospels who claimed authority. Jesus appears as one not demonstrably endowed with a particular charisma, nor as an office-holder within his nation, which might give him rank or status. Again and again, the only backing for his words or actions is Jesus himself. Yet, for all that, Jesus comes over with complete assurance and resolute authority. He teaches directly without seeking to cover himself; he acts not by precedent but as the occasion requires; he summons people to follow him and they do so immediately. He challenges the scribes to argument, as if he has no need of instruction himself. Before Pilate, it is Jesus who has real authority over the greatest authority in the known world. There's no public position to confine him or support him. He acts with complete freedom as the person he is, yet with complete authority. He has no need to fall back upon external force of arms, angels or miraculous signs. He expresses his sovereignty in every situation in which he finds himself. His authority expresses his mysterious nature and evokes awe, astonishment, intrigue and terror. Before him the power of the demons is broken, sin is ruthlessly exposed and rendered impotent. And those with insight are thrown into a crisis of decision.

When questioned about the source of his authority, Jesus is reticent. Only once did he hint at his source of authority – at his trial, at precisely the moment when nobody would believe him. He is uniquely the one who needs no justification for his authority in terms of human considerations. His authority speaks for itself – it is self-authenticating. It is, of course, the authority of God by which he speaks and acts, but there is no way that we can ever know this apart from and independent of Jesus.

Authority over and shared with the Church

The Church has frequently tried to circumscribe or silence the radical voice of Jesus, to water down the offensive demands he makes, and sometimes has even claimed to assume uncritically that it has the authority of Jesus. The Church that fuses or confuses itself with Jesus can become idolatrous. For Jesus still exerts his authority over his Church. The memory of his words and the power of his Spirit still go on interrogating us, calling us to fresh growth and change. So, in acknowledging Jesus as the man of authority, we acknowledge his authority over us. It's an authority that demands that we relativize every other authority over us, including our own self-serving wills. And there's one thing more: Jesus shares his authority with his followers. We who follow Jesus and are led by his Spirit are given authority to speak and act in his name, so that the world may hear, see and meet the living Jesus. Many people outside the institutional Church are excited by the person of Jesus. It's time for more of those inside the Church to catch up.

Roger Spiller

Suggested hymns

I, the Lord of sea and sky; May the mind of Christ my Saviour; Lord, you give the great commission; Forth in thy name, O Lord, I go.

Fourth Sunday of Epiphany   31 January
Second Service   **The Light was Still Burning**
Ps. 34 [*or* 34.1–10]; **1 Sam. 3.1–20**; 1 Cor. 14.12–20;
Gospel at Holy Communion: Matt. 13.10–17

A long silence

When we are facing political uncertainty, loss of faith, change or conflict, the opening chapters of 1 Samuel speak to us of God's presence and grace.

When the threat of the Philistines' military power became the catalyst for change, a new era in Israel's history began. Through the period of Judges, God was Israel's sovereign. Yet now we stand on the threshold of the story of Israel's monarchy. Ambiguity about whether the monarchy is a good or bad status for Israel circumnavigates these histories, which also relate the ambiguity of the relationship between monarch and prophet. But it is significant that these stories of political, military and religious quest begin in the first chapter of Samuel with a very human story: a woman longs for a child and calls out to God. Samuel's story begins with Hannah, a woman whose longing initiates a promise that her child will be dedicated to the Lord. So begins the next great chapter in the story of a nation's relationship with God.

Today's reading tells us that the voice of God was not often heard in those days: 'The word of the LORD was rare in those days; visions were not widespread.' I wonder how we would equate those words to our own time and place? Much of history depends on whose voices are heard and whose voices are silenced.

A call in the night

Eli, the penultimate Judge of Israel, to be succeeded only by Samuel before the institution of the monarchy, is losing his sight. But the lamp of the Lord had not yet burned out. This description denoting evening is also a note of hope. Despite the apparent silence and lack of vision, the lamp of God had not quite been extinguished; some spiritual life still existed if only faintly. There is a tradition in the Talmud based on Ecclesiastes 1.5 that before one righteous life is extinguished another is lit. So Eli, despite his faults, failings and weaknesses in his responsibility to Israel and lack of accountability for shameful and abusive actions of his sons, yet witnesses that God has provided the new light to Israel in the boy Samuel.

Credit where it is due – Eli does realize this. He can no longer hear God but he recognizes whose voice is calling to Samuel. It must have come as a deep wound to Eli as well as a comfort. Samuel, despite ministering before the Lord for most of his life, is still young and untried and assumes that the voice he hears in the night is the voice of his ageing mentor. Samuel's concern for Eli is apparent, for three times he rises from his bed and goes to Eli – 'Here I am. Do you need me? I heard you calling.' Puzzled, Eli denies that he called the boy. But the third time it dawns upon the old man that while the boy doesn't recognize the calling in the night, it must be One whom Eli can no longer hear. Allegiance has changed. The torch has been passed on. Whatever his personal grief, Eli gives Samuel the guidance he needs, perhaps the last time he will do so. 'When you hear the voice again, say, "Here I am, Lord. Your servant is listening."' Eli must have some idea of what God will need to say to Samuel that cannot now be said to Eli. It will not be good news for him or his sons. It takes courage to bow to the inevitable with the grace he showed.

A greater story

The life of the Church needs to remember that. Our ministries come and go, our light waxes and wanes, our individual callings may change. We can hold on to our private kingdoms so tightly believing they define our usefulness, our *raison d'être*. Yet our calling is always to the greater good, and sometimes we are called to let go, change direction or encourage and nurture someone else. Succession planning is something we learn from Christ.

It takes wisdom, integrity, grace and courage to recognize when the light is to be passed on to another and to enable others to recognize it for themselves. And it takes love and compassion and an appropriate marking of past services to enable some to let go. The story of Samuel reminds us that our individual callings are part of the great story in which the grace of God can be revealed to many. A woman's longing for a child, a nation's longing for a king, a priest's longing to hear the voice of God. These are also the themes of Epiphany. We are called to be lights in the world so that God can say through us, 'Let there be light'. A light that even the darkness of political turmoil, military power, and past abuse of position cannot put out.

Carey Saleh

Suggested hymns

Lead, kindly light; Longing for light, we wait in darkness (Christ be our Light); Light of the world, you stepped down into darkness; Like a candle flame.

Second Sunday before Lent   7 February
Principal Service   **The Centrality of Jesus**
Prov. 8.1, 22–31; Ps. 104.26–end; Col. 1.15–20; **John 1.1–14**

The Christmas season has ended. We've celebrated Candlemas, the crib is packed away. We've begun to journey towards Lent and Easter. How strange that today we have John 1 – the Christmas Gospel. We're being reminded that Jesus isn't just for Christmas. John 1 goes beyond the birth of Jesus, pointing us to everything that Jesus was and is, and his centrality in our lives. All three readings today remind us that God in Jesus is over all, in all and through all. However far we go back in time or forward into eternity, God was, God is and God shall be. We're reminded that it's through Jesus that we come to see and begin to understand God. If you want to know who God is, take a long, hard look at Jesus.

Jesus: the Word

John writes of the Word – who was with God and who was God. John picks up on both the Jewish idea of Wisdom being an integral part of creation, and the Greek idea of the word as the principle underlying the universe. John is saying that the abstract principle – Wisdom or Word, which holds everything together – is no longer abstract, but made flesh. The principle becomes tangible in the person of Jesus. Human words have existed for about 2 million years. We've only had them written on paper for about a thousand years, and we've only had them printed for about five hundred years. But 'the Word' goes back to before the beginning of time. Nothing was made without the Word. God spoke, 'Let there be light', and there was. What God says, 'happens'. In Jesus, God is saying again, 'Let there be light', and creation and light and hope and healing come to reality in Jesus Christ in whom we experience the fullness of the glory of God. We learn what God is like by looking at the life, death and resurrection of Jesus. The Word was in the beginning with God. When we look at the beauty of creation, or watch nature programmes on TV that take our breath away, they are reminding us not just of God the Creator, but also of Jesus – the Word – instrumental in creation too. Proverbs speaks of Wisdom, at the dawn of time, as a co-worker delighting in God, and in humanity.

Jesus: supreme and sufficient

The Colossians grasped the importance of Jesus but were still looking for the next thing – so St Paul reminds them that Christ is supreme and sufficient. Everything needed to belong fully to God can be found in following Jesus. He is the beginning, the origin, the firstborn from the dead. In him we see eternal life with God promised and fulfilled. No one has to strive to achieve this. In Jesus, God loves us as we are, completely, unconditionally. God in Jesus comes to us and brings us home. Nothing and no one is outside the range of God's love and reconciliation. This is incredible life-changing news for the whole cosmos. First-century Christians realized that. For them, following Jesus meant a completely different lifestyle: a dramatic change of direction. It was dangerous: there was persecution and ridicule, loss of family, friends and status, even martyrdom. That's still true in parts of the world today. It's very demanding to be a Palestinian Christian, it's very dangerous to be an Egyptian Copt. African and Asian churches are bursting at the seams despite persecution. To be Christ's disciple means everything.

Jesus: first in all things

A body can't survive without a head. We can lose limbs and even organs but without a head there's no life. If Christ is not our head – and we no longer put him first in all things, as our origin and goal, then other lesser things will flood in and steal our attention. Worship, prayer, service, witness can become 'a take it or leave it hobby', and those around us who know we're Christians will think faith is marginal, rather than central to life itself. Is Christ above all things for you? Does Jesus underpin your thoughts and words, actions and decisions? Ask yourself – is Jesus Christ Lord in my life? Lent begins on 17 February – Ash Wednesday. Lent is a good time to renew our relationship with Jesus. All good relationships require time and effort, sacrifice and commitment. There are various spiritual disciplines you might cultivate during Lent. Read the Gospels again or for the first time – those stories of Jesus that we think we know so well. Make a commitment to be faithful in worship. Pray to Jesus: keep in contact with him like you do with someone you really care about. Do good, generous, kind and sacrificial acts for others. Be filled with hope. Look for the best and celebrate it. And if you're really new to faith, or returning after a long time, start by asking Jesus to come into your heart and be part of your life. Jesus is the blueprint for humanity, and in him we're called to discover what being truly human, made in the image of God, means in practice. The more we open ourselves to Jesus and allow his Holy Spirit to be within us and shape us, the more we will become the body of Christ in this place and in our world.

Catherine Williams

Suggested hymns

Jesus is Lord; In Christ alone; Christ, whose glory fills the skies; Meekness and majesty.

Second Sunday before Lent   7 February
Second Service   **'Only Human'?**
Ps. 65; **Gen. 2.4b–end**; Luke 8.22–35

'We're only human!' It's what we say when we're caught out for some mistake or indiscretion we've committed. Aren't we bound to fail and fall? Isn't this just what we're to conclude from the story of the Fall? If it's part of our humanity, then mustn't we accept it and stop lacerating ourselves for our failures and sins?

Falling

We can't posit a 'fall' in any factual sense, but neither can we deny the evidence of our fallenness, at least as a self-serving gravitational field that spreads self-destructive patterns of conduct across our whole world. Set in an idyllic, blessed, garden of delight, a single prohibition and limitation unleashed wilful opposition to God's legitimate authority over the two occupants of the garden. That is the theme we see enacted in every home, school, church, company or any other organized gathering of people. The story of the Fall is, and arguably was intended to be, a profound diagnostic tool to bring insight and healing to our human condition.

One-sided

But on its own, the Fall can be a one-sided interpretation of the gospel and justify our excuse to be 'only human'. The Church has been overoccupied with sin and has used it to manipulate its control on society. It served the interests of those who administer the Church's sacraments to emphasize the excesses of the human condition and maintain their control. An exclusive focus on sexual sins and more trivial transgressions has often drowned out the voice that commends and rejoices in the intimacy and fulfilment that faithful relationships can bring. There's been much less interest in structural sin and the failure to call people to take collective responsibility for our social and economic systems that exploit and dehumanize people. We have been exercised by personal transgressions while we failed to notice the degradation of the planet.

Damage done

This has led to a widespread epidemic of self-loathing. It has fed a widespread sense of unworthiness, of being profoundly ill at ease with ourselves. Too many people suffer from the chronic anxiety of not being good enough. This has come to backfire on churches, because the feeling of not being 'good enough' is often the underlying reason why people are not going to church, rather than a reason for coming. The long-running advert for women by L'Oréal, 'Because you're worth it', reflects a culture where people are unsure of their own worth and value. People don't lack for a sense of fallenness or culpability. They know this already. Instead, they are caught in a spiral of self-criticism, inferiority, worthlessness and guilt.

The call to rise

If we continue to speak of original sin, we can do so only by extolling original grace. 'The creation is not a fall, but a positive act of God's will,' writes Pope Benedict.[20] God's image, however defaced, still bears the marks of our maker. Not only sin itself but an exclusive emphasis on human sin denigrates the potential of our grace-filled, God-given humanity. One of the most used words for sin in the New Testament is missing the mark. It gives us a more generous and hopeful reading of human nature. It's not so much a mythical Fall, but a failure to rise and to be what we're meant to be. It's our future potential that counts, not our past lapses. We're not to hide behind a fixed, determinist condition and claim that we are 'only human'. Rather, we're called to accept the divine and daring invitation to rise up and claim ourselves as God's sons and daughters. The writer Søren Kierkegaard said that the only real sin is 'the despairing refusal to be one's self'. In the creation story it's not so much in terms of eating the forbidden fruit but the prior surrendering of power and responsibility to the serpent. So the primordial sin is more to do with sloth than with pride. It's the timidity of overdependence, victimhood and setting more store by trifling sins than by glaring omissions.

Bearers of the divine

Since Christ shared our humanity we can never again say we're 'only' human. It was, after all, in his humanity that he offered perfect obedience to his Father and shared the divine life. Humanity isn't opposed to divinity; they don't run in parallel, because God has lifted us to the life of God. We are the crown of creation, 'little lower than God' as the Psalmist declares, and still bearers of God's image and likeness. How, then, dare we use the tawdry excuse that we are 'only human'. Since Christ has assumed our humanity, we don't have that option. Yes, we fall, we're fallen, but by God's Spirit we are raised with Christ, called to rise 'to the measure of the full stature of Christ'. That's what those chained down by guilt, shame, low self-esteem and worthlessness need most to hear.

Roger Spiller

Suggested hymns

Lord, your voice in Eden's garden; Let all creation dance; Great God, your love has called us; And can it be, that I should gain.

Sunday next before Lent   14 February
Principal Service   **Clouds of Glory in the Fog**
2 Kings 2.1–12; Ps. 50.1–6; 2 Cor. 4.3–6; **Mark 9.2–9**

So much mystery

So much in life is mysterious. I often don't even understand the terms. Neutrinos are the fundamental particles that make up the universe. Black holes are regions of space–time from which nothing can escape, not even light. Pseudo-randomness are numbers that look random but aren't. And what is the Higgs Boson – the so-called God particle – anyway? And that's just a tiny selection of the science archive of that extraordinary radio programme about ideas, *In Our Time* – never mind the philosophy, culture, history and religion sections. Humanity knows such a lot, and yet the more we know the more there is to know. So much is mysterious.

So much fog!

Whatever else this account of Jesus transfigured is meant to convey to us, mysteriousness must surely be the first thing – his appearance was changed as they looked; even his clothes shone with an out-of-this-world radiance; and it is as if Moses and Elijah, both dead centuries ago, were actually there, talking to him; and then even God spoke. Mysterious indeed. No wonder we're told a cloud formed! Could anything be more clouded in mystery? And that's perhaps a key. We assume that this workaday, worrisome world is far removed from the joys and wonders of heaven, but maybe it isn't? Maybe eternity is only hidden, as if by a fog, only to suddenly break into view when so unexpected. Last week I had to drive home in thick, grey fog; then in a moment as I came over the brow of a hill the fog was gone, and all was streaming bright sunshine. A mile later and I was into grey fog again. Could it be that our lives are so often fogged up with things that we can't see the bright rays of eternity through them?

Fog warning

Just before this transfiguring incident in Mark's Gospel, Jesus had been very explicit about his coming suffering and death. The reality of the cross was made plain – all too plain for Peter, if you remember. Peter had rebuked Jesus; which in turn called forth a strong rebuke from Jesus. Jesus' saving action will take place in a fog of despair, hurt, envy and anger that will be deadly. Jesus is setting his face towards Jerusalem, despite the loud and accurate fog warning. No wonder Peter is overcome. He doesn't know how to respond, and like most of us in such a situation he's eager to find something to do; his making of tents perhaps a first-century equivalent of 'I'll just make a cup of tea, shall I?' – something done when no words or actions are adequate to the loss, the hurt, or indeed the wonder.

63

The mountain-top experience is awe-inspiringly bright, but it points to things they will experience that are far from bright. Somehow these things have got to be held together: the mountain-top vista of splendour and the grey, cold clamminess of perplexing hurt. Our human inclination is always to wish away the costliness of glory, but it cannot be. It's as if God is saying to Peter, James and John, 'Here's a glimpse of glory; here's something to be amazed at; something to instil in you the realness of the eternal; something to buoy your spirits because you see it for yourselves.' Glory, splendour, majesty, beauty, the ineffable – and you've seen it for yourselves.

Splendour and apprehension

And to underline the experience there comes a heavenly voice, 'This is my Son, the Beloved; listen to him.' And notice at what point the voice comes. They are already shadowed in cloud. This cloud is at one and the same time the cloud in which the holy presence of God is known and the cloud of despair that signifies the cross that is to be. Overshadowed by God, a reminder of what happened to Moses; and overshadowed by the coming cross, a reminder of what Jesus has declared his destiny to be. Wonderful and worrying; sustaining and suspicious; heart-warming and heart-wrenching.

Mysterious – a place of longing and apprehension, of conviction and confusion – a place from which Jesus and his friends will journey towards Jerusalem; a place to which we must journey too if we are truly his disciples. Keep company with the one whose glory we know; keep company with the one who gives even his very self in the cause of that glory. Hold together the splendour and the despair. And when the tension is too much, and the costliness too hard to bear, remember Jesus the Beloved striving ... and winning through.

Trustful imagination

These words from Wordsworth ('Ode on Intimations of Immortality') seem to both sum it up and give pause for thought about how we forget:

Not in entire forgetfulness,
And not in utter nakedness,
But trailing clouds of glory do we come
From God, who is our home:

Heaven lies about us in our infancy!

...

Our noisy years seem moments in the being
Of the eternal Silence.

...

Hence in a season of calm weather,
Though inland far we be,
Our souls have sight of that immortal sea
Which brought us hither,
Can in a moment travel thither,
And see the children sport upon the shore,
And hear the mighty waters rolling evermore.

We come trailing 'clouds of glory' indeed. But this mountain experience recorded by Mark must stir our hearts and minds to such carefulness of each other and ourselves that it is not only in the seasons 'of calm weather' that we have sight of that 'immortal sea' that brought us here. Peter, James and John can't yet make the leap of imagination and trust so as to hold on to glory through the worst of weathers and the terrors of the storm. But they will. For now, 'they kept the word to themselves', though they did discuss 'what "to rise from the dead" could mean'. They will come to know, but for the moment it is only a glimpse of glory, and that must be enough, as hard as it is.

'Trailing clouds of glory do we come', always, but always.

Christopher Burkett

Suggested hymns

Christ, whose glory fills the skies; O wondrous sight! O vision fair; Christ is the world's light; Jesus, take us to the mountain.

Sunday next before Lent   14 February
Second Service   **God's Fugitive**
Ps. 2 [99]; **1 Kings 19.1–16**; 2 Peter 1.16–end; *Gospel at Holy Communion*: Mark 9.[2–8] 9–13

'The grandest and most romantic character that Israel ever produced.' Doesn't it make you want to know about this person? He is the prophet par excellence. He appears with Jesus, along with Moses, at the transfiguration. He is taken up into heaven in a whirlwind and was sometimes thought to make a reappearance in the guise of Jesus or John the Baptist.

Elijah lay low for a couple of years after obeying God's call to move to Israel. But then God summoned him to present himself to the king and that was when all his troubles began. King Ahab was a successful military leader and secured tributes from all his conquests. But he'd married Jezebel from a neighbouring country and she was opposed to the religion of Israel, and took action to kill off the prophets of the Lord. When Elijah appeared for his tête-à-tête with Ahab the king, Elijah's reputation had gone ahead of him and the king greeted him with the words, 'Is it you, you troubler of Israel?' Elijah replied that the problem was on the other foot! It was he the king who had troubled Israel by forsaking the commandments and following idols.

A fugitive from God

Elijah wasted no time in calling 'all Israel' to assemble at Mount Carmel, for one big showdown between the false prophets of Baal and the prophets of the Lord. Although that proved decisive for Elijah, it did nothing to endear him to Jezebel. She promised that within 24 hours Elijah would come to a bitter end. So begins the adventure depicted in our reading.

You might have expected Elijah to trust in the God who had delivered him such a decisive victory. But memories of such blessing can be short-lived. Instead, Elijah was afraid and fled for his life, right out of Israel and into Judah in the south, a journey of some 100 miles. Elijah arrives in the wilderness. It's a pitiful scene with Elijah sitting for shade under a solitary broom tree, feeling sorry for himself, with an exaggerated sense of victimhood, pleading to be allowed to die. But God isn't going to leave him alone and unsupported. There's cake! And that was a speciality for Elijah, since he'd already got the poor widow to produce some before getting down to bringing her son back to life. Once he'd eaten and recovered his strength, he was directed for 40 days and 40 nights to Mount Horeb, which was the scene of other of God's epiphanies.

Still hiding from God

Well might Elijah have assumed that he was following God's instructions. But he heard a voice. Just as soon as Elijah was back on his feet, there came the question, 'What are you doing here, Elijah?' It's one of God's favourite questions, asked of Adam, Abraham and Jonah. Elijah seemed to be taking refuge in a cave, against another disturbing confrontation with God.

But Elijah is already armed with his plea of mitigation and a self-justifying litany. Haven't I done enough for you already, he infers, as if to warrant a break. What more do you want? 'I alone am left,' he sighs, 'and they are seeking my life to take it away.' The sense of dejection, isolation and self-pity is palpable, for one who dares to think that he's the only person left in the country who honours God. Yes, there are times when serving God in some capacity we feel alone, overwhelmed and abandoned; carrying the whole weight of responsibility, convinced that if we withdraw, everything will fall apart. In such times we need the voice of the divine presence to refresh us so that we can recalibrate the pattern of our lives.

God in the unexpected

Elijah is beckoned by God to do what he failed to do the first time, and stand on the mountain before the Lord. There wind, earthquake and fire were paraded before him; great archetypal and dramatic portents of God's presence. But once again, the Lord was not where Elijah expected him to be. Not in the predictable forces associated with divinity does God appear, but in a 'sound of sheer silence'. God appears in silence. Did the unexpected encounter with God unnerve Elijah? He did, after all, hide his face, wrapping it in his mantle, and took his place against the entrance to the cave. And once again we catch the humour, the divine voice speaks, repeating his question, and evoking a repeat of Elijah's self-righteous plea. No one is allowed to underestimate the persistence of God, who is like a hunter in pursuit of his prey.

God's surprise plan

But there's no escape for Elijah, nor for any of the followers of the God and Father of our Lord Jesus Christ. A new commission follows swiftly after the last. Elijah is directed to go back to where he came from, back to the royal court from which he'd fled. But there are surprises. He's to anoint a new king of Israel, and a king of Aran. And he's given notice that he'll then be relieved of his duties, and will anoint a new prophet – Elisha – as his successor. And as a final surprise and touch of divine humour, God reminds him that there are seven thousand people in Israel who have not submitted to the false god Baal. Of course, he will have another assignation on a mountain, when this vulnerable figure will stand with Moses, to represent all God's faithful prophets in the company of Jesus Christ.

We see Elijah in his strength and in his vulnerability, and we see through him the activities of God who is present in might and in tenderness, to challenge and confront, but also to protect and to bless.

Roger Spiller

Suggested hymns

We sing your praise, eternal God; Come, living God, when least expected; Dear Lord and Father of mankind; Guide me, O thou great Redeemer.

Lent

Ash Wednesday   17 February
The Second Pancake

Joel 2.1–2, 12–17, *or* Isa. 58.1–12; Ps. 51.1–18;
2 Cor. 5.20b—6.10; **Matt. 6.1–6, 16–21**, *or* John 8.1–11

The story is told of a woman who was making pancakes for her two young sons, Kevin and Ryan; and while she was busy cooking, the two boys started arguing about who should get the first pancake. 'I'm the oldest,' says Kevin, 'so I should have the first pancake.'

'No, but I was here first,' says Ryan, 'so *I'm* the one who ought to get the first pancake.' Their mother, sensing an opportunity to teach them a good moral lesson, turns the gas down for a moment and says, 'Now listen, boys: if Jesus was here, he wouldn't say, "Give me the first pancake," would he? He'd say, "Let my brother have the first pancake and I'll have the second one."' Kevin thinks about this for a moment and then he says, 'Ryan, you be Jesus.'

Grow inwardly

Most of the time, most of us are like Kevin: we feel we're owed the first pancake. It's all about me. Lent gives us a chance to be different: to go for the second pancake, and to find that we're happier as a result. What we should give up for Lent is our persistent desire to put ourselves first. But that's much easier said than done. In today's Gospel reading, Jesus points out how easy it would be to take on some new challenges during Lent – such as giving more money to good causes, or fasting regularly – out of pride: your real motive is not to grow spiritually but to show off. We still want to get the first pancake. Instead, he wants us to grow inwardly, not drawing attention to ourselves but serving God 'in secret'. But what might that mean in practice?

Involuntary suffering

Jesus doesn't talk about 'growing spiritually' – he talks about taking up our cross. Basically there are two kinds of suffering: involuntary and voluntary. Most suffering is involuntary, things we don't choose and don't want – getting cancer, losing a job or a loved one, living with arthritis. All of us will have to cope with this kind of suffering at some point in life. And in order to cope with what we can't choose, we need a strong spiritual life, for the test of any healthy spiritual life is precisely how far it helps us cope with what we don't want to happen.

How do we cope with it? By choosing to live with less; by learning to let go of a way of life we'd become accustomed to, and live more simply, but above all by *adapting* to circumstances we can do nothing about. When we suffer, we have to learn the difficult art of adapting without conforming; and Jesus shows us the way. He *adapted* to the terrible reality of arrest, show trial, and execution. But he didn't *conform* to the cruel values of those who did this to him. Those who've described the unspeakable horrors of life in gulags or concentration camps like Auschwitz tell us that the people who survived (other than those who were lucky, or so selfish that they didn't care about anyone else) were those who learned how to adapt (to realities they could do nothing about) without conforming (to the evil ideology that confronted them). So it is with being bereaved, or being in hospital: you have to adapt, and accept what's happened to you; but you don't have to conform, or succumb to apathy, or become a helpless victim. You are still you; and you are still loved.

Voluntary suffering

But, wait a minute – I hear you say – this still begs the question of what we are to do in practice. That brings us to the other kind of suffering: not the involuntary suffering that is forced upon us, but voluntary suffering that is freely embraced – what Jesus calls taking up our cross; and this is where Lent comes in. If we can learn to live with less things voluntarily, and adjust our lives accordingly, discovering in the process that we can manage without things we'd always taken for granted – if we can learn to do this voluntarily, we are much more likely to be able to do it when involuntary suffering comes our way – and to help others to do the same.

Finally, learning to give things up in this way, to carry our cross freely, may not only equip us for what lies ahead, and help us to grow spiritually: it may actually make us happier, more fulfilled people. We may find there's far more joy to be found in being second-pancake people than in constantly demanding the first one. St Paul puts the central paradox of Ash Wednesday beautifully in today's second reading: 'We are treated ... as sorrowful, yet always rejoicing; as poor, yet making many rich; as having nothing, and yet possessing everything.'

Gordon Mursell

Suggested hymns

Take up the cross, the Saviour said; Hear me, O Lord, in my distress; From the deep places, hear my cry; Jesus, lover of my soul.

First Sunday of Lent 21 February
Principal Service   **Into the Wilderness**
Gen. 9.8–17; Ps. 25.1–9; 1 Peter 3.18–end; **Mark 1.9–15**

The baptism and temptation scenes stand together to illustrate the paradox that vocation to God comes through the crucible of trial and temptation. Jesus is 'driven', according to Mark, into the wilderness, to experience deprivation from food, drink, companionship, human support. There his vocation is formed in the stark loneliness of his environment. The temptations that come to him right at the end of his 40 days of endurance are timed to find him at his weakest. They offer a repertoire of messianic actions that try to deflect him from his divine calling.

The wilderness

The wilderness is initially a negative encounter. The inhospitable stretch of land between the Judaean hills and the Dead Sea was called 'the Devastation'. There the self was compelled to live on the basis of unseen realities. The wilderness is the place of ambiguity and surprise. The wild vastness is where illusions are smashed, clutter is jettisoned and the real self is finally confronted in all its solitariness and nakedness. Only in the wilderness does a person discover what they really value and in whom they really put their trust. No wonder, then, the wilderness was the formative place for the birth of Israel. It became the training ground for the great prophets, Elijah, Elisha, John the Baptist. In Christian history it was in the dessert that the fathers and monastic communities kept the faith of Christ alive when it was being compromised in Constantine's Roman Empire. It's the wasteland of the spirit, a place where even the bare hint of light, water and vegetation is seen as a promise and a gift. A place that demands resourcefulness as the price of survival, where 'those going through the valley of dryness can use it for a well' and where the wastes 'rejoice and blossom like the rose'.

A metaphor for spiritual growth

The wilderness is not simply a place but a metaphor for spiritual growth, a programme for intensive spiritual education. And not only for spiritual giants, but for all who seek to follow Christ. It's not because God is vindictive, but because he loves us too much to allow us to become too flabby, too cluttered, too attached to our familiar world that we are unwilling to take the next fateful step, to move on and to grow.

Jesus was driven into the wilderness, according to St Mark. It was involuntary. And the big calamities of life can drive us, kicking and screaming, to our own wilderness experience – a serious sickness, an examination failure, a harsh appraisal, an unexpected redundancy, a long period of unemployment, a mid-life crisis, the loss of a life partner, the collapse of our faith in God. Anything can drive us into a wilderness experience – the breakdown of our routine, our means of support, the sense of isolation that nobody on earth can know what we are going through. It can provide a sharp interrogation of our life, who we are and where we're going. It tests to the limits the faith we'd taken for granted. It forces us to leave behind the false trappings of religion that have kept us from facing reality. And it leaves us no option but to make friends with the wild beasts, the demons that occupy our lives. The growing points of our lives are the times of spiritual emptiness. It's when we are in the wilderness that we come to distinguish the things that hold body and soul together from the baggage that weighs us down.

The temptation is always to escape and, like temptations put to Jesus, to eat and drink our way out of it, or to pin our hopes on a magical cure or a short-cut, or to collude and make accommodations so that we defend ourselves against the harshest features of the experiences. There is always the temptation to want to move on, in the illusory hope that we leave the wilderness behind, when, of course, we would only take it with us. Wilderness can be a gift, it forms us, if we will allow ourselves to live through it and learn from it.

Lent in our own wilderness

Lent is the wilderness season, the time when followers of Christ are invited to enter a focused, intentional wilderness period through the discipline of study, prayer and self-examination. It's a journey we make in the company of fellow Christians, sharing perhaps in home groups, in a guided retreat, in the daily routine of a religious community or church that says the daily offices. For others it may involve an 'escape' alone to a wild and desolate place, or to devote time to systematically reading the Bible. It may, for some, be a time to address an issue we've long been avoiding. I heard one bishop, still in office, say that he was devoting his time in Lent to preparing for death. But whatever we do, it will require us to make fresh demands upon ourselves, be ready to leave our 'comfort zone', to declutter our congested lives, and be more open and honest with ourselves and with trusted friends. The wilderness is a formative experience. Let's not pass by the chance of making 'a good Lent' and finding a new sense of radiance and freedom.

Roger Spiller

Suggested hymns

Forty days and forty nights; Above the voices of the world around me; Hear me, O Lord, in my distress; Jesu, lover of my soul.

First Sunday of Lent   21 February
Second Service   **Does the Snake Speak with a Forked Tongue?**
Ps. 119.17–32; **Gen. 2.15–17; 3.1–7**; Rom. 5.12–19,
or Luke 13.31–end

In my mind's eye I'm transported back to my childhood and I'm watching Walt Disney's *The Jungle Book*. Kaa, the snake with the hypnotic eyes, is singing 'Trust in Me'. In the film, Kaa is one of the boy Mowgli's trusted friends and protectors; he sings Mowgli to

73

sleep. Despite his sinuous movements and his lisp, he's not a sinister character.

In the book of Genesis the scenario is somewhat different. The talking snake is not a protector, instead it becomes the catalyst for the woman's contravention of God's ruling. Despite it being expressly forbidden, she is persuaded to eat of the fruit of the tree of the knowledge of good and evil.

The pictures in my mind change and I can see various Gothic and Renaissance paintings that would have taught our forebears about the story of Adam, Eve, the snake and the tree. Like Kaa, the snake is often represented coiled around the tree in the centre of the picture. Adam and Eve stand either side, with fruits in their hands and usually they are depicted 'clothed' by leaves. The scene where the snake speaks to the woman is the pivotal point in the narrative. Hence, the artists were endeavouring to give a visual account of the primary teachings of the story. Maybe we should note that a picture can indeed be worth a thousand words! Beguiling as the depictions are, let's explore the words of the passage more closely.

God, the man and the garden

The verses from Genesis 2 help to set the scene. God places the man in the garden. Most English translations say that he is put there to cultivate and guard it, but that traditional reading may be somewhat misleading (it is later, towards the close of this episode in the story of Adam, Eve and their expulsion from the garden, that Adam is made a farmer). At the outset, Adam is put in the garden as a place of safety. There he is to worship and obey God. God says that he may eat of the fruit of any of the trees except for the tree of the knowledge of good and evil. The man's enjoyment of the garden is contingent upon his obedience.

The snake, the woman and the tree

In chapter 3 the snake is introduced as a cunning and crafty character. He asks the woman whether God really forbade the eating of the fruit of the tree. She replies that not only are they not to eat the fruit but that they are not even to touch it, on pain of death. The snake (who speaks only twice) then tells her that that won't happen, that God doesn't want them to eat the fruit because if they do so they will be like God, knowing what is good and what is evil.

The woman sees that the tree is beautiful and the fruit looks good to eat. She thinks it would be good to be wise. She eats the fruit and then gives her husband some fruit to eat too. Having eaten, they do receive knowledge and understanding. Realizing their nakedness, they clothe themselves.

How do we interpret the story?

It's difficult to set aside centuries of Christian teaching about 'original sin' and 'the Fall'. Yet the passage makes no mention of either. Many Christian preachers, however, will read those understandings into the text (Augustine and Milton have much to answer for!).

Placing the passage in its context, later in chapter 3 we read of how God punished the snake, the woman and the man. In the case of the snake the punishment is to crawl (slither) on the ground. So on one level this is an aetiological story, an explanation of origins, (like a 'Just so' story about how snakes first began to slither).

But what of humankind: the woman and the man? In our story, the snake told the woman the truth. She then became the primary human actor: she saw that the fruit looked good. Despite her initial fear of immediate death, she chose to eat to gain knowledge. She was curious and so she made an active decision.

The woman's husband is the weak and passive character in the story, meekly accepting the fruit and eating.

Adam and Eve (they are named later in the chapter) begin the story as innocents, living in the garden, protected by God from the knowledge of evil. By their actions they become knowledgeable, but they destroy the harmony of the garden.

The story tells how the exercise of human choice (free will) in disobedience to God can result in unintended consequences. Having eaten the fruit they now know not only good but evil too. Their knowledge will be costly, bringing pain and (eventual) death. Their original state of innocence is ended and they become aware of their nakedness. They see themselves, become self-obsessed and self-centred, turning their concentration away from God.

Is this story about 'original sin' or is it that we see in Adam and Eve people who, like ourselves, make ill-judged choices that distance them from God? Hence, we do not have to be called to be like them: we are like them. We too experience a world that is out of kilter, imbalanced by human choices made because we want to be like God.

May God forgive us.

Wendy Kilworth-Mason

Suggested hymns

All hail the power of Jesus' name; God in his love for us lent us this planet; God of Eve and God of Mary; Praise to the Holiest in the height.

Second Sunday of Lent   28 January
Principal Service   **Suffering to End Suffering?**
Gen. 17.1–7, 15–16; Ps. 22.23–end; Rom. 4.13–end;
Mark 8.31–end[21]

Peter's objections make sense. He and his brother Andrew had already made considerable sacrifices to follow Jesus. They had left their thriving fishing business and the security of their lakeside Galilean home in response to Jesus' invitation, 'Follow me'. They had staked their very lives on the assumption that Jesus was the long-awaited Messiah, the one who would restore the fortunes of Israel and save the people.

Everything they had seen up to this point suggested that their sacrifice was prudent, a good investment. They had watched with excitement as Jesus cast out demons, healed the sick, cleansed the lepers, taught with authority, calmed the storm, raised a young girl to life, fed the multitude, walked on the water, opened the eyes of the blind, made the deaf to hear. These were only the foretaste of the coming end of suffering, poverty and oppression, and they were on their way to glory.

The Son of Man and suffering

When Jesus asks, 'Who do you say that I am?' Peter's answer seems obvious: 'You are the Messiah.' Does Jesus commend him for his faith and his readiness to speak out to others? He does not. He enjoins strict silence upon the disciples and, as if to distance himself from the confession, Jesus starts talking a different kind of language. 'Then,' Mark tells us, with an emphasis as decisive as a newsflash, then Jesus 'began to teach them that the Son of Man must undergo great suffering, and be rejected by the elders, the chief priests and the scribes, and be killed, and after three days rise again'. And instead of the secrecy about Peter's confession, we're told that Jesus 'said all this quite openly'.

Just what exactly is going on here? We're halfway through the Gospel, where the power and authority of Jesus has been manifested, and now Jesus speaks of powerlessness, hostility and suffering, ending in murder. Jesus, who has been alleviating pain and suffering, acting in the belief that suffering is contrary to the kingdom, now speaks of bearing pain and suffering himself.

A clash of expectations

Peter objects, and well he might. It's only sensible that he should do so. Suffering was no part of the vocation of the Messiah. A Messiah who is brought down by suffering cannot fulfil his long-awaited vocation to overthrow the political order, liberate his country from Roman rule and restore peace and well-being to his people. That's what came to be expected in a Messiah. And Jesus seemed to have the power and authority to fulfil the role and be God's anointed. And that's what Peter and the other disciples, and we too, if we were followers of Jesus, would have expected. There was simply no other way of thinking about the Messiah.

Peter objects, but so do we. Isn't there already more than enough suffering in the world today? What of the millions of displaced people or people in war zones or makeshift camps? We want the end of suffering, and instead we're following One who speaks as if the crowning fulfilment of his vocation is suffering and death. No wonder this talk of suffering shook Peter and his fellow disciples to the very foundation. And, even though we know the ending, it should shake us too. Because if it doesn't, if we see the story of Jesus only from the resurrection looking back, we will misread the resurrection itself.

The sacrifices that spare others' suffering

When Jesus introduced himself as Son of Man, he was pointing us back to the idea in the book of Daniel that the suffering of the righteous would create a surplus of merit that would spare others. Although it's a strange idea, we do know of examples where innocent suffering is the means of defeating suffering. The medical research scientist who risks and often loses her own life in trialling new drugs that can be used for the cure of thousands; people like Maximilian Kolbe, who came forward in a Nazi war camp to be shot in the place of the person selected to die; men and women who risk their lives in exposing atrocities and rescuing others. We can see how a person killed in hostile circumstances can absorb and neutralize hate and loathing and call a halt to further suffering and wickedness.

Jesus bears suffering

Jesus was implacably opposed to suffering and spent time healing 'all' who were sick and suffering. He himself recoiled from suffering, but he did conclude that in the mystery of God the suffering and death of the Son of God was the means by which God would defeat the powers of suffering and wickedness. If God suffers in the self-giving of his Son, the option of a quick fix or dramatic intervention is not an option. That this should be the destiny of God's only Son is staggering and unthinkable. It confounds all we could expect of God's ways.

So what if anything can we dare to say of the suffering in the world? Because God can use even suffering as the raw material of his redeeming purposes, because Jesus has borne the brunt of human wickedness and outlived it, because God is intimately identified with us in our suffering, because in the greatest calumny and miscarriage of justice in human history it was love that had the last word, we can know that God is at work to defeat suffering and transform our war-ravaged, unjust and brutal world. And the costly, selfless action voluntarily undertaken for others is part of God's healing, redemptive presence in the world.

Roger Spiller

Suggested hymns

Body broken for our good; Jesus, in your life we see you; Though hope desert my heart; We cannot measure how you heal; Earth's fragile beauties we possess.

Second Sunday of Lent   28 February
Second Service   **When God Says Go**
Ps. 135 [*or* 135.1–14]; **Gen. 12.1–9**; Heb. 11.1–3, 8–16;
Gospel at Holy Communion: John 8.51–end

Have you ever felt that God is calling you? Maybe the voices you hear are those of friends and family, but their words seem imbued with additional meaning. In the passage from Genesis, Abram knows that it is God who is calling him.

The context of the passage

Genesis 12 is a transitional passage, it marks the end of the 'pre-history' (Genesis 1—11) and recounts this first episode of the story of Abram, whose name was introduced at the close of the previous chapter. In Jewish tradition Abraham is the first of the patriarchs, so his story marks the beginning of the patriarchal history and of the history of Israel.

In the earlier chapters a variety of old traditions have been drawn together by the redactors, from a number of sources. They form a collection of stories about how curses have come upon humankind. In contrast, in the story of Abram we learn that God wants, yet again, to bless humanity.

God spoke to Abram: we're not told whether it was a face-to-face meeting, but that's implied since there is no mention of a dream, or of friends, or of heavenly messengers.

Abram's story

What's the message? God tells Abram, 'Go'. He's to leave his home and his family and head to an unknown destination that God will reveal to him. Think about it: would you set out on that kind of mystery tour? Maybe the young would relish the opportunity for a great adventure but Abram is an old married man of 75, he has wealth and slaves; in other words, he's settled in Haran.

God promises that he will show him where to go (a promise of land is implied). Abram will have numerous descendants who will become a great nation. God will bless him and make him famous. He'll become a blessing to all nations.

To want to have a family is a common human desire. In the culture of the ancient Near East it was believed that someone's name would quickly be forgotten if they died without children. Abram wanted descendants so that he would be remembered. He likely thinks that if he becomes the forebear of great nations he'll surely go down in history.

That outcome would be a blessing, but God also offers a wider generic blessing – to make him a blessing for others. In order to receive these rewards, to fulfil his god-given potential, Abram must be obedient.

A nomadic pastoralist?

The latter part of our passage reveals that Abram did set out for the land of Canaan. When he arrived he didn't settle in one place but travelled the land. At Shechem God appeared to him and confirmed that this was the land he was going to give to Abram's descendants, so Abram built an altar there.

The account of his entry into Canaan is a very selective one, it mentions three particular places: Shechem, a place between Ai and Bethel (where he built another altar) and the Negev (the southern part of Canaan). Interestingly, these are locations that will feature again in the story of the patriarchs; Jacob visits them when he returns to Canaan. They are later among the sites occupied by Joshua. So Abram's story is intertwined with that of Jacob and Joshua.

What's this story to us?

How do we identify with a Middle Eastern nomad who lived around four thousand years ago? Our lifestyles and contexts are very different; however, we have in common a sense of God's calling. Do we see ourselves as the sons and daughters of Abraham?

When God called Abram he required him to 'Go'. When does the God of the Bible ever ask people to take a seat, rest and relax? He doesn't sound like a God who prizes those who have 'always done it this way'.

If Abram obeyed, God was going to do something new through him. What if we were to become the people through whom God does something new and blesses the world today? It might require of us that we give up certain of our treasured traditions, we might have to move, leaving our safe places and our familiar friends. How far would you go for God?

The story in Genesis is not so much about Abram as it is about God and God's blessing. The mission for the people of God is to obey him and thus convey his blessing to the nations. So, in what ways do we offer God's love to others? Are we a sign of his presence in this fractured world?

God promised Abram land, descendants and blessings. Surely his promises hold true for us too. Give thanks for all your blessings, they are God's gifts.

Wendy Kilworth-Mason

Suggested hymns

Deep in the shadows of the past; God it was who said to Moses; Hills of the North, rejoice; The God of Abraham praise.

Third Sunday of Lent   7 March
Principal Service   **Church Cleansing**
Ex. 20.1–17; Ps. 19 [*or* 19.7–end]; 1 Cor. 1.18–25; **John 2.13–22**

Jesus appears in the unlikely guise of a vicar, in a reworking of the gospel. He's being reminded of his record. 'I'm rather afraid, Vicar, you haven't been a great success. We'd expected full churches with your reputation as a preacher. But not a bit of it. You seem to be emptying the church if anything. Why, look at the register. Congregations are right down on this time last year. Eli's family have left. They used to be staunch supporters. And Annas' family have gone too. They used to run all our raffles and jumble sales. Even Caiaphas' family have left, and we were relying on them to raise money for our new church tower. In fact apart from Mary Magdalene and the old woman who puts a few coins in the collection, you've more or less emptied the whole church.'[22]

The caption explains: 'Anyone who has Jesus for a Vicar is due for a lot of emptying.' There's no more dramatic example of that than the cleansing of the Temple. Jesus is on the rampage, equipped with a handmade whip to overturn tables and drive out money-changers and cattle. But why? What does it mean?

Sharp trading practices?

It seems to be a protest like that conducted by the prophets against the abuse of God's house. But was there an abuse? The other Gospels who have the story certainly thought so. They cite a text from Jeremiah: 'My house shall be called a house of prayer for all the nations. But you have made it a den of robbers.' So sharp trading practices and overcharging may have been meant. But we can't conclude from John's account that dishonest practice is the issue. Rather, the Temple provided a much needed service for pilgrims arriving from distant places who needed to change currency to pay the Temple tax in shekels and to purchase animals for the sacrifices.

Another prophet, writing after the exile (Zech. 14.21), envisages a day when the whole world worships at Jerusalem; no merchants are found in the Temple, the Temple is cleansed and it is reclaimed as a place of prayer. Stop making my Father's house a marketplace, says Jesus.

Marketizing the Church?

Does the market intrude in more subtle ways in the life and worship of the Church in our times? Do the values of the market shape our relationship to the Church? Has the McDonaldization of Christianity arrived, as some have argued? With the market comes choice, plurality, shopping around for what suits us. Have we become consumers of religion rather than worshippers? Do our needs, choices and expectations override a prior commitment to the duty, obligation and commitment to the wider faith community? Do we insist on an à la carte religion that offers the forms of worship, hymn choices, leaders and preachers and service times that we prefer?

The market is obsessed with numbers, throughput, footfall, numerical growth, market share. Has the Church, and have we, succumbed to this? Do we then replicate the competitive, fevered, activist, noisy, mercantile world, rather than provide a healthy alternative to it? And how does the market influence what we offer and how we present ourselves? Are there spectacular events and installations in our ancient edifices to attract attention, or do they only confirm the suspicion that we have lost our purpose? Markets shape and constrain the products we offer. Just as we select the packages of religious goods that suit our lifestyles, so is the Church, as provider, tempted to serve pre-packaged, easily accessible, undemanding versions of the Christian gospel. Jesus reclaims it as a house of prayer. It's sometimes hard to do this amid the chatter and clatter of weekly gatherings where sociability is paramount. Do we need to safeguard the Church as a serious, safe, spacious environment for all who want space to pray, reflect, debate, learn and enlist in an apprenticeship in discipleship?

A temple not made with hands

Jesus has cleansed the Temple, at least for the time being. But he goes on to challenge the institution of the Temple itself. It has failed the purposes for which God intended it and will be subject to this judgement. Instead, Jesus will replace the Temple, and he will be God's dwelling place. What might this mean for us?

Jesus relativizes the Temple, so should we relativize the Church as a symbol, building and institution? Jesus does not replace the Temple by his own person only to have it reappear in the shape of the Church. If we think of the Church as a building, institution or organization, as the focus of our faith, then we're living in pre-Christian times. We rightly value our church buildings; they, together with our cathedrals, are sermons in stones, holy spaces, 'monumental representations of the truth of Christianity', sturdy reminders of an alternative lifestyle to the frenetic pursuit of wealth. Empty churches are not the worst thing that can happen for the Church or for us. Ceasing to be a place of prayer, a serious place, is. After all, God doesn't inhabit temples made with hands, but he inhabits human lives.

Roger Spiller

Suggested hymns

O thou not made with hands; Be still, for the presence of the Lord; Let us build a house where love can dwell; Christ is our cornerstone.

Third Sunday of Lent   7 March
Second Service   **Confidence and Credentials**
Ps. 11, 12; Ex. 5.1—6.1; **Phil. 3.4b–14**, *or* Matt. 10.16–22

One of those fearsome ice-breaking exercises involves people in a circle, finishing off the sentence, 'I'm proud that …'. There's scope for people to shock, surprise and impress other participants with their assets and achievements. We may not be drawn into this particular exercise, but I suspect we're likely to do some such listing of the things we're proud of, anyway. St Paul, too, has a ready list of his credentials. We can imagine him counting them out on his fingers for extra emphasis. They were sure to silence those who questioned his authority and send any detractors who might have wanted to take him on scurrying away for cover.

Credentials displaced

If St Paul expresses his credentials, it's only to show the extent to which they have been displaced by a relationship that shows up their futility and emptiness. His indictment on his assets, as he reflects from his prison cell, is not that they were bad, but that they were good but their goodness kept him centred on himself. Losses have to be written off by banks and governments, but who would write off assets! Well, St Paul writes them off, as unrecyclable waste. It's not because he's making a cool calculation, as if he's totting up gains and losses in some ledger. It's quite simply that he's experienced the all-consuming power and presence of Christ, and in that light everything in the world has to be reassessed, revalued or simply discarded.

It's our strengths and goodness that do most to lead us astray, because they can seduce us to believe that we can find confidence and security in ourselves. People with prodigious talents know better than most just how illusory these supposed sources of confidence can become. National treasures like Stephen Fry and Clive James have said that they live in perpetual fear that any day someone will tap them on the shoulder and expose them as charlatans. But of course, we're not engaged in some market exercise on what promises to deliver greater self-confidence. Jesus isn't simply a more durable source of confidence. He is the one with whom our whole identity is completely reconstituted.

Confidence in Christ

The key for St Paul is the knowledge of Christ. But this is not simply knowledge about Jesus, knowledge we acquire. That, as Paul reminds us elsewhere, can feed our pride and set us on a false trail. Our knowledge even of Christ can keep him at arm's length and put us in the driving seat. Knowing Christ Jesus, as suggested by the warm and devotional language that breathes through Paul's words, is personal knowledge. It's the experience of being loved. It's knowing Christ alone as the only source of confidence. We know how a relationship of love between two human beings changes everything, and friends look on as the all-consuming relationship changes deep-seated habits, appearance, interests, values. It's the closest we have for understanding our relationship to Christ. Knowing Christ Jesus is not, of course, one more relationship in our life but our life being reconfigured around his inexhaustible life. The Christian's confidence is grounded in the action that God has taken. We have merely to embark upon the journey of a lifetime in appropriating the life and person of Christ as he makes himself known to us.

Confidence through community

Seeking confidence in Christ sits uneasily with a culture that is shaped more than ever by targets, outputs, performances, assessments – however beneficial some of these may be. The radical Christian alternative is only sustainable through communities characterized by mutual and unconditional love and affirmation. Churches are meant to embody just such relationships, but too often they merely emulate rather than challenge the wider culture. They can also be over-impressed by those among their number who are particularly successful, well connected or influential. Whether in churches or small groupings, it is the face-to-face experience of mutual love, unconditional acceptance and openness that renders the claims of St Paul believable and compelling.

We may go on taking quiet satisfaction in our gifts and successes but through Paul's testimony we know that there is an alternative to the daily battle to prove our worth, to win approval, to prop up our vacillating self-esteem. We may need to be persuaded to write off our gains, but we can at least discover through our losses that we are accepted, loved and affirmed. We are accepted on grounds that depend on Christ's life, death and resurrection. And we are enlisted in a race in which we are prepared to jettison everything in order to win the prize of knowing the One who has already made us his own.

Roger Spiller

Suggested hymns

Be thou my vision, O Lord of my heart; All I once held dear; All for Jesus; All my hope on God is founded.

Fourth Sunday of Lent   14 March
(For Mothering Sunday, see the Second Service.)
Principal Service   **'God so loved the world ...'**
(or may be used at the Second Service if Mothering Sunday readings are used instead of those for the Principal Service)
Num. 21.4–9; Ps. 107.1–3, 17–22 [*or* 107.1–9]; Eph. 2.1–10;
John 3.14–21

If there's one sentence in the Bible that generations of young Christians were taught to memorize and cite chapter and verse, it is that 'God so loved the world that he gave his only Son, so that everyone who believes in him may not perish but may have eternal life'. It's valuable to have a succinct distillation of the Christian faith in such few words and the mere repetition of them brings assurance in times of crisis. But, of course, even so short a text poses questions that must be faced. What belief is required in order for us to be saved? Conversely, what would lead to condemnation? What are we meant to understand by God's giving of his Son? And, when can we know that we have or will have eternal life? A full response would take us scuttling all over John's Gospel, but the few verses we read bring light on questions that otherwise remain to torment and trouble us.

God's self-giving

God 'gave his only Son', and the most characteristic way in which that is expressed is when the Son of Man is lifted up. When and where is the Son, Jesus, lifted up? It is when he is hauled upon a cross. That is the cue for our author to give us a flashback to the time of Moses and the curious account of a bronze serpent, familiar in the ancient world but strange to our ears. Moses erected it as a token of divine deliverance from serpents. So when the dying Israelites looked up and directed their gaze on God and put their trust in him, they were saved from venomous snakes. A strange story, but poisonous serpents caused many deaths, and that was interpreted as divine judgement. But the bronze serpent is set on a pole so that everyone who is bitten can look at it and live. Jesus is lifted up, high, so that we can look and live. The serpent has become associated with healing, and is depicted on the badge of the Royal Army Medical Corps. Jesus is lifted up on a cross and secures the salvation of the world. The world needs to be saved, saved from itself and from its captivity to its wilful patterns of self-destruction and violence. And God gave his only Son, to secure our deliverance and open the way to abundant life.

Judgement

How, then, does that relate to judgement? Many people view religion, including the Christian faith, primarily in terms of judgement and not salvation. Worse, we think that the terms of God's judgement rest on criteria that we cannot know until our destiny has already been fixed. We may also be unsettled by the seemingly opposing claims in John's Gospel that 'God did not send the Son into the world to condemn the world, but in order that the world might be saved through him'. But we also read: 'I [Jesus] came into this world for judgement.' How can these be reconciled?

A woman visiting a gallery of modern art, said to the curator, 'I don't like your paintings.' 'Madam,' said the curator, 'the paintings aren't on trial.' We judge the pictures, but then we realize that they are judging us – or at least our artistic sensibilities. Christ came to give light and life – not to judge. But when the light appears, we judge ourselves by our attitude towards it. His presence causes people to take sides for or against him. Jesus is the light who, as the Prologue to John's Gospel says, 'enlightens everyone coming into the world'. But people can reject that light and when they do so they bring judgement upon themselves. Because Jesus is light, he brings everyone the possibility of life and salvation. But when he is rejected and we move out of the light, Jesus becomes the agent of judgement. At his trial, the religious and political leaders thought they were judging Jesus. But, as John shows, when Jesus is lifted up on the cross in shame and ignominy, he is simultaneously raised up in exaltation and glory as the Lord and Judge of the entire world.

Eternal life

The judgement of Jesus is determined now, already, by our response to Jesus Christ. For those who believe and receive Christ, the judgement is past. There's no need to live with an uncertain destiny; fearful of judgement, anxious that we might be rejected and excluded by God. It doesn't change. It is accepted by the Father because he has given all judgement to the Son. Eternal life, for John, isn't consigned to life after death. It begins here and now. We embark upon eternal life, life in all its fullness, when we have a relationship to Jesus Christ. We know if we've entered upon a filial relationship with God and we're growing in his family likeness. We know if we look up to the cross of Christ and behold his glory. And we can know if we stake our lives on the conviction that 'God so loved the world that he gave his only Son, so that everyone who believes in him may not perish but may have eternal life'.

Roger Spiller

To God be the glory; God is love, let heaven adore him; The light of Christ is shining; And can it be.

Fourth Sunday of Lent   14 March
Mothering Sunday   **Soul-piercing**
Ex. 2.1–10, *or* 1 Sam. 1.20–end; Ps. 34.11–20, *or* Ps. 127.1–4;
2 Cor. 1.3–7, *or* Col. 3.12–17; **Luke 2.33–35**, *or* John 19.25b–27

Soul-piercing

I wonder how many people here have a body piercing. Many of you have probably had your ears pierced and some of you probably have piercings in other places too – it's OK, you don't need to show me! I'm much too boring and square to have indulged in any body-piercing – though I know a number of clergy who have piercings in a whole range of places! However, as a Christian and as a mum I think I do know a bit about 'soul-piercing' – that image which comes from today's Gospel. Simeon holds the Christ-child and recognizes that he is holding all heaven in his arms. He can die in peace because God has saved him. He tells Mary that the child will be a sign, a pivot-point in history. Because of Jesus some will fall and some will rise. That which is deep within people will come to the surface: into the light. For Mary: her soul will be pierced. Being a parent is soul-piercing stuff. Imagine the mother of Moses doing all she can to try to ensure her son's safety. How desperate must you be to hide your baby in a basket on a crocodile-infested river? Soul-piercing indeed! Or Mary at the foot of the cross, watching her precious child mocked, humiliated, murdered. Those of us who are parents or grandparents, or who have responsibility for children and young people, know about soul-piercing – have experienced it to a lesser or greater degree – and others of us can imagine it perhaps when we witness human tragedies on the television or in the press. Children bring a mixture of joy and pain, delight and agony. It's the way of humanity: living life in all its fullness.

Mother church

Today is Mothering Sunday: that pause in the middle of Lent when we draw breath from our Lenten disciplines before launching headlong into Passion Sunday, Palm Sunday, Holy Week and Easter. It's a day on which to give thanks for our mother, and all she means to us. In the past it was also a day for returning to and giving thanks for your 'mother church' – which some would have seen as their cathedral, and others as their local parish. Young people in domestic service returned home to mum for the day, and to their mother church to worship. We are the mother church for our parish. For generations the people of this parish have identified with and cherished this church. What does it mean for us to 'mother' this community in which we are set? First, being part of the body of Christ makes us family – we are related to one another through our baptism. As a mother church we are family for everyone – a place where people can come and be at home. This is a place where people can be truly themselves, warts and all. It's a place where people can grow and develop, explore and question, get things wrong, know themselves forgiven, and make a fresh start. It's important not to be an exclusive and inward-looking club – but open, welcoming, warm and accepting of all. The people of this parish should be able to look upon this, their mother church, with deep affection and with a sense of ownership. They should be able to say, this is 'our church'.

Sorrow and joy

As the body of Christ in this place, we need to show that having the Holy Spirit at work in our lives makes a real difference to the way we interact with one another and with the wider community. St Paul, writing to the church in Corinth, reminds those early Christians and us that, because we bear Christ's sufferings, we also have Christ's consolation and we can offer that to others. We are to be people of encouragement and hope for our community. As a mother church we may find that we endure 'soul-piercing'. We may be cut to the quick by the sorrows and sufferings of those around us. The apathy and indifference of our neighbours towards the church can be difficult to bear. In-fighting and backbiting within our community, cruelty, hurt and injustice that is enacted around us, are all things that hurt our minds and souls. But because we are in Christ we know not just suffering, but also consolation – hope. We know that resurrection follows death and that a new heaven and a new earth are promised. However difficult life becomes, we know that through the power of God lives can be turned around. This is the message we carry and we state it every time we gather and whenever we celebrate the Eucharist. We celebrate not just for ourselves but always for the whole of our community, whether they come or not – whether they believe or not. We never give up on them; we never lose faith in them – that's what good 'mothering' looks like. When you receive the Eucharist this morning – give thanks for those who have mothered you down the years, and remember your calling to be part of this mother church offering new life to everyone.

Catherine Williams

Suggested hymns

For Mary, Mother of our Lord; Brother, sister, let me serve you; Tell out my Soul; Mary, did you know?

Fifth Sunday of Lent (Passiontide)   21 March
Principal Service   **Seeing Jesus**
Jer. 31.31–34; Ps. 51.1–13, *or* Ps. 119.9–16; Heb. 5.5–10;
John 12.20–33

In his book *From Christ to Coca Cola*, art critic and academic Martin Kemp argues that universally recognizable icons like Jesus are likely to become divorced from their origins. He warns that we don't want our cherished iconic figures to be destroyed, and so we are unwilling to confront what is known of the actual circumstances of their lives. Nothing, it seems, must be allowed to undermine the selective, contradictory images of Jesus that range from a Che Guevara figure to the 'gentle Jesus meek and mild' depicted in a thousand stained-glass windows.

Seeing Jesus

We are put on the right track to see Jesus as he wishes to be seen by the references to 'my hour' that punctuate John's Gospel and shape his ministry. We too speak of the hour or moment or time, like Churchill's 'finest hour', which is the culmination and high point of all we have longed for, planned and worked for and in the light of which we have decided the choices that were presented to us. The hour for Jesus is the time when he will be raised in exaltation, as he is raised to suffering and death. That 'hour' was for Jesus the decisive frame in which he understood and interpreted his daily life and vocation. Jesus could and can only be seen aright in the light of that hour. It is the hour from which he recoils, but it is also the consummation of a life lived in filial obedience to his Father.

Seeing Jesus is seeing Jesus lifted up on his cross and, as if to underline it, Jesus didn't grant the request of those Greeks to 'see Jesus'; instead, he went into hiding. They were not to see him apart from his cross, and neither are we. All that went before in the ministry of Jesus, procuring food and wine, healing and raising Lazarus from death, were signs of a reality that was made possible only through his death. But through his 'hour' of shame and glory, the way is opened for all people to be drawn to and to see Jesus. In Jesus, Jeremiah's promise of a new covenant is fulfilled, a covenant that offers the way for all people to know him.

Seeing 'through' Jesus

In his depiction of the crucifixion, Salvador Dali paints Christ's cross over the whole world. And that is precisely where he belongs. 'Since the event of Jesus Christ,' said Bonhoeffer, 'we cannot look at the world without seeing God or look at God without seeing the world.' We see Jesus, and through him, like the sun, we see everything else. Christ's cross is his judgement on, or, more accurately, his discrimination of, the world. Through it he brings us life and light. But the light exposes the dark machinations of the human spirit and shows up the self-serving ways that distort our seeing and ultimately consign us to death. To see through Jesus we have to follow him in that dying to false, worldly, self-serving ways of seeing, and to have our eyes trained through keeping company with him. A woman was making her way to the 'Seeing Salvation' exhibition that marked the new millennium. As she approached the gallery, she saw a homeless man begging on the Strand but did not pay much attention to him. In the exhibition she was particularly struck by the sixteenth-century sculpture *Christ on the Cold Stone*, showing Jesus seated on a rock, naked and vulnerable, awaiting crucifixion. On leaving the gallery she came across the same man in the Strand and found that the image of Christ came to her mind and she found that her reaction to him was transformed.

Facing Jesus

We have to see Jesus always from the vantage point of his cross, and subject all human experience to the testing and interrogation of the cross. But we have also to face Jesus for ourselves. There can be a one-sided concentration on what the cross means, what theories of salvation, what lessons for life we can deduce from it. But as we enter Passiontide, we are invited to face Jesus ourselves, imaginatively, through pictures, sculpture, theatre and interactive media. We don't have the detail of Jesus' physical face but we have plenty of evidence from those who did to appreciate what it would be like for us to be before his face. And we do so not just as spectators but as participants, and in John's Gospel as worshippers in particular.

The crucifixion of Jesus was a compulsive theme of some of the greatest medieval painters. They helped their viewers to observe the drama of salvation. But some of the greatest painters did more. They made it possible for their viewers not merely to stand outside the frame admiringly, but to come into the picture. Figures in the picture would draw you in with their eyes or beckon you with their hands. They created space for us to occupy and to become ourselves contemporaries in the drama and, in so doing, to face Jesus himself. Seeing Jesus enables us to see everything else aright. If we take up the invitation of this Passiontide to keep company with Jesus on his cross and to enter, in imagination and contemplation, the triumph of the Crucified, we will be drawn to him and find light and life and hope.

Roger Spiller

Suggested hymns

Jesus, we long to see your face; Come, see the Lord in his breath-taking splendour; Longing for light (Christ be our light); I am the Light whose brightness shines.

Fifth Sunday of Lent (Passiontide) 21 March
Second Service   Departures
Ps. 34 [*or* 34.1–10]; **Ex. 7.8–24**; Rom. 5.12–end; *Gospel at Holy Communion*: Luke 22.1–13

Some jobs (like being a vicar) require you to get good at moving house. Moving to a new home fairly frequently can be an exciting blessing, and you get practice at upping sticks and settling somewhere new (and decluttering too – which can itself be a Lenten discipline!). It's not easy moving from a familiar place to a new one, but every leaving, every arrival, is important both for individuals' ministries and for the churches and communities they serve. Moving on from old lives is a recurring story in the salvation history of God's people.

Exodus

This second book of the Bible has the title 'Departure' (the Greek word means 'journey out, away from'). The story of the Israelites leaving Egypt is crucial to both Jewish and Christian self-understanding. They had become a threat to the Egyptians, so Pharaoh treated them very badly, enslaving them and trying to put all their newborn sons to death. God has compassion for his people, and charges Moses and his brother Aaron with leading his people out of Egypt.

However, since the Israelites make up a large part of Pharaoh's workforce, he's not happy when Moses and Aaron ask him to let them go. So Pharaoh doesn't listen but rather makes the Israelites work harder. Any escape seems a long way off – it will require a miracle or two, and ten plagues sent to show the Egyptians the power of God. Only after the tenth plague – the Passover when all Egyptian firstborn males are killed – can the Israelites make good their departure.

Getting ready to be delivered

Part of this is for Moses to bring the Israelites back to their true identity – not as Egyptian settlers, but as God's people, the descendants of Abraham, Isaac and Jacob. Moses reminds them they are cared for by God, and they worship God.

93

Today's Old Testament reading is early in Moses and Aaron's relationship with Pharaoh. What to Pharaoh seems little more than magic tricks – the staff that turns into a snake, which gobbles up those that the Egyptian magicians appear to have created in the same way – is God's peaceful attempt to persuade Pharaoh that God is more powerful than anything else. But Pharaoh couldn't give two hoots. So Moses catches Pharaoh's notice down by the River Nile early in the morning: once Moses has given Pharaoh another chance to let the Israelites go, he declares that the River Nile will become a river of blood. The staff strikes again, and all the water everywhere is turned to blood. The first plague.

This story too is about drawing the Israelites back to worship the one true God. The River Nile was one of the gods that the Egyptians worshipped. The first plague shows God's power is greater than the divine river Egyptians thinks brings them life. This sign isn't just for Pharaoh's sake. This plague shows Egyptians and Israelites alike the power of the God whom Moses, Aaron and the Israelites' ancestors followed. That deepening of faith is necessary for the tale of departure that, after all the plagues, will come: the desert pursuit, and the 40 years more the Israelites spend wandering through the wilderness.

Renewing faith

The Israelites might have needed some time to get their heads round leaving. After all, despite being persecuted, they *do* still have homes and families and food. (They certainly manage to grumble a lot about what they're missing when they're wandering around the desert, as the book of Numbers tells us.) Sometimes we have to leave something that seems good. We have to take a leap of faith. We may not be entirely sure the grass *is* greener on the other side.

This is what we see the Israelites doing. They've witnessed the power of God through Moses and Aaron, they've heard that this is *their* God who is acting. They are called now to step out of what is hard but familiar, into the unknown future.

Our faith too may be scattered with callings to unknown futures. We may be in an unsatisfactory situation where we're not as close to God as we could be; but it's something we know. If we're called afresh daily to give our lives to Christ then we have to be prepared to step out of our comfort zones to come closer to him. And to rejoice not only in the good new things that may come our way, but also the things we miss – because they're a sign of an old life, which is not where God is calling us any more.

Today is Passion Sunday, the start of the last two, intense weeks of our Christian year when we remember how Jesus made that journey – to celebrate the Passover – to Jerusalem. Jesus left his ministry of teaching and working miracles to head to the great Temple to worship; to make his way to the place at the centre of his faith to which he would now bring extra significance.

Jesus models for us the courage that we may sometimes need – courage to step out for God into something new, whatever that might mean.

Megan I. J. Daffern

Suggested hymns

All ye who seek for sure relief; Through the night of doubt and sorrow; It is a thing too wonderful; Guide me, O thou great Redeemer.

Holy Week

Palm Sunday 28 March
Principal Service A Challenge to the Nation
Liturgy of the Palms: **Mark 11.1–11**, *or* John 12.12–16;
Ps. 118.1–2, 19–end [*or* 118.19–end]; *Liturgy of the
Passion*: Isa. 50.4–9a; Ps. 31.9–16 [*or* 31.9–18]; Phil. 2.5–11;
Mark 14.1—15.end, *or* Mark 15.1–39 [40–end]

What's Palm Sunday without palms? There's no direct mention
of palms in Mark's Gospel; only an improvised carpet of cloaks
and leafy branches from the fields. There's no donkey either; only
an unbroken colt that's hard to handle. And the triumphal entry
was a procession that began in Bethphage, a place we can't locate.
The crowd that now flanks Jesus are the country yokels, the people
who followed Jesus from the villages far away from the capital.
Their voices won't be heard in Pilate's courts on Good Friday, in
the places where power and decision-making occur. As always, they
will be silenced by the metropolitan elite.

But these common folk have experienced a presence so powerful,
a love so amazing that they are willing to make the arduous journey
to Jerusalem with Jesus and put their heads above the parapet with
no concern for the danger they're putting themselves in.

Topsy-turvy

There's something very odd, then, about the first Palm Sunday. You
may have learnt at school, as I did, the poem by G. K. Chesterton;
a donkey's-eye view of what it was like to be there at the first Palm
Sunday.

> When fishes flew and forests walked
> And figs grew upon thorn,
> Some moment when the moon was blood
> Then surely I was born.

Yes, being with Christ leads us into a topsy-turvey world, and the first Palm Sunday will convulse and shake the whole ruling establishment and force them to act. So what are we to make of it? Why, in fact, did Jesus go up to Jerusalem?

A challenge to the nation

He goes as a pilgrim. It's the Passover festival, the great annual fixture when God's chosen people celebrate God's liberation from oppressors in Egypt and keep alive their hopes that God will act again, finally, to rescue his people from Roman occupation. There's a swirl of expectation in the air, the atmosphere is electric, like a tinder box ready to ignite, with religious hot-heads always ready to inflame a dangerous situation in the hope of a showdown with the authorities and to force God to show his hand.

Jesus went to Jerusalem as a pilgrim, but it seems, too, that he went up to Jerusalem, on that last fateful journey, to present his nation with one last challenge – to make a final bid to save them from the disastrous course on which they had embarked, politically and religiously. Jesus didn't seek death; in fact right to the very end he recoiled from it, but he did pursue a way of life, in obedience to his Father, and with a selfless and single-minded devotion, so that it became ever more likely that it would terminate in a horrendous death. Jesus came into the world and went to Jerusalem, to call Israel to prepare for the inauguration of God's kingdom.

Street theatre

It's clear that Jesus choreographed everything very deliberately. So his procession begins at the Mount of Olives, the place linked to King David and where the Messiah is expected to appear. Jesus isn't riding a stallion, a war horse, as if he were leading troops into battle. He's on a colt, an unbroken, unmanageable creature, a beast of burden that speaks of service. He's mocking the Roman leaders riding on their lofty horses. Jesus seems to be parodying those who rule by force and parade their power, pouring scorn on the idea of brute force and coercion as the means to get things done. Jesus isn't making a protest, leading a demonstration; he's engaging in street theatre, a surprising, comedic, satirical exercise in unmasking the futility of self-centred living.

Jesus becomes king

So what is going on under the surface? Well, in his passion and death, Jesus becomes king, God takes back authority. He establishes his kingdom, reigns and saves and renews his people. He believed that his death was the way, the only way, by which he could defeat the principalities and powers of the world. Without the shedding of blood, says the Old Testament, there is no redemption. There's a cost to be met for reversing and redeeming all the malign, pernicious, accumulated forces of evil.

Palm Sunday is the first day in a week in which Jesus became our rightful king and Lord. Jesus will be decked in royal purple, wearing a crown, albeit of thorns, lifted up not merely in shame but in glory, and designated unwittingly the King of the Jews in the languages of the world, by the greatest power on earth. That's the topsy-turvey way in which God restores his sovereignty. Suffering love, self-sacrifice, self-emptying. Easter, then, doesn't reverse the ignominy and shame and suffering of Good Friday. It affirms it and says that death is God's way of coming alive. Good Friday is already Easter in disguise.

And what is our response? Is the cross more a question than a promise? That the man we will contemplate hanging on a cross at the end of the week is God's answer to the problems of the world? God's rescue plan for our human plight? As one writer says, it's as if the cross is hanging by a thread. Our faith is hanging by a thread. But the thread is Jesus. And to come to know that he loves us and gave himself for us defies description. Can we keep Holy Week so as to keep company with Christ's cross?

> Here might I stay and sing,
> no story so divine;
> never was love, dear king,
> never was grief like thine.
> This is my friend, in whose sweet praise
> I all my days could gladly spend.

Jesus went to the cross and made his way through death to something beyond life. Let's let him take our hand, empty, weak and worn, and his journey will be ours too.

Roger Spiller

Suggested hymns

All glory, laud and honour; There's a man riding in on a donkey; From heaven you came, helpless babe; My song is love unknown.

Palm Sunday 28 March
Second Service **A Sinister Song in a Vineyard**
Ps. 69.1–20; **Isa. 5.1–7**; Mark 12.1–12

Just imagine going to a party in a vineyard. You'd surely expect plenty of wine, good food, and, as the night wore on, wouldn't the celebratory songs, fuelled by the wine, become increasingly sentimental? However, what would it be like if the singer of what sounded at first like a love song suddenly introduced lyrics about murder, mayhem, injustice and judgement?

The (wine) harvest festival

The setting of our passage is the Festival of Shelters (Tabernacles/Booths) that celebrated the harvesting of the fruit crops, including the gathering of the grapes. The tents or temporary shelters that were built for the festival were a reminder of the years of the Exodus, when the people of Israel had dwelt in tents, before they had reached the security of the land of the promise. It recalled how God had brought them from the desert to a land flowing with milk and honey, a land of abundance. So, the festival was both a commemoration of the past and a celebration of (food) security. It's hardly surprising, particularly if the harvest was plentiful, that it was one of the most popular festivals of the year.

Perhaps, at this joyous time of the agricultural year, Isaiah had been invited to a vineyard to celebrate. Alas, it seems that the prophet really knew how to dampen the spirits of the partygoers with his song choice.

Hear the music

Isaiah is the singer and our passage is his song. In form it is like a three-verse poem. The first verse, narrated by the prophet who speaks as an observer, is about the 'Beloved', God, the owner of the vineyard who started his career with great enthusiasm, choosing a

99

fertile plot, preparing the ground for the vines, planting, readying a pit in which to tread the grapes and even building a watchtower to protect his investment.

In the second verse, the storyline of the song takes an unexpected turn: the vineyard is unfruitful. The voice of the owner of the vineyard takes up the telling of the tale and the effect is like that of a key change to a minor key in a pop song! Despite having planted the finest vines, the vintner discovers that all the grapes are sour. So God calls upon the people to judge between him and his vineyard. He asks what is surely a rhetorical question: is there any way in which he was negligent? The question demands a consideration of a further question: who's to blame?

Face the music

The concluding verse of the poem delivers God's judgement and tells of the destruction that is to ensue. The song, therefore, is a parable (with a sting in the tale), or an allegory, in which Israel is the vineyard and the people of Judah are the vines. God tended the vineyard (Israel) diligently and expected that the vines (the people of Judah) would produce fine fruit; instead, they have failed to do what is right and just, they have committed murder.

God, the Beloved, the farmer-nurturer owner of the vineyard, is also the righteous judge who has delivered his judgement. He will remove the defences from the vineyard, letting animals trample it. He will not tend it, nor will the rains fall on it, hence it will become overgrown.

God wants his people to be faithful. He prizes justice and righteousness. But Israel and the people of Judah have been unfaithful and unfruitful. Owing to injustice and unrighteousness, Israel is doomed.

Come to the party?

I'm sure that were we fellow guests at the party Isaiah's song would have gone down like a lead balloon with us too. If we were planning a celebration I doubt that we'd be booking someone like him as the entertainment.

Are we not like the people of Judah? We want cause to celebrate. We want to remind ourselves of the God of love who tends creation, the one who has provided abundantly for our material and spiritual needs. So we sing our hymns of praise and our love songs to Jesus.

But, as in Isaiah's time, are we guilty of partying and enjoying our plenty while injustice is rife? For example: was our harvest, back in the autumn, about enjoying a supper and a celebration for our friends? What did it do for the needy? Did we prayerfully consider food security?

Has God ceased to tend creation, because of our wickedness? Do we ignore illegal logging and land clearances devastating the Amazon, and the multinational petro-chemical industries' destruction of pristine habitats, as we celebrate abundance, at the cost of the sustainability of the world's agrarian systems?

What would the God of righteousness sing to us about our commitment to justice and righteousness? Where is the light in our darkness? Maybe we should invite Isaiah to our party.

Wendy Kilworth-Mason

Suggested hymns

Sing to him in whom creation; God in his love for us lent us this planet; We turn to you, O God of every nation; You are the vine, we are the branches.

First Three Days of Holy Week   29–31 March
Two Kinds of Love
(These are the readings for Monday of Holy Week but the sermon may be used on any of the three days.)
Isa. 42.1–9; Ps. 36.5–11; Heb. 9.11–15; **John 12.1–11**

The anointing at Bethany appears in all four Gospels, but in John it comes immediately before Jesus' triumphal entry into Jerusalem. It is during that entry that Jesus is acclaimed as king by the people. But where and when is he crowned? Here, at Bethany, Jesus is anointed, not by a priest in a grand religious building but by a lay woman at supper time.

At the anointing scene in John, Martha 'serves' Jesus: the Greek word is *diākonei*, from which comes our word 'deacon'. Her sister Mary serves Jesus too, but in a very different way. Martha's service is practical and essential, but inevitably utilitarian; Mary's service is anti-utilitarian, extravagant. Two kinds of love are revealed: the one robustly this-worldly, vitally down-to-earth, the other contemplative, utterly unconditional. Note also that Martha's love is directed towards the living Jesus, Mary's towards the dying Jesus (we will return to this). The loving service of both sisters is complementary; and both need to find expression in our lives and in the life of our Church. But it is all too easy, in a busy church's life, for the service of Mary to be undervalued, or even omitted altogether.

Facing death

'Why was this perfume not sold … and the money given to the poor?' Judas' question reflects a utilitarian, outcome-obsessed, approach to love and service. What's the point of spending all that money on someone who is going to die soon anyway? Yet that is exactly the point. Jesus replies to Judas by saying, 'Leave her alone. She bought [the perfume] so that she might keep it for the day of my burial. You always have the poor with you, but you do not always have me.' In fact Mary's extravagant love of Jesus does have a purpose: she prepares Jesus for his death – and, as we have seen, you can see her act of anointing as a kind of coronation. She knows he is dying; yet she still offers him this incredibly costly, seemingly wasteful, love. So when Jesus says, 'you always have the poor', he is saying: don't use the excuse of all the other competing demands on our time to avoid this most demanding and life-changing of gifts – helping someone to face death.

Adoration

Mary's service of Jesus is characterized by *adoration*, the offering of love and care and reverence to someone without looking for anything in return. Do you offer this to anyone? Who offers it to you? In terms of Christian pastoral care, adoration involves 'staying with' someone, keeping them company, rather than doing things for them or talking at them. It is the love we offer someone when we (and perhaps they) are not in control of what is happening. Intercession, penitence, thanksgiving and praise are all important – but adoration is the greatest of them. Adoration lifts us out of a narrowly me-centred world view, and adoration of the crucified Jesus cannot but elicit from us a personal response to what God in Christ has done for us – it is our response to unconditional love: 'love so amazing, so divine, demands my soul, my life, my all'. Hence it alone makes real change possible, because it involves giving our utmost attention and unconditional love to a significant Other; it involves relating to

God as God, not just to a kind of divine postal service. A century ago, the Anglican spiritual writer Evelyn Underhill wrote that all worship has a tendency 'to decline from adoration to demand, and from the supernatural to the ethical'.[23] Adoration is the opposite of a narrowly utilitarian, calculating service of others, a 'what-kind-of-return-on-my-investment-can-I-expect?' approach.

But adoration is costly: Mary's 'pound of pure nard' cost 300 denarii, a year's wages. And this brings us to the heart of the mystery of Holy Week. Like Mary, we are invited to offer Jesus the loving service of adoration, as he begins his journey towards death. All of us have to make this journey. All of us need help to face this most universal of human experiences. And adoration, unconditional love and reverence, is the highest and holiest help we can offer, for it makes us feel valued and loved even when – in fact, precisely when – we face the biggest challenge to any sense of love and value. And the mystery of Holy Week assures us that, whenever we offer someone that adoration and love in the name of Jesus, we open ourselves to the unimaginable new life of the resurrection that comes to us, not instead of death, but through it.

Gordon Mursell

Suggested hymns

Give to our God immortal praise; Fill thou my life, O Lord, my God; God beyond earth's finest treasures; Let all the world, in every corner sing.

Maundy Thursday   1 April
Principal Service   **Learn How to Receive**
Ex. 12.1–5 [5–10] 11–14; Ps. 116.1, 10–end [*or* 116.9–end]; 1 Cor. 11.23–26; **John 13.1–17, 31b–35**

It can be hard to receive from others

Have you ever had someone wanting to serve you and you've not wanted to be served? Have you ever been offered or given something that you've not wanted to receive? Has there ever been a time when someone has offered to help you, but you have not been willing to accept that help?

If that's the case, and I'm sure it is with most of us at some point, then there might be a variety of reasons for this. For example, it might be that you don't want people to think that you're incapable of doing things for yourself. It might be that you don't want to become dependent on someone else. It might be that you don't entirely trust that person's intentions, or may be that you don't trust their ability to do what they are offering to do. You might doubt their cooking skills, you might be worried that they will give you food poisoning, or that what they serve you might have peas in it. On the other hand, maybe your reluctance to be served is because you don't want to feel beholden to that person, or because you want to hold them emotionally at a bit of a distance, or because you are worried that if you accept what they are offering, people might think that you are accepting everything about them. There are all sorts of reasons why we might refuse to let someone wash our feet, so to speak. There are all sorts of reasons why we might be reluctant to drink from the cup of kindness that another wishes to place into our hands. There are all sorts of reasons why we might be unwilling to open our hands to accept the goodness of another person. Most of those reasons say more about us than about them.

Jesus' gift of himself

It was a bit like this with the events of that first Holy Thursday. Jesus wanted to give the disciples the gift of his entire self and he expressed it through the Eucharist and in the washing of feet. But while Jesus poured water into a basin, poured wine into a cup, and ultimately poured out his life the next day on the cross, the reaction of the disciples fell short of what you might expect of them. Judas left before the end of the meal, Peter didn't want Jesus to wash his feet, and the others, each in their own way, seemed terribly embarrassed to be on the receiving end of Jesus' self-giving. Theirs was not so much a reluctance to give but a reluctance to receive. It was almost as if they were already starting to distance themselves from him, that they no longer trusted him. In fact, you could say, that there is a rejection there. Most of us will also know how that feels, when we offer something and the other doesn't take it, or shows little interest, or even throws it back in our face. Jesus must have felt that too – yet later on, after he had risen, the first thing he did was to eat with them. At the lakeside, on the road to Emmaus, in the upstairs room, he gave them a chance to 'modify' their response, and, as we know, they accepted what he gave them.

A giving in receiving

There is a challenge and invitation here for each and every one of us – because Jesus wishes to give us the gift of his entire self. Now you might think that surely being a Christian is about serving others, about what we can do for others, but it works both ways. If we are to give properly, if we are to serve generously, if we are to help helpfully, then we too must learn how to receive. To receive requires of us a real openness and trust. It requires that we admit that we can't always stand on our own two feet and that we depend on God. There is a giving in receiving – and a receiving in giving. Sometimes we have to ask that question: Why am I not willing to receive, to be served, to be helped? Do I need to let go of my pride? Do I need to accept that I can't do everything? Do I need to admit that another person's help or expertise is necessary? Do I need to lower my guard, relinquish my control, and become vulnerable and trust another? For many of us that is quite hard – especially if there have been circumstances in our lives that have made trusting difficult. If we can do that, however, if we can learn to let Christ in, often through others, then we will be better able to serve and to pour out our lives for others too.

So as some of you put your feet out to have them washed, as you open your hands to receive Christ's body, as you hold the cup of Christ's blood poured out for you and for all, invite Christ in. Let him serve you, let him tend to your wounds; let go of what holds you back from trusting him completely. Only say the word and you will be healed.

Philip Dyer-Perry

Suggested hymns

An upper room did our Lord prepare; Meekness and majesty; A new commandment; Now, my tongue, the mystery telling.

Good Friday 2 April
Sorrow and Love Flow Mingling Down
Isa. 52.13—53.end; Ps. 22 [or 22.1–11, or 22.1–21];
Heb. 10.16–25, or Heb. 4.14–16; 5.7–9; **John 18.1—19.end**

O my God, I cry in the daytime

In the tumultuous narrative of the last three days of his life, it is difficult to imagine that Jesus did not weep. Surely tears fell from his eyes as his heart was wrenched and his body tortured? He had wept before, at the grave of Lazarus his friend, and he probably wept again as the universe turned on its axis and he was led like a lamb to the slaughter.

A whole world of pain, anguish and sorrow might have been seen in the tears that Jesus shed. Contained in each drop was his betrayal by Judas, Peter's denial, his own arrest and torture. Contained in each drop were the pains he must obediently endure, the nails being hammered into his hands and feet. Contained in each drop was his yearning for water, but the taste of vinegar and gall, a vision of cruelty beyond compare. Contained in each drop of Jesus' tears were the future faces of his mother, and Mary and Martha, and John and the disciples whom he loved, weeping this time for him, the faces of women weeping as he breathed his last. Perhaps in each of his tears Jesus could see his own face, calling to the Father from out of the deep, crying out to God in the daytime as the sky turned black. As he wept, both day and night, he only heard the mocking voices asking, 'Where is now your God?'

So perhaps in each one of Jesus' tears there was a shadow of all that had been and all that must be soon endured. Jesus might have wept again on the Mount of Olives, in the Garden of Gethsemane – the Garden of Tears. It was in that garden that Jesus, cried out, 'Father, if you are willing, remove this cup from me'; 'Don't make me go through this', he pleaded. 'Can there not be another way?'

And then through his tears he cried out to God again, 'Not my will but yours'. There in the Garden of Tears he chose to bear our heavy load, he chose to take up the cross. He cried, there in the garden, those tears we all cry when we know something difficult has to be done, when we know something is inevitable, when we offer up to God all that we are. And though we feel abandoned, we hope that God will hear our cry and gather up our tears into his bottle.

Drop, drop slow tears

Jesus wept again on the cross, and for whom did he weep then?

What can you see in his tears on that day, when they were mingled with his blood? Can you see his mother in pain as the sword that Simeon talked of pierced her aching heart? Can you see the disciples left alone to complete the mission he started? Or Pilate who chose power and politics over justice and mercy? Or Caiaphas who could not see the light?

Can you see in Jesus' tears from the cross the crowds who jeered and shouted 'Crucify him!', and the soldiers who cruelly mocked him as they put a crown of thorns on his head?

Jesus wept for all of these. They were in his tears on that day, when he pleaded, 'Father, forgive them; for they do not know what they are doing.' They were all in the silent prayers of Jesus' sorrowful heart, in words that only God could interpret.

Jesus wept for all these and more. He wept for all those who have betrayed him, and all those who have loved him. He wept for those who are in pain and sorrow, those who are lonely or lost, those who have their own cross to bear, those who would join him in paradise on that day and on every day since.

Perhaps Jesus also wept for himself as he was torn from the heart of his Father and left desolate on the cross, when he had done all he could do, and had given all that he could give.

Perhaps as Jesus wept that day on the cross, God his Father also wept as the sky turned black and the foundation of the Temple was torn in two, and perhaps in that moment the Holy Spirit, in a song of lamentation, hovered over Jesus' watery face.

On this holy day may we see the world through Jesus' tears and come to know in our hearts that the cross of Christ points to a new heaven and a new earth where crying and pain and death will be no more, and all tears will be wiped away.

Victoria Johnson

Suggested hymns

From heaven you came (the Servant King); Drop, drop slow tears; When I survey the wondrous cross; Be still, my soul.

Easter

Easter Vigil   3–4 April
The World Turned Upside-down

(*A minimum of three Old Testament readings should be chosen. The reading from Exodus 14 should always be used.*)
Gen. 1.1—2.4a *and* Ps. 136.1–9, 23–end; Gen. 7.1–5, 11–18; 8.6–18; 9.8–13 *and* Ps. 46; Gen. 22.1–18 *and* Ps. 16; Ex. 14.10–end; 15.20–21 *and Canticle*: Ex. 15.1b–13, 17–18; Isa. 55.1–11 *and Canticle*: Isa. 12.2–end; Baruch 3.9–15, 32—4.4 *and* Ps. 19, *or* Prov. 8.1–8, 19–21; 9.4b–6 *and* Ps. 19; Ezek. 36.24–28 *and* Ps. 42, 43; Ezek. 37.1–14 *and* Ps. 143; Zeph. 3.14–end *and* Ps. 98; Rom. 6.3–11 *and* Ps. 114; **Mark 16.1–8**

'And they said nothing to anyone, for they were afraid.' With these extraordinary words, the Gospel of Mark ends, for the verses that follow have been added on later by someone else. Some scholars have argued that there must have been another ending that is now lost; but there is no evidence that such a thing ever existed. You may well be thinking: if that really is where the earliest of the four Gospels ends, it's not exactly good news, is it, as we prepare to celebrate Easter? And besides, if the women who witnessed the empty tomb never said anything to anyone, how did the news of the resurrection get out?

Resurrection and failure

The first thing to note is that, if the women really didn't say anything to anyone, they were in good company: perhaps more than any other Gospel writer, Mark constantly shows us how Jesus' disciples let him down, or misunderstood him, or just got things wrong. You may notice how, in today's reading, the young man at the empty tomb (probably an angel) tells the women to 'go, tell his disciples *and Peter* that he is going ahead of you'. Why is Peter mentioned separately? Because he, more than any other disciple, failed his Lord and denied him after his arrest. But Jesus doesn't give up on him, any more than he gave up on the women who said nothing to anyone. It's the same with each of us. We fail Jesus again and again, and yet we're still loved, we're still called, we still have a future. And *that* is the miracle of the resurrection.

Resurrection and renewal

It's so easy to misunderstand Easter. You may know the story of the elderly couple who were visiting Israel on holiday when the wife fell ill and died. So the husband went to a local undertaker to arrange her funeral. 'How much will it cost?' he asked. 'Well,' said the undertaker, 'that depends. We could do you a lovely funeral here in Israel and it really won't cost you much. But if you want to have your wife's body flown home for the funeral, it will be very expensive – maybe ten times as much: it's up to you.' And the man thinks about it for a minute, and then says, 'I think I'd better pay to have her body flown home, even if it costs so much more. You see, I seem to remember reading about some guy who died here in Israel, and was buried, and three days later he came back to life again. And I ain't taking no chances!'

But the man had got it wrong. Easter is not about revival – as though Jesus was raised from the dead and just carried on from where he'd left off. Nor is it about survival – as though he never really died. It's about renewal – a whole new quality of life that emerges through death, and that death can never destroy. Everything is turned upside-down; so the young man in the empty tomb tells the women, 'He has been raised: he is not here.' No wonder they were afraid. And that brings us to the heart of the matter.

Resurrection and changed lives

The young man tells the women to 'go and tell' that Jesus has been raised from the dead. They do go, but they don't tell. So how did the news get out? *Because the real evidence for the resurrection is not words that are spoken, but lives that are changed.* Something about those terrified, wondering women must have convinced the other disciples that the tomb really was empty, and the Lord really was raised. So with you and me, here today at this Easter Vigil. You may have sensed Christ's living presence in the drama of this, the oldest of all Christian acts of worship on the greatest of all Christian feast days. You will almost certainly be about to renew the vows made at your baptism. You may have come to this service because something has made you believe that death and evil and sadness will never have the last word. Yet you can't put all that into words. *And you don't need to*; for the evidence of the resurrection is changed lives, failures who know they are still loved, people frightened about the future but who still dare to hope and look forward. For it really is true: Jesus Christ is risen, and all the world is risen with him. Alleluya!

Gordon Mursell

Suggested hymns

This is the night of new beginnings; Now the green blade riseth from the buried grain; Exult, creation round God's throne!; I will sing the Lord's high triumph.

Easter Day   4 April
Principal Service   **Complete the Story**
Acts 10.34–43, *or* Isa. 25.6–9; Ps. 118.1–2, 14–24
[*or* 118.14–24]; 1 Cor. 15.1–11, *or* Acts 10.34–43;
John 20.1–18, *or* **Mark 16.1–8**

We all like a happy ending to our novels, films and plays. 'Does it have a happy ending?' a son of mine always asks before agreeing to watch a film or take up a book recommendation. We don't mind how we get there, we may relish the surprising journey, but we look for a resolution, a satisfying conclusion. An elder brother played a trick on his younger brother that was new to me in the list of sibling menaces: he would rip out the last couple of pages of his younger brother's novels just as he was getting to the end of the story. There's a yearning in all of us for completeness, fulfilment, resolution to all the loose ends of our lives, and we hope at least to find it in a story.

A lost ending

The death of Jesus needs a happy ending if state injustice is to be reversed, love and goodness are to be shown to triumph and the hopes for salvation invested in him are to be believed. But the so-called resurrection story in our earliest Gospel, St Mark, finishes abruptly, without a happy ending. In the days when videos had to be purchased rather than downloaded, the suggestion was mooted that some videos might be made that would offer alternative conclusions, so that people could choose their preferred resolution. That, in effect, is what we have in the two alternative endings composed to try to complete the lost last act of Mark's Gospel. Both close on a triumphal note, and one has a heightened sense of the bizarre. Of course, we could have read the other Gospels, especially St John, the most widely used account of Easter Sunday, due to its heartfelt, happy and satisfying conclusion.

Incomplete lives

Mark's ending is abrupt. But so, for the most part, are our lives. Not many people find the fulfilment they seek within their span of life. There will always be aspirations that remain unmet, projects left unfinished, relationships only half discovered. What we seek to do and be can't always be completed in our few years of life, and if this life is all there is, we may have to reckon with a cruel and miserable incompleteness never to be resolved. Then, too, we think of the seemingly irreconcilable conflicts across the world, and the wars that stretch over decades; the genocide and ethnic cleansing that snuff out the lives of children before they've even had the chance to live. As someone said, here in this life all symphonies remain unfinished. While the tragic features of life still remain, Mark's ending can address the human reservoir of injustice, tragedy and loss that seems to go unchallenged. The three women at the graveside speak to and for us and our condition.

Finding Jesus in our Galilee

In Mark's Gospel the women at the tomb of Jesus are alarmed at encountering a young man with his message. Who wouldn't be terrified to find the grave you were visiting in a private garden open and empty and a rather direct and unaccountable young man delivering a blunt message, 'Gone away, meet you in Galilee'?

But why Galilee? Why not Jerusalem, where Jesus could vindicate his claims publicly and discredit and exercise some leverage over the powerful overlords? Galilee is the secular world; Jews called it 'Galilee of the Gentiles'. It was a racially mixed area, edgy, with a history of radical politics. There had already been an uprising there in Jesus' own lifetime. Galilee to the north of Jerusalem was where Jesus chose to live and work and was the place to which he was returning. That was far from the metropolitan elite and their pre-occupation with power-living in Jerusalem. Galilee is where faith is put to work, and where it is tried and tested.

Continuing the story

The abrupt and probably lost ending of Mark is fortuitous. For it tells us that space in the story is left for us. It resembles one of those tiresome game shows where contestants have to complete the story that was begun by someone else. Now the story is passed on to us and we are the ones to take it forward in the Galilees of our towns and communities. Jesus still goes before us, through his Spirit, and we are summoned to join him there. Facts, argument and evidence can satisfy us that belief in the resurrection is credible. But the resurrection can't be contained within the narrow bounds of reason and history. We will really only know the truth of the resurrection by taking up the call to follow Jesus. And discover where he takes us.

Jesus' resurrection heralds God's new creation, an alternative world order. But it doesn't eliminate our lost endings, unmet hopes and unfulfilled longings. It doesn't reverse Good Friday. Evil may still triumph, the ecosystem collapse and life on earth as we know it come to an end. Mark's Gospel embraces the tragic features of our lives and refuses to trivialize or deny them. It's a double-edged narrative which contains within it the vestiges of despair and fear.[24] All of life involves incompleteness, loss, death and bad endings, but these point us beyond the limits of our existence. They make us look forward to the day when our hearts will be filled with un-alloyed joy. That's the stupendous promise of Easter. May our hearts be full of the joy of Easter, so that we will ourselves be part of the continuing story of Jesus' risen life.

Roger Spiller

Suggested hymns

Ye choirs of new Jerusalem; Love's redeeming work is done; At the Lamb's high feast we sing; Jesus Christ is risen today.

Easter Day   4 April
Second Service   **You Shall Live!**
Morning Ps. 114, 117; Evening Ps. 105, *or* Ps. 66.1–11;
Ezek. 37.1–14; Luke 24.13–35

A difficult journey

Can these dry bones live?

What a reading for this Easter Sunday evening! This week may have been a difficult one for some. Holy Week can take its toll as we travel with Jesus through the events of those days and remember what happened with all its pain, horror and grief.

When Jesus walked the Emmaus road and opened the Scriptures to those disciples, was Ezekiel's valley of dry bones one of those passages Jesus brought to life causing the disciples to exclaim, 'Were not our hearts burning within us?'

Ezekiel was speaking to those in exile in Babylon, a conquered people, far from home, trying to hold on to their distinct culture as the people of Yahweh in a foreign land. Did they believe that all hope was lost, that life as they had once known it was over? To them God promises: I will raise 'you up from your graves, O my people. I will put my spirit within you, and you shall live, and I will place you on your own soil.' It is a promise of homecoming and new life. Surely a picture of salvation for this Easter evening.

Do we long to feel our own hearts stir within us, revived by the very breath of God? To be lifted from those things that feel like death to us, and find ourselves at home once more in our own bodies and minds and spirits? Have you known a form of exile, a dry spiritual death?

Breath of life

That exile in Babylon in fact produced great creativity. 'By the rivers of Babylon – there we sat down and wept when we remembered Zion … How could we sing the LORD's song in a foreign land?' They found a way to sing by writing down the stories of their people from the very beginning. They asked, 'How did this all come to be?' From that valley of dryness and death they wrote down the story of creation and life, abundance and growth; of a God who called us into being and breathed life into us. That was how these bones could live again.

Recognizing that divine spark within – the very breath of God – they were able to share the stories of a wandering pilgrim called into relationship. Stories of covenant relationship born through an apparently impossible promise to an elderly childless couple through whom all the nations would be blessed.

From such an exile, such a valley, came the writings of the Hebrew people – the gift of the Scriptures.

We may each know our own version of that valley of dry bones; our own experience of loss and despair, feeling far from God or from our own true selves. God asks us, 'Can these bones live?'

What would our answer be?

What could we bring from the dry depths to answer yes to that question? Even in our dryness, can we remember the Spirit who called us into being and calls us still?

Return

We have the story of Easter to remind us of what God can do. From the grief and anguish of Good Friday, from the desolation and silence of Saturday; from that dry parched valley we arrive at Easter morning. We find ourselves before the opened grave, an empty tomb. We turn and see a risen Saviour and feel new life breathed into us.

God longs for us to know abundant life. Yet the natural order of things, the way that Jesus came to reveal, is of birth, death and resurrection. Without death there can be no resurrection. We will inevitably come face to face with death in one of its many forms within our own lives. Grief and lamentation are therefore appropriate and necessary. An honest naming of such experience allows us to find some meaning and purpose beyond the suffering and becomes the very creative power that leads to life again, to resurrection. Many writers, artists, musicians, activists, scientists, advocates and visionaries have found this to be true – that from the dry valley there is a way back to life. And while it is impossible for us in our own strength, God invites us to participate. For within us there is that divine spark that can listen for the invitation. Can these bones live? God invited Ezekiel to speak into the valley, to call upon the four winds, to participate in the divine creative process of hope and life; to dream of what could be. Can we, as Easter people, find that breath within us and be part of the vision? The experience of coming home to life is our re-turn from exile. To turn again is the meaning of repentance. The graves are opened and the tomb is empty. For it is Easter Day.

Carey Saleh

Suggested hymns

Now the green blade riseth; This joyful Easter-tide; O Breath of God, come sweeping through us; Teach me to dance to the beat of your heart.

Second Sunday of Easter   11 April
Principal Service   **Doubting Thomas?**
Ex. 14.10–end; 15.20–21 (*if used, the reading from Acts must be used as the second reading*), or Acts 4.32–35; Ps. 133; 1 John 1.1—2.2; **John 20.19–end**

Misunderstood?

Thomas must be up there among the most misunderstood people of the Bible. He's so often called 'Doubting Thomas', with the distinct implication that this is some kind of fault. I can't let that go unchallenged. In the story of Thomas after the Christ's resurrection, Thomas never actually doubts the risen Lord! What Thomas doubts is the word and the witness of the other disciples. When the risen Christ turns up a week later, Thomas is filled with faith. 'My Lord and my God,' he proclaims. In this story, it is not Christ who causes Thomas to doubt, but Christ's disciples gathered there in the upper room. Thomas simply did not find his friends' story was credible.

Thomas?

Perhaps we need to step back to think a little more about this. We know precious little about Thomas from Matthew, Mark and Luke, except that Thomas was chosen by Jesus to be one of the disciples. Only the Gospel of John includes more about Thomas, and the story of Thomas after the resurrection makes more sense in the light of the other incidents that John has recorded.

The first mention of Thomas is in the eleventh chapter of John. Lazarus has died. Jesus has been summoned, and though he delays his journey back into Judaean territory, it's clear to his disciples that Jesus intends to go to Bethany, to the tomb where Lazarus has been buried. Some of the disciples think travel is really dangerous under the circumstances: the Jewish leaders were at that very moment seeking an opportunity to put Jesus to death. It is Thomas who realizes Jesus has made up his mind to go to his friends. It is Thomas who says to the others, 'Let us go to die with him!' Fearless Thomas we might call him; loyal Thomas; loving Thomas. Thomas is willing to stand by Jesus, even to the point of death.

A few chapters later, John records Jesus' prayer at the Last Supper. Jesus is preparing his disciples for his Passover through suffering to glory, but only in a veiled way. Jesus is talking in riddles. I don't have to imagine very hard to see a picture of Thomas, brows furrowed, trying to follow the implications of everything Jesus is saying, and finally blurting out, 'We don't know where you are going. How can we possibly know the way!' Surely Thomas wasn't alone? The others must have been just as perplexed, but perhaps they were afraid to show their ignorance, perhaps even afraid to call attention to themselves. Only a few minutes earlier Peter had protested that he would be faithful to Jesus until he died, and Peter had been cut down to size. Who would dare speak up? Yet Thomas is not cowed into silence. He didn't understand, and he wanted to. He can't follow Jesus unless he knows where and how. It's as simple as that. 'Straightforward Thomas' we could call him, or 'Simple Thomas', or how about 'Refreshingly Direct and Realistic Thomas'?

Context?

When we remember these two stories about Thomas, they give us a context for the appearance of the risen Christ in the midst of the disciples. The risen Christ arrives when Thomas is out. The disciples are gathered in fear behind locked doors. Jesus appears and fills them with joy. He gives them a mission and empowers them with his own Spirit to continue his saving work. At least that's what the Scriptures tell us.

But Thomas isn't there. He'd just stepped out briefly. Maybe he'd nipped out to Tesco for a pint of milk? Maybe none of the others would put a toe out of the door, but not Thomas. He ventures forth. He is either fearless or foolhardy, or maybe both; which may be what we also need to be, but that's to get ahead of ourselves.

Thomas returns, and the other disciples tell him they have seen the Lord, but for Thomas something doesn't ring true. If they have seen the Lord, why are they still locked up tight in that room? If they are filled with such joy, why couldn't he read it on their faces? If they have been empowered by the Spirit of God to complete Christ's work on earth, what are they waiting for? For Thomas to return? Surely not, or they would have been so breathless and eager that he would have seen the transformation in their eyes. So, Thomas says to them, in so many words, 'I don't believe you.' Thomas, simple, loyal, loving, straightforward, down to earth, direct, who didn't understand but wanted to, who longed to follow Jesus but who needed to know the way, Thomas didn't doubt the Lord; he doubted the word of his friends. Thomas found it highly unlikely that the Lord was risen because he was surrounded by a group of witnesses whom he simply did not find credible.

Ourselves?

There is an ancient saying in the Eastern Church: if you want to know if Jesus is really risen, look around you at the faces at the Easter Vigil. Thomas could not read the presence of the risen Christ on the faces of his friends. What would he read on our faces? What do we read on each another's faces? We need to look like credible witnesses, like a community that has seen the risen Lord and been transformed.

Michael Hopkins

Suggested hymns

Jesus, stand among us; Come, ye faithful; O breath of life; This joyful Eastertide; Christ the Lord is risen again.

Second Sunday of Easter 11 April
Second Service **The Thin Black Line of the Horizon**
Ps. 143.1–11; Isa. 26.1–9, 19; **Luke 24.1–12**

The end of the world?

I attended a funeral recently. The minister told a story of overhearing a little boy on a beach, gazing out at the thin black line of the horizon, asking, 'Daddy, is that the end of the world?' His dad replied, 'No, it's the beginning of something new.' I found the image comforting as I sat in the church. Later, as they lowered the coffin into the yawning grave, my inner cynic gained the upper hand, piping up, 'Thin black line, or deep dark hole?' As we threw earth into the grave, I wondered, 'New beginning or ultimate finality?' In these moments we face mortality in all its rawness. We are but dust and to dust we shall return. Is there nothing else? Looking up, I saw a gull soaring on an updraft, framed against the clear sky. It reminded me of my experiences of faith, of trust in the resurrecting Spirit of God, and the fear of the idle tale dissipated. But I empathize with the dismissal and doubt of the disciples in our Gospel reading.

An idle tale?

They write off the women's words as an idle tale. A silly hope. A pointless viewpoint. Made-up nonsense. How swift the disciples are to dismiss this possibility of hope. Why do they do this? Is it because the messengers are women in a male-dominated culture? Perhaps, but there is more going on here than prejudice. It's a matter of perspective and experience. The women see that the body is missing, they see the two dazzling men and bow before them, terrified. They hear the words, 'Why do you look for the living among the dead? He is not here but has risen.' They are reminded of Jesus' own words about this. The women have a significant experience of the spiritual amid the material, which shifts their perspective; the thin black line of death starts to look like the beginning of something new.

The disciples are locked in grief, shrouded in the despair that death can bring. In shock, faced with brutal loss, they have forgotten the bigger picture, forgotten hope, forgotten Jesus' words. Perhaps they never really understood them in the first place. So, the women's story is dismissed. Perhaps, for some, at that funeral I attended, the hope in the image of the thin black line was dismissed. Perhaps the liturgy that points to resurrection hope was never understood – just an idle tale we tell ourselves at funerals to fill the silence.

From deep dark hole to thin black line

But – so often so much hinges on that little word 'but'. 'But Peter got up and ran to the tomb.' He didn't dismiss the words as an idle tale but took them as an invitation; he went to see, went to find out more. What he discovers amazes him – he sees the empty tomb and the empty linen clothes. The text doesn't tell us what he thinks has happened, but we see he has moved into the beginning of new understanding. For him the deep dark hole is becoming the thin black line of something new.

The possibility of new horizons

It's easy to be so consumed by our certainties that we don't go and look. This might be as mundane as being sure we are right in an argument and not attempting to see the others' perspective. But this text is asking more of us. It is asking us not to be seduced by the notion that the material is all there is. It is beckoning us to look up from the dark graves of our experience to see the possibility of new horizons. It is inviting us to take Jesus at his word – 'Behold, I make all things new.'

The beginning of something new

We are just human. Of course, there are days when such hope seems just an idle tale. Jesus' first disciples had such moments. But (there's that word again) – we are encouraged not to remain in the doubt-ful, dismissive place of grief and fear, to leave behind the chains of cynicism, take a risk, step out and trust. Even when we don't understand – and mostly we don't – God is at work in, through and beyond our material world. The thin black line of the horizon is never the end of the story; it's the beginning of something new.

Kate Bruce

Suggested hymns

Now the green blade riseth; O worship the King, all glorious above; In Christ alone; Who breaks the power (This is amazing grace).

Third Sunday of Easter   18 April
Principal Service   **Wounded Resurrection**

Zeph. 3.14–end (*if used, the reading from Acts must be used as the second reading*), *or* Acts 3.12–19; Ps. 4; 1 John 3.1–7; **Luke 24.36b–48**

Entering the scene

They were in a maelstrom of confusion and uncertainty. Hopes they didn't dare hope churned around with scepticism, exhilarated joy, faint glimmers of understanding, unabashed terror and large chunks of complete bewilderment. Little wonder that when the risen Lord stood among them they were petrified. Suddenly he was there and they assumed it was a ghost, which is a reaction probably not far from one many people would have today. Faith was immobilized and strong tactics were called for. Our Lord opted for gruesome shock. 'Look at my wounds! See my hands and my feet. Touch me!'

Doubt slowly began to dissipate as Jesus effectively pursued his tactics and ate a bit of fish. We can imagine the fun Hollywood would have with the scene, but fortunately Luke spares us the overdone, amusing melodrama and offers the unfolding story of something far more powerful – and far more real. Having settled their minds about the reality of who he was, Jesus takes the opportunity to move the gathered disciples on in their grasp of what all this means: Scripture has been fulfilled in their sight, sound and touch.

Wondering about the scene

Good Friday's despair has been so rapidly transformed into Easter jubilation. It began with the story of the women who had been to the garden early that morning and the message they brought back from the two men in dazzling clothes. It moved on to Peter's puzzled viewing of empty grave clothes in a vacant tomb. Then late at night the two men who had left hours earlier for Emmaus rushed back into the house with their story: the risen Lord had joined them in conversation and a meal. And finally the fog of bewilderment was pierced; not by angelic messengers, not by an empty cave, not by compelling conversation or sacred meal, but by the sight of the horrifyingly familiar marks of crucifixion.

The whole extended scene is intriguing, not only because of what has been transformed but because of what is exactly the same. The risen Lord still bore the wounds of crucifixion. This was important evidence for the disciples that he was the same man: recently dead, now raised. For the early Christians, and ever since, the wounds have been an essential detail in our ministry of proclaiming a resurrected Lord. But the presence of those wounds is much more than evidence. The wounds bear a vital message for us and our faith, too.

This experience of the Eleven and their companions points us to the fact that Holy Week and Eastertide belong together – and not just because one follows the other in the calendar. The new life they witnessed in the risen Lord was only possible because he had been through the horrors of Good Friday. God had raised him from the dead, but he hadn't removed the marks that made Jesus who he was. His wounds were part of him. His suffering was not only borne in his limbs; it was carved in his character. And that suffering was brought into the resurrection life, not to be denied, not to be neutralized, not to be covered up, but to be transformed.

Embracing the scene

Our life as disciples is not a life free from pain, anxiety or distress. It's not a life in which we're immunized against the effects of sin – our own or other people's. We aren't spared the harshness of disease or the blights of illness. We're not promised an easy time or even a slightly cushioned time.

Of course, we know all that. The challenges, difficulties and sufferings that affect human life generally are as likely to affect us as anyone. But what we do have, what the resurrection offers us, is a new way of regarding the scars of life.

The wounds of crucifixion are the wounds of love – the indelible marks of what God was prepared to endure for love of us. By carrying them into his Easter life, Christ reveals to us another dimension of the love that will bear all things. Our God has descended to the depths, accepted the worst that could be done to him and carried those depths to the heights. Even horror is transformed, and horror's marks remain as a reminder of how powerful a transformation that is.

The experiences that scar our lives are as varied and numerous as any other experiences of life. What they have in common is their potential to be changed by the risen Christ from burden to grace. In the Easter event, he takes our pain, our bitterness and our anguish and transforms them with the love that resurrects us from the death of suffering. In doing that, he offers us a vision for living, not only with hope, but with a fullness of life that enriches us – regardless of our circumstances. Instead of life-limiting burdens, the resurrection recreates our wounds as life-giving signs of grace.

As we have been celebrating over the past weeks, the Easter life is a gift of God that not only changes our view of death, but changes how we live in the here and now. But it's a gift that is as full of mystery for us as it was for those puzzled, fearful, cautiously joyful disciples on the first Easter night. Exactly how our wounds might be transformed is something we can neither predict nor command. But how would they ever be a gift of God's grace if we could?

Brett Ward

Suggested hymns

Alleluia! Alleluia! Hearts to heaven and voices raise; The strife is o'er, the battle done; If Christ had not been raised from death; This is eternal life.

Third Sunday of Easter 18 April
Second Service **Love from of Old**
Ps. 142; **Deut. 7.7–13**; Rev. 2.1–11; *Gospel at Holy Communion*: Luke 16.19–end

Sometimes the Old Testament gets a bad press: there are too many gruesome bits, it's not an easy read, there seem to be lots of war and violence and disjointed stories that we can't understand at first glance. So it's good to be reminded that these were the Scriptures that shaped Jesus as he sat at the feet of the teachers in the Temple as a boy. The Old Testament isn't just about fighting, claiming land, and rituals that we can't get our heads around. The Old Testament is a lot about love. (It would have to have been, surely, if it was going to be the Scripture that Jesus – the greatest act of God's love – himself read and studied.)

An old story

Much of Deuteronomy is framed as a huge sermon that Moses preaches to the Israelites, just before they end their 40 years of Exodus wandering and reach the Promised Land. While it's unlikely that these were Moses' own words – at least in this exact form – or all one big speech, nevertheless it's likely that there is a deeply ancient text at its heart. It's a text that has endured throughout innumerable generations, about how God's people are called to keep covenant loyalty with God. They are called to love God and keep his commandments; while God loves his people and blesses them. That's the ancient covenant.

A simplistic introduction of what 'covenant' is all about might make us think that if we are having a hard time we are being punished by God for something we've done wrong; or that if we are having a good time we are being rewarded by God for something we've done well. But that's not how it works in God's sight. Instead, God in compassion is kind to us when we've gone off the rails. That's what *grace* is all about.

Covenant grace

Grace is easily seen in the New Testament. Jesus has lived, died and risen again, redeeming humanity once and for all, because he alone could keep God's commandments perfectly. Jesus took his place among people so that we in turn could be welcomed into the kingdom of heaven. By this grace of God, humanity can be saved by faith: not just by keeping God's commandments, because we will always fall short of those. That's why Jesus heralded a new covenant. And that is the new covenant we celebrate in Eastertide.

It would be easy to think that such grace that makes allowances for humankind's wrongs and mistakes came only in the new covenant in Christ. But there's a sense of grace too in the Old Testament, even if other words are used to talk about it. Moses reminds his hearers of this throughout Deuteronomy. It's not because of the Israelites' righteousness that they are reaching the end of their journey, the Promised Land. No: it's because of God's love.

In our first reading today, this is the message Moses starts teaching the Israelites. It's a variant on the theme: 'It was not because you were more numerous than any other people that the LORD set his heart on you and chose you – for you were the fewest of all peoples.' It's not your grandeur, your own impressiveness that has got you here, goes this old covenant teaching. It's the goodness of God, pure and simple.

It's grace.

Love not hate

Being reminded of our smallness in the bigger picture is helpful if we want to be in right relationship with our great God. Humility is a wonderful building block in all our relationships – having wonder that someone as amazing as our friends might actually want to be our friends; having a sense of awe every moment we are with our spouses, our lifelong partners; having a sense of the tremendous that God might actually have set his affection on us, chosen us, and loves us.

Because those are the things that God declares to his people in our first reading. There is so much language of affection and love in these few lines. Yes, God has set his heart on us, he has chosen us, he loves us, he keeps his promises for us, he acts for us, he is faithful, he 'keeps his covenant of love with those who love him'.

The Old Testament declares this truth too. This is what God does. This is who God is.

It comes as a surprise when the next verse is about hate. But this sudden incursion has a particularly ancient ring to it, and it brings balance and realism. If God is fully loving, then he will not tolerate hate. It's another way of demonstrating quite how loving God is. There is no room for hate in his kingdom.

God has loved perfectly from of old. And if we are to do our best to live lives of love worthy of him, then we will find ourselves in a place of contentment. Perhaps that's the most richly blessed place any of us can truly hope to inhabit.

Megan I. J. Daffern

Suggested hymns

God is love: let heav'n adore him; God beyond earth's finest treasurers; Loved with everlasting love; Love is the touch of intangible joy.

Fourth Sunday of Easter   25 April

(Mark transferred to 26th; see p. 306)

Principal Service   **Living Vocation**

Gen. 7.1–5, 11–18; 8.6–18; 9.8–13 (*if used, the reading from Acts must be used as the second reading*), or **Acts 4.5–12**; Ps. 23; 1 John 3.16–end; John 10.11–18

Vocation Sunday is always the fourth Sunday of Easter. Easter Day is three weeks behind us now; but the Easter season is only halfway through. Vocation Sunday lies exactly midway between the resurrection of Christ and the sending of the Holy Spirit at Pentecost, or Whitsun. These are days when we celebrate life in the flesh and life in the spirit.

First steps

Readings from Acts are always read throughout Eastertide. It's a way of drawing attention to the impact the resurrection, and the sending of the Holy Spirit at Pentecost, had on the disciples, now apostles, of Christ. These readings from the first chapters of Acts remind us that these were the very earliest days of what has now become known as the Church. And they remind us of the first acts of witness and ministry of the apostles.

Peter, just a few weeks ago, had declared he would be willing even to die for Jesus; and hours later had been shown up in his failure to do so. Now, however, with John, he is imprisoned because they were preaching and teaching that in Jesus there is resurrection from the dead. Far from fleeing danger, Peter now full of the Spirit apparently cannot stop himself teaching people about Jesus. Peter is a transformed man. Something extraordinary has happened.

It is not just the first few weeks of the Church's life. This is a new chapter of Peter's life. Can you remember what it was like when you first knew the transforming power of Christ in your life?

Living Christ

Peter, in Acts chapter 1, has become de facto leader of the first 120 Christians (probably all these numbers just account for the men). Peter is the one who organizes the selection of Matthias as the twelfth apostle. He is the one who explains to all the crowds at

Pentecost what God has done for them. He proclaims repentance and baptism for both the forgiveness of sins and for the gift of the Holy Spirit. He calls others to the promise of Christ. The now three thousand live a common life of prayer. Peter develops a ministry of healing as well as a ministry of preaching: he heals the lame man at the Temple gate. Peter speaks eloquently to make sense of what people have witnessed. He makes copious references to the Hebrew Scriptures. He's beginning to act like Christ, pray like Christ, heal like Christ, speak like Christ. It's as if he has inherited something of Christ's spirit. Which of course – at Pentecost – he has.

What things can you do in your life that show to other people the glimmer of Christ that is within you?

Speaking Christ

Peter is using his voice as well as his actions. It was his voice that denied Christ and now it is his voice that's proclaiming Christ and getting Peter (John, too) into trouble. Today's reading started just after their first night in prison for their Christ-like actions. Because Peter has been using his voice, at this point we learn 'many of those who heard the word believed' – now there are five thousand. A council of various Jewish sects is convened, and they ask Peter the crucial question: 'By what power or by what name did you do this?' Once again he is filled with the Holy Spirit, and in just a few sentences boldly proclaims the resurrection of Jesus Christ. Citing Psalm 118, Peter even goes so far as to declare that his powerful addressees have rejected Jesus, but that in Jesus is salvation. In Hebrew the very name 'Jesus' means 'salvation'. So the name Jesus is both the power and the name in which Peter is acting.

How do you use your voice in acknowledging and responding to the power and name of Jesus Christ?

Breathing Christ

Peter is literally inspired by Christ to speak and act as he does. He can do nothing else. And he seems more alive than ever before. There's no stopping him. Even the powerful rulers, elders, lawyers recognize this. They will ask Peter and John to stop talking about Jesus. But of course Peter and John won't be able to, and they say as much.

Peter is breathing Christ in, breathing Christ out. He is fully alive. And that is attractive to thousands. We are all called – to breathe in

Christ, to breathe out Christ; to be inspired by Christ. That can be a helpful thought in settling to a few minutes of silent contemplative prayer as you use your breathing to meditate on Christ, his power and name.

How does the breath of Christ in you transform you? What will you let the Holy Spirit do in you? What are you drawn to? What animates you? What will make you fully alive?

Such questions point to your true vocation. Whether that's a ministry in the Church or in the community, works of prayer, social action, teaching, pastoral care, or the many other possible expressions of ministry before us today, there will be something that will be life-giving for you.

Take a deep breath – and talk to someone about it.

Megan I. J. Daffern

Suggested hymns

All hail the power of Jesus' name; Jesus, the name high over all; Lord, speak to me that I may speak; Filled with the Spirit's power, with one accord.

Fourth Sunday of Easter 25 April
Second Service **Living Just for Today**
Ps. 81.8–16; Ex. 16.4–15; Rev. 2.12–17; *Gospel at Holy Communion:* **John 6.30–40**

Figures suggest that approximately 815 million people go hungry in our world for lack of access to adequate food supplies. That's not merely an economic and political problem, but a moral and spiritual problem too. That it's a spiritual problem is suggested by the complaints of the Israelites who were following God and then discovered that their lives were threatened by a lack of food. The story, in fact, is designed to show that God accepts responsibility and acts to ensure that his people have sufficient for each day. The regular, reliable daily supply of mana became a ground for trust in God's faithfulness. It was one of the benchmarks by which Jewish opponents of Jesus sought to contrast him unfavourably with Moses. Jesus responds in St John's account by rebuking the Jews for wrongly attributing the daily food supply to Moses. Instead it was the work of God. And in his feeding of the hungry multitude, the extraordinary supply of food pointed to the supernatural presence and beneficence of God.

Living for today

'Give us this day our daily bread,' we say, following Luke's Gospel. But Matthew seems to have it as 'give us today tomorrow's bread'. Either way, there is the same emphasis as that experienced by the Israelites, that the bread is given 'new every morning', fresh each day, a day at a time. Living hand to mouth demands awesome trustfulness that is often too much for us. We prefer to manage the supply and distribution ourselves. But when stockpiling, like the man in the parable who built bigger and bigger barns in the hope of guaranteeing his future needs, it all went wrong, just as it did when we had food mountains in Europe to secure future supplies.

God will have us live in the present, one day at a time, in a state of dependency, in immediate relation to nature. It was a lesson that St John Henry Newman learnt and teaches in one of his well-loved hymns. He was impatient to get home from a visit to Rome to continue his work in England. But he was forced to delay his departure for three weeks while waiting for a suitable vessel to become available. When he did finally embark on his voyage, the ship was becalmed and he endured another week's delay. It was then that he penned the lines of 'Lead, kindly light'. He called it 'The Pillar and the Cloud', so as to connect it directly with the years in the wilderness. 'I do not ask to see the distant scene; one step enough for me.' Again, he wrote: 'I loved to choose and see my path; but now lead thou me on.'

Agents of God

If we're to live in the present, trust God each day for our daily bread, what are we to say about the millions who are emaciated and dying from hunger? That, we've acknowledged, is a spiritual as well as an economic problem. As Mahatma Gandhi expressed it: 'There are people in the world so hungry that God cannot appear to them except in the form of bread.' Being content with food for today and refusing to fill our larders with long-life food helps to humanize the market and keep prices from ratcheting up. There is, after all, 'sufficient for our need, but not for our greed'.

But with adequate food supplies, it is we who are God's agents, trustees of the natural order, who must pursue the infrastructure for food distribution. The food banks set up and run largely by the people of God afford a glimpse of what is possible when God's people own their divine agency and mobilize to act in his name.

Meanwhile, we who are filled and fulfilled must recognize afresh that bread is sacramental; it acclaims God's goodness and his self-expenditure in the breaking of Christ's body for the life of the world. And it conveys the bread of life which is given today and promised for the great Tomorrow.

Roger Spiller

Suggested hymns

Lead, kindly light; Lord, for tomorrow and its needs, I do not pray; Jesus the Lord said, I am the bread; New every morning is the love.

Fifth Sunday of Easter   2 May
Principal Service   **New Branches**
Baruch 3.9–15, 32—4.4, *or* Gen. 22.1–18 (*if used, the reading from Acts must be used as the second reading*), *or* Acts 8.26–end; Ps. 22.25–end; 1 John 4.7–end; **John 15.1–8**

A 'chance' meeting

I'm sure you've had experiences where you're in exactly the right place at the right time. You have a chance encounter with someone and you sense that the meeting was meant – somehow planned without your knowledge. Philip had been preaching in Samaria when an angel told him to go south on the Wilderness Road. How did God's angel communicate this? We don't know. Perhaps Philip had a 'hunch'. On the road he meets a grand chariot, carrying an important official from the Ethiopian court. Again prompted, Philip gets into the chariot and discovers the Ethiopian puzzling over the book of Isaiah. Philip shows the man how the Scriptures have been fulfilled in Jesus. It's like when Jesus, on the road to Emmaus, showed the disciples how the Scriptures pointed to himself. Philip is copying his master. He opens the good news of Jesus Christ to one who is anxious to hear it – who is hungry for spiritual guidance – who is ready to receive new life. It all happens so quickly. The man is converted and asks to receive baptism as they pass by water.

Philip baptizes him and is then snatched away by the Spirit, and the Ethiopian continues on his way – back to court – a new man. Shining with new faith in Christ, he is ready to share Jesus with a whole new continent. The strength of the ancient Ethiopian Coptic Church suggests he did remarkably well.

The Vine

Before Jesus died, he left his followers a number of images of himself that they could remember and access after his death: pictures that would help them and us continue the work of building the kingdom of God on earth. One of these is the image of the vine. By the time of Jesus, the image of the vine was already the supreme symbol for the nation of Israel. Israel in the Older Testament is called God's special vine. A golden vine trailed over the entrance to the Temple in Jerusalem, and the vine was a picture on the coinage at the time. So, Jesus is saying that he is the vine – the new Israel – the one through whom all peoples and all nations will be saved. He says, 'abide in me as I abide in you', which means be part of Jesus the vine, and know that Jesus the vine is part of you – we are all wrapped up together in this image. Christianity is about community: we belong to one another. We are all branches on the vine: together we make up the plant. Therefore, we need to care for one another. We need to know each other and we should make every effort to work together for the good of all.

New branches

But the vine isn't just for us. New branches are to be grafted into the vine. This is what happened with the Ethiopian. As a eunuch, under the Jewish law he was considered unclean: he wasn't whole and therefore wasn't pure. He may have gone up to Jerusalem to pray but he wouldn't have been allowed in the Temple. Through baptism – through the working of the Holy Spirit within him – he has become acceptable. He's been cleansed from sin by the death of Jesus on the cross, and grafted into the vine by the word of Jesus spoken to him. He is a new branch, with new life, new responsibilities and new power. Philip is doing an excellent job at bearing fruit that God may be glorified. We're called to bear fruit for God too. Every branch that doesn't bear fruit God removes from the vine. Every branch that does bear fruit God prunes to bear more fruit. Pruning makes the vine healthier. Sometimes we need God to strip away particular habits or attitudes that we've allowed to get out of hand so that we can serve Christ better.

Abiding in Christ

Jesus reminds us that his words need to abide in us – to be part of us. Through Bible reading, prayer, regular worship and receiving Jesus in the bread and wine of communion, we remain in the vine. It's very easy to drift away and get separated from the things of Christ, but remember that without him you can do nothing. Those whom Jesus is waiting to graft into the vine are all around us. The Holy Spirit is preparing the ground just as she prepared the Ethiopian Eunuch and Philip to have that 'chance' meeting. We need to be in tune with the Spirit, and when we feel prompted to share our faith with someone, then we need to be courageous enough to do it. Philip's encounter was on the Wilderness Road, a barren and unpromising place. God opens doors of opportunity in the most unlikely and unexpected settings. Living in step with the Spirit always brings an element of unpredictability and surprise. Be open to that! We who gather around the Lord's table are the community of the vine: branches bearing fruit for God – growing the kingdom of God around us. It's both a gift and a task. We are called together to graft new branches into Jesus our vine and welcome new life into our midst.

Catherine Williams

Suggested hymns

You are the Vine, we are the branches; I am a new creation; Bread of heaven, on thee we feed; We have a gospel to proclaim.

Fifth Sunday of Easter 2 May
Second Service **A Worshipful Company**
Ps. 96; **Isa. 60.1–14**; Rev. 3.1–13; *Gospel at Holy Communion*:
Mark 16.9–16

O worship the Lord

Our world today often seems as if it is fragmenting and falling apart. Organizations and communities and old allegiances are being fractured. We increasingly exist in isolation, in atomized units without anchor or tether. More and more people are lonely, estranged from family and friends. The gap between the rich and the poor, the old and the young, the included and the excluded, the chosen and the disenfranchised, grows ever wider. Can anything bring us closer together? Can anything unite us? Is there anything at all that will help us lift up our eyes from ourselves and our own selfish desires? Is there anything that will help us remember we are part of one common humanity? We yearn for unity and community but perhaps we are not sure where to find it.

The vision presented by the prophet Isaiah suggests that the dispersed will one day be gathered in from the ends of the earth. The people who have been scattered far and abroad will stream to one place to greet the Holy One of Israel, their God. The vision suggests that people will be brought together when they bow down and kneel before the Lord their maker in worship and in praise. High and low, rich and poor, one with another. When they lift up their eyes, when they sing a new song, they will be brought into a great company, an awesome congregation of the beloved. It is the worship of God which is able to heal our fractures and bind up our wounds. It is the worship of God which lifts up our eyes enabling us to see beyond isolation to community. It is the worship of God which binds all things together and reminds us that we are all children of God.

Gather together all the earth

The Christian will read the words of the prophet Isaiah as pointing towards Christ, the light of the world, the one in whom the glory of the Lord has been revealed and his light acts as a beacon to all the nations and kingdoms of this earth. The Hebrew poetry also reminds us of the season of Christmas and Epiphany, giving us a flashback of the three kings bringing their gifts and bowing low before the newborn infant along with the ox and donkey, the sheep and the shepherds, angels and archangels. 'O worship the Lord in the beauty of holiness', cries the writer of Psalm 96, 'great is the LORD, and greatly to be praised'.

The beautiful vision of Isaiah extends beyond the people of Israel, it is a vision for everyone. It looks to a time when the whole earth – the trees of the field, the abundance of the sea, the wealth of the nations – will be gathered in and will worship together. The Psalmist puts this even more clearly. The trees will sing for joy, the sea will roar, the fields will exult, everything on this earth will ascribe glory and praise to God, and through that praise the earth and everything in it will be made one.

Made for worship

It becomes clear that it is through the worship of God that we are made one. Through worship, the dispersed are gathered in, the lonely find a home, the unloved are placed in the seat of honour. Through worship, heaven and earth are joined together in praise and thanksgiving. Through worship, we are also made one with creation itself. If we come to understand that even the trees and the fields and the seas were created for praise, we might give them more respect as members of the congregation of the beloved. It seems we were all made for worship. Everything is made for worship.

In the Westminster Catechism, it states that our purpose in life, our chief end, is to glorify God and enjoy him for ever. If we live into this common calling we will be formed into a worshipful company of believers. We will be made generous enough to open the doors and invite others to join us from the ends of the earth. When we sing together, when we pray together, when we stand and sit and kneel together before the Lord our God, we are no longer isolated and no longer alone. We are gathered into one body of many members, and within our worship and our praise we find the community for which we long, and for which we were made.

Victoria Johnson

Suggested hymns

O worship the Lord in the beauty of holiness; Here I am to worship; O worship the Lord, all glorious above; All people that on earth do dwell.

Sixth Sunday of Easter   9 May
Principal Service   **Fullness of Life**

Isa. 55.1–11 (*if used, the reading from Acts must be used as the second reading*), *or Acts 10.44–end; Ps. 98; 1 John 5.1–6;* **John 15.9–17**

Imagine that after months of political turmoil in our country, there has been a revolution. A dictatorship has been suddenly and brutally imposed. Tanks are rolling through the streets. There are police and military personnel everywhere. People have been ordered to stay indoors and told to listen to the news for further announcements. A kind of shimmering silence has fallen. Faces are peering out of windows. No one knows what will happen next.

On the television a disembodied voice announces that a glorious new day has dawned: stability and peace have arrived. There will be no more muddle; no more shilly-shallying. The cause of the difficulties over the past months, says the voice, has been that there has been no clarity, no certainty, no national, all-embracing purpose. From now on, certainty will be the watchword. All organizations that have promoted other ways of thinking are from henceforth proscribed and their superstitions, says the voice, will be destroyed for ever. Religious belief will be crushed. It has held people in thrall for centuries and is holding the nation back. 'Forward with certainty,' declares the voice.

On to the screen comes live coverage of a giant wrecking ball being swung from a crane and smashing against the western towers of Westminster Abbey. The camera moves rapidly to St Paul's where another wrecking ball is in action. Great blocks of stone are falling to the ground, sending up clouds of dust.

A face appears on the screen. 'For too long,' announces the pundit, 'our country has been in the grip of irrational forces. Today is the dawn of a new era where clarity will rule. Only the measurable matters … chaos is over; reason rules … Wait for further announcements …' The picture on the screen shows the wrecking ball continuing to pummel the Abbey, and through the dust we can see ashen-faced clergy being led away in handcuffs to unmarked vans.

Measurement is the new god

It's a grim, dystopian and fantastical picture that I have conjured up. But within it, barely hidden, lies a theme with which we have

134

become increasingly familiar. We have become obsessed by the need for clarity; only the measurable matters. We are deluged by messages about how schools are faring: one against another in league tables. Universities are required to turn out more and more students who will be able to compete with each other in producing new and more effective widgets. The economy is measured; output is measured, and television programmes judge their success by how many people have watched them. And, irony of ironies, the BBC now has a unit labelled 'Reality Check', which seems to consist of people who are committed to checking so-called 'facts' that have appeared on other programmes. Measurement is everywhere, and other values, such as truth and kindness, are being squeezed into non-existence.

Please don't misunderstand me. Measurement is important. If, for example, the constituent parts of a bridge are not measured with great care, the bridge could well collapse. But should we have allowed the obsession with measurement to have taken over every corner of our lives? Sport is the latest to go down this road: the best goal; the quickest try; the fastest serve; the most amazing run-out; the catch of the season … the desire to measure pushes joy to the margins.

And what has caused this mechanistic, joyless obsession with measurement? Perhaps it's because we feel threatened by things that are elusive and beyond our grasp; by measuring things, we can control them. We like that.

A burst of energy

It's a million miles from that situation where the early Church found itself. Then there were sudden explosions of social energy; radically new ways of looking at the world; those early Christians experimented with new, communal lifestyles. They were buzzing with possibilities. They believed that the risen Christ was leading them into fullness of life.

Now look at how they described this new situation: they referred to it as an outpouring of the Holy Spirit. And what images did they use for this? They spoke of the Spirit as being like tongues of flame; like a rushing, mighty wind. In their more reflective moments they described the Spirit as being like a pure, white dove, descending from heaven. All of these images are of a release of energy; a de-lightful sense of movement pervades them. The Holy Spirit cannot be pinned down, cannot be measured or manipulated or controlled.

135

Those early Christians referred to the Spirit as the breath of God. And in doing so they were echoing powerful descriptions within the Old Testament: did not God breathe into the nostrils of humankind the breath of life? And from that poetic moment onwards, men and women became living creatures, imbued with the very spirit of God. The idea is both very beautiful and very dangerous. Who knows what might result?

It is that prodigal uncertainty which informs and shapes our Christian lives. You and I, as followers of Christ, cannot know to what we might be called by God. But we live knowing that the future is in the hands of God, and that is all that matters.

A society that values only that which can be measured twists and starves the human spirit. Thank God, therefore, for the joy of living with and through uncertainty, living with and through the energy of the Holy Spirit, for that way lies fullness of life.

Christopher Herbert

Suggested hymns

O Thou who camest from above; Come down, O love divine; Lord enthroned in heavenly splendour; Now the green blade riseth.

Sixth Sunday of Easter   9 May
Second Service   **The Royal Wedding**
Ps. 45; S. of Sol. 4.16—5.2; 8.6–7; Rev . 3.14—end; *Gospel at Holy Communion*: Luke 22.24–30

I can remember where I was when I was able to catch a little of the wedding of Prince Charles to Lady Diana Spencer on the TV (Halls of Residence in Honolulu, Hawaii, because I was attending an international denominational meeting). Years later, I watched the broadcast of the wedding of the Duke and Duchess of Cambridge with a friend. In this day and age, whether you're an ardent mon-archist or not, the likelihood is that you will have seen some part of any significant royal wedding ceremony on the television (even if only as a brief news report). In the pre-television era, newspaper reports would have informed the wider populace of any royal event.

Why are we, who cannot claim friendship with the royal family, so interested in their marriages? We may say that our interest is in the fashion that is on parade, or that we are intrigued to note the celebrity guests. Is there, however, a lingering sense that these unions have significance for the nation?

Psalm 45, which is unique in the psalter, celebrates a royal wedding. It takes the form of a maskil: a song. It's a psalm that functions as a wedding song, a love song. The NRSV calls it an ode. As to authorship, it's attributed to the Korahites, hence it is part of an intriguing collection of psalms from a group whose identities are unknown. However, the content of the collection reveals that they were devotees of Elohim.

This is a piece of royalist propaganda penned by a court poet. It is reminiscent of the outpourings of poets laureate when they're obliged to write a poem to celebrate some state occasion. The author says, 'my tongue is like the pen of a ready scribe'. The language she or he employed, in praise of the king and his bride, is hyperbolic.

Who are the happy couple?

There is a debate about the setting for the psalm. Whose wedding is being celebrated? Clearly the psalm evidences the existence of the monarchy. A king (ruler) of Israel is marrying a foreign princess. Reference is made to Tyre, in Phoenicia, so it could be that the marriage is uniting Israel and her trading partner, Phoenicia. The biblical record tells of a marriage between a king of Israel, Ahaz, and a Phoenician, Jezebel, so it may be that this is an ode for their marriage. If this is so, then the psalm could be dated quite precisely. However, there is discussion as to whether this is a liturgy for all marriages or even for an annual cultic event.

The bridegroom

There is an idealized picture of the king, who is described in superlatives. He is handsome. His excellence is rooted in the Lord's having blessed him. He's a warrior leader who is expected to be the victor.

Importantly, he's successful because he's an anointed Davidic king who, in humility, keeps the covenantal relationship with God. His kingdom embodies God's kingdom on earth. The sceptre symbolizes the authority to rule with integrity. The words of verses 6–7 are quoted in the letter to the Hebrews, where they are used to refer to Christ, hence the description of the bridegroom may have messianic connotations.

As the king prepares for the ceremony he dons expensively fragranced robes. Music plays in the ivory palaces – the description of the palace is not necessarily an exaggeration: archaeological investigation has found ivory inlays in some of the buildings of Samaria. It's no wonder that the prophet Amos decried the pretentious extravagancies of Samaria. The bride is marrying into wealth and opulence.

The bride

Robed in finest gold (that from Ophir), the bride stands at the right hand of the king.

Echoing the understanding of the relationship between the man and the woman that is found in the Adam and Eve story in Genesis (and reprised in the stories of certain of the brides of the Patriarchs), the bride is adjured to leave her people and her father's house. Her new loyalty will be to her husband and his people (submission to the king will also mean the acceptance of his god(s)). This evidences that Israel was both patrilineal and patri-local.

The bride is adorned and readied for the ceremony. The bridal procession is briefly described, as she is led to the king, accompanied by her attendants. There is joy and gladness.

The psalm concludes with the hope for heirs to the kingdom and the promise that the king will be celebrated for generations to come.

Rejoice!

This psalm is not a lament but a song of joy.

Marriage, the uniting of two people or, in this case, two nations, is ground for hope for the future. Maybe that's why we give attention to royal weddings – because they make a statement about the future of the nation. We hope that the happy couple will exemplify all that is best in human relationships.

Maybe, just maybe, the wedding celebration will draw people together and allow them to re-evaluate what matters most to the people of the nation and to ordinary families.

In renewed relationships may we be a reflection of the love of God.

Wendy Kilworth-Mason

Suggested hymns

Come, Holy Ghost, our souls inspire; Crown him with many crowns; Let love be real; Sing we the King who is coming to reign.

Ascension Day   13 May
Principal Service   **When Going is Also a Coming**
Acts 1.1–11 (*must be used as either the first or second reading*), *or* Dan. 7.9–14; Ps. 47, *or* Ps. 93; Eph. 1.15–end; **Luke 24.44–end**

'Parting is such sweet sorrow' and those who have family members dispersed far away know the agony of parting at the airport. Of course we may breathe a sigh of relief when friends or relatives who've been staying with us depart. And there are some who can't decide when they're leaving and we don't know whether they or we are coming or going.

Jesus gone and the Church come?

Something of this uncertainty hangs over Jesus' long farewell discourses in John's Gospel. Jesus said, 'I am going away, and I am coming to you', in the same sentence. And then he went on to talk about leaving in a 'little time' and then coming back in the same brief timescale. Not surprising, then, that it's left many Christians unsure as to whether Jesus has gone or has come back. No wonder that many in church are puzzled about the meaning of the ascension. This is reflected in some of the hymns, where we are told that Jesus is ascending on his throne on high while we are languishing below.

> Christ is gone up, yet ere he passed
> From earth, in heaven to reign,
> He formed one holy church to last
> Till he should come again.
> So age by age and year by year
> His grace was handed on
> And still the holy church is here
> Although her Lord is gone.

So the Church is here said to stand in for its absent Lord! It's little wonder, then, why our thinking on ascension can be a little muddled.

Joy at the promise of 'power'

The parting of Jesus didn't create loss and despair, as we might have expected. Luke tells us that after Jesus was 'carried up into heaven' the disciples 'worshipped him and returned to Jerusalem with great joy'. And why were they joyful, when Jesus had left them physically? Why were they suddenly no longer cowed by fear of danger and persecution? It was because they were to receive 'power from on high'. And that power was going to propel them out by increments to the extremity of the empire, gathering vast numbers of converts along the way. It's an inspiring account told in the Acts of the Apostles. The apostles received power to speak boldly in the face of Roman prosecutors and Jewish opponents, performing miracles and following the explicit guidance and direction of God. Jesus' ascension was necessary for the Spirit to come to his followers. And his followers were, in turn, continuing and extending the racial, religious and geographical range of Jesus' own ministry.

But we must look to John to give us a more developed explanation of Jesus' coming and going. He tells us not merely that the power they received continues Jesus' work, but that Jesus says 'it is to your advantage that I go away, for if I do not go away, the Advocate will not come to you'. What is the 'advantage' to the disciples and to us that the Spirit or Advocate brings in place of Jesus' physical presence?

The abiding presence of Jesus

John tells us that Jesus and the Spirit are in a tandem relationship and that the departure of Jesus' physical life is the necessary condition for the coming of the Spirit. God's Spirit had always been active in the world, and has empowered key figures such as kings and priests. Now after the ascension the Spirit is to be poured out to all followers of Jesus. The Spirit will not be the impersonal 'power' of Luke. The Spirit will have the character, the alter ego, the personality of Jesus in our lives. The Spirit is, as it were, rebranded, and named as the Paraclete, which combines the roles of Advocate, Counsellor and Comforter. The Paraclete or Spirit imparts Jesus' continuous personal presence and fulfils the promise of Jesus to come again and dwell in the disciples. So there is an 'immediate and direct continuity between believers and Jesus'.[25] The Spirit is the indissoluble link between Jesus and his disciples. Every generation, including our own, is as close as the first generation of believers to the presence of Jesus. John's writings bear this out. They describe a community a generation or more after Jesus' ascension, whose vision, energy and vital religious experience leaps off the pages of John's Gospel and letters. This is for you, it tells us. Jesus' going is also his coming, but coming in a new way, as his personal presence.

'Wait' if we know our need

We must be honest and say that for most of us most of the time we are probably more likely to sense our distance from Jesus, and feel uneasy with the stupendous claims set before us. We are used to a humdrum life, on 'an even plain', where we are left to struggle through life on our own. And perhaps we envy those who speak of Jesus as if they are speaking of the friend next door. Is there 'more' that we have yet to receive, a power, a presence that can elevate us beyond the mundane routines of life that drain our spirits? Need we remain like orphans, when the Spirit of Jesus can abide in us and make us God's children?

Who could not be joyful even at the physical absence of Jesus if, instead, we are promised the immediate, vital, personal, spiritual relationship with God through the Spirit of Jesus? We can then become the visible and tangible witnesses of Jesus. If our present experience of Jesus and his Spirit falls short of his promise, then, like the disciples, we too must 'wait', stay where we are, wait with 'eager longing' until we, too, 'have been clothed with power from on high'.

Roger Spiller

Suggested hymns

Alleluia, sing to Jesus; Hail, festival day; Hail the day that sees him rise; Alleluia, sing to Jesus; At the name of Jesus.

Ascension Day 13 May
Second Service **Now it's Our Commissioning!**
Morning Ps. 110, 150; Evening Ps. 8; Song of the Three
29–37, *or* 2 Kings 2.1–15; Rev. 5; *Gospel at Holy Communion*:
Matt. 28.16–end

If you want to ask church folk to perform tasks, you would be well advised to remember that the Church is a voluntary organization. The Church is also a sign and agent of the kingdom, and as such its adherents are called and commissioned by their King and must be subject to his call. And on the day when we mark Christ's physical withdrawal from the earth, we hear again his commission to us to continue his own mission in the world.

There are commissionings given by Christ in each of the Gospels and in the book of Acts. Each of them reflects the distinctive character of their writings. Matthew's is so distinctive that the entire Gospel points to these final verses. And his so-called 'Great Commission' tells us that we are sent people, we are disciples who are, in turn, to make disciples, to baptize them and to teach them. And you'll recognize these themes that in recent years have become central to the way we think about our vocation, mission and ministry.

Go

The Church can look like a monument, museum or, worse, a mausoleum – moribund and anachronistic, beleaguered by fast-changing currents of belief and conduct. But we are truly a movement, a mission, a mobile agent of the coming kingdom. We are to 'go'. We once thought of missionaries as people who went somewhere, usually distant places, far from home. But 'go' is the main verb that determines the actions that follow. We don't have to go anywhere to fulfil it. It's a daily commission for every Christian. We are called to 'make disciples' wherever we are, at home, work, school, gym, sports club. We are all in a relationship with people who are not disciples of Christ and we have opportunities to bring them to discipleship.

Make disciples

This command is in keeping with the teaching about discipleship in the rest of Matthew's Gospel. Making disciples is not recruiting members to a community or a club of the likeminded. It's not recruiting other people to our branch of religion; it's alerting people to the universal reign of God. Making disciples means sharing in the Spirit's ongoing transformation of humankind. 'Making disciples' isn't merely influencing them; it's bringing people into a submissive, growing, living relationship with Jesus Christ.

Baptizing

We get a clearer idea of what is involved in discipleship through the ritual of baptism. Baptism is 'in the name of', which signals and cements a transfer of ownership. And Mathew alone tells us that that name is not that of Jesus only, nor even of our Father God. We are baptized into the name and life of the Trinity. Through baptism we are ritually moved from a network of autonomous, self-serving relationships to share in the mutual self-giving relationships of God's triune life.

Teaching

The centrality of teaching is no surprise to those who are familiar with Matthew's Gospel. His is a didactic Gospel, and not only in content but in his layout of material. His Gospel is formed by five great blocks of material that seem to replicate and answer to the five books of Moses, beginning with Genesis and known as the Pentateuch. This and other smaller orderings of material show his intention to aid memory and learning. And what is to be learnt is not primarily biographical details of the historical Jesus, nor any kind of discursive learning for its own sake. We are to learn those things that issue in obedience to what Jesus taught and will lead to a conspicuous change in our life and conduct. It's all undergirded by the promise that Jesus is with us 'always, to the end of the age'.

We would be mistaken if we thought making disciples, baptizing and teaching was a series of distinct activities. Rather, this is an expansion of what it means to 'go' and to be 'sent'. These are the vital ingredients of the self-same pattern of life that God's people are required to emulate.

Trinitarian

In Matthew's commissioning we go forth with the authority of God. In Luke's commissioning we go with the power of the Holy Spirit.

In John's commissioning, however, Jesus first shows his disciples his wounded hands and side before sending them out. So we go not merely with authority but with vulnerability. We are sent with the authority of God in Matthew's commissioning; with the vulnerability and grace of the wounded Christ in John's commissioning and with the Spirit's power in Luke's commissioning.

We celebrate today Christ's ascended and exalted life. And we celebrate, too, that we are invested with authority, power and vulnerability to go. Go, then, into a yearning and needy world; the world is waiting for its deliverance.

Roger Spiller

Suggested hymns

Alleluia, sing to Jesus; Lord, you give the great commission; Lord, thy church on earth is seeking; Filled with the Spirit's power.

Seventh Sunday of Easter
(Sunday after Ascension Day)   16 May
Principal Service   **Knowing Jesus**
Ezek. 36.24–28 (*if used, the reading from Acts must be used as the second reading*), *or* Acts 1.15–17, 21–end; Ps. 1; 1 John 5.9–13; **John 17.6–19**

Today falls in the middle of what is usually called the Novena of Pentecost – the nine days that separate Ascension Day from the Day of Pentecost, when we think of the disciples of Jesus gathered, together with the mother of Jesus and some others, awaiting the outpouring of the Holy Spirit. More recently, these nine days have become the focus for a major initiative called 'Thy Kingdom Come', when Christians across the world are encouraged to pray for more people to come to know Jesus. Today's Gospel reading, from the seventeenth chapter of John's Gospel, is part of Jesus' prayer to the Father. What does it tell us about how we might use these days for prayer? Three things: knowledge, union and converting the world.

Knowledge

First, knowledge. Jesus says to his Father, 'I have made your name known to those whom you gave me.' In the Bible, knowing someone's name means having access to a personal relationship with them (not easy, after all, to have much of a relationship with someone if you don't know their name). Jesus is saying that he has made it possible for people to come to know God personally – through him, for he really is God in our midst. But that begs a big question: what does it mean to know God? There are many different kinds of knowledge, and we all too easily confuse cleverness, or the acquisition of information, with true wisdom. You may know the story of the young Roman Catholic priest, fresh from seminary, who decided to use his first sermon in the parish to preach about the theology of marriage. And afterwards an elderly woman said sadly to the parish priest, 'Father, I wish I knew as little about marriage as that young priest.' The young priest was clever. The woman was wise. Cleverness may get you a job, or letters after your name. It's certainly better than ignorance. But it's no substitute for wisdom. And, for Christians, true wisdom means knowing God, in and through Jesus, who makes God accessible to us. And knowing God means one thing above everything else, the pearl of great price: it means knowing, feeling, discovering that you are unconditionally loved.

Union

How do you get to know someone really well? The surest way of all is by living with them. That is one of the major themes of John's Gospel: it begins by declaring that 'the Word became flesh and lived among us', and much of the rest of the Gospel is devoted to exploring what it means to live with Jesus – or, to use John's favourite word, to *abide* with him. So in today's reading Jesus prays that his disciples may be one, as he and the Father are one. But what does this mean in practice? The late Gerry Hughes, the Jesuit writer and teacher, used to ask: how do you think you might respond if Jesus were to call on you and ask to abide (or stay) with you for a while? At first, Father Gerry suggested, you'd be pleased that he'd chosen you: you'd invite him in and tell your friends. But after a while it might get embarrassing. You'd have to make space for him, change some of your habits. Jesus might start inviting some undesirables round for a meal in your house. And eventually, says

Father Gerry, you'd do what many so-called Christians have done down the centuries: you'd lock Jesus up in a tabernacle, or a broom cupboard, and genuflect or bow whenever you walked past, and proceed to carry on living your life exactly as you had done before he arrived.

But it need not be like that. Getting to know Jesus, living closely with him, is costly, because it involves *making space* for him. The test of a healthy church is whether it's a place where people make space for Jesus and for one another, and especially for the stranger. If it isn't, it's no better than a private club for an in-crowd. If it is, it can still change the world. Which brings us to the most important point of all.

Converting the world

So often, in John's Gospel, 'the world' is hostile to Christians. So in today's reading Jesus prays, 'I am not asking on behalf of the world, but on behalf of those whom you gave me.' But does that mean Jesus doesn't care about the world? No: it means exactly the opposite. Remember what Jesus says earlier: 'God so loved *the world* that he gave his only Son' – not just the Church, or even all humanity, but the entire cosmos, the whole creation. And Jesus' prayer to the Father ends with him praying that Christians may live in him 'so that *the world* may believe that you have sent me'. There is no contradiction here. Jesus came to live and die for the whole creation; but he needs you and me to make his love real. By coming to know Jesus, by learning what it means to abide with him and with one another, we begin to build communities of inclusive, unconditional love. They, and they alone, have the power to change and save our world.

Gordon Mursell

Suggested hymns

All I once held dear; Soul of my Saviour, sanctify my breast; O thou, who at thy Eucharist didst pray; As water to the thirsty.

Seventh Sunday of Easter
(Sunday after Ascension Day)   16 May
Second Service   **The Social Gospel of Christianity**
Ps. 147.1–12; **Isa. 61**; Luke 4.14–21

Could the 'good news' be anything other than 'social'? To be social is to interact; we are allies with each other, we do not exist alone. To be human is to be social – we are dependent on one another. We do not live in splendid isolation. It is this social fabric that obviously forms what we call a *society*.

Everything that Jesus says or does in the Scriptures is to a social end. He heals the sick in order to bring them back into society; he is attentive to those who are at the fringes of community life; he proclaims the forgiveness of sins to bring people into communion with God; he teaches and preaches to crowds of people; he travels around as part of a diverse company; and he inaugurates a new kind of social order, a new kind of kingdom, and he calls those who follow him to be citizens of this kingdom and, indeed, help make it a reality.

We can find evidence of Jesus' social vision throughout the Gospels. But there is one particular instance where he makes it very clear what kind of kingdom he is hoping to build. He stands up in the synagogue at the very beginning of his public ministry and, using the words of the prophet Isaiah, he sets out a manifesto that is both spiritual and political. He unrolled the scroll and read, that all might hear.

A manifesto for change

The poor, the captives, the blind, the oppressed – these are the people to whom Jesus will minister. Jesus is quite clear: his favour, his blessing, is with those who are neglected, or excluded from society; his favour rests with those who are at the edges of what we might want our society to look like. Until they are gathered in, God's will is not done.

This message is still challenging and troubling today, because as a society we still have our scapegoats, we still have people living on the edge, we still make our judgements on the poor, the prisoner, the persecuted, the weak, the stranger and the alien, and we set out our human-made boundaries to distinguish who is in and who is out. We think we know who God favours, who is deserving and who is not. But history has proved again and again that humanity's ability to build a fair society is always compromised. We need divine intervention.

We need Jesus to show us that everyone needs our respect, our care and our concern. We need Jesus to show us that, in order for his kingdom to be made manifest, we each need to take our personal commitment to Christ very seriously indeed. And as we respond to Christ personally, we also have to respond to what he is asking of us as members of his community and citizens of his kingdom.

We are not an island

It was always going to be thus: to build a better society, each person within it has to be fully participative and fully committed to the whole. Jesus asks each one of us to respond and play our part in building his kingdom. The choices we make as individuals affect society as a whole. How much are we as individuals willing to pay for, say, our food? Would we pay more if it was sustainably farmed? Or fairly traded? Do we like cheap clothes and shoes? Does it matter to us that they might be made in sweatshops? Do we really need two or even three cars? And what price should we be willing to pay for fuel and investment in alternative energy sources? Do we ever reflect on the likelihood that our choices here and now affect those on the other side of the world or indeed those who are yet to come? Are we concerned about the needs of our brothers and sisters in other countries, or do we switch off the TV in despair?

Part of our Christian calling is to raise the vision of our smaller units of community to the fabric of the larger community of which we are part. The gospel is social: it forces us to confront social problems and encourages us to make choices that alleviate inequality and injustice. The gospel does bid us to get involved, it encourages us as Christian's to participate and not sit on the sidelines. To be a Christian is to be social and to have concern for the social, and we show this concern through our personal choices.

We do not live in two separate worlds or spheres of existence. We live in one ever-present reality. We don't live in our Christian world on Sundays alone, and revert to a secular way of living for the rest of the week. This is a whole-life calling. It is a living theology, and we are called to witness to life in all of its fullness.

The good news, the social gospel of Jesus Christ, reminds us that our personal salvation through him is intrinsically connected to our corporate, social responsibility. It is the kingdom of God to which we point as an example of society as it is meant to be. We hope and pray that God's kingdom will come and bring about a new world order of justice and mercy, where peace and righteousness will roll down like waters. The challenge is to realize that we each have to play our part bringing this reality just a little bit closer.

Victoria Johnson

Suggested hymns

Beauty for brokenness; Jesus Christ is waiting; Bind us together; O God of earth and altar.

Day of Pentecost (Whit Sunday)   23 May
Principal Service   **A Bunch of Amateurs**
Acts 2.1–21 (*must be used as either the first or second reading*), *or* Ezek. 37.1–14; Ps. 104.26–36, 37b [*or* 26–end]; Rom. 8.22–27; **John 15.26–27; 16.4b–15**

Scared amateurs

Britain's Got Talent, *The X Factor*, *The Voice*: television talent shows like these grip the nation. We love to watch ordinary people performing before the judges and a live audience. The contestants are just a bunch of amateurs, and we're allowed to see their humanity. Fear, tears, anger, frustration, exhilaration, hope, joy. We see the whole range of human reactions to the challenging and scary situation of live performance.

Let's wind back two thousand years. Another bunch of amateurs in a challenging and scary situation. The followers of Jesus were very scared – even though they'd experienced the power of God in the resurrection, and witnessed Jesus' ascension. On the Day of Pentecost, 50 days after the Passover and the resurrection, Jesus' friends were all together in one place waiting for something to happen, which, going by God's past events, they could be pretty sure would be dramatic. It certainly was! Luke struggles to articulate what's going on. The power of God the Holy Spirit, experienced as fire and hurricane, touches everyone present and releases the talent to speak the languages of the known world at that time. These are amateurs: humble, uneducated folk from Galilee (a cultural backwater). People who were mocked for their local accent

– now sufficiently gifted to communicate with people from every part of the Roman Empire, so that God's covenant of love can be broadened and deepened to include all people. The disciples' new-found talent has a purpose – to reach out to everyone, everywhere.

Confident disciples

In the Gospel, Jesus promised his followers that he would send this power – this Advocate – who would witness to the truth – this Counsellor – who would go before and work alongside the disciples in their task of telling others about God in Jesus Christ. A special helper – God the Holy Spirit – sent from God the Father to lead people to the truth of God the Son. Look at Peter on the Day of Pentecost. Peter who was always getting it wrong, and getting confused, who denied Jesus and ran away (today's media would have loved him!). Look at him now, confidently and courageously standing and addressing thousands of people – making clever theological connections with the Hebrew Scriptures, and witnessing to the Lord Jesus in such a powerful way that three thousand people are converted. He nails it! That's what the power of God the Holy Spirit can do. Peter is beginning to enter into who he is truly called to be. Jesus saw the potential in Peter, and the Holy Spirit enables that potential to come to fruition. Peter is being a true witness to Christ, but he's no longer doing it in his own strength – we saw what happened when he tried that. It's the power of God in him that helps him lead people into the truth of Jesus, so that they can turn their lives around.

Empowered by the Holy Spirit

What about us – as we celebrate Pentecost today? We're a bunch of amateurs, too. That's good news because God works mightily through amateurs – those who know they can't do it alone, those who feel wobbly about their ability and are honest about their limitations. The Holy Spirit comes to each of us in different ways. We may have dramatic experiences of God to share with others, because the Holy Spirit can be like a rushing wind and flames of fire. But the Holy Spirit is also a comforter and counsellor, who brings peace, reconciliation and wholeness. Our experience of the Holy Spirit may be a quiet, deep-down nourishing, turning around and guiding to a place of truth. We received the gift of the Holy Spirit at our baptism and we grow into that gift as we grow deeper into God throughout our lives. The Holy Spirit enhances our God-given potential as individuals and as community. The Spirit enables us to be all that we can be and often takes us to new places within ourselves, our church and community life. We may need to take on new tasks that stretch us; we may need to change our behaviour or give more time to our relationships. Where the Spirit is at work, we will see barriers broken down, prejudices challenged, fears and anxieties relieved. When we are Spirit-filled people, we are fully committed to the journey of 'becoming' who God is calling us to be. Unity, building bridges and working for reconciliation will be passions for us. Where the Spirit of God is at work the Church isn't content with being cosy, but takes risks and is outward looking, always ready to take faith to another level. The gift of the Holy Spirit for each of us is given so that we can be sent out – as the Father sent Jesus – into our communities, workplaces and families, to witness to Christ at work everywhere. We are to speak the truth of Jesus Christ in a language that others will hear, understand and respond to. The bunch of amateurs in Jerusalem two thousand years ago took the world by storm. Filled with the Holy Spirit, they birthed a worldwide religious movement – the Christian Church. We're their descendants – today's bunch of amateurs – may God the Holy Spirit fill us and empower us to change our world too.

Catherine Williams

Suggested hymns

Holy Spirit, gift bestower; Spirit of God, unseen as the wind; O breath of life, come sweeping through us; Come down, O love divine.

Day of Pentecost (Whit Sunday)   23 May
Second Service   **Whole in Spirit**
Morning Ps. 145; Evening Ps. 139.1–11, 13–18, 23–24
[*or* 139.1–11]; **Ezek. 36.22–28**; Acts 2.22–38; *Gospel at Holy Communion*: John 20.19–23

We talk about getting a new hip, a new knee, a kidney transplant. But what about a new heart? A new mind? A new spirit? That's what Ezekiel says God promises to his people.

Good news at last

These are some beautiful verses within the book of Ezekiel. Around the time of the exile (deportations occurred over almost a 20-year period running up to 586 BC, then most of the educated ruling classes from Jerusalem were in captivity in Babylon until 539 BC), prophets like Ezekiel often gave quite dire prophecies in dramatic ways. For example, the symbolism of the siege of Jerusalem in Ezekiel 4: Ezekiel tells how God asked him to be a sign of the siege. He lay on his left side for 390 days, and his right for 40 days (the number of years that Israel and Judah respectively had sinned), and ate only a modicum of bread each day, which he baked over cow dung (an improvement he negotiated with God instead of using human excrement as fuel). Prophets often used astonishing actions to tell important stories, and weren't afraid to break bad news.

Ezekiel was among the exiles in Babylon. He prophesies woe and destruction among lots of different nations, not just the people of Jerusalem. But then he begins to speak of restoration to the people of Israel and Judah. In Ezekiel 34 he gives the word of the Lord that he will search for his sheep (his people) and look after them. Now in Ezekiel 36 he gives God's word that his people will soon come home to Israel; that God will gather them together again, bring them back, cleanse them and transform them.

A psychological transplant

God will make his people new. How often we yearn to be renewed, refreshed, reinvigorated! This is what he promises. The crux of this message is that he will give his errant people a new heart and a new spirit: he will remove their heart of stone and give them a heart of flesh.

They're not just heavy-hearted, their hearts have turned to stone over many years – first the years of their disobedience to God and then the years of their exile from Jerusalem. The human heart in Hebrew represents the seat of emotion, action, intellect, will. To have the core of their being as stone is to become unmoved, stationary, stuck. To have that cut out and replaced by flesh is to make the heart at one with the body: to be whole again.

We can often feel stuck. Stuck in our ways, stuck thanks to our own choices, stuck because of what others have done to us. Stuck because we can't see a way out. Unable to move on because of grief, or health problems, mental or physical. How much we would then benefit from having new hearts, replacing our cold, inanimate hearts with hearts full of life and love!

God offers his people a spiritual transplant.

Because God's worth it

Lest God's people start thinking that they somehow deserved this wondrous gift, our first reading started with God explaining why it was turning out like this.

All the peoples of the ancient Near East would have looked upon Israel and Jerusalem pityingly – since the devastation and exile that they had faced surely meant that their God was impotent and didn't care. While Israel and Jerusalem may have theologized their experience of exile, thinking of it as a result of their own disobedience to God, the rest of the world mistakenly thinks either that their God doesn't exist or that he's not up to much.

But God does care. He is not impotent. So he has to show these foreigners: he has to restore his reputation, his name, as well as his people. Oracles and prophecies in Ezekiel feature the refrain, 'the nations shall know that I am the LORD'. It's in our reading today. God wants to demonstrate his greatness and holiness. He does that through great acts of spiritual transformation in his people.

Culminating in the Spirit

After gathering his people together, God promises also to cleanse them. These words sound like a purity ritual, like the 'asperges' in some churches today, at the eucharistic confession, when the priest splashes the congregation with drops of water while Psalm 51 is said or sung. Psalm 51 further resonates with these words in Ezekiel, because it also talks about God creating in us a pure heart, renewed in spirit. After being cleansed, they are finally ready to receive their new heart, and this will be the vessel for the gift of God's Spirit.

As the Church today celebrates Pentecost, our Old Testament reading therefore helps us to think about how we can best receive God's Spirit and be healed, freed-up, made whole. Are we living our lives as well as we can? Do we have clean hearts? Are we ready to receive this most wonderful of all gifts – God's Holy Spirit – and thereby, like the message of good news in Ezekiel, to declare to the world that our God is the Lord?

Megan I. J. Daffern

153

Suggested hymns

Come, thou Holy Spirit, come; Purify my heart; Into the darkness of this world; Come down, O love divine.

Trinity Sunday   30 May
Principal Service   **Living the Trinity**
Isa. 6.1–8; Ps. 29; Rom. 8.12–17; **John 3.1–17**

Alan Bennett's play *Forty Years On* is based on a school review on the occasion of the headmaster's retirement. In one scene, the headmaster is interviewing a boy before his confirmation. 'Now, you're sure you've got the catechism all buttoned up, Foster?' asks the headmaster. 'I'm still a bit hazy about the Trinity, sir,' replies Foster. 'Three in one and one in three, perfectly straightforward,' declares the headmaster. 'Any doubts about that, see your maths master.' 'Yes sir,' says Foster, rather unconvincingly.

But the Trinity is not a mathematical conundrum. It's not about how three are one and one is three. People think that if they find an analogy for three and one they've understood the Trinity. But this sends us up a blind alley. So put away shamrocks and triangles and three-dimensional figures.

Trinity as community

God isn't one single entity who then presents himself to us as Father, Son and Spirit. God is not Father, not Son, not Spirit; God is all three, a community. And they are called 'persons', which, for all its complexity, indicates distinctive personhood. The 'persons' are distinguished from one another by their own peculiar characteristics, by the work they do, by the way they relate to each other, and by their origins. This is evident in all of our readings, long before the Trinity was formulated.

They are three and they are equal. They are equal, even though the Son and Spirit come from the Father's life in the first place. Try telling my sons that they're not equal to me, even though I provided the chromosomes that brought them life.

If God were not Trinity, he wouldn't really be able to relate to us, he wouldn't be part of our lives, nor we part of his. You see, we'd be forced to think of Jesus as like the curate to the vicar, as second best. But everybody wants a visit from the vicar – if not the bishop! Parishioners want to know they're dealing with the top person. But because of the Trinity, Jesus is all that God is, and the life of Jesus is the life of God.

Jesus

But for us, Jesus is the way in, the access point to our relationship with God. Jesus has entered our history, inhabited our life, and experienced our suffering. And he's not God's messenger, an intermediary, a second best, a dilution of God; he's a co-equal member of God's family. So, through Jesus we have the invitation to know God, God as he is in God's own self. Not an icon of God or a manifestation of God, but God's very self; or, as David Jenkins, former Bishop of Durham, used to say: 'God is as he is in Jesus.'

Participating in the Trinity through Jesus

The Trinity is at work not merely to help us to know God, but to bring us into the Trinitarian family. Jesus is God's only begotten son, but by the Spirit we too can be adopted sons and daughters. That's what St Paul promises: 'You have received the spirit of adoption.' The Spirit is the agent that secures our adoption into God's family. They say that dog lovers come to look like their dogs, but an adopted child will never look like his or her adopted parents – how could they? They only could by the process of birth. But rebirth is what Jesus told Nicodemus is the one thing necessary. The Father offers it, the Son models it, but only the Spirit, the secret agent who works on the inside of our lives, can bring it about. In other words, the Spirit gives us rebirth so that we belong in God's family. God the Father can't do it, it's the Spirit who seals our adoption, and then day by day the change begins, softening, breaking, mellowing, loving, and we begin to share his likeness and let his glory through. We probably can't see the change taking place, but it becomes second nature to want to talk to God in the intimate, informal language that we reserve for our closest relationships. The Spirit bears witness 'with our spirit that we are children of God, and if children, then heirs of God and joint heirs with Christ'.

The unity of God

If God is relationship, then can we say that God is open to our life and to change? 'God so loved the world' – that means that God relinquished his self-containment for openness, risk, pain, change. God lived our life, died our death, occupied our grave. God is not only the Lord of history, he is also the subject of history. So who God is, is in part shaped by God's experience of our history, and especially the cross, and all that happens through the Spirit until the end of time.

God is three, permanently, eternally three. God is not extended, like the three tubes of a telescope, as Son and Spirit, only to be retracted when their work is done. Oneness comes out of mutual self-giving, each acting for the other, each one mirroring the other.

The Trinity isn't a mathematical conundrum; it's a relationship, an experience, and a model for our thinking and contemplation. Trinity is the most important thing we can say about God. There's nothing else really asked of us than that our relationships with God and with one another should strive to mirror his family likeness and reveal his self-giving life where we live and work and have our being.

Roger Spiller

Suggested hymns

Father of heaven, whose love profound; Affirm anew the three-fold name; Father, in whom we live; All-creating heavenly Giver.

Trinity Sunday   30 May
Second Service   Heaven's Above
Morning Ps. 33.1–12; Evening Ps. 104.1–10; **Ezek. 1.4–10, 22–28a**; Rev. 4; *Gospel at Holy Communion*: Mark 1.1–13

We have heard read the curious first-recorded vision of the prophet Ezekiel. He received his visions in Babylon, where he was among the exiles brought there from Judah. Uniquely in the Old Testament, Babylon is the setting for all the sayings and all the actions in the book of Ezekiel. The book, therefore, gives us glimpses of the impact of the exile upon those who were among the first group to be seized and taken to Babylon in 597 BC. We learn of their despair and turmoil because of their loss of the land, the city of Jerusalem and their Temple. How they must have listened out for news of any reversal of Babylonia's fortune, hoping and dreaming that they would be freed to return to Judah.

Back in 922 BC the northern kingdom of Israel had fallen. Judah had been spared only to become vulnerable to various would-be conquerors. She clung on after Nebuchadnezzar's campaign of 597 BC, but remained in danger, as Ezekiel was to warn the people.

Ezekiel was the son of a priest and he would probably have been in training for the priesthood; a younger contemporary of Jeremiah, it's possible that they knew each other in Judah. As befits a member of the priestly caste, he has an interest in the Temple and in holiness. A would-be priest would surely suffer the dashing of his dreams because the exile had brought separation from the Temple, God's dwelling, the place of priestly service. However, Ezekiel's preaching will assure his fellow exiles that despite their losses they are still God's chosen people (they, not those who are left in the land: a land that soon will fall). Ezekiel teaches that they need a renewal of heart and spirit.

Ezekiel's insights took the form of visions, the visions inspired his prophecy.

The first vision

There are three visions of God's presence in the book. Ezekiel received the first vision in 593 BC (the book prizes itself on its dates). The vision gives rise to an attempt to describe the indescribable.

Ezekiel is summoned. He is awestruck by the theophany, the revelation of the holiness of God. In an electrical storm, a stormy wind, a great cloud with brightness and flashing fire, he sees 'something like' four living creatures. (A cloud often represents the presence of God, for example as in Moses' meeting with God at Mount Sinai.)

But who are these fantastical creatures? Each has four faces, a (dominant) human face at the front, a lion's to the right, that of an ox to the left and an eagle's face to the rear. Thus, they symbolize all creation. They have four wings, with a human hand under each wing. They are straight-legged and have bull's hooves. They sparkle like bronze. Spreading two of their wings, they stand in a square with wing-tips touching, and they move. The noise of their wings is overwhelming – even when they stop, the sound continues.

A Hollywood special-effects expert would have a field day attempting to depict such beings on film (perhaps they'd use computer-generated imagery). Apart from the verbal description in Ezekiel, which employs apocalyptic language and imagery, they could look for further clues in Isaiah's descriptions of the cherubim (beings with whom they are compared later in the book of Ezekiel). There is speculation that redactors of the book may have added to Ezekiel's description, drawing upon religious imagery from the ancient Near East, so our Hollywood experts could draw upon ancient Babylonian imagery.

Above these mythical creatures there is a dome that is made of crystal, the dome that separates earth from heaven. Above the dome there's a sapphire, or lapis lazuli, throne. Enthroned thereon is one who, says Ezekiel, seems to have a human form. Out of reverence he does not state explicitly that this being is God. However, the clues are in the language used: dazzling light often denotes the glory of the Lord.

Ezekiel has been brought into the presence of God. How, on earth, could one explain this ultimate mystery?

Catching the vision

Ezekiel's entire vision is an experience of God's glory. It is evidence that God is not confined to the Temple back in beleaguered Jerusalem, but that he is the King who is present to his people, even to those exiled in Babylon. If, as Ezekiel is to proclaim, the Temple is to fall, God himself will be their sanctuary.

God is not confined to temple, cathedral, church or chapel, but sometimes we behave as if he is. Are we lacking in vision? Do we, like Ezekiel, struggle to find words to express our relationship with God. The God who revealed himself to Ezekiel can show himself to us. We must do our utmost for him: for his glory.

Wendy Kilworth-Mason

Suggested hymns

God beyond our dreams, you have stirred in us a memory; Hosanna, hosanna, hosanna in the highest!; O worship the King, all-glorious above; The splendour of the King.

First Sunday after Trinity (Proper 5) 6 June

Principal Service **God's Family Values**

(*Continuous*): 1 Sam. 8.4–11 [12–15] 16–20 [11.14–end];
Ps. 138; *or* (*Related*): Gen. 3.8–15; Ps. 130; 2 Cor. 4.13—5.1;
Mark 3.20–end

The choice: be a slave to the system or live differently?

One of my greatest heroes of the faith is the nineteenth-century
African American preacher and evangelist Sojourner Truth. She
had been born into slavery, sold as a child to other masters and
forced as a young woman to marry an older slave she didn't love.
But then, some years later, she was liberated: a Quaker couple took
her into their home, purchased her from her master at a great price,
and then announced to her that she was a free woman.

Sojourner explains in her autobiography how she stayed on
freely with the couple after this, working as a help. They were
good people and treated her well. But as time went on she began
desperately to miss her old slave friends and family, and, for all
the horrors of her former life, still longed for their company. One
terrible night it all got too much for her and she decided to return
to her old life. But she was prevented from doing so by a sudden,
overwhelming experience of the presence of God, which pinned her
to the spot and kept her from going anywhere. This experience was
to change her life for ever. Instead of allowing her to return to
her slave's life where she would again serve the unjust values it
obscenely represented, God was to send her off in a new direction
to live in a wholly different way.

The choice Jesus makes

When I read the gospel story for today, it seems to me that if Jesus
chooses not to go out to his mother and brothers who – understandably – come looking for him, it is not because he has stopped
loving them or caring about them, but because to return home with
them would be to take a step backwards: it would mean returning
to the old value system and the divisive and unjust rigidity of its
traditions and boundaries. In the ancient world, a son was expected
to live in obedience to his father and follow his father's trade. This
signified his acceptance of religious, social and cultural norms, and
his willingness to conform to the status quo. But the purpose of

Jesus' ministry was not to support the status quo but to proclaim the kingdom of God. Using the image of 'binding the strong man', Jesus asserts that he is called to confront and overcome the power of evil in all its guises. A return to the old lifestyle is impossible.

The choice we make

As children, we often absorb our parents' values in a sponge-like way and, just as Jesus must have learnt strong and righteous values in the home of Joseph and Mary, the values we learn from our parents may well be good and true and set us off on the right track. Yet as we grow up, we naturally begin to reassess and test out attitudes that earlier we accepted without question. We may move away from certain values or take a stand against particular points of view that our parents never thought to doubt. This is an entirely natural and important process of our development and growth, and needs to continue throughout our life.

But when we journey away from the ways and wisdom of our parents, which ways and wisdom do we journey towards? It is all too easy simply to absorb the current attitudes of the society that surrounds us, and to exchange unquestioning acceptance of the values of the people who brought us up for those of contemporary culture – just replacing the flawed old status quo for a flawed new one. Today's Gospel reading invites us to take a different direction. When God calls us from the old ways, it is to free us to turn towards the values of his kingdom, standing against the powers of evil and seeking to 'bind the strong man' in whatever shape or form he manifests himself.

The choice and the call

The 'strong man' that Sojourner Truth was called to 'bind' was made known in the evil of slavery, and following her powerful and mysterious experience of God she became a passionate abolitionist, preaching to white audiences. By sharing her own experiences of slavery, she hoped to turn her listeners from its horrors. Yet, not unlike the Lord she followed, she was often vilified by pro-slavery members of her audiences who considered that if only she had a 'proper' relationship with God she would give up preaching and understand that slavery was all part of God's plan. In the face of violent opposition, she remained true to the values of the kingdom of God.

Just as Jesus refused to be turned from his course by those who thought he was off his head or in cahoots with the devil himself, we too are challenged to stay true to kingdom values. Many fears, hatreds and divides tear our world apart, while new forms of slavery never cease to rear their heads. As followers of Christ today, and as members of God's family charged with doing his will, we are called in our turn to recognize where evil is at work and to commit ourselves to 'binding the strong man'.

How and where shall we speak out? What action shall we take?

Mary Cotes

Suggested hymns

Will you come and follow me if I but call your name?; The kingdom of God is justice and joy; Jesus Christ is waiting; Jesus calls us o'er the tumult.

First Sunday after Trinity (Proper 5)   6 June
Second Service   **Ask for the Ancient Paths**
Ps. 37.1–17 [*or* 37.1–11]; **Jer. 6.16–21**; Rom 9.1–13; *Gospel at Holy Communion*: Luke 7.11–17

Despair at the outer world?

Do you ever look around you and despair? The world faces calamitous issues. The earth cries out. Starvation stalks many lands. Scorched earth. Barren land. Flooded landscapes. Food banks. Political fractiousness. Truth contested. Wars tear the fabric of peace into shreds. It's easy to feel a tad bleak.

Despair over the inner world?

Do you ever look inwards and despair, aware of your own divided heart? The desire to do good wrestles with the pull to please yourself. Aware of our complicity in environmental destruction through careless, selfish choices. Complicit in family feuds and self-centred narratives. Internally fractured, externally broken. Despair is an understandable perspective.

A Jeremiah of a sermon

All a bit bleak. This is indeed a Jeremiah of a sermon, but that might not be such a bad thing. Into this greyness the Scriptures speak such wisdom. Into our human condition they bring such comfort, such counsel. Listen up. The prophet Jeremiah calls out to his own people, and his voice takes wing across the centuries. Listen to his counsel: 'Stand at the crossroads, and look, and ask for the ancient paths, where the good way lies; and walk in it, and find rest for your souls.' Stubborn and rebellious, his people rejected this invitation, with a staggering and all too familiar bloody minded-ness: 'We will not walk in it ... We will not give heed.' Jeremiah warned them – the Babylonian army is coming from the North, a driving force of destruction and terror. The priests have failed the people, failed to call people back to God. Jeremiah urges all his hearers, then and now, to take responsibility and seek the ancient paths and the good way.

A balm to anxious hearts

Our psalm set for today has a similar message and we are invited to listen in. It's a real balm to anxious hearts. To those who look at evil and worry, who see the power and wealth of wrongdoing and wonder if they are on the right path, the Psalmist says, 'Don't fret'. Or to put it another way: 'Stop chewing on it.' Quit worrying. Reframe your perspective. Trust God. Now, lest you think this is going to morph into an 'all is well' piece of saccharine spiritualizing, stay with me.

I have an inner cynic. She brooks no pink and fluffy religious sentimentality. She won't buy into a perspective that says, 'It'll all be all right', while ignoring the reality of human pain: the truth of rapacious evil that harms children, batters the vulnerable, plunders the earth, twists language and distorts truth. She's on high alert for any reframing that cuts out of the picture these faces, these stories, these truths, with a 'there, there' pie-in-the-sky religious sentiment. No. However, our Psalmist is no peddler of religious opium.

Who are the wicked?

He doesn't airbrush out the wicked from the picture. He is fully aware. They plot. They gnash their teeth. They draw the sword and bend the bow. They take aim against the poor and needy. They slay the good. No soft soap here. The wicked are alive and well and causing harm. This begs a question. Who are the wicked? We rather assume it's 'them', those bad people over there. But what if it's me, you? Here is a call to look at the effect of our choices on others. To the small child who labours for little so I can have cheap clothing, I am the wicked. To the women who shell cashews for pennies, and burn their hands on the plant acids so I can have a snack with my gin, I am the wicked. To the kids involved in mining minerals so I can have another phone upgrade – I am the wicked. We are complicit.

Making a choice for good

The Psalmist calls us to trust in the Lord and do good. Doing good means thinking about our choices and their impact and doing it differently. He calls us to be careful. Don't align yourself with the wicked, those opposed to God. If we are only concerned for ourselves, we are those opposed to God. The Psalmist is clear about the how to of making better choices. Delight in the Lord. Be focused on God. Commit your way to the Lord. Align your actions to God's care for the poor. Trust in the Lord. Challenge internal worries. Don't fret. Sit before him. Wait patiently for him. Slow down, lean in and listen up. These are the ancient ways.

Because God

Do not 'fret' (that word again) when the wicked succeed in their ways. There is realism here. Evil is. At times it will seem to have won the day, but stand firm, because God. Because God is good, and God will overcome. Because God promises that the power of the wicked will be broken. The power of evil within us will be defeated. Standing firm does not mean looking away. It means looking at, leaning in, learning with; being aware of the situations of the poor and vulnerable, owning our own poverty and checking in with ourselves honestly. Am I seeking out the ancient paths – the ways of confession, penitence, prayer and contemplation? Am I walking the good routes of justice, care and mercy – in what I do and how I speak? Am I reframing my opinions, attitudes and actions around the will of God?

Showing consumerism the door

What am I doing with my money? Where is the focus of my heart? When I am envious, greedy and pursue wealth for its own sake, the Psalmist interjects: 'Better is a little that the righteous person has than the abundance of many wicked.' Let's show consumerism the door, and stop putting trust in tawdry baubles that rust. Trust in the living God.

Kate Bruce

Suggested hymns

Guide me, O thou great Redeemer; O Lord, the clouds are gathering; You are my hiding place.

Second Sunday after Trinity (Proper 6)   13 June
Principal Service   Speaking in Parables
(*Continuous*): 1 Sam. 15.34—16.13; Ps. 20; *or* (*Related*): Ezek. 17.22–end; Ps. 92.1–4, 12–end [*or* 1–8]; 2 Cor. 5.6–10 [11–13] 14–17; **Mark 4.26–34**

Jesus 'did not speak to them except in parables, but he explained everything in private to his disciples'. And aren't *we* his disciples? So if I, standing up here, am to be like Jesus, then I'd explain everything to you.

But how can I do that? How can anybody, even Jesus, explain *everything* – the riddle of life, the riddle of God? Wouldn't the explanation evacuate the mystery and reduce it to a formula?

And if I or anybody else *could* explain everything, why these parables, these everyday riddles that Jesus and other teachers are so fond of? Explaining a parable is like explaining a joke: once it's done, the joke isn't funny. Either you get the joke, or you don't.

Extraordinary in the ordinary

Well, it seems that many who listened to Jesus *didn't* get it. Why? Are these riddles so difficult? Surely, the material and the characters in his parables are from ordinary things and events around him: seeds and lamps, farmers and parties. But in those ordinary things and events, Jesus – and alert hearers of the parables – perceived the extraordinary, the strange truth, what Jesus called 'the kingdom of God'.

So it is with these two little parables we've heard: the mystery of unseen, miraculous growth. The amazing transformation of seed into tree, of earthbound weakness into a city for the birds. And it happens every day.

And perhaps that's the problem for the hearers who don't get it, precisely that it happens every day. The seeds are trodden underfoot and the mystery lost. After all, you can't actually *see* the growth and the transformation, and even the farmer, says Jesus, doesn't know how it happens. And if you can't see it, is it real?

Restless faith

This is where those awkward words of St Paul may help, even if they too don't 'explain everything'. 'We walk by faith, not by sight,' he says to the church in Corinth. What he calls 'faith' doesn't mean a denial of reason, nor does it mean subscribing to some ideology (which is often how 'faith' is presented by people suspicious of religion). As Paul and as Jesus present it, faith isn't something you take refuge and rest in. Far from it, faith is rest*less*, it means refusing to be content with how things are, refusing to assume that nothing can change.

So if we *do* make that assumption, that's the ultimate faithlessness. How often do you hear (or how often might you yourself have said), 'Oh, I can't alter my ways now', or, 'You can't change human nature', or, 'Corruption is the way of the world', or, 'There'll always be rich and poor'?

But no! If we walk by *faith*, then we're open, with divine impatience, to the possibility of transformation. The possibility of truth beyond what our eyes and minds can configure; the possibility of a world made new and made just; the possibility of what Jesus calls 'the kingdom of God'.

This restless faith is mind-changing and world-changing. 'Faith' is often allied with tradition (as in the phrase 'keep the faith'). But faith actually means sitting loose to old ways that are familiar to our eyes, and reaching forward to the new, the unseen. St Paul again: 'If anyone is in Christ,' (by which he means being baptized into Christ and living his way and fed by his body and blood) if anyone is in Christ, 'there is a new creation; everything old has passed away; see, everything has become new!' And the sign, the ratification of this newness, is in what we celebrate this and every Sunday: the ultimate transformation of death into life, the Easter miracle, which can't be seen but which energizes all life.

Repeat Jesus' way of seeing

So if we are to walk by faith and not by sight, what place is left for our *eyes*? Jesus *saw* parables, he saw the kingdom of God, in the ordinary world around him. And perhaps our calling isn't so much to repeat his parables, let alone explain them, but to repeat his way of *seeing*. In other words, to hold our eyes and our minds open to the parables scattered around us in our everyday world.

But we can't do that if we are rushing through the world, or trying to control it. Only if we're prepared to turn aside, to wait on signs of transformation. And then, even if we don't understand, to grasp them and celebrate the new creation. So R. S. Thomas celebrates it in what seems an everyday experience in his poem 'The Bright Field':

> I have seen the sun break through
> to illuminate a small field
> for a while, and gone my way
> and forgotten it. But that was the pearl
> of great price, the one field that had
> the treasure in it. I realise now
> that I must give all that I have
> to possess it. Life is not hurrying
>
> on to a receding future, nor hankering after
> an imagined past. It is the turning
> aside like Moses to the miracle
> of the lit bush, to a brightness
> that seemed as transitory as your youth
> once, but is the eternity that awaits you.

Will *you* be turning aside today? What parables of the kingdom of God might you discover? What will become new for you?

Christopher Burdon

166

Great Shepherd of thy people, hear; Now the green blade riseth; The kingdom of God is justice and joy; The Lord is here – he finds us as we seek.

Second Sunday after Trinity (Proper 6)   13 June
Second Service   **Inconvenient Truths**
Ps. 39; **Jer. 7.1–16**; Rom. 9.14–26; *Gospel at Holy Communion*: Luke 7.36—8.3

Jeremiah must have been an inconvenient fellow to have around. Put yourself in the shoes of one of Jeremiah's target audience. Imagine, everything is ticking along nicely ...

'We attend Temple on all the right occasions, sing all the right songs (sometimes three times over), chant all the right liturgy – we've got this religion thing covered. Then along comes this prophet claiming we are just giving lip service to God. Good grief, we are here, aren't we? There he is pointing the finger at what he imagines are our iffy business practices, claiming we turn a blind eye to the poor and the most vulnerable. What does he know? I do my bit. He implies that complicity with greed makes us wilfully harm the poor. As if we would do such a thing! He accuses us of being in bed with other gods. Why doesn't he just shut it? What's worse is he stands outside the Temple and hassles us as we come to God's house. Oh come on, Jeremiah, everyone has a pet god or two. It's just the way things are. Lighten up, buddy. We're here, aren't we? Have a go at those who don't bother to turn up at all. Jeremiah talks as if God wanted to do a deal with us. If you amend your ways, then God will dwell with us in the Temple. What kind of a transactional God is he on about? God is here – we don't have to do anything to earn his presence. He doesn't expect anything. Jeremiah makes God sound grumpy and demanding. All that ranting about other gods – you'd almost think God was jealous. Jeremiah, you are the exact reason religious people should steer clear of politics. "Amend your ways," you say. "Act justly." Jeremiah, you have no sense of how the business world works. You're naive. Eggs get broken to make an omelette. That's just life. Jeremiah talks as though it's our fault some people have a rough time. I'm sure we all do what we can. And anyway – we are here, in the Temple, doing our bit, showing up. As for all his doom and gloom and threats of destruction – I think old Jeremiah might have lost it a bit. He's always been a bit odd, ever since he was a boy. I think I'll have a word with the Temple police – he should be thrown out – he's becoming an embarrassment. A real inconvenience.'

Jeremiah: as inconvenient now as he was then

Yes. I can't help but imagine that Jeremiah must have been a very inconvenient fellow to have around. But sometimes truth is inconvenient. It disrupts the normal pattern. It says, 'Take another look.' Jeremiah is as inconvenient now as then. Unchecked, we humans quickly forget. We are not the authors of our own destiny. As the Psalmist today reminds us, our lives are fleeting, we are passing guests in God's world. Yet, we act as if we own it.

Jeremiah calls us to check in with ourselves and ask some hard questions. Is my worship empty, just rote words? Am I giving houseroom to gods of my own making? Am I two-timing God? Have I forgotten that God is for the most vulnerable – so I cannot airbrush them out of my picture of the world:

the family displaced in war-torn Syria
the woman slaving in a sweat shop, making cheap clothes for
   Western markets
the terrified infant separated from his parents in a refugee centre
the girl passed from hand to hand for sex
the man forced to risk his life on an overcrowded boat.

The widow, the orphan the powerless; the abused, the homeless, the refugee. If I do not care for them, can I really claim to care for God? Ah Jeremiah, your inconvenient truths are biting, but ultimately hope-filled.

Inconvenient, but hope-filled

Can you hear Jeremiah's glorious words of hope? 'If you truly amend your ways, God will dwell with you.' God will draw close again. God will make his home here, sharing our postcode. Helping us to help transform the world – one kind and generous act at a time. This is a call to confession, repentance and new relationship. It's a reminder that God doesn't do cheap grace. His love is freely given but expectant. Pass it on. Do something with it. Don't try and lock God up in a religious system and nod his way every now and then. Jeremiah's inconvenient truths build a bridge back, into deeper relationship with God. His inconvenient truths are bolt-cutters for those who listen, snapping through the chains that bind us to greed, worship of the self, the love of money, the very things that bring paranoia, obsession, worry. The very things that alienate us from God and torpedo genuine peace. Jeremiah's inconvenient truths are an invitation deeper into love. His inconvenient truths draw us to confession. So let us pray:

[*Preachers can insert here a set liturgical confession, or use a block of confessional worship songs. Giving people space to consider what they will do to put genuine action into their confession will be important. Preachers might give suggestions of ways people could reach out to the poor in the local area and wider world – through prayer, giving of time and resource.*]

Kate Bruce

Suggested hymns

The kingdom of God is justice and joy; All are welcome in this place; Brother, sister, let me serve you; Christ be our light.

Third Sunday after Trinity (Proper 7) 20 June
Principal Service **The Fear of Fear**
(*Continuous*): 1 Sam. 17.[1a, 4–11, 19–23] 32–49 *and*
Ps. 9.9–end, *or* 1 Sam. 17.57—18.5, 10–16 *and* Ps. 133;
or (*Related*): Job 38.1–11; Ps. 107.1–3, 23–32 [*or* 107.23–32];
2 Cor. 6.1–13; **Mark 4.35–end**

Watching a film of one of our round-the-world sailors a few years ago, battling alone with the elements and the great waves of the Southern Ocean was a riveting experience. He was battling, too, with the damage inflicted on his little vessel and, still more, battling with himself, his own instinctive fear and uncertainty, and then with the eventual sense of failure when he was forced to withdraw from the race.

The threat to life

The weather conditions on the Lake of Galilee – only the provincial Mark calls it a 'sea' – bear no comparison with the Southern Ocean. But it's notorious for sudden storms like the one experienced by the disciples of Jesus. So even disciples who are experienced sailors can become fearful and terrified out of their wits. What makes matters worse is that Jesus is asleep. He's actually occupying the seat reserved for the rower, and slumbering on a nice cushion. The disciples are gripped by fear; the boat is buffeted about and the water pours in, destabilizing the boat. They expect they will perish. And Jesus is asleep. We can find ourselves being irritated with people who can sleep through anything, while the rest of us are awake and restless and keeping watch.

Sleep can be a picture of trust and faith. It's a picture of letting go. I expect you've known people with fragile health who are reluctant to sleep, fearing they may just slip away without the chance to put up any resistance. The disciples interpret Jesus sleeping as uncaring and endangering their lives. But it was they who 'took Jesus' into the boat and, with a crew of experienced fishermen, had been entrusted to get them safely back to land.

Addressing the sea

When Jesus is woken up, he addresses the 'sea' as you would address a noisy child or an agitated adult: 'Quiet', 'Peace', 'Be still!' In reality, he addresses it as a demon. In the Old Testament, creation is described as a struggle between God and the sea. The sea is a monster, 'that great Leviathan'. But it's the mark of God's sovereignty that the sea obeys his orders. The disciples will ask, 'Who is this, that even the wind and the sea obey him?' They have yet to heed the psalm that gives the answer to their question. 'O LORD God of hosts … *You* rule the raging of the sea; when its waves rise, you still them.'

'Why are you afraid?'

Having calmed the sea, Jesus turns to the disciples: 'Why are you afraid?' It's the most frequent question in the whole of the Bible. We don't have to be caught in a storm on a lake to be fearful. Lives can be transfixed by internal feuds and fears, the fear of failure, of things getting out of control, of losing a job or even a partner. 'Why are you afraid?', asks Jesus. 'Have you no faith?' There is a lot of fear bottled up inside many of us. But what are we to do, what were the disciples to do? Does faith suggest doing nothing and leaving it to Jesus? Would Jesus have woken up just in the nick of time? Or was he saying that death is not the worst thing that can happen to us? Or does Jesus take us right to the edge so as to show us our need to depend upon him?

Fear of fear

If we're asked to let go of our fear and trust Jesus, we have to have reason to trust that Jesus will act. Jesus is asleep, in another world. Like the disciples, we can think of Jesus or God as being detached from us, absent, indifferent to threats to our life as we are tossed about by the waves of economic and social uncertainty, change, sickness, suffering, loss. And we say, 'Teacher, do you not care that we are perishing.' But it is our fear, not his care, that is in dispute. It's not that squalls won't happen or that we can be protected against them, but that we can survive and flourish if we know and live by the care that God has for us. It's not that there's 'nothing to be afraid of' but that being afraid is not the only option. As President Roosevelt's pregnant phrase has it: 'The only thing we have to fear is fear itself.'

The capacity to trust

Our ability to trust has its roots in our experience of the people we have trusted in the past and how far we have been let down. Our ability to trust even in God reflects how we have learnt to trust others. But there is One who is trustworthy, One who desires and deserves our complete trust and confidence, One in whom we can fully commit our very life. Jesus, whom the winds and waves obey, is acting with divine power. He is Lord not merely of human relations but Lord of creation.

Today the world stands on the brink of a potentially catastrophic threat to the entire planet. Trust in God's sovereignty over creation doesn't absolve us from responsibility to act, but it emboldens us to trust that actions we take make a difference. There's a world of difference between believing that there's nothingness and no one at the heart of the universe, nothing in, with and beyond unruly, uncreated matter, and the belief that the universe can be addressed 'Be still', because we know that at the heart of the universe there is a personal being. He is the One who neither slumbers nor sleeps, but is awake to our longings and will bring us safely home.

Roger Spiller

Suggested hymns

Jesus calls us o'er the tumult; No coward soul is mine; Be still, my soul; Will your anchor hold in the storms of life.

Third Sunday after Trinity (Proper 7)   20 June
Second Service   When Theology and Experience Clash
Ps. 49; Jer. 10.1–16; **Rom. 11.25–end**; *Gospel at Holy Communion*: Luke 8.26–39

There can often be a conflict between belief and practice, theology and experience. Once I was phoned by the hospital asking me to baptize a baby who was not expected to live. By the time I got there, the baby had died. Mormons baptize the dead, but our theology does not permit this. The parents are facing grief, and the refusal of baptism, due to the vagaries of time and traffic, would deliver a further blow.

The clash of the personal and religious

Negotiating our way around conflict leads to deep personal anguish and heart-searching. And in the letter to the Romans, we see Paul absorbed in a conflict that is racial, religious and deeply personal. The issue may not concern us as much as the way Paul attempts to handle it. He says that he has 'great sorrow and unceasing anguish' in his heart and would prefer himself to be accursed and cut off from Christ for the sake of his people, the Jews. They are in just that position, 'cut off from Christ', and it's breaking his heart. And, to add to his grief, he's facing charges that he's forsaken his own Jewish kinsfolk for the Gentiles. And the Gentiles think that he has been so carried away by the Jews that he has neglected them. He cannot win, but he will try. Since then he's often been attacked as anti-Semitic, but that's hardly justified by the three chapters he devotes to this in his letter. A brief summary is in order.

A summary of the argument

If Jews are excluded from God's promise, has his promise then failed? No. No Jew would have expected that everyone who was literally descended from Abraham would be saved, and many, like Paul, showed God's promise was being fulfilled.

Why are the Jews cut off from Christ? Paul says that it depends upon God's mercy, and God gives mercy to some and hardens the hearts of others. Any reasonable person would think this is unfair and arbitrary. But 'who are we to answer back' to God, says Paul. God's will is inscrutable, but humankind shouldn't accuse God of being unjust.

Paul doesn't give a rational explanation for what seems to be God's arbitrary decision. But he does see purpose in it. First, God's wrath shows up and brings into greater relief what he has done to show his mercy. So the Gentiles who don't seek righteousness have it through faith; the Jews who strive to gain righteousness by fulfilling the law don't find it. The second outcome is that it gives Gentiles the opportunity to proclaim his glory to the nations.

Has God rejected his people?

But is it open to Jews to call on God and be saved? Perhaps, it may be suggested, they should be excused because they haven't heard or, having heard, haven't understood the gospel? Yes, they have heard and understood, says Paul. So has God rejected his people? No, Paul himself is proof of that, and he is not alone. There is a remnant, an elect, already in the present, who have been chosen by grace, who will be saved. But the remainder of the people have their hearts hardened and are resistant to the gospel.

Addressing the Gentiles

The unbelief and 'stumbling' of the Jews has brought benefits to the Gentiles. This causes the Jews to be jealous. 'I glorify my ministry in order to make my own people jealous and thus save some of them,' says Paul.

Gentiles have taken the place that Jews were expected to occupy. Paul introduces the familiar image for Israel; the olive tree stands for the Jewish nation. Some branches of Israel have been cut off due to their unbelief, and space has been created for Gentiles to be grafted in, in their place. But this is not the fixed or final destiny of the Jews. Paul argues that if the exclusion of Jews means inclusion for Gentiles, how much more will the inclusion of the Jews mean. But he's already referred to a remnant of Jews, said that 'some' but not all Jewish branches have been cut off. On what basis, then, are the Jews saved?

Paul doesn't answer. Instead he warns the Gentiles not to boast that God has included them at the expense of the Jews. The Gentiles must recognize that we are included through faith, but still with the threat that we too might be cut off, and that we must not take our promise of salvation for granted.

Jews in a new Israel for all

Now Paul suggests that if Jews do not persist in their unbelief, they will be grafted back into the olive tree, which is the people of God. But the condition is that it must wait until 'the full number of the Gentiles has come in', incorporated into God's people. But then Paul takes a leap in developing his argument and declares that 'all Israel will be saved'. He's not thought to be claiming the ultimate destiny of every person, but declaring that the Jews as a people will be incorporated into the new Israel of God. And then the purpose of God's wrath is shown; God has destined everyone to wrath and everyone to mercy. God's severity is the means to bring home to us his mercy.

We may well struggle with Paul's tortuous logic; with the sudden shifts in his argument and with his attempt both to do justice to the gospel that is based on the grace of God received by faith alone and at the same time to the unique, historical role of his own people, without according them special privileges.

What more can Paul say? His argument is exhausted, his explanation runs dry. His logic has been confounded. Paul is emotionally wrung out. He can only surrender himself to the unsearchable God in doxology and praise.

Roger Spiller

Suggested hymns

When all thy mercies, O my God; God moves in a mysterious way; Can we by searching find out God; Immortal, invisible, God only wise.

Fourth Sunday after Trinity (Proper 8)   27 June
Principal Service   **Healing and Wholeness**
(*Continuous*): 1 Sam. 1.1, 17–end; Ps. 130; *or* (*Related*):
Wisd. of Sol. 1.13–15; 2.23–24; *Canticle*: Lam. 3.22–33,
or Ps. 30; 2 Cor. 8.7–end; **Mark 5.21–end**

We find in today's Gospel an account of two people preoccupied with health and desperate for a cure. We learn that Jesus had just arrived from the other side of the lake and a big crowd had formed. And at the same time, pitted against the demand of the crowd, was the personal need of just one man.

A sick child

We know the man's priority – the priority of any parent when their child is sick – they would do anything, go to any length, raise thousands of pounds and fly around the world in pursuit of a cure. The father is named Jairus, he's known to the crowd. He's one of the leaders of the synagogue, a sort of churchwarden who's responsible for the building and for ensuring that services are conducted. Officials of the synagogue would normally be a bit wary of Jesus, suspicious even. But Jairus is desperate and he has faith in Jesus. So he's prepared publicly to humble himself and kneel, and plead and petition Jesus to visit his home and lay hands upon his little daughter. And Jesus meets his request. There's a huge crowd that wants to be fed, but the healing of one person takes priority over the crowd. Thankfully, Jesus is no captive to numbers and popularity stakes or maximizing publicity, as his followers seem to be.

A desperate woman

But no sooner does he go in pursuit of one person's needs, than he is waylaid by another. He's mobbed by the crowd, herded around by a multitude eager to get close to him. But now attention has switched from one sick person to another. We learn three facts about her. First, she's had bleeding, probably from fibroids. Second, she's had that condition for 12 years. And third, she's spent her life savings on private medicine and, far from getting better, the doctors have made her worse. There was some scepticism about doctors in the ancient world, just as there is in some quarters today.

But she had faith in Jesus, perhaps even a superstitious faith, that the mere touch of his garments would transmit healing power. Why didn't she speak to Jesus and ask for healing? Was she too shy and reserved? Did she feel it would be unnecessary? She knew that someone in her condition was ritually unclean and wouldn't have wanted to pass this on to Jesus. But she also felt shamefaced and uncomfortable about what she'd done, as we learn from the way she reacted when the deed came to light. Mark says that when confronted by Jesus she told him the whole truth – as if to suggest that she had initially been a little disingenuous. But why, for his part, does Jesus want to identify her? Why does he add to the woman's fear and embarrassment? Why does he 'out her' – name and shame her? Without this, the woman would have lived her life with a sense of unease, guilt, shame – her healing in one area would have only opened up a sickness on another front. Her physical healing would have exposed her need to be healed in the way she related to other people. She might even have viewed all her relationships in terms of their usefulness to her. In any case, healing is incomplete until we are brought into a right relationship with God. And when she came forward, in fear and trepidation, she received the affirmation and blessing of Jesus.

The sick child again

Meanwhile, what has become of Jairus' daughter? Why is Jesus shown to have been side-tracked? After all, the purpose of the story seemed to be Jairus' daughter, and now her acute condition has all but been eclipsed by a less serious ailment of an older woman. Jairus has remained with Jesus, in the hope, perhaps, of steering Jesus to his home against further delays from the crowd. You can imagine what Jairus' family are going through as the minutes tick away, desperately willing Jesus to arrive before it's too late. And then discovering that it is too late. Anxiety turns to anger as they discover the child has died and is beyond the reach of Jesus' power to heal.

Of course the reader knows differently. Jesus will go in to the little girl – she's 12 years old, the length of time the woman had suffered from bleeding. And there we see the tenderness as well as the sovereignty of Jesus. How gently he addresses her – the original words in Aramaic are preserved, *Talitha cum*, little girl, get up. And we're told that immediately the girl got up and began to walk about.

Oh well, we say. It must have been good for that generation. How we wish we were accompanying Jesus around all the sick and suffering children and adults, for whom the National Health Service, medical science, tender loving care, is all too late. There are two things we have to remember. The first is that their state and ours is, according to Jesus, an interim one, not a final one. Jesus didn't routinely raise the dead – only a handful of cases are reported – and nor even did he systematically heal the sick. Those brought to life and healed had still to die, but it was about restoration to new life in the kingdom that Jesus was primarily concerned. And those sporadic examples of raising the dead and healing the sick were not only acts of compassion but action parables of that eventual healing that will encompass the whole creation. We rejoice in the success of the human genome project, but even when there are cures to so many known diseases, and life expectancy has been extended for 30 or more years, this is still only an interim condition.

It means therefore that our condition isn't fated or fixed or final. It will be transformed. But the transformation can already be begun. Our gospel is there to invite us to exercise faith in Jesus, to invoke him, entreat him, and trust him to act in the needs we bring to him. It sets out the sovereignty and tenderness of Jesus. It invites us to have faith that his sovereignty and tenderness will triumph universally and that it is already at work in the world, in us and, who knows, through us as well.

Roger Spiller

Suggested hymns

Christ's is the world in which we move; Lay your healing hand upon us; Jesus, in your life, we see you; The kingdom of God.

Fourth Sunday after Trinity (Proper 8)   27 June
Second Service   **Good Citizens: Good Neighbours**
Ps. [52] 53; Jer. 11.1–14; **Rom. 13.1–10**; *Gospel at Holy Communion*: Luke 9.51–end

Did you vote at the last General Election, or at recent local elections? Are you law-abiding? Do you keep to the speed limit, clean up after your dog, avoid fly-tipping and pay the appropriate amount of tax?

Do you love your neighbours? Do you love yourself? All questions raised by our challenging passage today from Romans.

Submit to civil authority

Paul, writing to the early church in Rome, encourages them to be law-abiding. Some have suggested that this passage has been added into Paul's letter by a different hand, but being obedient to the civil authorities is not a new idea – it runs throughout the New Testament. In the letters of Timothy, Titus and Peter, Christians are encouraged to pray for and submit to those in authority over them, not just in the Church but in the State too. 'I urge that supplications, prayers, intercessions and thanksgivings should be made for everyone, for kings and all in high positions,' we read in Paul's first letter to Timothy. This was quite a radical idea in a society where many dissident and disaffected groups were refusing to acknowledge the rule of the Roman Empire. Paul is suggesting that rulers are put in place by God, and under God's authority. The Emperor Nero believed himself to be a god and therefore under no other authority. Paul is acknowledging that God can and does work through secular rulers – Cyrus in the time of the exile is a good example. In John 19, Jesus says that Pilate's authority comes 'from above'. Positions of civil authority are part of God's plan: God institutes the office – but not necessarily the office holder, so the position deserves honour, even if the person who occupies it doesn't. This means that we don't have to submit to authority without exercising some discretion. There are times when it is entirely appropriate for our own good and the good of others that we use the mechanisms available to whistle-blow or change leaders.

Pay taxes

Paul urges the early Christians, and us too, to pay taxes. We are to pay the amount due and not try to fiddle the sums in some way. For the early Christians this meant paying public debts, which included a number of taxes: such as the tribute to the empire, ground tax, income tax and poll tax, and then local taxes such as custom duties, import and export taxes and so on.

Jesus in Mark 12 reminded his disciples that they should pay to Caesar what is Caesar's and to God what is God's. Paul refers to the need to pay private debts and not to owe anyone anything. In our society today it's almost a badge of honour to fiddle one's taxes – to pull the wool over the eyes of the tax office, and to get away with paying as little tax as possible. Corporations seem to be particularly good at tax avoidance and we are all up in arms about that. But we too are to be honest with our earnings and to remind ourselves that paying taxes enables flourishing for all. It's very easy to think that our life of faith as a Christian on a Sunday and the way we behave in society for the rest of the week are not connected. That's a grave mistake.

Love your neighbour

Paul moves from tax and debt to love. If we truly love God then we will automatically keep God's commandments, which put care and consideration for the other above our own desires. In our reading from Jeremiah, God reiterates the covenant of love that has been made with the people of Judah. Judah has broken the covenant by running after other gods, and not giving due weight to loving the one true God – Yahweh. Disaster will surely follow, suggests God. Loving God takes work and commitment. We are to work on loving God and others daily, doing no wrong to a neighbour. Who are our neighbours? They aren't just the people we live alongside – though that's a good place to start. Jesus, in the parable of the good Samaritan, indicated that anyone can be a neighbour to another, and neighbourliness doesn't necessarily go hand in hand with faith. Those whom society deems to be outcast can be the most caring. The homeless often say that those on the streets look out for each other, while those in positions to help and make a difference walk past. Being good and diligent citizens, exercising our democratic privilege and paying our taxes is one way we love our neighbours. It's the way in which our democracy works and our roads, schools, hospitals, social centres and resources are funded. When we can't be bothered to vote, we take no interest in politics or we cheat the tax office, we hurt our neighbours and ultimately ourselves. 'Love your neighbour as yourself,' writes Paul. Let's treat those around us in the way we would wish to be treated ourselves. When we love ourselves, then we are sufficiently secure to love others and to long for the best for them. God is sovereign over all things in time and eternity. Let's remember that nothing and no one is beyond God's reach and outside God's plan for salvation.

Catherine Williams

When I needed a neighbour; Brother, sister, let me serve you; God is love, let heaven adore him; Bind us together, Lord.

Fifth Sunday after Trinity (Proper 9) 4 July
Principal Service **Jesus on His Terms, Not Ours**
(*Continuous*): 2 Sam. 5.1–5, 9–10; Ps. 48; *or* (*Related*):
Ezek. 2.1–5; Ps. 123; 2 Cor. 12.2–10; **Mark 6.1–13**

Returning home after a time of change is often an apprehensive as well as an exciting experience. Whether it's returning to our home church, neighbourhood, school or circle of friends, we can't always be sure of the reception we'll receive. Relationships are not likely to be the same as they were before we went away.

Jesus home in his own synagogue

Jesus came home, which we assume is Nazareth, the place where he was brought up. He'd caught the eye of the public and gained a reputation for healing and teaching. And he'd acquired a retinue of disciples who accompanied him and confirmed his growing influence. But they kept their opinions to themselves. It was only when, on the Sabbath, Jesus taught in the synagogue that strong reactions were provoked. It's hardly surprising. Ask yourself how you would feel if one of the young people you'd nurtured in the youth club or Sunday school was standing up and preaching to you? You might be proud. On the other hand, you might say, 'Why her? Why not me?'

Grassroots or centre?

I was involved in ministry as local ministry schemes were being developed. This meant that we would look to the local church to identity a candidate who had the active support of the congregation to train with a view to authorized local ordained ministry. The idea seemed sensible, and was a healthy departure from the normal practice of parachuting people into parishes where they were unknown. Congregations took pride and satisfaction that 'one of their own' would be their priest. But, it was when their newly ordained candidate got into the pulpit and started preaching that at least some congregations became less comfortable with their fellow member and friend, now standing before and probably above them and, in a real sense, set over them. Power dynamics had sprung into action. We shouldn't have been so surprised. Hadn't Jesus cited a well-known saying at the time, that 'Prophets are not without honour except in their own town'?

The home crowd were 'astonished'

It started off well. Jesus delivered a stonking sermon. And the congregation were 'astonished'. Well, perhaps not all of them. 'Many' were – which could mean 'all those present', but it could equally mean more than half of them.

Reactions to preaching are worth analysing. Most of us preachers are more than satisfied if we get a reaction other than 'Thanks' or 'Thanks for keeping it short' or 'I could hear every word you said' – which could just mean, 'but I wished I couldn't'! The one response I positively dislike is the comment 'Well done'. It suggests that the preacher is being assessed, which, of course they are, but it probably also indicates that they are paying attention to the medium not the message. Being 'astonished' might suggest a similar response, if it's a comment not on what Jesus said but on who it was that was speaking. They go on to ask, 'Where did this man get all this? What is the wisdom that has been given to him? What deeds of power are being done by his hands?' Their minds are still on the person of the preacher rather than the substance of the preaching. But if they even felt 'astonishment' and acknowledged that Jesus was the recipient of a divine 'giver', that would have been an enormous step in their religious education.

The carpenter creates a scandal

But now, maybe others who were not part of the 'many' piped up with their put-down. 'Is not this the carpenter?' We thought that Jews had a high regard for manual workers, but were they scorning this mundane, working-class man? In Matthew's Gospel Jesus is the 'carpenter's son', whereas Luke omits the title altogether. This and other material shows that Jesus' trade was a sensitive issue and suggested the early Church had difficulty in accepting that an artisan could be the Messiah. But then they drag his mother into it, sneeringly naming her and possibly hinting that because the father isn't named, Jesus might be illegitimate. And then they mention his brothers and sisters, which we'll come back to shortly.

The conclusion was that those present were not merely provoked by Jesus; they were scandalized by him. They couldn't see beyond his humanity. Their rejection of Jesus was tantamount to a rejection of God. And who are the ones who are scandalized? 'A prophet is not without honour except in their home town', and – note this – 'among their own kin and in their own house'. Jesus is rejected by his own relatives and in his own house. Earlier in the story Jesus' family declared him to be out of his mind and set out to find and restrain him. If that was the judgement of the family on Jesus, it's understandable why the people added them to the witness evidence against the identity claimed for him.

Mark shows us that his humanity, his suffering and rejection is a scandal and stumbling block. His followers must accept, in Paul's words, that the foolishness of God is stronger than the wisdom of men and women. And there is one more surprise. Jesus is also a realist. He doesn't dispute the truth of the proverb; he uses it to explain and perhaps excuse his misguided hearers. The saying also exists in a shorter form: 'No prophet is accepted in his village, no physician heals those who know him.'[26] I'm married to a physician and I can vouch for the truth of that!

Roger Spiller

Suggested hymns

God moves in a mysterious way; Lord of all hopefulness; The Son of God his glory hides; We have a gospel to proclaim.

Fifth Sunday after Trinity (Proper 9)   4 July
Second Service   **Between a Rock and a Hard Place**
Ps. [63] 64; **Jer. 20.1–11a**; Rom. 14.1–17; *Gospel at Holy Communion*: Luke 10.1–11, 16–20

Jeremiah is on the scene during the catastrophe of the last days of Judah, which culminated in the destruction of Jerusalem and the Temple in 587 BC. That crisis is the dominant event in the Old Testament and Jeremiah is God's reluctant spokesman, to deliver the unpalatable final warning of judgement that rained down hostility and violence upon him. But what of the man himself and the impact his uncongenial calling is having on him? We're drawn to look at the most intense of his anguished 'confessions'. These are addressed, mostly to God, in shockingly accusative, abrasive, language. They show the human side, the personal cost, the anguish of the vocation that serving God can entail.

A fool for God's sake

At the beginning of the first of the confessions, we need to add words to try to do justice to the original Hebrew. 'O LORD you have enticed me and I was enticed, you have overpowered me and you have prevailed. I have become a laughing stock all day long, everybody mocks me.' We're already told that he's been placed in the stocks in a prominent place for physical public humiliation. He's saying that God has enticed, seduced, duped and made a fool of him. He's been compelled to pronounce judgement but it has yet to happen and his hearers are repudiating his fake news. Jeremiah feels deceived because he is squeezed uncomfortably between a compelling word from God and the refusal of people to hear; he is beset by the word of God on the one hand and beleaguered by antagonists on the other.

The message must be delivered

Might he have refused to speak, and disobeyed his call? He complains that he doesn't have that option. 'If I say, "I will not mention him, or speak any more in his name", then within me there is something like a burning fire shut up in my bones; I am weary with holding it in and I cannot.' God's word has become his word, and so he would fail to be himself were he to keep silent. And so he admits that God has outwitted and overpowered him. Perhaps we too have felt pressure within us to speak a word that would attract opprobrium and opposition, even though we feel we cannot remain silent. Or perhaps we try to contain it within us and live with guilt and anguish for failing to speak as we knew we should.

Trapped in the crossfire

Jeremiah feels duped by God; he didn't fully realize what he was getting himself into. God's call has placed him in the direct line of fire, trapped and squeezed between two parties with opposing agendas. He is repudiated by his nation, on the one hand, and denied all visible support and solace from the God in whose service he is acting, on the other. He feels 'high and dry'. He recognizes that God's word will prevail, even over his persecutors, but that doesn't reduce the anguish of his vocation, especially as deliverance seems a long way off.

The divine commission causes Jeremiah to play the fool, a laughing stock to everyone. He is ridiculed and censured. He is the subject of a whispering campaign. And his message that 'terror is all around' is thrown back at him, as though it was self-evidently discredited and needlessly alarmist. People are out to get him and even his close friends lie in ambush to catch him out.

Jeremiah knows that God is with him 'like a dread warrior', and so the machinations of his persecutors and erstwhile friends won't prevail. He knows, too, that testing is a component of all significant relationships, and must be characteristic of his own relationship to God. But no sooner has he reasserted his trust in God than the torment of his vocation reasserts itself, and he concludes with a lament directed at the day of his birth and a wish that he had not survived the womb. When the word of God does come, the pressure is on Jeremiah to keep speaking without regard to how he feels.

A crisis of vocation

Jeremiah's is a crisis not of faith but of his vocation. It is echoed in the experience of many prophets and preachers who dare to voice a disturbing word. Bonhoeffer took this text in addressing his German congregations in England when he felt bound, like Jeremiah, to stand against the German church authorities who were supporting the Nazi party. But whether as preachers or hearers, Jeremiah's heartfelt, personal confessions give us all permission to direct sharp questions at God for laying on us vocations that set us unbearably in opposition to the popular mood; a vocation that must denounce the unserious optimistic, self-belief of our day that gives no space for a dissonant and demanding word from God.

Roger Spiller

Suggested hymns

Put thou thy trust in God; Filled with the Spirit's power; From the very depths of darkness; O God of earth and altar.

Sixth Sunday after Trinity (Proper 10)   11 July
Principal Service   **When People Get in Our Way**
(*Continuous*): 2 Sam. 6.1–5, 12b–19; Ps. 24; *or* (*Related*):
Amos 7.7–15; Ps. 85.8–end; Eph. 1.3–14; **Mark 6.14–29**

The beheading of John the Baptist is hardly a theme anyone would wish to choose as the subject of preaching. True, it's an intriguing tale, but the violence is too graphic and the event too tragic to read as good news. It's the only passage of any length in the Gospels that is not focused on Jesus. Of course there are parallels between John and Jesus, Herod and Pilate. Both John and Jesus suffer at the hands of vacillating political figures. Both are killed for speaking the truth. And John's death prepares for Jesus' coming trials, and those of the disciples. In the case of today's Gospel, Mark is fascinated by the relationship between the three main characters, excluding John himself, and it leads us to face some deep and disturbing features in ourselves.

Sibling rivalry

Herod, we're told, wanted to take Herodias, the wife of his own brother, as his second wife. It sometimes happens that a man finds himself more attracted to his brother's wife than his own. Herodias evidently felt the same way and wanted to ditch her own husband. But in comes the prophet John who condemns the union, not simply on strict legal grounds but because Herod is acting against his dispossessed brother. In part it's a story of sibling rivalry. They fight over the same crown, the same wife. Herod wants above all to triumph over his brother, even more than gain Herodias. You can tell that because the moment he has secured Herodias she loses all direct influence over her new husband. She can't secure the death of this turbulent prophet.

The new wife's hatred of John

Herodias feels denied and obliterated by the words of John. But Herod shields the prophet from her vengeance. John's in prison as much for his protection as for punishment for his audacity. But this only intensifies the woman's hatred. Intrigued and fascinated as she is with John, her mind is set on his destruction. She can think of nothing else. But she knows she can't persuade her new husband to grant her desire. Desire is only interested in that which gets in the way. John the Baptist is that obstacle. Herodias won't be put off. She can think of nothing other than John, but she must enlist her young daughter in a terrible plot to influence Herod

Like mother, like daughter

Herodias' daughter, known as Salome, is a young woman. Forget the idea of her as a professional seducer. She's been transformed into a second Herodias. Like daughter, like mother. Violence has been handed down a generation and grown in intensity. She has pleased Herod by her dancing and Herod makes an exorbitant offer – to give her anything that she wants. But Salome has no desire of her own. So she asks her mother what she should desire. Is she an innocent intermediary, carrying out her mother's terrible errands? No, she's been transformed. Her uncertainty disappears, she hurries back, feverish and impatient, worried that the king might go back on his promise. Her mother's desire has become her own. Her desire has become more intense even than her mother's.

Dance is the means of winning Herod to her violent intent. Dance expresses the freedom we dream of, ecstasy, joy. But it also heightens desire. It took possession of Herod and left him a mere puppet. And it puts all the guests under Salome's spell. The guests feel that they are satisfying their own desire. But they mistake the object of their desire because John's head feeds their appetite for violence. There is always an appetite for sacrifice, a scapegoat to destroy or a victim to behead.

The king never anticipated Salome's grim demand. Herod doesn't have the courage to say no to his guests. The guests comprise all the elite of Herod's court. At the supreme stage of crisis, only the crowd could intervene. But the crowd have become murderous. Violence has spread. And the desires of Herodias, Salome and now the crowd can only be assuaged by the destruction of the victim. When he was alive, John disturbed all their relationships and in his death he facilitates them, making them of one mind.

Hidden things brought to light

If Mark had simply wanted to remind us that following Jesus involves cost, sacrifice and even death, he wouldn't have needed to include this story. But we're not cast as victims of actions done to us because we're Christ's followers. We're cast as perpetrators of violence done to others. We are all, like Herodias, obsessed with some John the Baptist figure. Scapegoating, exclusion, imitation, corporate murder is never far away. The gospel works to bring hidden things to light, to help us name, acknowledge and displace the rivalries, jealousies and violence we may not name. The gospel speaks the truth and exposes our falsehood and that of the people who cast their spell over our lives and render us timid and intimidated. Discipleship concerns the inner life as well as the life we mirror to the public world.

Roger Spiller

Suggested hymns

The great forerunner of the morn; Walk with me, oh my Lord, through the darkest night; Teach me to dance to the beat of your heart; We shall go out with hope of resurrection.

Sixth Sunday after Trinity (Proper 10)   11 July
Second Service   **Boasting in Christ**
Ps. 66 [*or* 66.1–8]; Job 4.1; 5.6–end, *or* Ecclus. 4.11–end;
Rom. 15.14–29; *Gospel at Holy Communion*: Luke 10.25–37

Why is the word 'ambition' so often frowned upon within the life of the Church? If you are a Christian, do you have to settle for second best? Do you have to keep quiet? Do you have to downgrade your aspirations? Is it wrong to talk confidently about our faith with others? Is it wrong to be hopeful in Christ?

Perhaps we are scared of ambition because our definition is drawn from worldly perceptions of what this word means. When we hear the word 'ambition' we might call to mind aggressive and competitive behaviour or the selfish pursuit of wealth and power. These ideals run counter to what we think it means to be a Christian person. The word ambition is often used pejoratively.

Whether this perception is true or not, perhaps the Church should reflect on what it means to be ambitious and to be confident, not in ourselves but in Christ alone. What does holy ambition look like? Is it wrong to want the best for our church and give of our best? Is it wrong to want to live into our calling in Christ and even to boast about it? If we are confident in the reason for our ambition and if we are confident in the foundation of our hope, we may be more able to inhabit it as something holy and righteous and channel it, and use it, for the greater glory of God and for the building up of the kingdom.

Holy ambition

Henry Thoreau, the American poet, philosopher and essayist commented that if he was prone to boasting more than was becoming, his excuse was that he was bragging for humanity rather than himself. Perhaps we can frame our Christian ambition in that way, except that we are bragging (or, to use the biblical word, *boasting*) for Christ rather than for ourselves.

Of course, there are ways and means of bragging and boasting. Similarly, we find in St Paul's writings inspiration and justification for being confident in Christ and proclaiming the gospel boldly and without hesitation. Christ had died, and Christ had risen. If one could gain no confidence from this, then surely our faith is in vain.

Paul was not bragging for himself either, he was boasting in Christ and was not embarrassed or ashamed of that calling. Paul understood his own weaknesses and limitations very well, and he also knew and understood the weaknesses of the communities he was ministering to, but beyond those weaknesses and flaws and limitations, he saw the vast possibilities that were opened up by having complete confidence in the risen Christ.

A gospel to proclaim

Paul speaks only of those things that Christ has accomplished through him. He takes no glory for himself, for, in the words of Job, God 'does great things and unsearchable, marvellous things without number'. It is to God that glory belongs.

Paul's vocation is to be ambitious in Christ and to proclaim the good news, not where Christ has already been named but to those who have never heard. He believes his faith is worth sharing. His confidence and his ambition for the gospel propels him to be determined in his mission and confident in his calling.

If we are able to find our confidence in Christ we become apostles and teachers and preachers and missionaries in his name. We are able to preach boldly and proclaim loudly what the Lord has done for us. We are given the freedom to be ambitious in the name of Christ and share the wonders that the Lord has done.

If we are able to shape our ambitions and our hopes by the power of the cross and in the light and glory of the resurrection, then anything is possible and that is surely something to boast about?

Victoria Johnson

Suggested hymns

Go forth and tell; We have a gospel to proclaim; In Christ alone; When I survey the wondrous cross.

Seventh Sunday after Trinity (Proper 11)   18 July
Principal Service   **Restoring the Future**
(Continuous): 2 Sam. 7.1–14a; Ps. 89.20–37; *or (Related)*:
Jer. 23.1–6; Ps. 23; Eph. 2.11–end; **Mark 6.30–34, 53–end**

You may have seen the T-shirts that say 'Jesus is coming. Look busy'. They're available in all shapes and sizes online. You can even get the same message on coffee cups and fridge magnets. It's clearly struck a chord with a lot of people. And you could argue that today's Gospel reading reflects it. Certainly there's a great deal of bustle going on. The apostles of Jesus 'had no leisure even to eat'. Crowds of people, seeing where Jesus was going, 'hurried there on foot'. Later on, more people recognized Jesus, 'and rushed about that whole region', bringing the sick for him to heal

A restored church

The bustle is understandable. Jesus is a celebrity, an attractive figure; and people rush after him in search either of teaching or of healing, or of both. The Church has not always reflected that attractiveness; but then it hasn't always succeeded in keeping Jesus at the heart of all that it is and does: so often, other priorities, like institutional maintenance, get in the way. Today's reading suggests that if the Church is to be truly Christ-centred in every aspect of its life, it will have at least two vital attributes: it will be a compassionate church and it will be a healing church (6.56). But neither of these attributes will be of any value unless it first learns to be a *restored* church.

What does that mean? Well, notice that it's not just the crowd who are busy in today's reading. The disciples are too. They 'were

189

coming and going, and they had no leisure even to eat'. Many Christians, including clergy, will recognize that description. The crucial point here is that *this is not what Jesus wants*. He doesn't want his disciples to 'look busy', let alone to be busy all the time. He tells his disciples to 'come away to a deserted place all by yourselves and rest a while'. The Greek word translated 'rest' here (*anapauō*) occurs in only one other place in Mark's Gospel, in Gethsemane, when Jesus finds the disciples asleep and rebukes them: 'Are you still sleeping and *taking your rest?*' The moral is clear: the disciples were so busy for so much of the time that, when Jesus really needed them to keep him company, they fell asleep and failed him.

Sabbath time

At the heart of the biblical idea of rest is the Sabbath, the seventh day of the week. It's part of the DNA of Jewish life, now as then. The Hebrew word *Shabbat*, from which 'Sabbath' comes, simply means 'stop'. You don't keep Sabbath just because you've earned it, or because you're tired. You keep it because it's part of the God-given rhythm of creation. God knows, that's not easy: God knows, because even in today's reading, Jesus' plan for the disciples to 'rest a while' was thwarted by sheer human need. A church that practises compassion and healing will find that its work is never finished. But that's precisely why all of us need to find, and help each other to find, a right balance between rest and busyness. Christians should try to keep one day out of every seven as a Sabbath day – not a 'day off' but a 'day on'. Begin it the evening before, perhaps with a family meal or a treat. Make sure the Sabbath itself is characterized by play – that is, activities or experiences that are designed purely for their own sake, not in order to achieve something or get something done. And there's an even more important point.

Restoring the future

The Sabbath is not just about rest: it's about *restoration*. We tend to use that word in connection with the restoration of buildings, or works of art. That kind of restoration is usually about restoring the past. But Jesus wasn't interested in restoring the past. He wanted to restore people's future – to give a new future to those who must have felt they had nothing to look forward to at all. His ministry of compassion and healing was all about restoring their future. No wonder the crowds came after him. Now as then, so often people judge one another on the basis of their past: where they come from, what they look like, and so on. Jesus didn't seem to be much interested in that. He wanted to know where they were going, or rather where they could go if they could believe they were loved and valued. You don't have to settle for fishing for fish, he told the disciples: you could fish for people. He hated the restrictions, the diseases, the stereotypes, that stopped people from becoming the unique individuals they were created to be. He wants us to continue that work today.

But we can't: unless we first accept our own need for forgiveness and healing, and even before that our own need for restoration. A frenetic church, an overworked priest, a group of people who look busy, is good news for no one. A community of Christians who have the energy and vision to engage in Jesus' ministry of compassion and healing can still change our world. But that work doesn't begin with looking busy, or even with being busy. It begins by recognizing our own need for stillness, our own need to be restored in body, mind and spirit – our need for Sabbath time. Jesus has a new future in mind for every human, indeed every creature. Including you and me.

Gordon Mursell

Suggested hymns

Be still, my soul: the Lord is on your side; Dear Lord and Father of mankind; Sweet is the work, my God, my King; O God, you search me and you know me.

Seventh Sunday after Trinity (Proper 11)   18 July
Second Service   **Shaking the Foundations**
Ps. 73 [*or* 73.21–end]; Job 13.13—14.6, *or* Ecclus. 18.1–14; **Heb. 2.5–end**; *Gospel at Holy Communion*: Luke 10.38–end

You are probably wearing on your wrist a watch that either has a quartz movement or a mechanical movement. If it's a quartz-based watch then you can trace its history back to 1969 when the first quartz watch, called the Astron, was made by the Japanese company Seiko. Go a little further back to 1957 and we come across an American watch called the Hamilton 500, the first ever battery-powered retail wristwatch. Go back about 130 years to 1812 and you discover the very earliest wrist watch created by Breguet for Napoleon's sister Caroline Murat, the Queen of Naples. Travel back further to the late seventeenth century and you will discover a man called Thomas Tompion from Northill in Bedfordshire, known as the Father of English Clock-making, who made intricate and wonderfully engineered clocks. Further back still, in the fourteenth century, Abbot Wallingford of St Albans created a remarkable astrological clock (there is a replica in St Albans Abbey), and if we travel back further still as we search for the origins of time-keeping, we should come across, somewhere in the world, a person who stuck a stick upright in the ground and followed the shadow the stick made. It is said that the earliest sundial dates from about 1500 BC and is to be found in Egypt.

So there we have the history of time-keeping in just a few sentences.

A history of ideas

Now, that has been a relatively easy history to write. It centres on an everyday object, but suppose instead of giving consideration to the history of an object, we switched our attention to the history of ideas. That is a much more complex and elusive process. But ideas do have origins, and in some cases we can trace their history reasonably accurately. Think of Plato and Aristotle, for example, and you can see how ideas had certain beginnings and then were developed over succeeding centuries.

In today's Epistle we can see exactly the same process at work. The author, a Jewish Christian believer, is writing to some fellow Jews who are perhaps wavering in their Christian faith, and trying to persuade them of the absolute importance of Jesus. So, how can he do this?

He decides to use an idea with which his readers will be entirely familiar: the high priest in the Temple. Jesus, he says, is the high priest, the one who makes expiation for sin. Now, the idea of the high priest in the Jewish religion can be traced back for centuries before Jesus. The classic account is given in the book of Leviticus, where, in chapter 16, the role of the high priest is spelled out in some detail (it is likely that this particular chapter was written in the late 570s BC, but no doubt the idea of the centrality of the high priest goes even further back).

But what was the function of the high priest in Leviticus? It was to be the one who stood before God on the Day of Atonement (Yom

Kippur) and via a series of carefully delineated sacrifices purified himself and then interceded with God so that Israel's sins should not be held against them. As part of the holy ritual two goats were taken. One was sacrificed and its blood was smeared on the cover over the Ark. The other goat was placed in front of the high priest. He laid his hands on its head and confessed over it all the sins of Israel. And then the goat, the scapegoat, was driven away into the wilderness, led by a specially chosen man who eventually pushed it over a rocky precipice where it fell to its death. The whole process of ritual sacrifice was to ensure that, for the moment, the great gap between the holiness of God and the wickedness of humankind was done away with.

A new archetype?

So, taking this archetypal idea, the author of the Epistle develops it in a new and radical way. Instead of one of the Levites – they were the traditional caste of priests from whom the high priest was elected – the author says that Jesus is the new high priest. He is the one who atones for the sins of the world not by sacrificing bulls and goats, nor by selecting a scapegoat, but he selects himself to be the sacrifice offered to God.

One can imagine how shocking such an idea would be to the first readers of the Epistle. They were being asked to believe that a man who was not a Levite, a man who had been crucified, was somehow a high priest. It was an idea that would have shaken the pre-conceptions of their minds like an earthquake.

But the author pushed the idea even further. Jesus, he says, was a man who experienced death not only in himself but on behalf of all humankind. As high priest he stands before God as the representative of humanity, embodying us all in himself; through his sacrifice he bridges the gap between the holiness and purity of God and the wickedness and sin of human beings.

The claim is huge. It verges on the outrageous, but it needed an idea as stunning as this for the author to get his first readers to understand who Jesus was and what he achieved.

The question is one we need to ponder deeply. If those first Jewish Christians needed such an idea to shake them into new modes of thinking, what might our ideas of Jesus be that need similar upheaval?

Christopher Herbert

The King of love my shepherd is; In Christ there is no east or west; There's a wideness in God's mercy; With joy we meditate the grace.

Eighth Sunday after Trinity (Proper 12)   25 July
(For James the Apostle, see p. 331.)
Principal Service   **Feed the Hungry**
(*Continuous*): 2 Sam. 11.1–15; Ps. 14; *or* (*Related*): 2 Kings 4.42–end; Ps. 145.10–19; Eph. 3.14–end; **John 6.1–21**

Jesus climbs up a mountain and sits down with his disciples. That's the signal for Jesus to start teaching, and the large crowd coming towards him expect it. That must be gratifying for any preacher. But Jesus is not seduced by popularity. The acclaim that can make us self-satisfied can also disable us from seeing the immediate needs of those we meet. The crowd of people who wind their way up the side of the mountain appear fit enough to make the journey. But Jesus perceives their physical need and concludes that it must be met. The only question is how: 'Where are we to buy bread for these people to eat?' The writer inserts a note forestalling any suggestion that Jesus was out of his depth and uncertain as to how to respond. Jesus was testing his disciple Philip, says the writer. All the same, it's entirely characteristic of Jesus to pose awkward questions and to enlist others in working with him to alleviate human need. And here, facing the crowd, there is a great gulf between demand and supply. A twofold problem: access to the markets – 'Where are we to buy bread …?' – and then cost – 'Six months' wages would not buy enough bread for each of them to get a little.' But why did Jesus see this as his problem and not the responsibility of the crowd? And isn't our priority with the bread of life, rather than with the bread that perishes?

Jesus is at one with Moses and his Old Testament forebears, that basic subsistence needs must be met. That's why we find there's a big emphasis upon food, feeding and table celebrations in the Bible. It's why Christianity is 'the most materialistic religion', as William Temple put it. It's why, today, the churches are leading in running food banks. Set against the resources, the need is inexhaustible. And the offering of five loaves and two fish seemed pitiable. Like the disciples, we can be paralysed by the scale of human need. But surprising things can happen when we launch out boldly with the fragments that we have.

Hunger, a theological problem

Those who are hungry are enslaved to a cycle of deprivation that affects their health, education, life chances, career prospects, longevity, and also, ultimately, their capacity for personal fulfilment. The preoccupation with finding food to feed a family absorbs the time that might otherwise be available for the kind of reflection that enables people to embrace life in all its fullness. There's a hierarchy of need, argues Maslow, that means that lower levels of need – food, drink, shelter – have to be met before we have the capacity to embrace higher levels. Put more plainly, 'You can't hear the gospel on an empty stomach.' But perhaps we can go further and suggest that feeding the hungry is intrinsic to the gospel? Being fed, even with perishable food, is the necessary sign and symbol for discovering a more permanent and personal feeding. The experience of hunger can erode trust in the faithfulness and credibility of God. As Gandhi said, 'To those without food, bread is the only form in which God dares to appear.' The unmet condition of hunger, then, turns out to be a theological issue. God's goodness and faithfulness, his very reality, is put in doubt in the minds of many who battle daily with the curse of hunger and impoverishment. Feeding the hungry, then, is the necessary precondition that opens the way for discovering the gospel. And we ourselves are enlisted to work with God so that through us God's promise to 'fill the hungry with good things' can be realized.

Hunger for the Bread of Life

The feeding, then, is the overture to a drama that it will take the following four Sundays to unfold, and we mustn't anticipate its conclusion. But a freestanding note in our gospel is a clue to where John is going to take us. John tells us that the Passover was near, and we know that the Christian Passover was the Eucharist, and then we spot the eucharistic language of breaking, blessing and distributing. So, a story of the feeding of the multitude becomes the vehicle for bringing us John's account of the Eucharist. Jesus gives bread to the hungry, but he gives something even better; he gives the bread of life. But even more than that, he is himself the Bread of Life. The bread is transposed, but it is not discarded, replaced. Even the fragments of bread left over are garnered and hallowed. And so, still today, the Eucharist is like a bread queue, a line of people who are prepared publicly to declare their hunger for the Bread of Life. The wonder is that through the sign and material of bread our lives are filled with Christ's divine life and we are nourished with his body. How this occurs and what it means will be unfolded in the following Sundays.

Roger Spiller

Suggested hymns

Jesu, thou joy of living hearts; Bread of heaven, on thee we feed; Jesus the Lord said, I am the bread; O food to pilgrims given.

Eighth Sunday after Trinity (Proper 12)   25 July
Second Service   **Job's Search for Vindication**
Ps. 74 [*or* 74.11–16]; **Job 19.1–27a**, *or* Ecclus. 38.24–end; Heb. 8; *Gospel at Holy Communion*: Luke 11.1–13

I once visited a woman who was terminally ill. But death held no terror for her because she had a strong Christian faith and she had had a consoling out-of-body experience. She told me that she had decided to offer her body for medical research. Being a meticulous sort of person and not wishing to burden her only daughter with complicated arrangements after her death, she wrote to the Birmingham Medical School to enquire what would happen were she to die on a bank holiday. She read out the reply: 'Dear Madam, Thank you for your enquiry. You will be pleased to know that we do remain open on bank holidays for the collection of bodies. When you die you have only to phone us and we will arrange the collection of your body.'

We may well admire, and envy, her clear-sighted confidence in the face of death. But what of those who have faced the torment of deprivation and false accusations in their lives and the prospect of dying without any hope of redress? That was the prospect that faced each of the Israelites throughout most of their history. Any hope of an afterlife was at best a shadowy, indeterminate state with no prospect of a continued personal existence.

Job's plight

If there is one figure who embodied the cruellest suffering, deprivation and injustice imaginable, it was the figure of Job. We needn't linger on whether Job was a historical person or a literary creation. There have been many Job-like figures, whose sufferings and injustices have gone unresolved, and Job is the supreme and sharpest embodiment of them all. We too can try to enter his world through the book that has been branded the greatest literary achievement in the world.

Suffering and sin

We know that in a wager with the devil God permitted the devil to deprive Job of everything – child, wife, home, cattle, livelihood, health, reputation. That imaginary negotiation was designed to establish whether Job's righteousness was genuine or merely self-serving. The underlying view of suffering that prevailed was that suffering was retribution for sin. So if you suffered, the ineluctable conclusion must be that you had sinned. That pernicious view is echoed in the complaints of some who suffer: 'Why am I made to suffer?' 'What have I done to deserve this?' And it's the view taken by a trio of Job's so-called friends, and then by a brash young man who thinks he knows all the answers. They will not be diverted from the rigid logic of the prevailing view that suffering results from sin. They show what happens when we stick rigidly to abstract dogmas and disregard the actual human condition before our eyes. Job persists in claiming that he is righteous, but his friends insist that he is deceived, and they go to ludicrous and ingenious lengths to insist that Job sinned whether he recognized it or not.

Living with false accusations

No suffering, arguably, is more unbearable than false accusation leading to the loss of reputation, public shame and social exclusion. We have witnessed decent public figures in our country facing interminable years seeking justice while their lives are plighted, kept on hold, as a result of false accusations.

Our reading from the book of Job is a defiant, abrasive diatribe that lambasts all who cold shoulder and shame him. Even God himself is not spared. 'He has put me in the wrong and closed a net around me.' But then, suddenly, when Job has reached rock bottom and has spewed out all that is on his heart, a new and inconceivable note is struck. It's perhaps the newest and most unexpected in the whole of the Hebrew Bible. It's a phrase we know and love, brought to audiences worldwide in the soprano solo in Handel's oratorio *The Messiah*: 'I know that my Redeemer lives.'

The hope of vindication

A ray of light enters the gloom, but this isn't the dawn. This isn't resurrection as we know it. The logic of his faith in God, which has persisted throughout his sufferings, convinces him that the Vindicator will arise to establish Job's innocence. He hopes and believes that he will be present in person so that he will be able to see God with his own eyes. Job does indeed see God, though not in the way he might have expected. When he stands before God he realizes that all attempts to explain the problem of suffering are futile. Job is suffering not merely to vindicate himself but also to vindicate God's trust in him. Seeing God, he knows there must be a solution; that is enough. The hardest part of suffering need not be the sense that God has deserted us. In prosperity Job thought he knew God, but he realizes that that was nothing compared with what he has discovered through his experience of suffering.

The story of Job is well on the way to being a preparation for belief in the resurrection. The fact of innocent suffering, and the triumph of injustice, seems logically to require that God raises the dead.[27] But, as Job shows, that hope comes not merely from logic but from the experience of God. It was just such a deep experience of God that enabled my dying parishioner to take delight in the crude letter from the medical school and to face the future with hope.

Roger Spiller

Suggested hymns

My God, I love thee; Have faith in God, my heart; Within our darkest night; Through the night of doubt and sorrow.

Ninth Sunday after Trinity (Proper 13)   1 August
Principal Service   **With God it's Always Bread Week**
(*Continuous*): 2 Sam. 11.26—12.13a; Ps. 51.1–13; *or* (*Related*):
Ex. 16.2–4, 9–15; Ps. 78.23–29; Eph. 4.1–16; **John 6.24–35**

Bread is an age-old staple. Its aroma speaks of homecoming, belonging, of sustenance and warmth. There is nothing quite like breaking
open a loaf of freshly baked bread – crusty on the outside, soft and
warm on the inside. Filling and comforting. No wonder bread week
on *Bake Off* is always a favourite.

Bread week

Trevor Dennis tells a wonderful story about a man who dies
and goes to heaven. He wanders the streets looking for God and
eventually finds a house with music and people spilling out into
the streets. He notices that all the people have white handprints on
their backs. He enters the house and discovers God. She is baking
bread, her hands floury. She embraces each person, hence the floury
handprints on their backs. With God it's always bread week.

Our Gospel reading takes place the day after Jesus has fed around
five thousand people with just five barley loaves and a couple of
fish. Imagine. A huge crowd are given all they need to satisfy their
hunger. They're stuffed. No wonder they seek him out again the
next day. Jesus understands the motive exactly. They are interested
in a free lunch, but rather less focused on what the sign of the feeding might mean. Their focus is rather more material, not unlike
their ancestors in the wilderness.

Just over two weeks after the Israelites had been freed from captivity, we see them in distress. They are hungry and their material
need overwhelms them. They moan and complain. 'At least there
was bread in Egypt. We are going to starve out here in the middle of
nowhere.' If I'm honest, I can hear my voice among them. Perhaps
we like to think we'd have trusted in God on the basis of all the signs
we'd witnessed – the plagues, the Passover and the Red Sea parting.
The truth is that humans are pretty forgetful. How many of us have
experienced God's loving kindness in multiple ways, but forget all
that when the chips are down? They needn't have worried. God
provides their fill of bread each morning in the form of the manna
they find on the ground. This becomes a story handed down, a story
to remind the hearer of God's loving kindness. Notice how Psalm

78 stresses God's abundant provision. The grain of heaven is rained upon them. They ate and were well filled – just like those whom Jesus fed. With God it's always bread week.

'You are my bread'

But Jesus takes the image of bread and does something remarkable with it. He applies it to himself. 'I am the bread of life.' Interesting that he was born in Bethlehem, which literally means 'the house of bread'. He is urging his hearers to see him not simply as a source of a free lunch, but to read what the sign says about him; they need to look beyond full stomachs; 'work for the food that endures for eternal life'. 'What is this work?' they ask. Jesus tells them – it is belief. 'Believe in him whom he has sent.' This belief is more than passive assent. Belief is active work. Belief says, 'You are my bread. You are my homecoming, my belonging, my sustenance and my warmth. You are my fill and my comfort. You are all these things for the world. With you it is always bread week.'

This belief is not a one-off. It is active and continuous work. So easily we forget. So easily we are seduced by that which is not bread. We come again and again to the Eucharist, to see bread taken, blessed, broken and given. To hear again, 'This is my body broken for you.' To remember again that Jesus, the bread of life, gave himself to restore us to the embrace of God. We come to open our hands and receive again. This eucharistic rite that takes place in the church is repeated again and again each day. We come in prayer with empty hands, needing the provision of God's bread. In tight spots we cry out, aware that we need God's resourcing. God is always ready to press into our hands exactly what we need. So today we are invited to renew our trust in God. We are invited to tell him of our hunger and need. To whisper our deepest longings for homecoming and belonging, comfort and warmth, and to talk to God about our worries and concerns for those around us. We can be confident that when we seek God's bread we will be satisfied. With God it is always bread week.

Kate Bruce

Suggested hymns

I am the Bread of Life; Guide me, O thou great Redeemer; The Lord's my shepherd; Faithful One.

Ninth Sunday after Trinity (Proper 13)   1 August
Second Service   **Wisdom**
Ps. 88 [*or* 88.1–10]; **Job 28**, *or* Ecclus. 42.15–end;
Heb. 11.17–31; *Gospel at Holy Communion*: Luke 12.13–21

The Little Book of Wisdom is the title of an expanding set of little books garnering the memorable words of such people as the Dalai Lama, Kahlil Gibran, C. S. Lewis, Pope Francis, Jesus and A. A. Milne. A bite-sized word of wisdom is considered just about as much as people can cope with in our high-pressured culture. For those who, in a world drowning in information, ask with T. S. Eliot, 'Where is the wisdom we have lost in knowledge?', such books offer the appeal of easy consolation.

The search for wisdom

It's perhaps wiser to doubt that you possess wisdom than to attempt to dispense your own wisdom between the covers of a book, even a small one. Where is wisdom to be found? That's the subject of an exquisite hymn to wisdom that breaks up the text and mundane defences mounted by Job in the book of his name. 'Seek wisdom and pursue it,' someone said. After all, wisdom is an entity, something one can obtain, possess, like gold or silver. Well, our poet puts that invitation to the test. He imagines a mine for precious metals, hidden, in darkness, with a miner opening a shaft letting in light as the intrepid miner sways on ropes connected to the ceiling. After a poetic odyssey, the writer has drawn a blank. He can only ask, 'But where shall wisdom be found?' Suggested sources of wisdom are contemplated and then dismissed. Mortals can't find it; nature's sources don't possess it; it cannot be exchanged for precious jewels or metals; it is, quite simply, beyond price.

The failure to find wisdom

So our poet repeats his question: 'Where does wisdom come from?' The riposte is that it's hidden from the eyes of all living; even the birds, with powerful receptors that give acuity of sight, cannot see wisdom. The most that can be said is that the spokesperson for Death admitted hearing a rumour about it.

Now then, when human ingenuity and searching is exhausted, we are ready to hear where wisdom comes from. 'God', we're told, 'understands the way to it and he knows its place.' In much of the wisdom literature, wisdom is a gift of nature. If prophets showed that God was seeking people, the wisdom teachers argued that it was humankind that was seeking God. The genre of writing that appears in several books of the Old Testament and in some of the Apocryphal writings offered human instruction not divine commands; not proclamation but discourse between humans. For the most part, wisdom was a discourse between humans, a sharing in the accumulated insights gathered from the practical experience of negotiating a way through the business of living. Wisdom was prudence in managing relationships and handling the vicissitudes of the human condition: adversity, uncertainty and helplessness. Wisdom was rooted in the existential, in the here and now, not in a future or a past. It discarded an abstract and comprehensive understanding of the whole of life, settling instead for a practical, domestic way of submitting to nature, and trusting, if at all, in an omniscient creator.

Wisdom and God

But now, in identifying where wisdom may be found, Job gives testimony to the all-powerful, all-knowing God. And he brings his glorious hymn to a close with the refrain, 'Truly the fear of the Lord, that is wisdom; and to depart from evil is understanding.' Although the wise teachers expressed themselves in a secular, humanistic manner, they never thought that wisdom could function independently of their faith in God. They were simply unaware of any reality that was not controlled by God.

The search for wisdom within the constricted sight of secular humanism is bound to lead to disappointment. If we're urged to seek wisdom, it is so that we realize the foolishness of an unaided human quest which refuses to reckon with the overwhelming, breathtaking wonders of the natural order; and the foolishness of refusing to accept the reality of a mind greater than our own human minds.

Job shows that wisdom is intimately bound up with God; something that God alone knows, sees, searches out and declares. Human beings can't search it out and know it. We may know and possess so much knowledge, learning and ingenuity. But wisdom is where our truest well-being is to be found, and in which our deepest aspirations are met. As St Paul says: 'Has not God made foolish the wisdom of the world? For since, in the wisdom of God, the world did not know God ... Christ the power of God and the wisdom of God'. And, 'He is the source of your life in Christ Jesus, who became for us wisdom from God.'

Roger Spiller

Suggested hymns

The works of the Lord are created in wisdom; Oh, the life of the world is a joy and a treasure; O Lord of every shining constellation; O Lord my God, when I in awesome wonder.

Tenth Sunday after Trinity (Proper 14)   8 August
Principal Service   The Bread of Life
(*Continuous*): 2 Sam. 18.5–9, 15, 31–33; Ps. 130; *or* (*Related*):
1 Kings 19.4–8; Ps. 34.1–8; Eph. 4.25—5.2; **John 6.35, 41–51**

Bread church

A few years ago a Methodist minister, Barbara Glasson, was appointed to inner-city Liverpool. She felt dwarfed by the huge buildings, intimidated by the task. Her thoughts turned to yeast – something tiny can make a huge difference. And the idea formed in her mind that she would rent some rooms, get an oven and gather a few friends together to make bread. They made a huge mound of loaves and gave them away. People who received a deliciously free, freshly baked loaf asked why. And some of them joined in. A small community evolved. While the bread was rising, people raised questions about important issues in their lives. People would read from the Bible, pray for one another. They became companions, which means, literally, *cum panis*: with bread. Some of those who were given free bread and were drawn into the group were homeless, and their lives were turned round.[28]

Bread as a sign to the world

Barbara said:

Making bread has taught us so much – the process of baking mirrors so much in life; the pummelling and proving is about how we engage with one another, the waiting for the dough to rise is about how we give each other time. Churches are a bit obsessed with numbers and outcomes. But the bread makes us wait ... it needs to rest, to rise. In the waiting time the smell of the bread triggers memories and facilitates story so that people quite naturally talk to each other. And every loaf we make is different. Bread is a sign to the world.

And now there are bread churches springing up all over the place. It's not good news for churchgoers who like to keep their religion in their head, but it's making an impact where churches have lost their freshness and warmth.

If you've seen the film or read the book *Chocolat*, you'll get the idea. In that case a chocolate shop was set up close to a church, a church that had grown harsh and judgemental. But the chocolat cafe was open, inclusive, welcoming, lifegiving, celebratory. And the viewer was left asking which of the two is the real church.

Back to bread. It's the staple diet, the essential food for life, and it's clear why Jesus spoke of himself as the 'bread of life'. We can see, too, why making bread, living with bread, being a bread church, can teach us so much not merely about bread but about Jesus himself. We eat bread, symbolizing the way that Jesus feeds, fills and nourishes us. And although John doesn't have an account of the Last Supper, his feeding of the multitude had unmistakable eucharistic overtones.

The body of Christ

But St John goes further: 'Whoever eats of this bread will live for ever, and the bread that I will give for the life of the world is my flesh.' So most Christian churches have agreed that this isn't merely a symbol, but a sacrament, and a sacrament is something that effects what it signifies. A kiss is a sign and symbol that expresses love, but it's more than that: it not only expresses love, it generates it. A flag symbolized nationhood, but it's more than that: it inspires and produces patriotism, a love of country. Words in the Book of Common Prayer catch the meaning of the sacrament, when we pray 'that this bread and this wine may become for us the body and blood of our Lord Jesus Christ'.

Christ's living presence

Christ is really and truly present with us in this Eucharist, in the form of bread and wine. He is, of course, present, alive and loose in the world, but here he is pledged to meet us, in this sacrament. He meets us not only in the bread and wine but in the whole enacted drama of this service. The bread and wine become for us the body and blood of our Lord Jesus Christ. It is so, objectively, whether we feel it or not, whether or not we're in a right relationship with God. But as the Gospels remind us, we need to be 'in love and charity with our neighbours' if the sacrament is not to become a judgement on us rather than a gift of grace. The meaning of the Eucharist has been the locus of disagreement and division, but we should at least take John's words seriously and receive the body and blood of Christ in a state of expectancy and preparedness. And, as former Archbishop Michael Ramsey said, 'It's not what we make of the eucharist that matters, but what the eucharist is making of us.'

The invitation to Christ's love feast

And then we come to Christ's love feast. It's like an altar call, or a bread queue, a line of people who are prepared publicly to express their need of God. By presenting ourselves with empty hands we are acknowledging our complicity in the death of Jesus. We're saying that Jesus died for me. And then we who have fed on Christ's body are to allow him to shape us all into his Body the Church. As St Augustine memorably expressed it in an Easter Day sermon:

> You are the Body of Christ. In you and through you the work of the incarnation must go forward. You are to be taken. You are to be blessed, broken and distributed, that you may be the means of grace and the vehicles of eternal love.

Bread churches may be a good thing but, if Jesus is the living bread, all our churches can become sources of Christ's fresh and living bread that satisfy our deepest hunger.

Roger Spiller

Suggested hymns

The trumpets sound, the angels sing, the feast is ready to begin; Author of life divine; Just as I am, without one plea; God is here! As we his people.

Tenth Sunday after Trinity (Proper 14)   8 August
Second Service   **The Big Picture**
Ps. 91 [*or* 91.1–12]; **Job 39.1—40.4**, *or* Ecclus. 43.13–end;
Heb. 12.1–17; *Gospel at Holy Communion*: Luke 12.32–40

Our readings today remind us that we are not the centre of the universe. We are encouraged to recognize that there is far more going on in the kingdom of God than we are aware of, and it doesn't all revolve around us. We need to look up and out in order to see the big picture, reconcile ourselves to our place within it, and learn to trust in God's providential care for all.

Walking with Job

The story of Job is one of the oldest parts of our Scriptures. Job has endured all sorts of things – sickness, bereavement, loss and disaster. In earlier chapters, Job shouts at God demanding to know why so many terrible things have happened to him and asking God the age-old question, 'Why?' Job's friends walk alongside him but struggle to give helpful answers. Towards the end of the book, in chapters 38 and 39, God responds to Job with a surprising reply. God puts Job in his place – with a 'Who do you think you are?' response. God asks, 'Where were you when I laid the foundation of the earth? ... Have you commanded the morning since your days began?', and in today's chapter questions Job's knowledge of wildlife. God asks if Job understands the mountain goats, and the wild ass and ox, the ostrich, the horse and the hawk. Does he understand the life cycles of different animals, their habitats and feeding habits? God reminds Job of his place in creation alongside all whom God has made and provides for. Creation is rich and diverse; much of it we cannot grasp, but God is involved with it all and so it is to be trusted even when things don't go the way we want, when seemingly bad things happen or when God seems absent. God is perhaps suggesting that Job needs 'to get over himself', its not all about him! God's plans are much greater than we can possibly imagine. Job recognizes that he is very small and realizes he is in no position to argue with the Creator of the cosmos. He submits to God's sovereignty. Recent television programmes about the beauty of our planet, together with the deep concern about climate change and our stewarding of creation, remind us that we need to remember our place within the ecology of our world and not imagine that we are the centre of everything that happens. Looking around us and connecting with the wonder of the created order helps us to reverence, value and protect God's handiwork.

Running the race

The passage from Hebrews takes us beyond the visible creation to remind us that we are part of eternity, surrounded by a great cloud of witnesses – those who have gone before us in the faith. The writer to the Hebrews encourages the early Christians, who are undergoing persecution, to keep going. The analogy of a race is used. The saints cheer on those who run the Christian race. My daughter has recently run her first half marathon – and we are the least sporty family imaginable, so this is some achievement. After crossing the finishing line, she spoke with considerable emotion about the hundreds of people who turned out to watch, lined the route and cheered on the runners. They kept her going – especially from three-quarters of the way in when she was really tired and wondered if she'd make it. God's followers throughout time and eternity are cheering us on, and we are encouraged in our Christian pilgrimage not to give up. When we are weary or lose heart, we are to look to Jesus who is both the pioneer and perfecter of our faith. It's through Jesus that we come into a living relationship with God and it's through Jesus too that our faith is made perfect and complete. It's not through anything we achieve ourselves, but through what God has done in Jesus on the cross. Again, we are encouraged to see the big picture – its not all about us! We run the race of faith along with many others, and always it is Jesus that we look to. As with Job, we are to trust in God's providential care and not rely on our own all-too-human resources. We are God's children, suggests the writer to the Hebrews, and as with any good parenting sometimes boundaries need to be set and discipline administered in order to keep us safe and help us grow to maturity.

Taking stock

Do you know your place in the universe? Do you look with wonder and awe at all God has made and commit to protect it? In what ways can you walk lightly on the earth, acknowledging your connectedness to the created order? Do you trust that God works in all things for good, and that nothing is beyond God's transforming power in Jesus? And where are you in the Christian race? Can you imagine that great cloud of witnesses cheering you on? Remember, when all gets tough and you really want to give up, look to Jesus, who endured humiliation and death for us all. See beyond yourself, reach out for help, receive the grace that is offered and believe that God welcomes you at the finishing line, bringing your faith to perfection in Jesus.

Catherine Williams

Suggested hymns

For the beauty of the earth; Fight the good fight; How great thou art; Indescribable.

Eleventh Sunday after Trinity (Proper 15)
15 August
(For Blessed Virgin Mary, see p. 335.)
Principal Service **Living for Ever**
(*Continuous*): 1 Kings 2.10–12; 3.3–14; Ps. 111; *or* (*Related*):
Prov. 9.1–6; Ps. 34.9–14; Eph. 5.15–20; **John 6.51–58**

In a few minutes' time we shall be sharing in Holy Communion. And what we've just heard Jesus saying about this act may be heartening to you – or it may be alarming. 'I am the living bread that came down from heaven. Whoever eats of this bread will *live for ever*.'

Now, do you want to live for ever? Can you even conceive of time that goes on for ever?

Surely time is inexorable: the persistent, measurable chronology that fascinated Isaac Newton. Your computer or the atomic clock can tell you exactly what time and what day it will be a thousand years hence.

But at the same time our everyday *experience* doesn't really tally with this scientific accuracy; so that, even though the clock ticks with precise regularity, we can speak of time 'rushing by' or of time 'dragging'.

How can this be? We are born in time and formed by time, and, especially if we are working or commuting, we may be ruled by timetables. Yet that time seems infinitely elastic. If you're waiting for a bus, or sitting an exam, the last thing you'd want is for it to go on for ever. Yet if you're reunited with somebody you deeply love, or if you're experiencing a sunset of amazing beauty, what you want is for it never to cease. And it seems we can't achieve that: the sunset will fade, the lover will depart, and the world of the timetable will resume its control.

Words for 'time'

But really, I'm talking about two very different sorts of time. And since the New Testament was written in Greek it uses two quite different words, which confusingly we translate with the single English word 'time'. The first word is *chronos*, from which we get 'chronology' and 'chronometer': the time of the clock and the timetable, which can be precisely measured – and which, to be fair, is very helpful in managing our life and work. But the second Greek word is *kairos*, and *kairos* cannot be measured: it is a moment, an event, an intensity, perhaps even a glimpse of eternity, a time within time that goes beyond time.

Such a time, a *kairos*, was the event that leads in the Gospel to Jesus speaking those words about living for ever – that is, the feeding of five thousand on the hillside. Such was the time when around the table he spoke the words to his friends, 'This is my body'. Such was the time he rose from death.

Theoretically you could date all those moments and locate them in *chronos*. But that would miss the whole point. And when Jesus talks of *living for ever*, what he's describing isn't immortality, nor an everlasting wait at the bus stop. It's living *in time* with a new quality, a new intensity of life, living in the presence of God. In this Gospel of St John it's called '*eternal life*'.

Eternity is often imagined as a state of timelessness and disembodiment – which is why it's so hard to imagine, since all our experience is within time and within the body. But as Jesus presents and lives eternal life it doesn't mean leaving the world. His language about it is insistently *physical*. 'Whoever eats this bread will live for ever; and the bread that I will give for the life of the world is my flesh.'

Flesh – bread – eating – drinking – dying. This Gospel, and our religion and our worship, are insistently physical too: Christianity, 'the most materialistic of all great religions', as Archbishop Temple said many years ago. And that matters because our living of *eternal* life is celebrated and practised *in time* – with our neighbours, with our money, with the work of our hands.

Living wisely

'Be careful how you live, not as unwise people but as wise, making the most of the time,' says the writer to the Ephesians (which we heard in our first reading). 'Time' there is *kairos,* so 'making the most of the time' doesn't mean constantly watching the clock or trying to cram each day with activity. No, it's *a quality of living*, the quality of eternal life, which is also the practice of true *wisdom*.

'Live not as unwise people but as wise, making the most of the time.' Perhaps William Blake was thinking of that same verse when he wrote, 'The hours of folly are measured by the clock, but of wisdom no clock can measure.' In our thanking and eating and drinking here, we're being called into a more boldly loving, a riskier and wiser way of life, so intense that it can be called 'eternal'. 'Whoever eats of this bread will live for ever.'

Christopher Burdon

Suggested hymns

Light of the minds that know him; Thee we adore, O hidden Saviour, thee; Come, living God, when least expected; There's a spirit in the air.

Eleventh Sunday after Trinity (Proper 15)
15 August
Second Service   **The Fear of God**
Ps. [92] 100; **Ex. 2.23—3.10**; Heb. 13.1–15; *Gospel at Holy Communion*: Luke 12.49–56

Sometimes, only music will do. Recall the menace created by the music from the film *Jaws.* The opening bars say it all: the drumming, the muted French Horns, those double basses sawing away, the sudden clashing sounds of the trumpets ... and that terrible, insistent, underlying beat – it sends shivers down one's spine. Perhaps a little less menacing, except for young children, is the music that introduces *Dr Who.* Again, it's probably the underlying, opening beat that conveys a sense of drama and menace, followed by that screaming, electronic noise an octave or so higher.

From a classical music perspective, if you want to think of fear, think of Elgar's *Dream of Gerontius*. It does not convey menace, but it carries a powerful sense of the holiness of God and the terrifying moment of divine judgement. Let me just read part of the poem written by St John Henry Newman, which formed the basis of 'Gerontius'; it is the Angel of the Agony who speaks:

> Jesu! by that shuddering dread which fell on Thee;
> Jesu! by that cold dismay which sickened Thee;
> Jesu! by that pang of heart which thrilled in Thee;
> Jesu! by that mount of sins which crippled Thee;
> Jesu! by that sense of guilt which stifled Thee;
> Jesu! by that innocence which girdled Thee;
> Jesu! by that sanctity which reigned in Thee;
> Jesu! by that Godhead which was one with Thee;
> Jesu! spare these souls which are so dear to Thee;
> Souls, who in prison, calm and patient, wait for Thee;
> Hasten, Lord, their hour, and bid them come to Thee,
> To that glorious Home, where they shall ever gaze on Thee.

St John Henry Newman's poem, written in 1865, attempts to convey the fear and hope that embrace Gerontius as he lies on his deathbed contemplating the judgement of God that lies ahead. Surrounded by angels, whom Newman describes so winsomely as 'least and most childlike of the sons of God', and screamed at by demons creating a horrible dissonance, Gerontius awaits that moment of bliss as he encounters God himself. The angel tells him that the sight of God, 'that sight of the Most Fair, will gladden thee, but it will pierce thee too'.

The encounter at the burning bush

Turn from thinking about the terrors and joys of Gerontius – eventually, he is caught up in the rapture of the hymn, 'Praise to the holiest in the height' – and think of Moses who was encountered by God in the epiphany of the burning bush. He is told to take off his shoes because the ground on which he is standing is holy; God announces who he is, the God of Abraham, Isaac and Jacob, and at that point the storyteller says that Moses hid his face, for he was afraid to look at God.

Now ask yourself a question: when did you last feel a frisson of fear in relation to God?

Somehow, as a generation, we have lost our sense of awe. It's rarely encountered in our churches. Why? Are we afraid of awe? Is the possibility too overwhelming? Is our God too small?

In the secular world, perhaps the only place where awe is felt is among space scientists as they contemplate the scale and immensity of the universe. But awe in religion seems to be no longer part of our experience.

Why this might be the case I leave to you to ponder, but if we have no fear of God, does this mean that we are also losing our sense of holiness? Is our faith too anaemic, too gentle, too caught up in the self-regarding, narcissistic culture of our age, so that the sheer otherness of God, his majesty and beauty, are beyond our capacity to imagine?

The contrast between us and God

But when we consider our own weaknesses, our own sin-filled-ness, our own selfishness, our greed and pettiness, and then hold those against the purity and holiness of the Almighty, should there not be just a glimmer of existential terror?

St John Henry Newman's poem was, of course, a product of his time. A time when the Church was going through agonies about its own origins, asking questions about tradition and authenticity, struggling to come to terms with huge societal changes. It is the kind of poem that could be written in the mid-Victorian era by a man struggling with his own theological torments, but it simply could not be written now; our sense of irony, our scepticism, our cynicism are perhaps too strong. But what if Newman's poem, what if Moses' epiphany, point us to a dimension of our faith that we need to contemplate? Is there any harm in doing so?

Christopher Herbert

Suggested hymns

Praise to the holiest in the height; Angel voices ever singing; Judge eternal, throned in splendour; Just as I am, without one plea.

Twelfth Sunday after Trinity (Proper 16)

22 August

Principal Service   **'Those who eat my flesh ...'**
(*Continuous*): 1 Kings 8.[1, 6, 10–11] 22–30, 41–43; Ps. 84; *or*
(*Related*): Josh. 24.1–2a, 14–18; Ps. 34.15–end; Eph. 6.10–20;
John 6.56–69

'This is my body, this is my blood.' What more majestic words are there than these? For millions of people worldwide, in many cultures and diverse conditions, these words heard week by week, at the administration of Holy Communion, bring comfort, healing, elation and renewal. This is the drama of the Christian Church, and we are enlisted and drawn in as participants. The suffering and death of Jesus is re-enacted before our eyes. This is a multisensory experience that touches people more deeply than they can express. It was noticed that the great composer Olivier Messiaen walked into church in Paris looking rather ruffled and forlorn. When he emerged from Mass, he looked different, focused, more alive. I think we all feel changed after sharing in the drama of the Eucharist and encountering God at some level of our being.

Believing and feeding

John doesn't use those awesome words, 'This is my body', but he assumes them in a discrete section in a long discourse on bread.[29] He had been telling us that eternal life comes from believing in Jesus. Now he says that new life comes also through feeding on his flesh and blood. Word and sacrament go hand in hand; understanding and experience together. It's arguable, then, that we don't need subtle theological explanations about the Eucharist. We don't go to the theatre to learn about a play; we go to experience it, and the experience of the play, like the Eucharist, defies all attempts to put it into words. The 'word made flesh' cannot be turned back into words. But reading the play and studying it does enhance our capacity to appreciate it when we see the performance. So, too, with the Eucharist. It does make a very big difference to us whether we regard the communion as symbolic or as sacramental; whether we believe that Jesus is represented by the symbolism of bread and wine or whether he is specially and really present in some way, in the bread and wine.

213

'Eat my flesh'

'This is my body' has been the focus of disagreement and division, creating a fault line between the great communions and church traditions across the world. A rite of unity has become the source of division. The subject of the Eucharist is so sensitive that preachers are reluctant to step into the minefield. But John has opened that door to us this morning and we must walk through it and see where it takes us.

It's more than surprising; it's really shocking that John speaks of 'eating' Christ's 'flesh' and 'drinking his cup'. To eat someone's flesh in the Bible signifies hostile action. To drink blood was regarded as horrendous and forbidden by God's law. And for non-Jews, too, John opened himself up to the frequent charge of cannibalism. He used the realistic word 'flesh' rather than the word 'body'. Scholars believe those were the words in Aramaic that Jesus himself used. They reproduce the words of the other Gospel, 'Take, eat; this is my body ... drink ... this is my blood'. Jesus, who became 'flesh', gives the same flesh to us and the living bread. The language seems to many to rule out a spiritual meaning. There is a realism, here, that echoes the Passover meal where the flesh of the sacrifice was literally eaten and the blood daubed on the doorposts as a means of deliverance.

Sharing in God's own life

John spells out the result of sharing in the Eucharist. 'Whoever eats me will *live* because of me', and, 'Those who eat my flesh and drink my blood *abide* in me.' Our regular participation in the Eucharist brings us closer to Jesus, as many will attest from their own experience. But it's far more. Communion with Jesus is the means by which we ourselves share in the intimate communion that exists between the Father and Son. In the communion Jesus gives us a share in God's own life. And we also enjoy eternal life already because we have the life of God within us.

That should heighten the sense of drama, awe and anticipation as we come to receive the broken bread and wine. We're not expecting to restructure our theology. What we are given in Scripture is too rich, too sprawling, too paradoxical for that. It would impair the communion were we all to reach conclusive agreement as to its meaning or to attempt to pin down what we think God is up to in the Eucharist. But we are all expected to be stretched. God's ways are always more not less surprising than we think, and he has demonstrated in the incarnation that he is able to transfigure the ordinary, fleshly material of his creation into his likeness.

We're not always what we believe, but we are what we eat. And can there be any more direct and intimate way of sharing God's life than through the sacrament of his broken body?

Roger Spiller

Suggested hymns

Body broken for our good; Here, O my Lord, I see thee face to face; Lord, enthroned in heavenly splendour; All for Jesus, all for Jesus.

Twelfth Sunday after Trinity (Proper 16)
22 August
Second Service   **Moses and Aaron: The Plan is Set in Motion**
Ps. 116 [*or* 116.10–end]; **Ex. 4.27—5.1**; Heb. 13.16–21; *Gospel at Holy Communion*: Luke 13.10–17

A bridge in the conversation

These few verses are a bridge between two significant dialogues. On one side the dialogue between God and Moses at the burning bush, and, beyond, the dialogue that Moses and Aaron will attempt to have with Pharaoh. Our reading today is the bridge that makes it all sound so possible. The elders of Israel brought together by Moses and Aaron for the demonstration of signs and wonders are impressed. They believe. They worship.

Our reading ends with a refrain that will sing through the rest of the narrative – 'Let my people go.' It is not a request or a plea. It is a revelation of the character and nature of God – the God who desires freedom and liberation for God's people. We know the story isn't going to be that easy. The verses that follow straight on from our reading will reveal Pharaoh's contempt. 'Who is this God who demands I release slaves? Never heard of him.'

Moses will rage at God. But God will continue to work through those who didn't even want to be called.

Moses didn't want to return to Egypt. Nothing would have taken him back there. Even when God speaks to him from the radiance of the burning bush Moses finds every reason not to go until he finally cries, 'Please send someone else!'

God is setting in motion the great defining story of deliverance and abundant life, but first God must contend with a reluctant prophet. In that dialogue they begin to get to know each other. The man who is afraid that he just isn't up to the job; and the God who will not take no for an answer. In the end God says, 'Fine, you can take your brother Aaron with you.'

Wilderness of our fear

God gets to work straight away on that. For our reading begins with God sending Aaron to meet his brother in a wilderness both physical and emotional. This wilderness is also the cause of Moses' low self-esteem, fear, reluctance and bewilderment at his calling.

This is our first introduction to Aaron. He was Moses' brother, older by three years. Events meant that their upbringing was very different. Aaron the son of a Levite slave, Moses the adopted son of an Egyptian princess. Yet Moses is the one lacking in confidence. Which is why God, with infinite understanding and kindness, sends Aaron to Moses, not the other way around. Aaron comes to find Moses, as though God said to Aaron, 'Your brother needs you. He's in a bit of a state. I've got a task for him and he doesn't think he's up to it. Have a brotherly word with him, will you? Listen and believe in him.' A vital role in the discernment process. Aaron goes to find Moses in that wilderness place. He listens to his brother's outpouring – all the words God has told him, all the signs with which he has charged him. Aaron rises to the occasion before the whole assembly of the Israelites, and later he will do the same before Pharaoh.

We know how Pharaoh will respond. But it doesn't change the rightness of Moses' calling or what Aaron did to enable Moses to receive it. Aaron doesn't, as far as we know, say to Moses, 'What utter rubbish! No one will listen.' Instead he believes in God's calling to Moses when Moses cannot yet believe it for himself. Aaron does what is needed. 'I'll come with you. I'll be there. I'll speak on your behalf.' Then, when the time is right, Aaron steps aside for Moses to lead the way.

A sign of solidarity

We cannot read today's verses in isolation. They are part of a greater narrative that is ongoing: God's deep involvement in the lives of individuals to transform and to involve us in bringing about the justice and righteousness that God created us to thrive within. Jesus will call it the kingdom. A kingdom that is as far from the Pharaohs of this world as it is possible to be. When God sends Aaron to his brother it is into a wilderness of Moses' low self-esteem, fear, lack of confidence and self-belief. Yet in that wilderness Moses will unfold to Aaron the great plan of God's deliverance that is to begin with them. Aaron is the sign that Moses needs – the sign of companionship and solidarity; the brother who will make it possible for Moses to take his place.

It may be that God will send an Aaron to us. Or it may be that we are called to be an Aaron for someone else.

God needs the Aarons of this world as much as Moses.

Carey Saleh

Suggested hymns

Be thou my vision; Guide me, O thou great Redeemer; Join the song of praise and protest; Jesus Christ is waiting.

Thirteenth Sunday after Trinity (Proper 17)
29 August
Principal Service   Living Inside Out
(*Continuous*): S. of Sol. 2.8–13; Ps. 45.1–2, 6–9 [*or* 1–7]; *or* (*Related*): Deut. 4.1–2, 6–9; Ps. 15; James 1.17–end; **Mark 7.1–8, 14–15, 21–23**

'The service is straightforward, as set out in the service booklet,' they told me when I first went to an unfamiliar church to lead a service during a vacancy. But they didn't tell me that the choir sits at the back, that the banns are read before the intercessions, that the priest isn't involved in taking communion to sick people in the pews, that notices come before the blessing, that coffee is served in the hall and that everybody remains in the pews, including the minister, while the organist plays the closing voluntary. Yes, apart from that, it was all 'straightforward'. Nobody I spoke to imagined it was or could be done differently elsewhere.

Traditions

Families, clubs, churches and all human groupings have their traditions – little rules and rituals that are expected to be observed by those who belong. Once when I was a cathedral curate sharing the leading of worship, my senior colleague asked me to give the notices. Later when the dean got to hear about it, we were ticked off. We had inadvertently infringed a tradition: giving the notices was, apparently, the preserve of the most senior cleric present. But it was fine for me to read the Gospel, pray or preach! There's much to be said for tradition, as long as it serves the values of the gospel.

Cleanliness instead of godliness

'Wash your hands before you come to the table,' shouts Mum to her children. Yes, washing is also one of those practices that is shaped by tradition. And in our Gospel the Pharisees and some scribes, we're told, made the journey all the way from Jerusalem to the north in order to investigate the personal hygiene of the disciples. They noticed that at least 'some' of Jesus' disciples were eating without first washing their hands. Washing hands is a sensible thing to do, but Jesus saw that they were consumed by what could be seen, by a ludicrous scrupulousness for its own sake, while they were neglecting to attend to their interior life.

In the musical *Fiddler on the Roof*, Tevye, a bumbling patriarch and farmer, insists on being a matchmaker for his three daughters, against their will, and he relents. But when his youngest daughter marries a non-Jew, that's a bridge too far. Tevye is lost to his daughter. When she and her husband take refuge in America and visit her father, he is still anguished and turns his back on his daughter. There is to be no blessing, no reconciliation. Tevye is a good man but one for whom tradition is more important than the command of God to love and forgive.

Traditions to challenge

We think of hymns as traditional, but in the eighteenth century they were sending clergy to prison for daring to introduce hymns. Pews and organs can be contentious and time-consuming issues, and were largely introduced by the Victorians. And, if you're a church that has handwashing for the priest before the distribution of communion, and it gets overlooked, is the reaction allowed to undermine the impact of the Eucharist itself?

Traditions can ensnare the human spirit, they can place a moratorium on the life of the Church that means we're not free to adapt, change and explore new ways of being church that can address an unchurched generation. They can give us false comfort and satisfaction in our own convictions and conduct and can distract us from the really fundamental issues that cry out to be addressed at this time.

Inside out

Jesus directs us inwards, to examine our hearts and motives. The life he expects of us is lived from the inside out. Led by the Spirit, we can find freedom from the burden of overweening and redundant traditions. We will respect the sensibilities of others and the distinctive traditions that secure order and identity in our churches. And we will, of course, be scrupulous, in handwashing. But we will not be captive to the norms, traditions and expectations of others where they transgress the values of the kingdom and the impulses of the Spirit.

Roger Spiller

Suggested hymns

Lord, you are the light of life to me; Speak, O Lord, as we come to you; The heavens prepare God's glory; Lord of all power, I give you my will.

Thirteenth Sunday after Trinity (Proper 17)
29 August
Second Service **Blessed Reconciliation**
Ps. 119.1–16 [*or* 119.9–16]; Ex. 12.21–27; **Matt. 4.23—5.20**

Reconciliation might sound attractive but it's not universally liked. If warring peoples or individuals have suffered great hurts at each others' hands, their anger may be such that revenge on each other, not peace with each other, is what they want.

And reconciliation isn't just for times and places of war and hatred. It's also the Roman Catholic, or Anglo-Catholic, rite of making a personal confession to a priest. That's the Reconciliation of a Penitent with God.

It's also something that people who work with numbers or texts can do. When they see things that don't fit together when they think they should, they try and work it out so that they do fit together. That can be about making the accounts add up; or it can be about making apparently contradictory texts add up.

Reconciliation makes relationships right

Jesus says in the Beatitudes, early in the Matthaean Sermon on the Mount, 'Blessed are the peacemakers, for they will be called children of God.' Jesus paints the work of peacemaking as the work of God's family. Making peace with others is what helps us live together as God's family, to respect each other as children of God, our siblings in the heavenly family. Making peace may not mean that people who have fallen out now become best buddies and soulmates; it means getting the relationship right. We are called to relate to different people in different ways, to ensure peaceably that we relate rightly to one another. That a parent looks after a young child appropriate to their age and development; that a son or daughter cares for an elderly parent according to their needs. That we respect and appreciate people who have taught or given us things, and we seek to be generous in turn in passing such gifts on to others. That we rightly cleave to our spouses or partners; but that where a relationship is unhealthy we breathe distance and safety into it.

Let's explore the Beatitudes in this light. We could read them as right attitudes towards different kinds of people: holding in awe the poor in spirit; looking out for those who mourn; noticing the meek; admiring those who hunger and thirst for righteousness; reflecting on the mercy we see in the merciful; respecting those who are pure in heart; not disdaining the persecuted but wondering why they are persecuted.

Who's in this crowd anyway? Those who have sought Jesus out for healing, those who want to learn from him, huge crowds from 'Galilee, the Decapolis, Jerusalem, Judea, and from beyond the Jordan'. Jesus wants his disciples, gathered around him, to relate rightly to all of these: to live up to the fact of Jesus calling them the light and salt of the world.

A tall order

This is what we are called to do if we are the light and salt of the world, if we are in the family of God. Right relationships with each other – that's surely an integral step to being in right relationship with God, right? But it's a minefield. How on earth can we hope to get every single relationship right every single moment of our lives?

Our hearts perhaps sink further when we hear Jesus next declaring: 'For I tell you, unless your righteousness exceeds that of the scribes and Pharisees, you will never enter the kingdom of heaven.' He has just honoured every single element of the Law, the Torah, which he inherited. We have to be even more righteous than the most righteous person we can think of, if we want to get to heaven! A few verses on from tonight's reading, Jesus takes this argument to its most complete conclusion: 'Be perfect, therefore, as your heavenly Father is perfect.'

This perhaps gives us a clue. Jesus knows full well that all this is beyond us, really. We can do our best – but, let's be honest, we will get at least some things wrong. We will simply not manage to live perfectly right relationships with each other and God (and indeed ourselves). Where's the reconciliation now?

Christ's reconciliation

Jesus says, 'Do not think that I have come to abolish the law or the prophets; I have not come to abolish but to fulfil.' Jesus is claiming to make our reconciliation work possible. Not by our own power, but by his. By his fulfilling them, he honours the past – his ancestors, and the covenants God has previously made with his people.

So he reconciles the old and the new: the Old Testament and the new covenant. In a sense, he actually *becomes* the Passover sacrifice of our first reading. The law and the prophets are upheld. They can be perfectly fulfilled only by Jesus, who is sinless, who alone perfects reconciliation – reconciliation with each other, reconciliation with God, and the reconciliation of texts and promises old and new.

Here is our reconciliation – in Christ. We are called to be the agents of Christ's reconciliation – the salt and light to help true reconciliation spread to the world.

Megan I. J. Daffern

Suggested hymns

Put peace into each other's hands; Blessed are the pure in heart; Blessed those whose hearts are gentle; Jesus Christ is waiting.

Fourteenth Sunday after Trinity (Proper 18)
5 September
Principal Service **'Be Opened!'**
(*Continuous*): Prov. 22.1–2, 8–9, 22–23; Ps. 125; *or* (*Related*): Isa. 35.4–7a; Ps. 146; James 2.1–10 [11–13] 14–17;
Mark 7.24–end

Jesus touched a deaf man's ears and his disabled tongue and said 'Ephphatha', 'Be opened'. And the man heard again and spoke clearly. 'He has done everything well,' say the people.

Well, *everything*? In the story Mark tells immediately beforehand, Jesus seems to be guilty of racial discrimination. He avoids healing a woman's daughter because she doesn't belong to the children of Israel: he even refers to her and other foreigners by the highly offensive term 'the dogs'. It's only when the mother cleverly hits back that he relents of his discrimination.

The difficulty of not judging

This is puzzling, coming from the teacher who had said 'Do not judge': a teaching that proves pretty hard to observe, even for him, it seems. And when you think about it, is it really possible to go through life *without* judging? Some of those judgements will be thoughtful and considered, working out what is right and true. But many of our judgements are immediate and instinctive discrimination, based on appearances.

Admit it. Just passing somebody in the street, don't you assess them by the way they talk or the clothes they wear? Such instant judgement or discrimination is hardly a new problem; nor, sadly, is it one to which the Church is immune.

Listen again to what James, their pastor or prophet, writes to some early Christian communities:

If a person with gold rings and in fine clothes comes into your assembly, and if a poor person in dirty clothes also comes in,

222

and if you take notice of the one wearing the fine clothes and say 'Have a seat here, please', while to the one who is poor you say 'Stand there' or 'Sit at my feet', have you not made distinctions among yourselves and become judges with evil thoughts?

Like much of St James' short letter, that hits home hard and sounds very modern. For, the same cultivating of the rich and deference to the powerful goes on today, the same celebration of wealth and so-called 'celebrity', the same thoughtless discrimination against people who are poor or scruffy or ill-spoken.

Wherever you go in human history and culture and religion, it seems that discrimination is endemic. Discrimination between rich and poor, between respectable people and the rest, between faithful and heretics, outsiders and insiders, us and them. And this discrimination provides a crude kind of security, for we know who to look up to and who to look down on.

Down with the walls!

The letter of James, indeed the whole Christian gospel and this sacred meal where we all share one table and the same food, they present a radical *dismantling* of that hierarchy that human cultures have internalized. We keep erecting walls so that we know our place and 'they' do too. But then come prophets and Gospels and sacraments to knock them down.

Jesus himself, it seems, discovered one familiar wall knocked down by a woman's witty reply after he'd called her people 'dogs'. The same division between clean and unclean, insider and outsider, was overthrown for St Peter by a vision, and for St Paul by the appearance of the Jesus he was persecuting. The chequered history of the Church, and our own knowledge of its life, show that we *still* need the knocks of experience or the sharp words of people like St James to jolt us out of our lazy judging.

A sharp letter

Starting last week, and continuing for the next three, that pungent little letter of James, sent to some early Jewish Christian communities, is being read Sunday by Sunday here and across the western churches. You may want to spend some time this week reading the whole letter through and sensing how it can speak to us today.

That may not be a comfortable experience. As the letter goes on, it becomes a kind of tirade against the rich and a celebration of the poor, whom he calls 'rich in faith'. But faith, believing – is that all, is it enough? As James so clearly says, 'faith without works is dead'.

For there is no faith, no baptism or creed or religious status, that dispenses us from the practical love of our neighbour. And our neighbour may be the man in fine clothes or she may be the despised outsider, the Samaritan.

In other words, *nobody* is an outsider. Perhaps Jesus' command, 'Be opened', isn't addressed just to one deaf man but to all the human world. *Be opened* to greet the poor, the foreigner, the misfit. And then together we can say, 'He has done everything well.'

Christopher Burdon

Suggested hymns

When I needed a neighbour; There's a wideness in God's mercy; City of God, how broad and far; In Christ there is no east or west.

Fourteenth Sunday after Trinity (Proper 18)
5 September
Second Service   **Looking Back and Looking Forward**
Ps. 119.41–56 [*or* 119.49–56]; **Ex. 14.5–end**; Matt. 6.1–18

Sometimes it is good to look back. For anyone who has ever reflected on their vocation, or their journey of faith, looking back into our own personal histories helps us discern the presence of God in our lives. We might, with the gift of time and hindsight, see patterns which indicate to us that God was at work, even in the midst of challenge and danger. When we look back, we come to recognize that God is working his purpose out within us, and through us and around us.

It is also good for communities to reflect on their history. Where have they come from? How have they got here? What is their story? The book of Exodus recounts an important moment in the history of the people of Israel.

The people had been released from the service of Pharaoh and took flight. But before they had even gone a day's journey, Pharaoh had changed his mind and set about to pursue the Israelites with his horses and chariots in order to recapture them.

It says very clearly that, as Pharaoh drew near, the Israelites looked back. What might they have felt as they looked back to see their captors behind them? Were they destined to be slaves for ever? What might they have felt when they looked forward to see an uncertain future in the wilderness? Were they going to die hungry and homeless? Whichever way they turned, they were in trouble. Fear was on every side. To whom could they turn for help?

Rescue and redemption

Moses offers the people of Israel comfort and hope. He encourages them to have faith in the Lord their God. He says to them, 'Do not be afraid.' He tells them to 'be still' and let the Lord accomplish that which he purposed. Moses lifts up his staff and stretches out his hand over the sea, and from the chaos and the fear a path is forged in the mighty waters, and the Israelites pass through. Their rearguard is a pillar of cloud and light that protects them and guides them, and they are delivered from the dominion of darkness into a place of light, hope and freedom.

If we take a step back and look at this remarkable story, we might come to see that it is a story of rescue and redemption. This is a story where God's purposes are made known through challenge and calamity. When hope seems almost lost, God does something incredible and new. This is a story about perspective, and about the past, the present and the future.

This is the story told in our churches on Easter Eve, the night when we remember that Christ rose again from the dead and became the source of rescue and redemption for the whole of humanity. This is our story too.

Our light and our hope

Underneath the Paschal candle, in a darkened church, the deacon sings, 'This is the night when once you led our forebears, Israel's children, from slavery in Egypt and made them pass dry-shod through the Red Sea.' This story is part of our history. This story is our song and part of our looking back and looking forward, alive to what God can do with us and for us, and what God has done and will do for all who put their trust in him.

This story reminds us that in Christ we are set free and released into a promised land, and whatever darkness we face, and whatever uncertainties we have, we need not be afraid. This is a story that pre-empts the rescue and redemption that Christ offers us through the cross, through whose power all people are set free into a new life and a new future.

This is the story that is told over the waters of baptism as we remember that Christ stood over the deep waters of death and opened for us the way of salvation.

In all of our uncertainties, in moments of confusion and chaos and utter darkness, Christ says to us, 'Do not be afraid.' We are encouraged to lift up our eyes and turn to him. We look back to stories such as this and remember what God has done, and this should give us confidence in what God can still do, yesterday, today and for ever.

Victoria Johnson

Suggested hymns

Guide me O, thou great Redeemer; Do not be afraid; Through the night of doubt and sorrow; The God of Abraham praise.

Fifteenth Sunday after Trinity (Proper 19)
12 September
Principal Service   **Declaring Your Identity**
(*Continuous*): Prov. 1.20–33; Ps. 19 [*or* 19.1–6], *or Canticle*:
Wisd. 7.26—8.1; *or* (*Related*): Isa. 50.4–9a; Ps. 116.1–8;
James 3.1–12; **Mark 8.27–end**

Today's gospel story is the turning point in Mark's Gospel. It's the turning point in the earthly ministry of Jesus and soon he will face his passion and death. Jesus and the disciples are on the border between pagan and Jewish territory known today as the Golan Heights. The border is the place for identity checks. And that is what Jesus is doing. He's giving an identity check to his followers: 'Who do you say that I am?'

What we say of others reveals ourselves

If I were to ask you, in today's parlance, 'What do you think of David Attenborough?', to select a not-quite-random example, I could learn a lot about you. I could discover whether or not you loved the natural world, maybe your favourite animal or species, where you stood on climate change, and perhaps also your lifestyle choices affecting the planet, shopping, flying, travel choices and food consumption. Questions of identity tell us more about the respondent than about the subject about whom they are talking. We learnt more about Peter's hopes and expectations than we did about Jesus when he answered Jesus' question.

The titles and words we use to address God in private prayers, in leading intercessions in church or in talking about our faith with others, similarly tells us a lot about ourselves and about how Jesus features in our lives. Words, as the writer of James, reminds us, are the signals that can reveal our true identity. And didn't Jesus say, 'Out of the abundance of the heart the mouth speaks'? Often it's only through being cornered and asked exactly what we think of this or that person, or, most significantly, of Jesus Christ, that we get to nail our colours to the mast and can listen to ourselves voicing the convictions that we may well not have fully recognized before. As E. M. Forster said, 'How can I know what I think until I see what I say?'

Coming face to face with a former poet laureate at a poetry reading a few years ago, I broke the ice by saying I found that her poetry had been *transformative* for me. She was surprised, and muttered the words 'transformative, ah', a few times. This led me to want to withdraw my remark for a much more modest assessment.

Confessions that reveal our faith

The New Testament writers show that natural, spontaneous confessions of faith can decide our identity. It may only be the title ascribed to Jesus, 'My Lord and My God', 'Master-Rabbouni'. Or, 'When he cried "Abba! Father!" it is that very Spirit bearing witness with our spirit that we are children of God.' Or this: 'No one can say "Jesus is Lord" except by the Holy Spirit.' There are identity-giving words which are revealed that simply cannot make their journey on to our lips and into the ether without being borne by the Spirit. So Paul can say 'one confesses with the mouth and so is saved'.

Jesus certainly warned those who said 'Lord, Lord' but did not heed his words. But there are confessions that are so daring in their implications, so intimate in their origin, that they can only come from God.

When words dry up

When I was interviewing a man offering himself for public ministry in the Church, I asked him what he would say if I happened to lead the worship in his church and were to invite him to come out to the front and share a few words about what Jesus meant to him. Immediately he became uncomfortable. He said he would feel inadequate. 'I don't have words to say.' He said he could talk easily about other things: his church activities, how things are for him. He wouldn't be comfortable talking about Jesus. Did he need an anointing of the Spirit, so that he could be released to speak about his faith? Or did he have the experience locked inside him but lacked the language, the vocabulary and the confidence to share it?

If we are tongue-tied in sharing our faith, our identity, don't despair. It's not a judgement on us. It's an invitation to seek a new freedom in the Spirit. The Church is the community that provides the opportunity to practise speech, to share and interpret our stories, and to rehearse and give voice to our confessions of faith. And we know that Jesus Christ will always far exceed our human efforts to communicate him. But even our faltering attempts to speak can be demonstrations of the Spirit's power to save.

Roger Spiller

Suggested hymns

Thanks to God whose word was spoken; Lord, speak to me, that I may speak; Go forth and tell, O Church awake!; Tell out, my soul, the greatness of the Lord.

Fifteenth Sunday after Trinity (Proper 19)
12 September
Second Service   **The Management of Love**
Ps. 119.73–88 [*or* 119.73–80]; **Ex. 18.13–26**; Matt. 7.1–14

In a course on adult education we were taken aback when the lecturer handed round a copy of today's Old Testament set reading. In it a father-in-law gives advice to his son-in-law so that he doesn't burn himself out and become unable to support his wife. The father-in-law is named Jethro and we don't need any information about his son-in-law. It's Moses. The lecturer told them that

Jethro gives a litany of reasons why an overworked Moses could delegate much of his work and spread the load to others.

We may be just as surprised to be confronted by this text as the students on the course, thinking that it belongs with management, not the gospel.

Planned withdrawal

Moses is being asked to adjudicate in disputes between people, and the demands on him are interminable, stretching from morning till night. He is the one who is trusted and sought out by the people, and feels he has no choice but to keep faith with the people. It's a flattering but deceptive approach, one by which many in leadership positions are seduced. We congratulate ourselves that we're being sacrificial, but Jethro warned that it's not good. An American pastoral theologian wrote, 'Busyness is a symptom of betrayal, not commitment, like adultery.' 'We're busy', he argues, because 'we're either vain or lazy'.[30] That may be harsh but it's noticeable how Jesus knew when to accept pressure and when to walk away from it. Even God is known more for his absence than for his presence, and by the sense of his absence we learn how much his presence matters to us. Being always available, we can paradoxically be less truly available when people need us most.

Empowering others

It's not good, also, because it creates a dangerous overdependence and disempowers others. Why won't other people share the load? It's usually because we're unwilling to teach, train and share vital information. Information is power, and it serves those who are naturally controlling to keep information to themselves. Jethro advises Moses to teach others the 'instructions of God', so that many more people would be able to resolve the disputes for themselves.

Jethro has concern for the welfare of his son-in-law and God has concern for our welfare and proper flourishing. He wants us to be an animating and capacious presence among the people with whom we live and move. As it happens, the role models in my formative years have been exceptional people with indefatigable energy and a capacity to fill every waking hour with purpose, and who have the capacity to excite and energize others. Nathan Soderblom, once Archbishop of Uppsala, told his clergy: 'Work yourself to death, but do it slowly.'

Moses is advised by his father to reconfigure his role. He is the resource and teacher of others who will act on his behalf, and that will release him to be priestly to his people, to represent his people before God and to be their intercessor. If we don't keep time with God, as Michael Ramsey said, we don't have anything useful to say when we are with people.

Discernment

It's all very well, we say, to reduce our workload, while ensuring a proper oversight that maintains what we call 'quality control'. Jethro proposes a tiered accountability structure. Most important decisions can be left to Moses and his senior colleagues, and lesser decisions apportioned to others. Are we doing what we are gifted, called and intended to do? Or are we captive to the endless, trivial round of inconsequential decisions, while the strategic and far-reaching decisions get shelved? Brother Lawrence commended the idea of 'planned neglect'; areas of work and decisions that would intentionally not receive attention but would nevertheless be announced and planned for so as to avoid guilt and confusion.

Another Ramsey, Ian, was Bishop of Durham after a brilliant career in mathematics and philosophy. He was a warm person who would excite us in expounding his distinctive approach to issues of faith and life, illustrating often with equations and diagrams. Few doubted that he would become Archbishop of Canterbury. He was called on for many and varied tasks, including writing a guidebook to the north of England. When in a university mission one of the speakers had to withdraw, Ramsey stepped in at short notice, as well as enthralling us in his own lecture. Ramsey died suddenly while poring over his papers for a meeting at the BBC. Ian Ramsey was felt to lack one thing: the capacity to distinguish between the important and the secondary. And so his premature and hugely lamented death deprived the Church of his formidable personal and intellectual gifts.

Jethro recognizes that we will need discernment, above all things, if we are to differentiate what is important and deserves our attention from what is secondary and can be left to others or left in a state of 'planned neglect'.

The way we manage ourselves and others has to be shaped by God's care and love for us all. After all, Christ has set us free, shouldered our burdens, cast away our fears and imparted his abundant life, and that must be the reality and the embodied message of all who follow him.

Roger Spiller

Suggested hymns

All-creating heavenly Giver; By gracious powers so wonderfully sheltered; With joy we meditate the grace; For the healing of the nations.

Sixteenth Sunday after Trinity (Proper 20)
19 September
Principal Service   **A Little Child**
(*Continuous*): Prov. 31.10–end; Ps. 1; *or* (*Related*):
Wisd. 1.16—2.1, 12–22, *or* Jer. 11.18–20; Ps. 54;
James 3.13—4.3, 7–8a; **Mark 9.30–37**

A little child. What kind of example is that to those fumbling disciples, or to us?

What can a little child show us of *achievements* in life? Or of power? Or of wisdom?

Conventional role models might be great statesmen, or great artists, or indeed great parents or great friends. But a little child? Here, once again in St Mark's troubling story, is Jesus' crazy reversal of the world's values.

Jesus lived in an age of empire. The venerable Greek and Roman styles of democracy were long gone, as was the Jewish people's independence. The Emperor's face and title were seen on every coin, his soldiers on the streets. Below him, authority belonged to strong male rulers in province or in household. Women and slaves counted for little, children for nothing.

Who is first in such a world? Below the Emperor himself, the masters of society are those who gain his ear, and those who inherit wealth, and those who craft their way to citizenship or business success.

Which, alarmingly, is not *so* different from who comes first in our own day. Aren't we all tossed around in this heap of power relations?

First and last

More awkwardly still, Jesus says to those first-century disciples arguing about who's the greatest, as to us twenty-first century disciples concerned for our own flourishing: 'Whoever wants to be first must be last of all and slave of all.'

These are not just words. This is the way Jesus will tread in the flesh; the way of child-like, slave-like powerlessness. Hasn't he just said, for the second time in this Gospel, that he is to be betrayed and killed? But his disciples miss the point entirely with their concern for greatness – just as they had in the story from Mark we heard last Sunday, when Peter objected to Jesus' talk of suffering, and just as they will when he speaks of it a third time and two of them ask for the top places in his kingdom.

Power or wisdom?

No, Jesus' words are utterly serious, and they will be fulfilled in Jerusalem in utter, painful seriousness. Which means that his way is *not* a religion of power, and therefore that our God is not a god of power. Rather, as we hear so often in the Bible, a God of wisdom.

And this wisdom God invites us to share is that of a child. 'Show by your good life that your works are done with gentleness born of wisdom,' says St James in our second reading. This is divine wisdom, 'wisdom from above', he goes on. It is 'first pure, then peaceable, gentle, willing to yield, full of mercy and good fruits, without a trace of partiality or hypocrisy'. Hardly the usual criteria for power in the world.

That short letter of James was written to a very early Jewish Christian community, who must have been unsettled by its pungent, practical wisdom.

As may *we* be, hearing it read Sunday by Sunday this month. For what James celebrates, with his talk of the wisdom from above, is the opposite – yes, of the values inculcated by the Roman Empire – but the opposite too of many of the values inculcated by *our own* economic system: by its advertising, by our own valuing of power and celebrity, even by much of our education.

What *is* the wisdom of the world? Fulfilling yourself? Perfecting your CV? Exercising power and influence? Gaining wealth? Yes, but by the *alternative* wisdom of James and of Jesus these all count for nothing; indeed, for less than nothing.

Two unglittering images

This wisdom from above is not an easy way, glittering with images of success. Instead, we have before us just *two images*.

One is a little child, held by the Messiah in the midst of his group of slow learners. The second image is that Messiah condemned and crucified. And in a way the two images are the same: 'Whoever welcomes one such child in my name welcomes me, and whoever welcomes me welcomes not me but the one who sent me.'

Notice, in neither image is there any trace of a crown or a throne, or a smart suit, or an investment portfolio. Rather, 'Whoever would be first must be last of all and slave of all.' Think this week: in our world of power relations, how can I hear these words? And how can I live them?

Christopher Burdon

Suggested hymns

It is a thing most wonderful; I come with joy, a child of God; Beauty for brokenness; The kingdom of God is justice and peace.

Sixteenth Sunday after Trinity (Proper 20)
19 September
Second Service   **Jesus the Storm-bringer**
Ps. 119.137–152 [*or* 119.137–144]; Ex. 19.10–end;
Matt. 8.23–end

At first I thought this sermon would focus on Jesus as the bringer of calm into life's storms, but as that sermon was being born, another address emerged, gripping its heel and usurping it. An uncomfortable reflection which kept pushing the focus away from the theme of calm, to the storms that Jesus himself creates. Jesus the storm-bringer.

First, let's zoom in on the disciples after the storm has been stilled. There they are, hair plastered down by lake water, crouching in a half-submerged boat, its hull caressed by gentle wavelets. I don't think the calm on the lake is matched by calm in their hearts. 'This guy just stilled a storm. The Old Testament is clear that only God himself has power over the waters. Jesus stands before them. Who is he? He has power over the elements. He is God himself.' Jesus the storm-bringer.

A storm to awaken us

Do we shrink Jesus down until he is dashboard sized and manageable? Have we forgotten that the Lord of heaven and earth, God almighty, is only a heartbeat away? Where is our faith? Sometimes we need a storm to wake us up. Jesus is a storm-bringer. He brings a tempest of realization that tears up our self-reliance, uproots our pint-sized idols. 'What sort of a man is this, that even the winds and the seas obey him?' Who is this and what will following him mean? All our old ways of living and being are rearranged, reordered around him. What will this mean? What will it cost? Where will this take us? The men in the boat were amazed. What of us?

Let's look now at that second story. The two possessed men in the Gentile land of the Gadarenes – roaring and raging among the tombs; disturbed and disturbing. Jesus sends the demons into the pigs. We are not told what happened to the demoniacs – though certainly, the demons leave them and perish. So, we might think, all is well – the storm-tossed souls are stilled. All calm. Job done.

But no ... Jesus is a bringer of storms. Matthew tells us that the people 'begged Jesus to leave their neighbourhood'. Begged? That's a strong word. Jesus, a Jew, is not perturbed by being on Gentile turf, with pigs around, facing two demonic men ranting and raging in the place of death. Jesus comes into the place of uncleanliness, because the men matter. Why do the people push Jesus away? Perhaps because he implicitly asks them to rethink what is important – profitable pig farming or two local weirdos? The people are left with a choice. Will they embrace the once mad men into their community, work together to survive the damage to their local farming industry, hear what this powerful healer has to teach, find out who he is, reorientate their lives around him? No chance. It's all too much. Too frightening. This man Jesus is powerful and dangerous. He brings change. The set ways are challenged. Our calm existence is disturbed. Deeply disturbed. They ask him to leave – and he respects this. But notice that they show no hint of celebration that the men are restored. No whiff of thanksgiving. Not a suggestion of welcome. Not an iota of joy. They can't get shot of Jesus fast enough.

A superficial calm?

Jesus is a storm-bringer. His power uproots expectations and challenges convictions. But in that storm we have a choice. We can either push Jesus off, far from our shores, or we can ask him to dwell with us, helping us to endure the tempest that demands a change of heart, mind and perspective. Perhaps we have cosied up to a comfortable outlook, with a pint-sized Jesus we can manipulate at will? Perhaps we have ended up in a place where our calm and well-being matters more than the cider drinkers in the cemetery. Perhaps we have settled for a superficial calm that allows us to bury our meanness and lack of love.

Jesus is a storm-bringer – bringing challenge to our perspective, to who and what we value. Have we the wisdom to pray for a storm and for the faith to ride it out with Christ? Have we the guts to pray, 'Jesus – cook up a storm and lead us on'? Perhaps we lack courage – but it's worth remembering that a calm life can be boring, dull, predictable and empty, and storms can be exciting, wild, energizing, invigorating and transforming – and he is always present in the storm.

Kate Bruce

Suggested hymns

O Breath of life, come sweeping through us; Jesus be the centre; All hail the power of Jesus' name; Blessed be your name (Matt Redman).

Seventeenth Sunday after Trinity (Proper 21)
26 September
Principal Service **The Practice of Community Discipleship**
(*Continuous*): Esther 7.1–6, 9–10; 9.20–22; Ps. 124; *or* (*Related*): Num. 11.4–6, 10–16, 24–29; Ps. 19.7–end; James 5.13–end; **Mark 9.38–end**

Welcome to the kingdom of God, a bizarre, paradoxical and weird sphere! Come and join the self-mutilated citizens of this kingdom, either maimed or lame, or without an eye. If you are not fond of self-mutilation you have an option to be thrown into a permanent abode where one never dies and the fire is never quenched. Or you could choose to throw yourself into the sea with a great millstone hung around your neck.

This is definitely not the invitation you should hear from our Gospel reading today. The language here is symbolic, hyperbolic and deliberately scandalous. Jesus is stretching the language to breaking point. He has already announced his imminent suffering and death, but the disciples are in denial. They cannot grasp the paradox of losing life for gaining it. So Jesus offers them images shot through with mystery and awe. Arresting metaphors are used here in order to force the hearers to serious reflection.

Inclusivity

An earlier episode in the chapter tells the story of the disciples' failure in the ministry of exorcism, and now they want to restrain a successful exorcist! The reason could be professional jealousy or the feeling that there is a threat to their own status. But the pronounced reason is that the successful minister does not belong to their group. In John's words, 'he was not following us'. The case is not about the exorcist not following Jesus! John thinks he knows the boundaries of divine power. His attitude denies the radical freedom of God's Spirit to move and work as God wills. Jesus urges them not to draw dividing lines between themselves and others. Disciples have no corner on the ministry of healing and liberation, and, therefore, should without prejudice work alongside those whose practice is redemptive. Neither have we got the monopoly of goodness in this world. The power of Jesus is not the property of a hierarchy. God rejects our undue ill will towards people who do not belong to our circle of believers. Jesus challenges us to examine our view of others as competitors or rivals in the reign of God. As disciples, we need to nurture the gift of graciousness and generosity. We should resist the general human tendency to draw the circle of friendship far too narrowly and to secure our own positions by excluding others.

Hospitality

To serve as Christ serves means recognizing and caring for those who are the focus of Christ's care. Hospitality was to be practised freely and with minimal requirement. Even a cup of cold water given and received was not unnoticed or unrewarded. Such hospitality is part of Christian servanthood and is done and received 'in Christ's name'. Jesus proposes a radical servanthood of all believers. John is entertaining 'holier-than-thou' delusions, but Jesus points to the fact that his followers may find themselves on the receiving end of compassion. We need to have the humility to accept the 'charity' of others as Jesus himself did many a time.

Jesus insists that it is not important to be recognized by others, but to recognize others. The desire to receive recognition can corrupt our best intentions and blind us to the needs and accomplishments of others. There is, too, the danger of looking for 'recognizable' services, ignoring the 'smaller' actions of hospitality in the community. Smaller services offered often quietly, like making a cup of coffee for an elderly worshipper after the Sunday Eucharist, or offering a welcome handshake or a smile to a newcomer in the pews, can be important.

Care for the weak

Instead of criticizing and judging outsiders and their ministries, the disciples are invited now to engage in a bit of self-criticism. By all means recognize the good 'outside', but also look for the bad 'inside'. They should look at their own style of life and ministry. Is there anything they say or do that would be a stumbling block to fellow believers, particularly the weak and young? The warning is against leading others astray. A stumbling block is literally something one falls on, a trap or hindrance placed in another's way. Anything that stands in the way of community solidarity must be dealt with.

The practice of community solidarity in this way involves special concern for the weak and the young. 'Little ones' Jesus speaks about may be understood as either the child that he placed among them or, more generally, as a follower of Jesus, someone young in faith. Children are still the most likely victims of abuse, slave labour and neglect. Christian community solidarity demands that we are to be concerned for the well-being of the 'least of these', who have no one to advocate on their behalf.

Moral earnestness

Jesus is dead serious about sin. But his exhortation here is not about self-mutilation but about self-mastery. The life of a disciple must be morally earnest inasmuch as our present behaviour has eternal consequences. Nowhere in the Gospels is the language of Jesus more vivid and emphatic than in these calls to self-discipline. The disciples are called to a distinctive lifestyle. They are urged not to lose their distinctiveness, not to give in to the pressures to adopt the standards and ethos of the world.

Salt makes food palatable. It is also used as a preservative and often as a medical remedy. Fire refines and purifies. Salt and fire represent the character of Christian discipleship. The medical use of salt and fire to close amputation wounds in ancient times is well attested. In the community of disciples, some amputation would be required, but it is a place of healing and restoration. Salt is a sign of peace, too, as represented in the passing around of salt at the dinner table.

Conclusion

In the Gospel today, Mark insists that the good from 'outside' should be appreciated, and the bad 'inside' dealt with. In all situations, it is imperative that Jesus' community works for conflict resolution and the re-establishment of unity and peace. An inclusive and caring community, which is serious about its mission of hospitality, will not have much time for petty games and rivalries.

John Perumbalath

Suggested hymns

The kingdom of God is justice and peace; Father welcomes all his children; Seek ye first the kingdom of God; The Lord is King, lift up thy voice.

Seventeenth Sunday after Trinity (Proper 21)
26 September
Second Service **All the Words that the Lord has Spoken We Will Do**
Ps. 120, 121; **Ex. 24**; Matt. 9.1–8

The passage we've read today doesn't read like a continuous narrative, so it can be confusing as the story goes back and forth. It's a bit like watching a film that has both flashbacks and glimpses of the future. Unfortunately, however, the film's continuity person doesn't seem to have been very attentive. It's still evident that various versions of the story have been edited together; maybe as many as three different sources have been melded together by the biblical redactors.

Our story begins with God speaking to Moses, inviting him to bring Aaron, his two eldest sons (Nadab and Abihu) and 70 elders to worship at a distance. However, before this worship takes place, part way up the mountain, there is a ceremony that is held at the foot of the mountain for all the people.

The blood ceremony

Moses tells the people the words of God and they promise that they will do as God asks. Moses then writes down the words of the Lord (presumably he didn't have time to pen the whole of the Pentateuch). He then changes from 'lawyer' mode to that of a priest as he builds an altar and sets up 12 stones, one for each of the tribes. Then there are burnt offerings and a blood sacrifice. Half the blood is dashed on the altar: a ritual of purification. Then Moses reads the 'book of the covenant': it's not clear what that is, but at the very least it was presumably a reading of the Decalogue (the Ten Commandments). The people responded, 'All that the LORD has spoken we will do', as they had said before, but now they add, 'and we will be obedient'. Their commitment is then sealed when Moses dashes the remainder of the blood on the people. The covenant has been cut in the blood of the sacrifice.

The meeting with God on the mountain

The passage now recounts the meeting between God and the leaders and elders (resuming the narrative that was paused at the end of verse 2). They see God, but are not allowed to draw near. This is a silent encounter, God does not speak and perhaps the people are awestruck. Maybe the point is that a meeting with God is indescribable. What is described is the pavement on which God stands, the sapphire or lapis lazuli that is the dome of the firmament (separating the upper waters from the waters below). They see God, he doesn't harm them (despite the belief that those who see God are doomed to die), and then they eat and drink before descending the mountain.

Moses meets with God

In the final 'scene' of the story Moses is invited to come to the summit of the mountain to receive the two tablets on which the law is written. Joshua accompanies him part of the way. They leave

Aaron and Hur with the elders. The cloud covers the mountain for six days, evidencing the glory of the Lord, and on the seventh day Moses is drawn into the light that looks like fire; he remains with God for 40 days.

What has the passage to say to us?

God really met with his chosen people, Israel, at Sinai. The meeting gives rise to three acts of worship: the blood ceremony at the foot of the mountain, where the people pledge their allegiance and promise to be obedient; second, there is the silent, awestruck encounter that is ratified by a (ritual) meal; and, lastly, there is Moses' mountain top one-to-one encounter with God that includes the gift of the tablets of the law.

This story forms a bridge between that of the group of freed slaves who had wandered the desert and that of the covenant community that will travel from Sinai to the Promised Land.

The people of God must accept his laws and commit themselves to obedience if they are to live in a 'land' of promise. If the covenant is the mark of God's people, what is our covenantal relationship with God? In some Christian denominations there is an annual covenant service that requires an act of commitment: thankfully it is a bloodless service, but nonetheless a solemn one.

The covenant makes explicit what our commitments should be and asks us to be obedient to God's laws, in order that we may be God's people.

Wendy Kilworth-Mason

Suggested hymns

Author of faith, eternal Word; Come, let us use the grace divine; Here am I, Lord; I am a new creation.

Eighteenth Sunday after Trinity (Proper 22)

3 October

Principal Service   **The Key to Mark's Gospel**

(*Continuous*): Job 1.1; 2.1–10; Ps. 26; *or* (*Related*): Gen. 2.18–24; Ps. 8; Heb. 1.1–4; 2.5–12; **Mark 10.2–16**

Mark and the other Gospel writers would, I think, be very surprised to know that we divide their Gospels into small chunks for reading, preaching and study. It's a serviceable way of expounding Scripture. But it isn't the only or even, perhaps, the best way. Mark and the other Gospel writers expected their readers to read their Gospel as a whole. And if we don't from time to time do so, we risk missing what each Gospel most wants to say to us by its choice and shaping of material.

Identifying with the disciples

After Jesus' baptism, he wastes no time in choosing his disciples. His disciples are central to Jesus' mission and to the dramatic story that Mark has created. Mark shows them in a favourable light so that we will identify with them; the disciples stand together against the opposition of the scribes and Pharisees. The disciples and others 'around Jesus' are favourably contrasted with his natural family. And when Jesus shares the mysteries of the kingdom of God, he does so only with the disciples, excluding those 'outside' who neither see nor understand.

'Have you no faith?'

But, like all good stories, the plot deepens and we who hear and read the story have some hard thinking to do. There are three boat scenes, and they focus down exclusively on Jesus and his disciples. In the first there is a storm and Jesus is asleep in the boat, indifferent to the plight of the fearful disciples. The disciples are terrified and wake Jesus, who calms the sea but rebukes them: 'Have you still no faith?' he says, for they were afraid. And 'filled with awe', they ask, 'Who is this ...?' They still don't know who Jesus is. When they arrive on land, Jesus meets a man possessed of an unclean spirit who recognizes who Jesus is, by contrast to the disciples.

A great multitude who turn up to hear Jesus become hungry and need feeding. The disciples want Jesus to send them away, but Jesus hands responsibility over to them. 'You give them something to eat,' he says. But they can only suggest a visit to the shops. Jesus has to step in to multiply the loaves and fishes.

A second boat scene

In a second boat scene, there is some repetition of the previous pattern. This time Jesus instructs his disciples to get into a boat to go to the other side of the lake, while he dismisses the crowd, goes off to pray and is alone on land. But when Jesus sees the disciples 'straining at the oars' against a strong wind, he walks towards them in the early morning light. But they mistake him for an apparition and are 'terrified'. Once more he tells them not to be afraid, steps into the boat and the wind ceases. They don't understand the feeding miracle and now their hearts are hardened. When they land, more healings take place, as before, and after a contretemps with some Pharisees, Jesus suggests that the disciples have no more understanding than the Pharisees.

Two more miracles follow. The healing of a deaf man makes a pointed comparison with the deafness of the disciples. And then there's another feeding of the multitude, this time four thousand. But they ask: 'How can one feed these people with bread here in the desert?' It's as though they had never witnessed the miraculous feeding.

A third boat scene

Jesus and his disciples get into a boat a third time, for another confrontation. This immediately follows from the feeding of the multitude, and we learn that the disciples have forgotten to bring bread – well, except a loaf. And as the disciples dig themselves into a big hole, Jesus delivers four leading questions. The inference is that they still lack understanding, their hearts are hardened, they do not remember and they neither see nor hear who it is who is with them.

Blind and faithless

We've now arrived at the critical turning point in Mark's Gospel. But when Jesus begins to speak about suffering, rejection and death, he is opposed by Peter. The spokesperson for the disciples is now speaking for the devil, says Jesus! And then a man brings his dumb and possessed boy to the disciples and they can no longer heal him. But now they are intent on stopping those who do, although they're not part of their set. And, in today's Gospel, they also try to stop people bringing their children to Jesus. By their actions they show they still lack the child-like trust that is needed for entry into the kingdom of God. Soon their discipleship will degrade into a self-serving, jostling for position in the kingdom, and their discipleship will end in failure.

The author intends that we identify ourselves with the disciples. As characters in his story, they open up possibilities for our own lives. Are we fearful, faithless, uncomprehending, forgetful of past experience of Christ's power and grace, deaf and blind to his presence, unsure of his identity? Let Mark's deceptive and glorious Gospel, whether as a whole or part, illuminate and shape our own discipleship.

Roger Spiller

Suggested hymns

Will you come and follow me, if I but call your name; Lord, we know that we have failed you; Take my life and let it be; Put thou thy trust in God.

Eighteenth Sunday after Trinity (Proper 22)
3 October
Second Service **Moving Closer to God**
Ps. 125, 126; **Josh. 3.7–end**; Matt. 10.1–22

> Follow [the Ark], so that you may know the way you should go, for you have not passed this way before. Yet there shall be a space between you and it, a distance of about two thousand cubits; do not come any nearer to it. (Josh. 3.4)

Get ready for some simple mathematics. Here we go: multiply 2,000 by 17.5 inches, or, if you prefer, multiply 2,000 by 45.7 centimetres. The answer, to put you out of your misery, is that 2,000 × 17.5 inches equals 35,000 inches, and 2,000 × 45.7 centimetres equals 91,400 centimetres. In imperial measurement, 35,000 inches equals about 2,916 feet, and in the metric system, 91,400 centimetres equals 914 metres.

Congratulations! You have been measuring in cubits. A cubit, in biblical times, was reckoned to be the distance from the elbow to the outstretched tip of the middle finger. It was a useful measurement if you didn't have a tape measure or a calculator handy.

The capacity of our forebears to create simple and memorable measuring devices was remarkable. Here's another example taken from the twelfth century AD. When the first Cistercian monks set out to construct their earliest monasteries and churches they too followed a simple architectural formula. The width of the crossing in the church was the key. In their ideal plan the monks could design their churches in multiples or quarters of the central square. That square frequently measured 16 metres each side. The height of the main vault of the church, it was declared, should be equal to twice the width of the nave. So, if the nave was 16 metres wide, the vault should be 32 metres high. This wasn't just so that unskilled monks could know what size their church building should be, it was because the proportions of the church were intended to echo the Benedictine belief in order and equilibrium.

But let's return to the concept of the cubit: the distance from the elbow to the tip of the outstretched middle finger. The people of Israel, according to today's first lesson, were required to walk no closer to the Ark than 2,000 cubits or 2,916 feet or 914 metres. It all seems impossibly precise, but presumably this was believed to be a safe distance between the people and the holiest object they knew, the Ark of the Covenant. It also became the measurement used to define the distance of a Sabbath day's journey.

Distance as a metaphor

But before we begin to feel impossibly superior to our ancestors, try considering whether we also use measurement metaphors for some of our most important experiences. Think of a couple in love. We might describe them as being 'very close'. We aren't measuring the physical distance between them in either feet and inches or in centimetres, we are using the language of measurement as a way of helping us to understand their relationship. Or, go to the other extreme; think of someone whose character you might describe as 'distant'. Again, this has nothing to do with physical measurement, it's just a useful way of describing a personality or a relationship.

And now, let's press this idea further. Consider the use of measurement terms to describe your relationship with God: do you feel 'close' to God or 'distant' from him?

Of course, at this point, metaphors based on measurable distance break down, for if God be God then he is neither far away nor very close. God is that which surrounds, upholds, informs and inspires us. He is the source of all being. Or, as Tennyson once wrote, 'God is closer than breathing, nearer than hands or feet.' In other words, to use terms from the world of measurement to describe the relationship between God and us is to fall into a form of sterile literalism.

Perhaps if we want to think of 'nearness' or 'farness' in relation to God, we should try abandoning that kind of language altogether and instead refer to 'Emmanuel', God with us; or refer to God as Abba, Father, as Jesus did. Measurement inevitably implies fixed physical distance, whereas metaphors drawn from relationships imply much more complex, dynamic, interpenetrative interactions that have more of the characteristics of a dance than they do of a relationship characterized by distance.

A gap between us and God?

But before we completely abandon metaphors from measurement, it might be worth pondering that 2,000 cubit distance a little more. Might that distance be a reminder to us that, in spite of all our talk of relationship, there is indeed a kind of inevitable gap between us and God? We are mortal, God is immortal. We are finite, God is infinite. We are bounded by time and space, God contains all time and space. We can only know in part, God is omniscient.

In philosophical terms, the gap is ontological; that is, there is a gap between God's being and ours, which we, from our side, cannot cross unaided.

But suppose that gap has already been crossed by a fellow human? Suppose that there is a person who has created an indestructible bridge, across which he accompanies us towards God? Suppose that this is what the death and resurrection of Christ achieved. Then, are we not hugely blessed? No longer alienated; no longer suffering from being the wrong side of an existential abyss, we have one who is in reality God with us; the one who, having conquered the dark unknowns of death, has opened the kingdom of heaven so that on faltering steps we can come into the presence of God and with thankful adoration fall on our knees before him, the Redeemer and Saviour of us all.

Christopher Herbert

Nineteenth Sunday after Trinity (Proper 23)
10 October
Principal Service　**Salesman or Lover?**
(*Continuous*): Job 23.1–9, 16–end; Ps. 22.1–15; *or* (*Related*):
Amos 5.6–7, 10–15; Ps. 90.12–end; Heb. 4.12–end;
Mark 10.17–31

I'm not sure whether anybody here is a professional salesperson. But most of us will have been approached by one. And to be a successful salesperson I suggest there are three things you need. First, a snappy slogan. Then an offer or a product that's really attractive. And then a good price. So: 'Make a friend for life,' the seller might say. Then, 'look at this gorgeous cuddly teddy bear. And it's yours for just a tenner.'

Now, Jesus was far more than a salesman, but he *was* in the business of attracting and persuading people. So if for a moment you think of him as a salesman, you could say that he was brilliant on the first two requirements.

The salesman's tools

He had the slogan you hear in the Gospels: 'The kingdom of God is close at hand.' Then he held out the offer of entering that kingdom or rule of God. The promise of living in a new and just world, liberated from human tyrants, forgiven and free, one with the Creator, and so answering the plea we heard from Job in our first reading: 'O that I knew where I might find him!'

But when it comes to the third salesman's requirement, the attractive price, Jesus was atrocious.

Atrocious, especially if you follow Mark's Gospel, as we are week by week this year. Last Sunday we heard Jesus say, 'Whoever does not receive the kingdom of God as a little child will never enter it.' The price seems to be complete loss of power. Who's going to pay that? Then today, he looks at his friends and says, 'How hard it will be for those who have wealth to enter the kingdom of God!'

And, he goes on, 'It is easier for a camel to go through the eye of a needle than for someone who is rich to enter the kingdom of God.'

A steep price

As far as we know, his followers weren't rich themselves, and according to Peter they had indeed left everything to follow Jesus. But they were still aghast at this steep price. In response, Jesus says they will indeed have rewards: brothers and sisters in the new family of God's kingdom, even eternal life. But, awkwardly, he also adds, 'with persecutions'.

'With persecutions' – really? Yes: for it is false salesmanship to present the gospel of Jesus as something that will make your life easier or bring you comfort. Weren't we warned in our second reading that 'the word of God is living and active, sharper than any two-edged sword' – not consoling but piercing? I'm increasingly sure that it's harder to live as a follower of Christ than to be one of those who admire him from afar or simply ignore him.

That's what the rich man in today's story found out. He was a good man, he desired eternal life. But the price was too high. 'Give away all your wealth, then come and follow me.'

Losing everything

How literally should we take this? A young man called Antony in third-century Egypt heard this same story read in his church. That same day he gave away all his belongings and went into the desert to live as a hermit, working with his hands, facing demons, and inadvertently becoming the founder of Christian monasticism. A thousand years later a rich young man called Francis did something similar in Assisi.

They realized what the man in the Gospel found it too hard to accept. That what Jesus calls 'the rule of God' or 'eternal life' isn't just a matter of keeping commandments or living a virtuous life. It means stripping away anything and everything that I put in place of God and God's rule of universal love and justice. It means a radical iconoclasm.

For this man in the Gospel, that idol was his wealth. For another person it might be career, for another the search for popularity. What is your most precious or most pernicious idol?

247

The patient lover

That may sound harsh, and Jesus' words are often harsh and piercing. But there's another side to the story. When the man says he's kept all the commandments, we're told, 'Jesus looking at him, loved him'.

He loved him; loved this would-be disciple who fails the test. For Jesus is *not* a salesman, trying to cajole us or trick us or profit from us. He is our lover: desiring our healing and our companionship, but refusing to coerce, and being honest about the potential cost.

And, as we heard from the letter to the Hebrews, that cost he is prepared to pay himself, a high priest in our own flesh and blood. So, as his followers, often trembling and failing ourselves, let us – again as that writer says – 'approach the throne of grace with boldness, so that we may receive mercy and find grace to help in time of need'. The grace, the comfort, is not cheap. But, patiently, at his table, our lover awaits us.

Christopher Burdon

Suggested hymns

O for a closer walk with God; Take my life and let it be; The Lord is here – he finds us as we seek; Word of God, renew your people.

Nineteenth Sunday after Trinity (Proper 23)
10 October
Second Service   God's Faithfulness and Historical Evidence
Ps. 127 [128]; **Josh. 5.13—6.20**; Matt. 11.20–end

'Joshua fought the battle of Jericho', as the well-known African American spiritual has it, 'and the walls came tumbling down.' 'But did they?' is the question we're most likely to ask. The unexpected blast of seven trumpeters and a screeching mob can deliver quite a shock, but would we expect it to cause thick fortified walls to collapse into the ground? Of course, what the writers of the story were wanting to say was that God was responsible for giving the land to the Israelites. That holds true whether or not the walls of Jericho came down. It would be irrational of us to deny the supernatural simply because we struggle to understand it, but we are right to question how it happened and how God's will is exercised when the immediate causes seem incredible.

What happened?

In asking what happened, there are two lines of enquiry open to us, or at least to the biblical scholar. The most obvious is to take a close look at the text itself. When we do, inconsistencies come to light; different tribal traditions have made insertions in the text. In our text, some scholars have concluded that what we have is an account of a liturgical procession to remember God's gift of land to Israel, rather than an account of how semi-nomadic people used a ruse to breach the 5-metre-high double walls of the city.

But what of the findings from extensive archaeological research in Jericho? Early excavations discovered a section of the collapsed wall, which was thought to be evidence for Joshua's conquest. But then it was found that the walls dated from hundreds of years earlier than the time that Joshua could have been around. And so there is no evidence of the attack described in the book of Joshua. There is the argument from silence. Was there evidence for mud brick defences that have eroded or does the unlikely disappearance of any traces of the wall suggest that the wall itself did not exist? The best that can be said is that it's neither probable nor impossible that the fall of Jericho could have taken place.

What does it tell us about God?

Faith may require us to live with openness to truth and the vagaries of historical inquiry rather than to a literal interpretation of every aspect of biblical history, even if that requires straining the text and defying the uncertainties of historical investigation. But we don't rely on historical truth in forming judgements for most of our lives. Truth can only be told in the form of pictures, stories, narrative; truth depends not merely on what happened at a particular event but what meaning can be made of it. The most important lesson from this story is not whether it is historically true, but how it reflects Israel's belief in God. The purpose of the compilers of this and other accounts was not to collect and edit facts in order to reconstruct a particular situation. The purpose was to show to a community the actions that God had carried out through the history of humankind, and especially through his 'chosen people'.

249

If semi-nomadic Israelites arrived in Jericho and found it sparsely populated, its city walls already breached, and simply infiltrated the land without military conquest or bloodshed, as may be a more accurate description of what happened, then that is itself a miracle. It was felt to be an action of God, whatever the precise means that brought it about. That was sufficiently new and surprising that it led the Israelites to create a liturgy, a procession, to memorialize and celebrate the actions of God.

What every interpreter of this strange text can agree is that the most important truth our text is telling us is that Israel's God, who promised his chosen people the gift of land that was not their own, fulfilled his promise. This attested to the astonishing, gratuitous and personal character of God. But it must also be true that such a conviction could not have been arrived at without there being a consistent basis for it in history. The God of Israel, the God and Father of our Lord Jesus Christ, sets himself a high watermark when he makes his promises. There can be no escape clauses, no weasel words that give room for manoeuvre. God promised the one thing that is most important to people and nations: their own land. For semi-nomads occupied in rearing animals, their most basic need is to possess land. This narrative was compiled at the very time when the land of Judaea was most at peril, at the time of the exile. So this and other Hebrew texts serve to acclaim that God's promise remained in force, against all expectations. And today, when it is we who despoil the land, it tells us that the land is not so much a right to exploit but a sacred duty to treasure.

Roger Spiller

Suggested hymns

Rejoice, O land, in God, thy might; Guide me, O thou great Jehovah; There is a land of pure delight; Through the night of doubt and sorrow.

Twentieth Sunday after Trinity (Proper 24)

17 October

Principal Service   **Why Did Jesus Die?**

(*Continuous*): Job 38.1–7 [34–end]; Ps. 104.1–10, 26, 35c
[*or* 104.1–10]; *or* (*Related*): Isa. 53.4–end; Ps. 91.9–end;
Heb. 5.1–10; **Mark 10.35–45**

Why did Jesus die? Since the cross is the cornerstone of our faith, it's a crucial question and one that deserves our consideration.

At one level, we can say he died because he offended the Jewish authorities. He died because he was viewed as a danger by the Roman authorities. But we need to go deeper. Was a violent death inevitable from the start? It seems that Jesus had to agonize his way through his vocation. There simply wasn't the sombre comfort of a predetermined script that he was called to play out. Sometimes when death seemed close, he would slip away. Even as late as the night before he died, in the Garden of Gethsemane, he wrestled with God over whether obedience must at this late hour incur a cruel death.

The prospect of a violent death

Of course, he knew that his self-giving obedience to God would lead to a big showdown with the authorities. He knew the fate of prophets and told parables like that of the wicked husbandman, in which the son of the owner of the vineyard was killed. He would have reckoned with his own imminent death at least after he received news of the murder of John the Baptist. So death was a likely part of his vocation. He didn't seek it, but neither would he abandon his self-giving obedience to avoid it. He recoiled from death. It wasn't death as such, but self-giving service and obedience that motivated him.

The purpose Jesus saw in his death

It is unthinkable that Jesus would have said to himself, 'If I carry on the way I am doing, I will be put to death.' If Jesus had no more to say about his death, he would, surely, have withdrawn long ago. Jesus not only announced his death, but he must also have interpreted it; that is, seen some reason why it might be necessary in terms of the long story of the search for the redemption of humanity.

Scholars believe we come closest to the words of Jesus when Jesus speaks in terms of the Son of Man. It's an enigmatic phrase, mainly from the seventh chapter of the book of Daniel, and used almost without exception only by Jesus himself. It's one of only two sayings by Jesus, the other at the Last Supper, on the meaning of his death, and takes us as close as we can get to what Jesus revealed about the purpose of his death.

'A ransom for many'

'The Son of Man came not to be served but to serve, and to give his life a ransom for many.' It's a slender phrase but one that remains the focus of extensive study. But what, briefly, does it tell us? We hear today of the word 'ransom' when we hear demands made, usually to governments, in order to secure the release and safe return of people who have been abducted, imprisoned and who often face the prospect of violence or murder.

What lay behind this phrase? An Old Testament idea was very much in the minds of the contemporaries of Jesus. It declares that 'without the shedding of blood, there is no redemption'. It expresses the conviction that human transgressions and the almost physicality of evil, guilt and shame cannot simply be absolved by mere words of forgiveness. It demands a cost, a ransom. The sacrificial system was just such a mechanism, and required men and women to make a blood sacrifice. But, as the reading from Hebrews tells us, it could only be of limited effect and needed to be repeated. Even the high priest who presided over the sacrifice needed to offer a sacrifice for his own sins. And in the later period of Jewish history, the period of the Maccabees, the idea developed that a righteous person who met martyrdom died not only on their own account but accrued a surplus of merit that could extend to others. It's such fragmentary and alien ideas that helped to inform Jesus about the meaning of his death.

Jesus offered himself, not needing to make the sacrifice on his own account, but for the sake of others, for 'the many' in the sense of 'for all'. By his death we can be free from our captivity to sin, guilt and shame and, with the whole cosmos, can be free from what St Paul called its 'bondage to decay'.

The impact of his death

The first disciples of Jesus were devastated by Jesus' death. But they did not have long to wait before they had their fear and confusion overturned. Three days after Jesus' death, they became convinced that he had been raised from the dead. They themselves knew that their sins had been forgiven. The life and teaching of Jesus had been vindicated. They experienced a sense of new life, the coming of the Spirit, which enabled them to become changed people, a 'new creation', embarking upon the re-created world set in train by the resurrection of Jesus. They were convinced that his dying had brought them to new life. And we are left to this day with the question as to how this peripatetic teacher who suffered an ignominious death goes on exercising such a tremendous and unique and unsurpassed influence across the world. An influence that must be evident and visible through the selfless serving of others.

Roger Spiller

Suggested hymns

Come, wounded healer; Take this moment, sign and space; King of kings, majesty; Brother, sister, let me serve you.

Twentieth Sunday after Trinity (Proper 24)
17 October
Second Service   **The Purposes of the Heart**
Ps. 141; Josh. 14.6–14; **Matt. 12.1–21**

Why do we do what we do? Every day we carry out hundreds of tasks and actions, at work, at home and in every arena of our lives. We make thousands of decisions and choices that have an impact both great and small upon the world around us. Whatever we do, and whatever we say, what are the deep-seated intentions which lie beneath our every word and action?

Because we are human, there will be times when our actions and our intentions diverge. We do something because we have to, or we are told to, or we do something automatically without even thinking at all. We do things because we have always done them; we resist change because it is easier not to ask questions. We say things we do not really want to say, words spill out of mouths and then we regret their harshness or insensitivity. To ask the question, 'Why do we do what we do?' or, 'Why do we say what we say?' is to unravel our motivations and our inspirations, and reveals how we view the world that we live in.

Jesus questions the intentions and the motivations of the Pharisees when they challenge his disciples about what they are doing on the Sabbath. They claim that plucking the heads of grain off the corn and eating them is unlawful. The law says that the Sabbath is holy and a day of rest.

The Pharisees, not content with Jesus' answer, challenge him again. This time they question his healing of a man with a withered hand on the Sabbath. 'Is it lawful to cure a man on the Sabbath?' they ask. Jesus responds by reminding them that the law is enlivened by the Spirit. Intentions are perhaps more important than regulations. For it is the intention that reveals the purposes of the heart and points towards the kingdom of God. Jesus' intention, through his words and his actions, is to inaugurate a new kingdom and a new way of being for those who chose to listen to him.

Mercy not sacrifice

Jesus reminds the Pharisees of the words of the prophet Hosea, 'I desire mercy and not sacrifice.' Jesus seems to be saying that he does not wish an empty-hearted conformity to rules and regulations. He is not so interested in the letter of the law. He is seeking to build a kingdom where the love of God is at the centre of all things and fulfils all that the law had promised.

Rather than following rules for the sake of it, his desire is that we first love the Lord our God with all of our heart, our soul and our strength, and all other decisions and actions will flow from that. This action is the beginning of a new creation, where all are healed, forgiven and restored.

Love is his law

In his life and ministry, Jesus sets about to bring to the light the things hidden in darkness and disclose the purposes of the heart. He exposes our intentions and our meanings and causes us to question our motivations. Jesus said that the Sabbath was made for humankind, not humankind for the Sabbath, and he is Lord even of the Sabbath. This puts into the right perspective the rules and regulations that the Pharisees were rigidly adhering to. There is a bigger picture to be seen which is expansive and generous and full of mercy and love. This can be the intention behind all of our intentions and the meaning beyond all of our meanings if we choose it to be so and follow the commandments of Christ, whose law is love.

In the light and mercy of Christ, we might then reassess and realign our response to God and to our neighbour. We use, as our law and our guide, the first commandment, to love God with all of your heart, soul and strength, which is outworked into the second, to love your neighbour as yourself. As Jesus himself said, there is no other commandment greater than these.

When we reflect on why we do what we do, and why we say what we say, we might return to this first principle. We might use it to question and interrogate our own intentions and motivations and bring to light the purposes of our own hearts.

Victoria Johnson

Suggested hymns

There's a wideness in God's mercy; O God, you search me; Love is his word; Immortal love.

Last Sunday after Trinity (Proper 25) 24 October
Principal Service **What Do You Want Me to Do for You?**
(*Continuous*): Job 42.1–6, 10–end; Ps. 34.1–8, 19–end
[*or* 34.1–8]; *or* (*Related*): Jer. 31.7–9; Ps. 126; Heb. 7. 23–end;
Mark 10.46–end

See Bartimaeus the blind beggar, crouched in roadside dust, face turned to the sunlight. He sits in darkness, hoping for a crust or a coin dropped into the cloak spread out before him. The bustle and babble of a crowd approaches, heading out of Jericho on the Jerusalem road.

'Did yer hear about that bloke from Nazareth? They saw he heals people.' 'You'll never believe what happened in Bethsaida, to the blind fella. Jesus put his hands on the bloke's eyes and now he can see.'

Jesus, Son of David!

You can almost hear the flare of hope spark up in Bartimaeus. To have sight means no longer to beg at the roadside. No more stumbling and tripping. Light for those who walk in darkness – a theme in the ancient promises. Hope for the physically and spiritually blind. Hope for those in exile, far from home. Hope for a descendant of David to embody these promises. Bartimaeus discerns the connections and sees clearly who Jesus is. 'Jesus, Son of David,' he cries. Bartimaeus might be blind, but he has 20/20 insight. He sees something of who Jesus is. More than a travelling rabbi, more than a healer, here is the One who bears the hopes of Israel. This insightful blind man is calling for mercy.

Jostled by the crowd, Jesus hears a voice bawling out: 'Jesus, Son of David. Have mercy on me.' Jesus stops still: 'Son of David'. This title is resonant with messianic meaning. New sight. New hope. New life. So many have not understood. But here a disembodied voice is crying out for mercy from the Son of David. And the Son of David does not pass on by.

Jesus urges those around him to call the man over. 'Take heart; get up, he is calling you.' See the cloak falling aside as Bartimaeus rushes into the arms of those who will guide him to Jesus. Tugged and shoved he hears a voice, 'What do you want me to do for you?' 'My teacher, let me see again.' Again – that single word tells us much. Bartimaeus had sight, but lost it. In that single word 'again' is a whole world of pain, sorrow, memory and loss, as well as rich hope. Jesus' response is swift: 'Go, your faith has made you well.' Immediately, Bartimaeus can see and he follows Jesus. From sitting by the roadside, he is walking on the way. The way will lead to Jerusalem and beyond. For all its suffering, it is a way of new sight, new hope, new life.

Who is Jesus for us?

And so what? What does this story mean now? Who is Jesus for us? The writer of Hebrews paints a fabulous picture of Jesus as one who is a priest, not any old priest, but *the* priest. He holds his priesthood for ever, because he is eternal. Add to this – the writer tells us that Jesus is both priest and sacrifice. In the Old Testament the priests offered sacrifices every day, being human and flawed. But Jesus offered himself once for all. Jesus saves completely all those who approach God through him. He always lives to pray for us.

If someone says they will keep me in their prayers, I am always deeply encouraged. In that promise they are saying, 'I will keep your concerns and situation in my heartspace, and bring that to God for you. You matter and I care for you.' In Jesus we have one who is saying, 'I live to pray for you always.' Hang on a minute. Are you saying that Jesus, Son of David, restorer of sight to the blind, feeder of the hungry, King of Heaven, high priest for ever, lives to pray for me? Me? In a world of humdrum stuff – doing the shopping, cooking the kids' tea – me? Doing my exams? Me? Looking for a job? Me? Getting mad with the family? Me? Struggling with depression? Me? Are you saying that Jesus, high priest, holy, blameless, undefiled, separated from sinners, exalted above the heavens, prays for me – earthy and earthbound?

Yes. I. Am.

The Jesus of Nazareth who stopped and asked Bartimaeus the blind man, 'What do you want me to do for you?' is the same yesterday, today and for ever. Jesus, risen high priest asks us, 'What do you want me to do for you?'

Half the time we don't bring to God the things we desperately need from him. Often we sit quietly on the kerbside – blind and silent. Perhaps too proud to shout out, or too ashamed. Or maybe we have cried out and been told to be quiet by others. Picture yourself sitting next to Bartimaeus. Listen as he yells, 'Jesus, Son of David. Have mercy on me.' He knows his need. How about you? Will you walk through the crowd and stand before Jesus? When he asks, 'What do you want me to do for you?' What will you say? Take some time to consider that.

Kate Bruce

Suggested hymns

What a friend we have in Jesus; Light of the world (You stepped down into darkness); Amazing grace; In Christ alone.

Last Sunday after Trinity (Proper 25)   24 October
Second Service   **Before the Days of Trouble**
Ps. 119.121–136; **Eccles. 11 and 12**; 2 Tim. 2.1–7; *Gospel at Holy Communion*: Luke 18.9–14

You aren't allowed to forget when you approach old age. Leaflets start coming through your letter box offering you free tests for hearing aids. Suppliers entice you to consider installing a stair lift. Letters arrive from estate agents offering to sell your house, and glossy brochures invite you to make an appointment and book your place in a care home. You know when you struggle to get upstairs and can't remember why you were making the effort, and when you bend down to tie your shoelaces and bring on back pains and you still can't reach your feet, and you can't remember where you left your reading glasses and have to be reminded that they're caught in your hair.

Life in the old house

The writer of Ecclesiastes, known as Qoheleth, has a very colourful way of reminding us of our mortality and the loss and diminution that ageing brings. He describes the body as if it were a house and leaves the reader to crack the code and guess the clues as to what he is saying. Be warned, the text isn't always clear and so scholars disagree, but let's have a little Bible study and attempt to see what our sober writer is trying to tell us.

He begins by invoking a Palestinian winter, which is a metaphor for the winter of life, when the years draw down and darkness eclipses our remaining, failing years. A house provides no comfort. The house of which he speaks is like our ageing bodies and minds, in a deteriorating condition. Our writer then goes through some of the features of a house and leaves us to infer to which parts of the body he refers. The 'guards of the house tremble', by which he probably means arms or other trembling limbs. 'Strong men are bent' evokes the image of awkward, wobbly legs. 'The women who grind cease workings.' What grinds? It's 'teeth', of course, but 'they are few', and there's a problem with chewing. The 'windows' of the house represent the 'eyes', but they, like the house, enable people to see only 'dimly', as sight deteriorates. What are 'the doors on the street' that 'are shut'? This may refer to ears where hearing is fading and people don't hear the knock of the visitor. The 'grinding' is back, but this time it's the sound of the voice, not probably 'low' but more usually translated as 'high', high-pitched, child-like sounds. The rising up 'at the sound of a bird' suggests the sleeplessness of the elderly, who wait for the sound of the bird that signals that morning has arrived. 'Fear of heights and terrors on the road' is a clear reference to the increasing fears faced by the elderly, the risks of falling on steep slopes, poor conditions on the road or from miscreants. The blossom of the 'almond tree' is linked to the whitening of the hair. The grasshopper or locust eats so much that they 'drag themselves along' and suggest the old person walking sluggishly, in the manner of a shuffle. The reference to desire fading hints at impotence and perhaps a more general contraction of life's attractions. Mention in some translations of the caper berry may also allude to its use as a stimulant, but one that no longer takes effect. The severing of the chord or thread of life conveys death, and when the 'pitcher is broken at the fountain, and the wheel broken at the cistern' the water of life can no longer be drawn and life is extinguished. For a shorter litany on the loss of old age, we might look to Shakespeare and the end of Jacques' soliloquy on the 'seven ages of man' in *As You Like It*: 'Sans teeth, sans eyes, sans taste, sans everything.'

A message to the young

Qoheleth, our writer, describes decay and death, but can bring no comfort to the elderly. But he does address the young person, and wants them to remember God before they grow old and 'before the days of trouble come'.

I once heard a headteacher of a famous private school stating the purpose of schooling: 'To prepare students for death.' It might seem premature to disturb the carefree character of youth with thoughts of our demise. But we need boundaries, even young people need boundaries, limits within which to flourish and form judgements. Death is just such a boundary. If we don't reckon with death before it overtakes us, we might regret a life overtaken by trivial pursuits and decadence. As our writer says, the outer parameter of our life ought to inform the way we conduct our lives, lest we are crippled by remorse in old age. Growing up with God, knowing him as our unwavering parental figure through all the turbulent stages of life, brings security, hope and blessing.

Roger Spiller

Living God, your love has called us; When memory fades and recognition falters; When all thy mercies, O my God; Lord, for the years.

Bible Sunday   24 October

(May be celebrated in preference to the Last Sunday after Trinity.)

Principal Service   **Route Map and Signpost to Jesus**

Isa. 55.1–11; Ps. 19.7–14; 2 Tim. 3.14—4.5; **John 5.36b–end**

The Bible is the top seller in the world, with sales figures ranging from 2.5 billion to over 6 billion. But why should we read it? You can, said Jesus, in effect, read the Bible until you're blue in the face, and only get a blue face for your pains. The Jews were assiduous in searching their Scriptures, thinking that through them they would obtain eternal life. But they didn't find Jesus, though (said Jesus) the Scriptures 'testify of' him. So the primary reason for reading the Bible is not for teaching, nor for finding comfort, but so that we may be directed to Jesus.

Old Testament pointers

The Scriptures that were being talked about were, of course, what we call the Old Testament. Jesus said, 'If you believed Moses, you would believe me, because he wrote about me.' And of the two forlorn disciples on the way to Emmaus, we're told, 'Then beginning with Moses and all the prophets, he interpreted to them the things about himself in all the scriptures.' It's not at all obvious to us what texts these might be. But Jesus didn't simply fulfil particular prophecies; Jesus was the fulfiller of the Old Testament in a profounder way than by simply matching texts. In the experience of his followers, Jesus embodied a perfect relationship with God that God's people had failed to achieve. He occupied the position that had always been intended for Israel and for all people. So we read the Old Testament because it points us to Jesus. And it's the essential background for understanding Jesus' vocation and the new covenant that he has sealed between God and humankind.

Gospel pointers

But it's the four Gospels that present Jesus most clearly. What are the Gospels? They're not mini-biographies of Jesus. They give us information about Jesus and the impact Jesus had on the different groups he encountered in his day. But they're not there primarily to give an accurate and exact account of his public ministry. They are there to point us to Jesus. What we have are four portraits of Jesus, a plurality of images of Jesus, each one drawing out different features of him, as seen by the writers and with an eye on the audiences for which they were first written.

It's surprising that there were four Gospels rather than one harmonious Gospel. It leads us to note differences, discrepancies between the Gospel writers. But in opening us to that possibility, the existence of four Gospels witnesses to the fact that Jesus transcends even the witnesses of the Bible. He, not the Bible, is the supreme authority, the one to which the Scriptures point. And he is the one by whose Spirit alone we can understand the Scriptures aright.

Witness to Jesus

What could we know of Jesus without the Bible? What false and fanciful ideas might we attribute to him without the correction reading the Bible brings? What but the Bible can bring us the truth about Jesus? And what but the Bible is there to critique and expose the self-serving failures of the Church?

The Bible points us to Jesus, and it does so because Jesus brings us life. The first ending of John's Gospel expresses it thus: 'these are written so that you may come to believe that Jesus is the Messiah, the Son of God, and that through believing you may have life in his name.'

Read as story

How should we read the Bible in order to realize the purposes for which it was intended? Most of the Bible is in the form of a story told. It's been estimated that nearly 90 per cent of both Testaments are narrative. Stories don't ever tell us what to believe; they don't deliver teaching, or issue commandments or moral instruction. Stories involve their readers. They take us on a journey. They give us space in which to engage with the imagination. We have to read ourselves into the story, follow the plot and identify with one or more of the characters. And we must be caught up in the surprise, shock and disturbance of the story. Any story can help us to emerge with a changed perspective, changed values, occupying an alternative 'world view'. But the Bible, uniquely, leads us to Christ, who brings us the fullness of life.

There is, perhaps, no better advice than that of biblical scholar J. A. Bengal in 1734. It sounds better in Latin but it will be translated: 'Te totum applica ad textum: rem totam applica ad te.' 'Apply your whole self to the text: apply the whole text to yourself.'

Roger Spiller

Suggested hymns

God in his wisdom, for our learning; Speak, O Lord, as we come to you; Lord, thy word abideth; Thanks to God, whose word was spoken.

Fourth Sunday before Advent   31 October
Principal Service   **Love for God**
(*or* All Saints' Sunday; for All Saints' Day, see p. 351)
Deut. 6.1–9; Ps. 119.1–8; Heb. 9.11–14; **Mark 12.28–34**

Most people seem to think that Christianity is about keeping the Ten Commandments. The scribe who came up to Jesus would have been handling some 613 commandments, which acted like a protective fence around the shorter list, to minimize the risk of inadvertently breaking them. The Jewish law spoke of love, but it was Jesus who concentrated all the commandments into this one dual commandment: love God and love neighbour.

'Which commandment is greatest of all?', asks the scribe, and he agrees with Jesus that the command to love God has primacy. But why, and is this still applicable?

Love of neighbour

Many people in our society would declare that they broadly try to love people, whether or not they love their actual neighbour. All responsible people in the world could subscribe to that. And is that command the way we may also fulfil our duty to love God? John's words suggest this. He writes: 'Those who do not love a brother or sister whom they have seen cannot love God whom they have not seen.' 'We cannot know whether we love God,' said St Teresa, 'but there can be no doubt about whether we love our neighbour.' Those who served the needy in the well-known parable in Matthew's Gospel discovered that they were at the same time loving God and also serving Jesus. This makes clear that we love God by loving others: love of God through love of neighbour.

But do we only love God through our love of others? It's been suggested that our relation to God is based on faith, not love. How can we love God? There is nothing that we can add or give to God. In that case the first command to love God would be duplicating the second, to love neighbour, and we could unite believers and non-believers alike around the single commandment, to love your neighbour.

Love of God

The witness of Scripture is clear that we can and must love God as well as and independent of loving our neighbour. Indeed, love for God is often the motive for love of neighbour. Says John: 'The commandment we have from him is this: those who love God must love their brothers and sisters also.' But how could we express our love to one who is beyond our senses and limited human capacities? 'There exists some point at which I can meet God in a real and experimental contact with his infinite actuality; and it is the point where my contingent being depends on his love.' So wrote the monk Thomas Merton. That rings true for many theists as well as Christians, who experience a presence that is at once awesome, immediate and personal.

The physicality of loving God

The command to love God specifies the way our love for God should be expressed: we are to love with heart, soul, mind and strength. Three are inward motives, dispositions, attitudes, but there is also the physical dimension that is involved in our love for God: the expenditure of 'strength', time, effort and energy, in prayer, study, exercise and reflection. There's a physicality of relationship that exceeds the merely inward. 'Present your bodies', says St Paul, 'as a living sacrifice'; Paul, who bore the marks of following Christ in his own flesh. God makes unlimited, unconditional demands on us that extend to every activity of our lives and at every moment, but though the demands may be onerous, unwelcome and costly, they can also satisfy our deepest desires, since God intends that we find ourselves through surrendering to him.

God's love through us

Our love for God is a direct consequence of God's love for us. We love because God first loved us. That is the irreversible chronology and sequencing of the gospel. The love we exercise is simply the overflow and reflection of the love that God has poured into our lives. It's not, then, our love for God that is sought, but the love of God that animates our own lives and works to convince us that we are loved, worth loving, loved unconditionally, for no other reason than that we bear his image and we are his adopted children. So we love God through the love God has for us. As St Augustine expressed it: 'That you may love God, let him dwell in you and love himself through you.'

Love, the indissoluble unity

Two commandments, then, but we can't play off one against the other. Love for God and love for neighbour are an indissoluble unity. We cannot block the love we receive from God from freely flowing out to our neighbours. Nor can we love our neighbours with the paucity of our natural affection, without seeking the love of God that will reach unconditionally and without discrimination to all our neighbours, whether or not they receive and return our love.

The scribe in our story was an honest and serious seeker whose wisdom Jesus commended. 'You are not far from the kingdom of God,' Jesus said. And neither are we if God's love, the love we receive from God, flows in and through us.

Roger Spiller

Suggested hymns

God is love: let heav'n adore him; O love that wilt not let me go; O love, how deep, how broad, how high!; Love is his word, love is his way.

Fourth Sunday before Advent 31 October
Second Service **Trust Our Heaviness**
First Evening Prayer of All Saints
Ps. 1, 5: Ecclus. 44.1–15, *or* **Isa. 40.27–end**; Rev. 19.6–10

A warm wind

How do eagles fly? And why? Birds don't fly just for the fun of it. They fly to find food, or to migrate, or to find a safe place to build their nest and raise their young. They fly as a means of survival. Birds must teach their young to fly; to leave the nest. And the eagle with its huge wingspan must also learn to fly in its environment and conserve energy. It learns to fly without needing to flap those huge wings by learning to wait for the wind thermals. An eagle will launch itself into the warm current and as the warm air rises the eagle allows itself to be borne up higher and higher. It can therefore cover great distances at high altitudes without flapping its wings or wasting energy. It can do this because it is designed to do so.

Eagles teach their young to fly by bearing the chicks on their backs up to those warm air currents, and then the adult bird drops away leaving the chicks to experience the fall in the air. The parent will swoop in again, catch the birds and rise again, drop away – repeating this process until the young eagle suddenly realizes what it can do, and will rise on the warm wind itself, higher and higher.

At these great heights the air can become turbulent and stormy. Then the eagle is able to lock its wings and brace itself into the wind so that it is carried safely to where it needs to go.

The writer of Deuteronomy compares God to the parent eagle bearing us up on her wings and teaching us to fly. It is an image of trust and relationship as we learn who we are and come to understand the nature of a God who nurtures us and protects us and teaches us the way we should go.

Written in exile

This fortieth chapter in Isaiah is part of Deutero-Isaiah. Believed to date from the time of Israel's exile in Babylon, the writer declares God to be God of the whole universe. The chapter begins with a cry of comfort, a call to the levelling of justice, a comparison between the frailty and brief lifespan of humanity with the everlasting creator God. It reminds the Israelites of who they are and where they come from. In exile they may feel that there is no hope, but the writer reminds them that the nations and their leaders are nothing, can be brought to nothing by the God who created all that is.

'Lift up your eyes', is the exhortation. 'Lift up your eyes and see.' The journey home may be long and difficult, and to do it in your own strength would seem impossible. But the God who has always known you, who nurtured you and taught you who you were, will be the wind on which you can launch yourself and will bear you home.

Our trust in the turbulence

What is your experience of exile, I wonder? Do you feel far from home, far from yourself, your own centre and integrity? Are you exhausted at this stage of your journey? Have the turbulent winds of illness or grief or loss or disappointment or anxiety tossed you around and left you adrift?

Sometimes in such circumstances it is difficult to pray, to find any words to offer either of praise or petition. We may feel only a need to lament, rage or call out like small birds who have fallen from their nest and cannot remember how to fly. Intercession can be like launching ourselves on to those warm currents. We may have forgotten they were there in the very nature of creation. But if we lean out, stretch our wings, we find them again; the familiar rhythm that is not of our making but part of the created universe in which we may find our place and path again. We don't need to pray in our own strength but in the strength of the spirit who knows each one of us so well and draws close to comfort us. It is the paradox of finding ourselves strong in weakness; we stretch our wings into the wind and find we are lifted up higher to the very heart of God.

As we launch ourselves into the vastness of God we find our place, our identity; we can spread our wings in trust to the warm embrace of God's strong and life-giving current.

Rilke begins his poem *The Book of Hours: Love Poems to God* with these words:

How surely gravity's law,
strong as an ocean current,
takes hold of the smallest thing
and pulls it toward the heart of the world.

And ends it with:

This is what the things can teach us:
to fall,
patiently to trust our heaviness.
Even a bird has to do that
before he can fly.

Carey Saleh

Suggested hymns

God is our strength from days of old; She sits like a bird; Jesus, be the centre; Praise to the holiest in the height.

Third Sunday before Advent   7 November
Principal Service   **Out of the Depths**
Jonah 3.1–5, 10; Ps. 62.5–end; Heb. 9.24–end; Mark 1.14–20

Now Nineveh was an exceedingly large city, a three days' walk across. Jonah began to go into the city, going a day's walk. (Jonah 3.3–4)

Some of the best-loved stories in the world begin with the phrase 'Once upon a time', and the child listening knows that, although they may be snuggling down in bed before the lights are switched off, or sitting cosily on their parent's lap, they are about to be magically transported to a parallel world where giants dwell and where fairy godmothers come to the rescue of the hero or heroine, and where animals can talk. The phrase 'Once upon a time' sings with delicious promise.

The story of Jonah, probably composed sometime after the Jewish exile of 597 BC, falls into a similar category. It is a 'Once upon a time' story; not, repeat *not*, to be taken literally. But if someone insists that it must be based on fact, just point out to them that the city of Nineveh was not an urban sprawl that required three days of steady walking to cross it. Archaeologists estimate that, at the height of the city's importance, it was less than three miles in extent. And if your interlocutor insists on trying to pin you down and insists on facts, then you can tell them that Nineveh was an ancient Assyrian city located in Iraq, very close to what is now Mosul. But we would be much closer to understanding the way the word 'Nineveh' is used in the story if we think of it as 'Hogwarts' or Tolkien's 'Middle Earth' or even Winnie the Pooh's '100 Acre Wood'.

To think of the story of Jonah as factual is to miss the point entirely. If you are interested, this is known in academic literary and philosophical circles as a 'category mistake'.

A morality tale?

But because the story of Jonah is not factual and has elements of 'Once upon a time' about it, it doesn't mean to say that we should treat it lightly. Like 'Once upon a time' stories, it has a moral message. In fact, there are at least three morals to be drawn from it:

1 If God calls, you cannot escape that call. No matter how much you want to run away, or wriggle or squirm, God knows what he wants you to do.
2 Wherever you are, even in the belly of death, God hears your cry.
3 God's plans are probably opaque to us, but we should not pretend that his will and what we ourselves want are one and the same.

Unfortunately, in reading the Jonah story we get so caught up in the notion of Jonah being swallowed by a whale that we are deflected from what is really going on. But it's not only the flow of the story that is significant; it's the very structure of the narrative that is also important.

The narrative structure consists of three parts: the first is when Jonah tries to escape from God; the second is a poem; the third is when he feels sorry for himself and fails to comprehend the merciful nature of God.

It's the second part of the narrative structure on which I want to focus our attention. It's a poem of great beauty; a poem that explores the realities of our human condition. It expresses in just a few stanzas those moments of absolute despair and anguish that all of us experience – times when we are at our lowest, when life has become impenetrably dark, when we feel we are going under.

This is how the poem puts it:

The waters closed in over me;
    the deep surrounded me;

weeds were wrapped around my head
   at the roots of the mountains.

Just 22 words, each word pulling its weight, capture our feelings of utter misery. But then, when we feel that we are surrounded by absolute darkness, the poem suggests that there is another truth waiting to be discovered:

yet you brought up my life from the Pit,
   O LORD my God.
As my life was ebbing away,
   I remembered the LORD;
and my prayer came to you,
   into your holy temple.

Words of hope

Thirty-three words of hope, an epiphany of the very nature of God: God rescues, God redeems, and God makes new.

It is no wonder that the story of Jonah lodged itself in the mind of Jesus. Remember that moment in Matthew's Gospel when he prophesied about his own death: 'For just as Jonah was three days and three nights in the belly of the sea monster, so for three days and three nights the Son of Man will be in the heart of the earth.' Nor is it any wonder that when some of our early Christian ancestors were considering what visual imagery to use to decorate their tombs in the Roman catacombs, the story of Jonah featured strongly.

Jonah may be a 'Once upon a time' story with moral messages, but it is richer and more wonderful than that, for it holds within its tender embrace truths about God that are life-giving and profoundly healing.

We may be left wondering about who wrote it, but whoever the author may have been, we offer our thanks and praise, for within this gorgeous story, God is revealed.

Christopher Herbert

Suggested hymns

Eternal Father, strong to save; O praise ye the Lord; May the mind of Christ my Saviour; O thou who at thy Eucharist didst pray.

Third Sunday before Advent   7 November
Second Service   **St Jude's Question**
Ps. 46 [82]; Isa. 10.33—11.9; **John 14.1–29 [*or* 23–29]**

Living with questions

Today's long Gospel reading may at a first hearing (or reading) sound like a monologue, set in the context of the Last Supper, with Jesus doing all the talking. But look more closely and you'll see that three of his disciples all play a part. All three sound puzzled, not understanding what Jesus is saying. There's a vital point here: if Jesus' closest companions felt free to bring their questions and doubts into their relationship with him, then so can we. In fact it wouldn't be much of a relationship if we could only bring our successes and our certainties, and leave everything else outside. Thomas speaks first. He wants to know where Jesus is going, and what way he will travel to get there. Then comes Philip. He wants to see Jesus' heavenly Father before committing himself to following Jesus. Both of these disciples have a key part to play, not just in honestly sharing their uncertainties but also in eliciting from Jesus profound answers to the questions they pose.

But it's the third disciple who matters most. He's described as 'Judas (not Iscariot)'. Not much of a moniker, is it? Imagine going through life with a label on your jacket that says, 'I'm not Iscariot. I'm the nice guy. I'm not the one who betrayed him.' Perhaps that's why this disciple, usually known as St Jude, ended up as the patron saint of lost causes. Unless the Letter of Jude really is by him, this is the only place in Scripture where he speaks. But it doesn't matter, because his question to Jesus is even more important than those of the other two. He says, 'Lord, how is it that you will reveal yourself to us, and not to the world?' In other words: what's the point of the Church? It's a good question – one that most of us will have asked from time to time, and some of us all of the time!

Abiding

Jesus' answer doesn't immediately seem relevant. 'Those who love me will keep my word, and my Father will love them, and we will come to them and make our home with them.' The word translated 'home' is the Greek *monē*, from the verb form *menō*, which means 'to abide', and the noun a place to abide. The verb in particular plays a crucial role in the Gospel of John, occurring around 40 times; but because it's not always translated with the same word in English we don't notice how common and how important it is (if you read John's Gospel in the King James Version, which is much closer to the original Greek, you will see how often the word 'abide' appears).

Why is it important? Because when people abide with Christ, or Christ abides with people, lives are changed. In the Gospel's opening chapter, two people approach Jesus, calling him 'Rabbi' (which, we are told, means 'teacher'), and they ask him, 'Where are you abiding?' He says, 'Come and see.' They came and saw where he was abiding, and they abode with him that day (the Greek word *menō* comes three times in two verses). The result? They are changed from spectators to participants; they now see Jesus not as 'teacher' but as 'Messiah', and they bear witness to others. The same thing happens with some Samaritans, who ask Jesus to 'abide' with them; and 'he abode there two days'. The result? They become believers. To abide in Christ means to make your home in him, which is life-changing – as it so often is when we make our home with someone.

But Christ doesn't just want us to make our homes, to abide, in him. He wants to make his home in us. Hence his reply to St Jude's question: 'Those who love me will keep my word, and my Father will love them, and we will come to them and make our home [or 'abide'] with them.' You could say that the whole message of John's Gospel is that Jesus left his home in heaven and came to make his home in us: if we are willing to admit him. And here's the point. To have someone abide with you, or to be at home with you, means *making space* for them, giving up your own autonomy, rearranging your inner furniture. That's not easy – especially in a world full of the sound of doors closing on refugees and migrants and those seeking asylum. Remember the old hymn: 'O come to my heart, Lord Jesus; there is room in my heart for thee.' But is there room in my heart?

Let's go back to where we started. Jesus' answer to Jude's question is this: the point of the Church – the *only* point of the Church – is to be a community of mutual abiding, a place where we freely choose to make space for Christ, who comes to us in the Eucharist, in the word of God and in our neighbour – and thus to discover that he has already made space for us. The Church is a place where all should be able to feel at home, to feel safe (which is why the abuse of children and others is such a peculiarly wicked crime), and above all to feel loved. A community of unconditional love, of mutual abiding, in a world full of barriers and xenophobia: that really *is* good news for the world.

Gordon Mursell

Suggested hymns

Great God, your love has called us here; Jesus calls us here to meet him; Thou didst leave thy throne and thy kingly crown; Lord of the Church, we pray for our renewing.

Second Sunday before Advent   14 November
(For Remembrance Sunday, see p. 274.)
Principal Service   **Hope for the World**
Dan. 12.1–3; Ps. 16; Heb. 10.11–14 [15–18] 19–25;
Mark 13.1–8

We are daily reminded that we live in a violent and imperfect world. We are faced with the needless loss of innocent life and humankind's inhumanity. The sorrow and evil that we witness can cause us to despair. What can we do? How can we help? How will this all end? In our reading from Mark's Gospel, Jesus presents the disciples with a picture of what is to come: wars and rumours of wars, earthquakes and famines. It's sometimes difficult not to wonder whether we are living in these end times today. Many have thought much the same as they have journeyed through the violence and conflict of ages past, but have found in the words of Christ hope for the world, and hope for the coming of his kingdom.

In his life and ministry Jesus was always pointing beyond the here and now to a world of peace, mercy and justice. Christ called his disciples to keep on praying and never lose heart, to lift up our eyes and hope that goodness can arise from evil, peace can emerge from war and the light will overcome the darkness we are sometimes witness to.

Thy kingdom come

Jesus always knew that the future for those who followed him would not be easy. He knew they would face persecution and hardship, and this is why he prophesied against the Temple. He was trying to tell his disciples that faith was more important than anything else. The Temple in Jerusalem was shiny and new and impressive, adorned with golden pomegranates and the finest marble. It was, on first appearances, a fitting and perfect tribute to God, the very best that money could buy. But appearances can be deceptive.

The danger was that the Temple had really become a tribute to King Herod, who throughout his reign spent the equivalent of millions of pounds on the Temple in Jerusalem as a trade-off to the people he was trying to control. If he made their Temple beautiful, they might just do as he said. Jesus saw through all of this. He understood the politics of the day, he was aware of the corruption and he knew that this was not the kind of response God required of those who loved him. This was not what faith was about, this was not the kingdom he had come to proclaim. None of this really mattered. Jesus came to turn this kind of world order upside down. The mighty would be brought down from their thrones and the lowly and humble lifted up.

A new temple

Jesus predicted the destruction of the Temple in Jerusalem, which would eventually come to pass in AD 70, about 40 years after his death. It would never be rebuilt. About 30 years later, the early Church would have looked back at this recent history and come to realize Jesus was right all along. Jesus also predicted earthquakes, wars and famines, and he knew that Christians would be persecuted and denounced and hated because of his name; they would even be betrayed by their own family. This wasn't a shiny kind of Christianity, which promised perfection, prosperity and wealth. There was no gloss here. The new temple, Jesus predicted, would be of flesh and blood. This is what the writer of the book of Hebrews is telling us. The temple would no longer be a place of worship – it would be Christ himself. A living temple, a holy sacrifice that would be nailed to the cross and raised from the rubble three days later.

Children of hope

Faith opens our eyes to the real world as it really is, bruised and broken, and yet full of glory and grace. We will all face desolation and destruction, uncertainty, doubt and sadness. But do we give up? Or do we persevere with patient endurance? Are we not all children of hope walking by the light of our faith? Is this not where the cross of Christ leads each one of us?

The writer of Hebrews says that we must encourage one another, provoking each other to love and good deeds, meeting together more and more and holding fast to the confession of our hope. Jesus gives his people a new hope in the future, he gives a troubled world the promise that his kingdom will come, that his people will be delivered and protected. He calls us to follow him into the hard places of the world, because it is in him that our hope is founded and it is through him that we become a community of hope.

We continue to look for hope on the horizon as our forebears have done. We are about to enter the season of watching and waiting – a season of hope – and now more than ever we pray that Christ will come again on earth to reign. As we approach Advent, we begin to yearn for Christ, we beckon his coming and we continue to work to make his kingdom come on earth, as it in is heaven.

Victoria Johnson

Suggested hymns

All my hope on God is founded; O God, our hope in ages past; Come, living God, when least expected; Thy kingdom come, O God.

Remembrance Sunday   14 November
The Centurion's Confession
Mark 15.33–39[31]

> Now when the centurion, who stood facing [Jesus], saw that in this way he breathed his last, he said, 'Truly this man was God's Son!' (Mark 15.39)

There's something extraordinary about those words, spoken by someone who witnessed Jesus' death. The Roman centurion, broadly what we would call a senior NCO, would doubtless have been responsible for getting Jesus crucified. And at the very moment when the job was done, and the victim was dead, the centurion wonders who he was: 'truly this man was God's Son!'). There are others in Mark's Gospel who come close to the truth about Jesus:

Peter calls him 'the Christ', the blind Bartimaeus calls him 'Son of David'. But – apart from the demons, who recognize him just before he drives them out – there's only one person who sees the full truth, that this Jesus is the divine Son of God. That person is not a disciple, not even Jewish, not someone likely to have been remotely interested in who Jesus was, until that moment: a foreigner, a soldier, a representative of the hated occupying power, is the one who gets it right: 'Truly this man was God's Son!'

How he came to believe

And what's even more remarkable is how it is that the centurion comes to believe this. In Matthew's version of the story, the centurion is convinced by the dramatic events that take place as Jesus dies – the earthquake and the dead arising from their tombs. In Luke's version, he just concludes that Jesus was a good man. In John's Gospel, the centurion doesn't appear at all. But in Mark's Gospel, the earliest of the four, the centurion becomes convinced that Jesus is the Son of God not by dramatic events such as the veil of the Temple being torn apart but by the way Jesus died (when he 'saw that in this way he breathed his last'). Centurions might not be expected to know much about theology. But, like their equivalents all over the world, they would know a thing or two about human suffering, about courage and cowardice, and above all about what happens when people die a violent death (things most of us prefer not to think about at all). We don't know exactly what impressed that centurion about Jesus' death: it may have been the way he died without pleading for mercy, without any complaint or calling down of vengeance on those who were killing him. What we do know is that this foreign soldier looked at the dead body of the man he'd just crucified and said, 'Truly this man was God's Son.'

The power of reconciliation

Now, what does this mean, and why does it matter for us on Remembrance Sunday? Two things are worth saying. First, the centurion shows us the power of Christian reconciliation. He isn't some innocent bystander who happens to come across a crucifixion taking place and stays to watch. He is responsible for it. Jesus is not just a foreigner to him. He's his enemy. Yet he sees, *precisely in him*, the presence of God. Today we remember those who gave their lives in the horrors of war, especially in two world wars. But

Christians can never be satisfied simply with the remembrance of those who died 'on our side', or for our land. The only kind of remembering that will help to ensure that such wars never happen again is to call to mind, and pray for, the victims of *every* land, and to commit ourselves to seek the face and the presence of Christ in those who in worldly terms were our enemy.

On this of all days, we are right to remember and give thanks for the courage and dedication of those who served (and still serve) in our armed services, both during two world wars and today. But we also give thanks for those who have been able, like that Roman centurion, to see something of the presence of God not only in those on their own side but even in those they are fighting against – all those who have seen the suffering Christ in Passchendaele or Hiroshima or Syria, and have been able to speak across the barriers of war and nation and to say, like the centurion: surely this person too was a child of God. And above all we give thanks for all those who inspire us to see that there can be more to life than just thinking about me, and that there is something I can do to challenge the powers of evil and despair.

The power to change hearts and lives

For there's one more thing to be said about the centurion's confession, which brings us even closer to the heart of Christian faith. At the very moment when the centurion thinks that Jesus, this Jewish trouble-maker, has been got rid of, he suddenly realizes that the opposite is true: that there was something about this man that death could not defeat. Wars and fighting are always tragic, and sometimes necessary: they can change situations, but they can't change hearts and lives. Only one power can do that: the power of unresisting, unconditional love – the love that God offers us by sending his only son to die for us. What the centurion witnessed was a love that would outlast imperial Rome and would one day bring its rulers to their knees in worship. As we remember today those of all nations who gave all they had to give in the service of a cause they believed in, we commit ourselves afresh to the God whose love alone can change our world and heal its wounds, and in whose love we and all who have gone before us are for ever safe.

Gordon Mursell

For the healing of the nations; In Christ there is no east or west; Holy Spirit, storm of love; Forth in the peace of Christ we go.

Christt the King 21 November
(Sunday next before Advent)
Principal Service **The King Who is No King**
Dan. 7.9–10, 13–14; Ps. 93; Rev. 1.4b–8; **John 18.33–37**

We're celebrating the feast of a king. Yet what *are* kings, what are they for?

Surely monarchs have fallen on hard times in the past few centuries. There aren't many kings left, and those that are still around haven't much power.

One or two, as in Saudi Arabia, still rule as autocrats; but most absolute monarchs succumbed to popular revolution ages ago, as in France and Russia. Wiser monarchs compromised with representatives of their people, as in Britain and other northern European countries. But then they and their heirs were reduced to a mainly decorative role, so they risk looking like overdressed anachronisms.

Either way, kingship has lost much of its force as an image for power and glory.

And that suggests that much of the imagery in the Bible has lost its force and is growing stale. For, again and again, God is depicted there as *king* of his people, even of the universe. He is the supreme ruler, the mighty warrior. And, despite the abysmal record of the kings of Israel, the almighty Monarch is to send his Messiah, that is, a new anointed King; and the Messiah will vanquish all his enemies and bring 'the whole created order to worship at his feet' (as today's Collect has it).

The rule of the Messiah

Is that really what we believe about Jesus and how we picture him? Or has that whole triumphant story lost its power, as have the kings of Europe?

This feast of Christ the King was instituted by Pope Pius XI in 1925 as a way of shoring up the confidence of Christian Europe against the threats of revolution and atheism from Soviet Russia and from sceptics within. As in that Collect, and in some of our readings today, there's a strong streak of triumphalism in the feast. How does that tally with what we read about Jesus in the Gospels, and how we see him on the cross?

Jesus himself eventually confronts monarchical power, in the person of Pontius Pilate, representative of the Roman Emperor. We've just heard part of the very strange conversation between the two. Jesus is accused of claiming to be a Messiah or king, which would be an act of rebellion against the occupying power. But when the imperial governor asks him if this is true, Jesus is rather like a government official today: he will neither confirm nor deny the claim.

'Not from this world'

Or rather, he speaks of kingship in mysterious terms, which sound very different from those of Caesar. 'My kingship (or my kingdom) is not from this world.' If you *do* want to call me Messiah, he's saying, then forget all your worldly notions of kingship and power and glory, forget about bowing and fancy titles and leading troops into battle. You, Pilate, not I, you say that I am a king. 'For this I was born, and for this I came into the world, to testify to the truth.' You know all about power, Pilate. But it's not *about* power; it's about *truth*.

So when we call Jesus the Messiah, the Christ, when we sing to him as our king, what we are celebrating is the *truth* that comes from his lips and from his life. A truth that sidelines the claims of Pilate and Caesar, and of any earthly monarch or ideology or system. If we are faithful to Christ our King, then none of these can be accorded any absolute honour.

In earthly terms, of course, they have more power. Pilate is able to condemn to *death* this strange man, who is a king but not a king. But *there* is the greatest reversal: it shines out so insistently in the climax of St John's Gospel. That the glory lies not in a throne or sceptre, not in any of the clutter of earthly monarchy, not in any kind of power. No, glory radiates out from our suffering lover, the speaker and liver of truth, lifted up on Golgotha.

'No monarch thou'

The Christian poets and hymn writers of the Middle Ages (an age when earthly kings made such ambitious claims) loved to dwell on this extraordinary and saving paradox: that the maker of all things is confined in a baby's crib, that the king of the world is nailed to a tree. And so, in our own age, does the preacher and poet Bill Vanstone, concluding his hymn to God:

Thou art God; no monarch Thou
Thron'd in easy state to reign;
Thou art God, Whose arms of love,
Aching, spent, the world sustain.

So thanks and praise and glory be to our King who is no king, with the Father of Love and the Spirit of Truth.

Christopher Burdon

Suggested hymns

Morning glory, starlit sky; From heaven you came, helpless babe; Beauty for brokenness; Jesus shall reign, where'er the sun.

Christ the King 21 November
(Sunday next before Advent)
Second Service **The Voice of the Lord**
Morning **Ps. 29**, 110; Evening Ps. 72 [*or* 72.1–7]; Dan. 5; John 6.1–15

The voice of the LORD is powerful;
the voice of the LORD is full of majesty. (Psalm 29.4)

Ask Google a question and it's amazing the answers you will receive. For example, ask Google the question, 'Who is the greatest drummer in the world?' and you will be offered the following list: Ginger Baker of Cream; Mike Portnoy of Dream Theatre; Lars Ulrich of Metallica; Dave Grohl of Nirvana, Foo Fighters and Them Crooked Vultures; Keith Moon of The Who; Neal Peart of Rush; and John Bonham of Led Zeppelin.

You will notice that the drummers named, of whom you might or might not have heard, are all drummers in rock bands. There's no mention of drummers from the classical music world – which all goes to prove that Google is biased and is not omniscient. So, there's no mention of the Austrian percussionist Martin Grubinger or of Dame Evelyn Glennie.

A voice like a drum beat

So, why begin a sermon with a brief discussion about drummers? Because of today's psalm, Psalm 29. That psalm has only 11 verses, but within those 11 verses, one phrase, 'The voice of the LORD', occurs no fewer than seven times. It's just like a drumbeat. It bangs its way insistently and rhythmically into our consciousness. The psalm is sometimes called 'The Psalm of the Seven Thunders'.

The author of the psalm obviously has a great and violent storm in mind as he seeks to describe the glory and might of God. It's a storm which whips up the sand in the wilderness, which makes the cedar trees dance, which stirs up the fury of the sea. It's a powerful metaphor for the voice of God, made even more powerful because the phrase 'the voice of God' is repeated so often.

Voicing different sounds

There are other moments in the Old Testament when the voice of God is mentioned. For instance, in that haunting account of Elijah who discovers that God is not in the earthquake, nor in the fire, but in the still, small voice. And there's that equally moving story of Adam and Eve being encountered in the Garden of Eden.

> They heard the sound of the LORD God walking in the garden at the time of the evening breeze, and the man and his wife hid themselves from the presence of the LORD God among the trees of the garden. But the LORD God called to the man, and said to him, 'Where are you?' He said, 'I heard the sound of you in the garden, and I was afraid, because I was naked; and I hid myself.'

A naive question: how did Adam know that it was God who was in the garden? What kind of sound did God make so that Adam had no doubt about who was there?

And in the New Testament, while we are given no clues about the timbre or quality of the voice of Jesus, we are left in no doubt about the power and authority of what he says. For example, in the account of the storm on the Lake: 'He woke up and rebuked the wind, and said to the sea, "Peace! Be still!" Then the wind ceased, and there was a dead calm.'

At the crucifixion each of the Gospel writers describes what Jesus said when he hung on the cross, but again, we aren't told what the tone of his terrible cries might have been. Was 'It is finished' a triumphant roar? Was 'My God, my God, why have you forsaken me?', by contrast, an agonized, soul-juddering whisper?

There was a lovely medieval belief that newly born baby lions were born dead but were brought into life when their parents roared. It is probably that notion which gave C. S. Lewis his inspirational idea for Aslan: the Voice of God which, when uttered, like a roar, brought life and the created order into being.

The Psalmist, with great literary skill, brings to our attention the might and glory and power of God.

Reverberations within the soul

The concept of sound as the origin of things is not limited to the Judaeo-Christian tradition. Within Hinduism, the word 'Om', which some say is like the sound of a drum, refers to Ultimate Reality, to Brahman, the Creator of all that is.

There is something about primordial sound (which is what the sound made by a drum is) that reverberates intensely within our souls. Paradoxically, it takes us deeper into ourselves and at the same time out of ourselves, and leads us towards a more mystical place. Perhaps this is what the Psalmist is trying to suggest with his repetition of the phrase 'the voice of God'. It is the author's way of directing us to that unfathomable part of our being that seeks communion with the Divine. It is a phrase which, because it does not then express itself with further explanatory words, ensures that our ideas of the Almighty are enlarged. The 'voice of God' is about majesty and awe and the beauty of holiness, and the essence of that music at the heart of all creation that calls us to plunge into God's mysterious and passionately lovely Being.

Christopher Herbert

Suggested hymns

How sweet the name of Jesus sounds; Above the voices of the world around me; For the music of creation; Lord, your voice in Eden's garden.

Sermons for Saints' Days
and Special Occasions

St Stephen, Deacon, First Martyr   26 December
Costly Discipleship
2 Chron. 24.20–22, *or* **Acts 7.51–end**; Ps. 119.161–168; (*if the Acts reading is used instead of the Old Testament reading, the New Testament reading is* Gal. 2.16b–20); Matt. 10.17–22

Today is Boxing Day. We are still in the Christmas season. We are still singing carols, eating up leftovers, opening presents and watching Christmas television. Traditionally Boxing Day is the time for a long walk. Some are doing that today, others are sleeping off Christmas excess, still others are rushing to the sales – eager to buy yet more. Today, however, the Church moves from the baby in the manger to focus on the martyrdom of Stephen. During these days immediately after Christmas, the Church commemorates Stephen, the first Christian martyr, the massacre of the Holy Innocents and the murder of Thomas Becket. The birth of Jesus, the Messiah, brings both celebration and conflict. The baby in the manger doesn't stay a cosy story for Christmas. Jesus grows up and calls his disciples to a life of service and sacrifice.

Stephen – the deacon

Everything we know about Stephen comes from Luke's account in chapters 6 and 7 of Acts. Stephen is one of seven followers of Jesus in Jerusalem chosen to have hands laid on them by the apostles in order to be appointed as deacons. Luke describes Stephen as being a man full of faith and the Holy Spirit. As a deacon he carries out acts of service for the community, waiting at tables and caring for widows and the vulnerable. More than this – Stephen is full of grace and the power of the Lord. He also does great wonders and signs and, when challenged by those in the synagogue on his beliefs, he is able to debate with great wisdom and skill, in a way that causes the elders and scribes to feel threatened. Those against the new followers of the way cry, 'Blasphemy'. They accuse Stephen of teaching against Moses, the law and the Temple.

Stephen – the disciple

In the Gospel set for today, Jesus tells his disciples that they will be handed over to synagogues and councils, and brought before governors and kings because of their belief in him. They are not to worry about how they will testify because the Holy Spirit will give them the words they need at the right time. Jesus warns his followers that they will be hated and persecuted. He promises that they will eventually be saved. Stephen is his master's disciple. He is indeed brought before the assembly – the main council in Jerusalem. Asked to make account, he gives a detailed and thorough retelling of the history of salvation starting with the glory of God and moving through Abraham, Moses, the Temple and finally to Jesus the Messiah. The Holy Spirit is indeed giving him the words to say and they are inflammatory. The Jews are furious to be told that they have opposed the Holy Spirit, broken the law and betrayed and murdered the Righteous One. Stephen's faithful discipleship leads him on a very dangerous trajectory. Luke tells us that Stephen has the face of an angel – his fate is sealed.

Stephen – the martyr

Imagine the crowd: enraged and gnashing their teeth. Imagine Stephen filled with the Holy Spirit, radiant and almost luminous. Such contrasts. Stephen is looking to heaven not earth, and he sees Jesus standing at the right hand of God ready to welcome him home. Rocks are thrown. Stephen is battered and crushed to death. He calls on Jesus to receive his Spirit, just as Jesus on the cross called to the Father. Like Jesus, Stephen asks forgiveness for his murderers – practising love for enemies and persecutors. It is in complete contrast to our passage from 2 Chronicles 24 where Zechariah – who is also stoned to death – calls down the Lord's vengeance. With Jesus, forgiveness and reconciliation are key tenets of faithful discipleship. On one level Stephen's death is a disaster, a tragedy. Family and friends will have been sickened and distraught by his murder. But this first Christian martyrdom takes place in the light of the resurrection and, like the crucifixion, Stephen's death is not the end of the story. His martyrdom leads to the early Christian community being scattered, and from there the good news of Jesus Christ is spread far and wide. But closer to home, too, Luke records that at the stoning of Stephen witnesses laid their cloaks at the feet of a young man named Saul. Surely Stephen's extraordinary courage and witness to Christ laid the foundation that led to the conversion of Saul the persecutor into St Paul the apostle.

Beyond the Christmas story

It's very easy to leave the baby in the manger – to pack away Jesus for another year with the tinsel and decorations. But the Christ-child calls us to grow up with him. We are called to grow a mature faith that is prepared to go on adventures into the unknown, following Jesus our master. We probably won't be called to martyrdom – though Christians around the world die for their faith every day. However, as we follow Jesus we will certainly be called to witness to our beliefs and to stand up for our faith, sometimes in hostile environments. Don't be afraid! Jesus promises that the Holy Spirit will tell you what to say and do. And if it feels like your witness is a failure, remember Stephen's martyrdom, remember Jesus' resurrection – God can turn even the most terrible events into extraordinary new beginnings.

Catherine Williams

Suggested hymns

Good King Wenceslas; Once in Royal David's city; Jesus, lover of my soul; When Stephen full of power and grace.

St John, Apostle and Evangelist   27 December
The Beloved Disciple
Ex. 33.7–11a; Ps. 117; 1 John 1; **John 21.19b–25**

'There are also many other things that Jesus did; if every one of them were written down, I suppose that the world itself could not contain the books that would be written.' With these remarkable words, both personal and world-embracing, the Gospel of John closes. But what do they mean? Is St John really saying that it would take all those books to set down the sayings of a man whose public ministry only lasted a couple of years? Or is it a piece of literary exaggeration? And does it matter anyway? Let me suggest that, no, it wouldn't take all those books; no, it isn't a literary exaggeration; and, yes, it does matter. But we'll come back to that in a moment.

The peril of envy

Let's return to that reading. It begins just after the risen Jesus has told the apostle Peter that when he (Peter) was young, he used to go wherever he wanted, but that when he grows older, he will find himself having to go where he doesn't want to go. Jesus is predicting Peter's martyrdom in Rome. And Peter, understandably, is unimpressed. So he looks round and sees 'the disciple whom Jesus loved', by tradition also the writer of the Gospel, who doesn't look as if he's going anywhere. So Peter says to Jesus, 'Lord, what about him?' It's a very understandable reaction in life. 'What about him – he's only got half a workload compared to me', or, 'That couple seem to sail through life without a cloud in the sky'. Envy will always be around, because there will always be someone who seems to get a better deal in life than you or me. But it doesn't help you face the future *you* need to face. Jesus says to Peter, 'If it is my will that he remain until I come, what is that to you? Follow me!' Don't spend your one life thinking 'If only I were him' or 'What about her?' God has other plans for them.

Following and abiding

What these verses offer us are two complementary ways of being a Christian: you can *follow* Jesus, like St Peter; or you can *abide with* Jesus, like St John (the word translated 'remain' is the Greek *menō*, one of the key words in John's Gospel, which means to abide or be at home with). The Church needs its active, outgoing mission-minded members like Peter, as well as its contemplatives like John, whose ministry is more hidden but no less fruitful. In fact all of us need to find the right balance between the two: there's a Peter and a John in you, a time in your life for world-engaging discipleship and a time for reflective Christ-centred withdrawal. We don't know much about the Beloved Disciple except for the fact that he was loved; and that's the single most important reality in anyone's life. Millions never know, or can never believe, that they are loved, because no one has ever told them they are, or shown them that they matter. Because he knew he was loved, St John was free from the need to compete in strenuousness with his fellow disciples; free to live into the love God had for him, and through his life and his writing to extend that love to others.

Witnessing

But today's reading tells us one more vital thing about John. He was a witness (this is the disciple who is *testifying* – literally 'witnessing' – to these things). The Gospel of John begins and ends with witnesses: John the Baptist at the start, John the Evangelist at the end. They bear witness, by their lives and their words, to Christ, and then step out of the way. Notice something else: the only place in the Gospel where its author actually appears is in the very last verse: 'I suppose that the world itself ...' The 'I' pops up on stage just as the curtain begins to fall, and then steps out of the way: because it's not about him, and it's not about you or me, either. Which brings us back to where we started.

'There are many other things that Jesus did; if every one of them were written down, I suppose that the world itself could not contain the books that would be written.' This is not a piece of empty rhetoric: the reason the world will not be able to contain the books that would be written is that *the story goes on after the Gospel ends*. That's what St John is telling us as he leaves the stage. It's over to you now, he says, as he bids us farewell – and to others after you. And one day the world will be transfigured, filled to overflowing, through the stories of lives that were changed as his was, by the risen Lord who is his God and ours.

Gordon Mursell

Suggested hymns

Come, thou Redeemer of the earth; A great and mighty wonder; In heavenly love abiding; Christ is the world's light, he and none other.

The Holy Innocents 28 December
Who Do You Want to Murder?
Jer. 31.15–17; Ps. 124; 1 Cor. 1.26–29; **Matt. 2.13–18**

Have you ever fantasized about murdering another person? I wouldn't have dared pose that question but for the fact that an academic, Julia Shaw, has suggested that most of us have done just that at some time. Perhaps the thought has crossed your mind even this past week, with your extended family gathered in your home. Well, today, our attention is focused on a person who was a serial murderer. Right in the middle of Matthew's telling of the Christmas story we find Herod initiating the mass murder of infants. It's there right in the middle of Matthew's account of the nativity, and it's as much part of the story of Jesus' birth as that of the 'wise men' and the good news of the angels. And it's there to remind us that if we don't reckon with the worst manifestations of the human condition, we can't begin to grasp the scope of Jesus' mission to bring salvation to a troubled world.

Is it true?

The perpetrator of this brutality was one, Herod, who ruled Judaea in the years leading up to Jesus' birth. Herod had backed the wrong side at a crucial battle won by Anthony and was unexpectedly made a puppet king, living from day to day in fear that his crown would be revoked. There are no independent records of a massacre in Jerusalem, but the numbers of male children under two years, an estimated 20 or so, may not have merited a report in the long annals of Herod's brutality. But the report of the massacre is, at least, in keeping with what we know of him already. He tracked down and murdered all who threatened him, and after a period of peace, when family feuds returned, he became embittered and murdered his wife, mother-in-law and three sons.

True to experience

So the account of Herod is plausible and in character with what we know of him from other sources. The very mention of a new king of the Jews rang alarm bells for Herod. After all, he was the son of a mere Idumean adventurer; he had no ancestral right to the throne, and even his claim to be Jewish was a matter of dispute for many Jews. Even if the tale of the Magi was plausible to Herod, it would clearly be a long time before Jesus would be in a position to threaten Herod's kingship. But reason brings no consolation when we feel threatened. In those moments of paranoia everyone on two legs poses a threat to our life and well-being.

The wise men didn't return to give Herod details of the whereabouts of Jesus and his parents, and it was the feeling that he had been 'tricked' that resulted in Herod authorizing the murder of all male children aged two and under, in the region. The person under threat goes to ludicrous lengths in order to protect himself and safeguard his position. For Herod, survival is everything and he will stop at nothing in order to maintain his existence.

Fears and phantasies

That's Herod, the man who, through disorder in his own life, had no place for Jesus. The man with an identity crisis that led him to fear the identity of everyone else. So, then, does the conduct of Herod, however exaggerated, at least resonate with us in our insecurities and vulnerability? Have we, indeed, fantasized about murdering another person – the boss, neighbour, spouse, child, parent or slow driver ahead of us, or person at the checkout keeping us waiting while she seems to have a counselling session with the cashier?

Perhaps there are echoes of Herod in all of us. We all have our little empires, we're all kings in some areas of life, however small. We cherish and guard the territory in which we function, and we can be sensitive to threats, so sensitive that we imagine threats where they don't exist. When we see a group of colleagues or acquaintances talking quietly together and looking sheepish when our eyes meet, do we fear we're being discussed unfavourably, perhaps the object of some concerted action against us? Do we lie awake imagining rings of hostility designed to frame or expose us? Are there people who remind us of other people and who then become the unwitting target for enacting all our negative projections?

We may not only feel the threat to our person, power or position. Like Herod, we can overreact to defend it. We can unleash excessive force to attack or neutralize the threat we perceive from others. We can spend all our powers surmounting threats, real or imagined, so that we become paralysed and disabled by our imagining of others.

Living from a secure base

Fantasizing about eliminating those who threaten us may be a necessary start on the long journey of self-discovery, and can temper our irrational and impulsive emotional responses. Herod had real and powerful opponents, but even he could have found a secure relationship to exorcise his false and imagined perceptions. The good news is that God's coming down to earth offers us that secure relationship that casts out our fear and stills our troubled lives. We are accepted and acceptable, not simply in and by ourselves but through the indwelling of the Son of God.

Roger Spiller

Suggested hymns

Brightest and best of the sons of the morning; In the night, the sound of crying; Our Saviour's infant cries were heard; Thou who wast rich beyond all splendour.

Naming and Circumcision of Jesus   1 January
The Power of Names
Num. 6.22–end; Ps. 8; Gal. 4.4–7; **Luke 2.15–21**

> After eight days had passed, it was time to circumcise the child; and he was called Jesus, the name given by the angel before he was conceived in the womb. (Luke 2.21)

During the early 1470s a banker called Tommaso Portinari, who was head of the Medici Bank in Bruges, commissioned an artist in Ghent to paint an altarpiece. The artist was Hugo van der Goes. The huge painting that resulted, measuring 253 by 304 cm (roughly 8 feet by 10 feet), was destined for the Santa Maria Nuova hospital in Florence, a hospital which had been heavily supported by the Portinari family for generations. The altarpiece eventually reached Florence in 1482.

The painting depicts the story of the Adoration of the Shepherds. At the centre of the painting the naked Christ child lies on the ground next to his mother, surrounded by angels in eucharistic vestments. At the front of the painting are two small vases holding flowers, lilies, carnations and aquilegia – symbols of Christ's passion. Just behind the flowers a sheaf of wheat lies on the floor, a symbol of the Mass.

So, obviously, as an altarpiece, the Mass is central to our understanding of the painting. Nevertheless, our eyes keep straying away to the right-hand side of the central panel where three shepherds are shown: the oldest is kneeling, the second is in the process of going down on his knees, and the third is behind them, leaning over to get a view of the baby. It's their humanity that is so striking; rough and ready men, used to the outdoor life, hired by a rich farmer to care for his flock. The oldest of them has his hands held together as if in prayer, and his face is suffused with a kind of gentle, adoring radiance. It is a stunning portrait. You could gaze at it for hours.

Nameless people

One of the interesting things about Luke's story of the shepherds is that they are not named. We simply do not know who they were, though presumably they lived somewhere in Bethlehem. They are a critical part of the drama, witnesses of an epiphany of angels, but having played their roles they walk off stage never to be heard of again. They are the nameless ones.

Now let us cast our minds forwards to the final chapters of Luke's Gospel. There we find other nameless people, two disciples who encounter the risen Christ on the Emmaus road. We don't know their names either, and having delivered their message to the Twelve they too walk off stage

It's curious, isn't it? Nameless shepherds at the beginning of the story; nameless followers at the end. Was this carelessness on Luke's part, a bit of slap-dash writing, or might this have been part of his storytelling skill?

Let's return to today's reading because the departure of the shepherds is followed immediately by this sentence: 'After eight days had passed, it was time to circumcise the child; and he was called Jesus, the name given by the angel before he was conceived in the womb.' It's very specific. Note the words 'eight days', which refers to the legal requirements of the Jewish faith. The child is circumcised following Jewish tradition, demonstrating that he is an inheritor of the covenant made between God and Abraham.

After circumcision, the child is then named. He is called 'Jesus', the name delivered to Mary by the angel Gabriel at the annunciation. It's a name that echoes the prophecy in Isaiah 7.14: 'Therefore

290

the LORD himself will give you a sign. Look, the young woman is with child and shall bear a son, and shall name him Immanuel.'

The meaning of the name 'Jesus'

And what does the name 'Jesus' mean? Here we enter complicated territory. The name 'Jesus' is the Greek form of the Hebrew *yeshuah* (Joshua) and is probably best translated as 'God saves' or 'God is my help' or 'God is salvation'. In other words, the name given to Jesus is a descriptive one that both encapsulates and foretells his future ministry.

In Luke's account of the nativity, nameless shepherds encounter a child who, at the time they see him, is also nameless. He does not yet have a publically given name. He is, as it were, representative of all humanity.

Once he has been officially named, his name remains with him throughout his life, but ironically, in Luke's account of the crucifixion, it is then taken away from him. The label on the cross reads, 'This is the King of the Jews' (Luke 23.38). The name 'Jesus' appears in the accounts of the crucifixion label in Matthew and John, but in Luke, there's no name. Jesus has returned to namelessness again.

Now, it may be that we are reading too much into this, but perhaps not. Perhaps this is Luke's way of reminding his readers that Jesus was in solidarity with humanity at the very beginning of his life, and is in solidarity with us as he dies on the cross. He takes all of us with him on his journey through life and death and on into resurrection; which is why we rightly describe the story as 'good news', and why the name of Jesus should frequently be on our lips and in our hearts. As St Paul wrote in his letter to the young church at Philippi:

> at the name of Jesus,
>   every knee should bend,
> in heaven and on earth and under the earth,
> and every tongue should confess
>   that Jesus Christ is Lord,
>   to the glory of God the Father.

Christopher Herbert

At the name of Jesus; We have a gospel to proclaim; While shepherds watched; Jesus shall reign where'er the sun.

Epiphany   6 January
'Another King, One Jesus'?
Isa. 60.1–6; Ps. 72 [1–9] 10–15; Eph. 3.1–12; **Matt. 2.1–12**

How many kings were alluded to in today's Gospel? Three? Four? Five? Twelve? All those suggestions have seriously been proposed. What do you think? I think Matthew reckoned that there were just two. The Magi were astrologers not kings, despite all the pictures and carols depicting them as regal. And that leaves just two: King Herod and King Jesus.

King Herod

King Herod, puppet king of the hated Romans, reigned in Palestine for nearly 40 years. Known as Herod the Great, he brought his country a period of stability and peace during his long reign. He was a visionary who instigated colossal building projects, including renovating the Temple, extending the Temple Mount and constructing Masada. He could be generous too, once reported to have melted some of his gold to buy corn for people starving from a deep famine. But for all his achievements, Herod's position as king was precarious, dependent upon keeping favour with his Roman overlords and living daily in fear that others would plot against him and remove him from office. Even close family members weren't safe. And his wife, mother-in-law and three of his sons were murdered on his instruction.

The paranoia of power

So when magi or wise men from the East showed up, his paranoia went into overdrive. For Herod, there could only be one king of the Jews and that was him. No one should feel threatened by a newborn baby or by the claims of him made by mysterious Eastern visitors. But the risk was too great for Herod, and he gave orders to eliminate all potential threats to his and his family's control. The decree to slaughter all (male) children aged two or younger in the region of Bethlehem is meant to remind us of another king, long ago, one Pharaoh, who also decreed to murder all young males in the hope of removing Moses.

Knowledge and faith

The Magi go to Herod's court and enquire, 'Where will the Messiah be born?' And Herod's advisers know, of course. They were sitting on far-reaching knowledge but choosing to ignore it. When the Magi called in to seek directions to the birth, you might expect the religious leaders to have welcomed news of their coming king. They might have joined the wise men in their search for the king and Messiah that they had been waiting for. But they refused to act, to change, to make even the small journey that would have changed them for ever.

Herod stands for those who know but refuse to act. The wise men lacked knowledge but they had faith. They had the faith to act on no more than a hunch, an intuition, slender evidence, in order to pursue their dream and seek the king of another nation, not there own. Faith is often contrasted with knowledge. Our story shows that both are needed. But the search for knowledge, to know more, become more confident, gain more certainty, before we commit ourselves, can lead us to miss out on the encounter and worship of our true king who alone could satisfy our trust.

The true King is revealed

Herod's actions expose him as a false, illegitimate king and it takes wise men from a distant and alien country to expose him. Herod only pretends that he will come and worship him. But the Magi become the true worshippers of the infant King, Jesus. And they recognize him as the universal King. The pagan elite stand on the side of Jesus, while the elite of the holy people of Judaea oppose him. Herod seeks to murder the rightful king of the Jews; the men from an alien religion help to save him. And then the heathen land of Egypt becomes a place of refuge for Jesus as he flees from the rage of Israel's king. There is the supreme irony that heathen nations in distant lands, the Magi from the East and the Egyptians from the South help to save the life of Jesus, the true king of the nations.

Our king?

Who do we enthrone? Having discredited the existing king of the Jews, the Magi point us to our true king. And they teach us that discovering him involves a long and costly journey. But only through embarking upon this daring adventure will we discover the legitimacy of our quest. It cannot be known in advance, before embarking on the journey. The visit of the Magi sets before us two kings, two centres of power, two lifestyles. That's the choice that is always lurking in every decision we have to make. It's timely that we face it early in a new year, a year in which much of what will be most significant to us remains unknown. The magi, who proved to be 'wise men', returned to their own home changed, as T. S. Eliot's poem declares. It cannot be otherwise, when we encounter and worship Jesus.

How many kings were there? For Matthew there is only one king. There can only be room for one to be enthroned in our lives. The choice is clear, the stakes are high and the consequences profound.

Roger Spiller

Suggested hymns

O worship the Lord in the beauty of holiness; Bethlehem, what greater city; Wise men, they came to look for wisdom; As with gladness, men of old.

Week of Prayer for Christian Unity   18–25 January
The Unity for Which Jesus Prays
John 17

Here we are once more at the beginning of the Week of Prayer for Christian Unity – the one hundred and twelfth Week of Prayer: 112 years of Christians around the world from many denominations praying for unity. You might ask, as Archbishop Rowan did, on the centenary, 'Where has all this praying got us?' It is easy to forget just how far we have come. I don't suppose a hundred years ago anyone would have believed that an Archbishop of Canterbury would be planning a visit to the Sudan together with the Pope, or that a pope would take off his episcopal ring and put it on the finger of an Archbishop of Canterbury, or an Archbishop of Canterbury would take off his episcopal cross and put it around the neck of a pope. These lovely exchanges of gifts symbolize more than can be put into words about how far we have come in reconciling the terrible divisions of the past.

A long road travelled together

Who would have thought a hundred years ago that Lutherans and Roman Catholics would come to agree on the doctrine of justification that lay at the heart of the Reformation break? Who would have thought a hundred years ago that Christians here in towns across our country would work together in food banks or as street pastors to support those in need, or minister together in hospital and prison chaplaincies?

I could go on and on with stories of positive examples of changed relations forged over the last one hundred years. We have come out of our denominational corners. We have tried to understand the causes of our divisions; we are learning to receive gifts from other traditions and offer our gifts in a sort of gift exchange; we do act together in serving local communities; we do witness together to peace and justice – or at least we do when we remember that it is better together and more effective together.

Have we come far enough?

So, perhaps this is enough. Perhaps it's time to put an end to this annual Week of Prayer for Christian Unity – that's what many of my friends think. If you are tempted to think that, then stop. Remember the prayer of Jesus on the night before he died (John 17.20–21). It's one of the most moving passages in the whole of the Bible. We are placed in the most intimate of positions as we are drawn into Jesus' prayer to his Father. Jesus prays for his disciples then and for all those who will follow after them. That means Jesus prays for us – 'May they be one'. But, what does that mean? Jesus gives us three clues. He prays that we might all be one as he and the Father are one. We glimpse something of what that means as we follow Jesus' ministry and as we enter his prayer on the night before his crucifixion when, as he prays, facing what lies ahead Jesus comes to accept the 'Not my will but thine be done'. We see a loving conformity of minds and wills. Our unity is to be joined together, living with that same mind that Jesus shared with the Father.

One in the Trinitarian life

But Jesus prays not just that we might be one as he and the Father are one but more mysteriously, 'May they be one in us'. Our unity as Christians is a gift to be received, the gift of being drawn into that life of love that flows between the persons of the Trinity, to live in that life of love. In baptism, through the power of the Holy Spirit, we are joined to Christ. In the waters of baptism we die with Christ and rise to new life in him, with the Father, and with all the baptized. That unity is pure gift: a gift to be received and re-received, a gift we are called to live out together with all the baptized. Our unity is a unity founded in our common baptism, in our shared faith, ministered to by a common ministry, and nurtured in our eating and drinking around a common table which builds us up – we who are many are one, because we all eat of the same bread and drink from the same cup.

Sign to the world

And Jesus gives us a third clue about what our unity is as he prays to his Father, 'May they be one, so that the world might believe'. Our life together is to show to the world that it is possible to live together, loving one another, staying together even through differences that threaten to shatter our unity. There always will be disagreements as we are challenged by new theological, moral, political and economic issues. We are not called to uniformity but to a life of rich diversity, and in discovering that life we are called to 'disagree well', to listen to one another, to feel as others feel, believing the best of each other and not saying again, 'I have no need of you'. We are called to a life together that expresses the faith we believe and is modelled on the life of Jesus. We are called to express our common faith in action, caring for the vulnerable, the poor, the hungry, the migrants seeking refuge from violence and desperation. Our unity is to be a sign to the world of its own possibility.

So, this one hundred and twelfth annual Week of Prayer let's pray with Jesus: may we all be one as he and the Father are one; may we be one in them, enfolded in their love. May we be one so that the world may believe. Let's get on with it!

Mary Tanner

Living God, you word has called us; What should our greeting be?; O thou, who at thy Eucharist dids't pray; Filled with the Spirit's power, with one accord.

Conversion of St Paul   25 January
Good News

Jer. 1.4–10; Ps. 67; Acts 9.1–22 (*if the Acts reading is used instead of the Old Testament reading, the New Testament reading is* **Gal.1.11–16a**); Matt. 19.27–end

'Good News' was the name for a brand of chocolates for 30 years from 1960, presumably because it had sales appeal. It suggests you get something attractive, with a hint of freshness or discovery that implies you will want to pass it on to others. Long before it was named a box of chocolates, Christians were busy seeking to attract hearers by the promise of 'good news' or gospel.

At the present time all churches, especially in the West, seem to be reporting a decline in members, funding, resources, clergy. So, has good news gone stale or turned into bad news? When Christians sit down together to discuss what we need to do, the likelihood is that we talk about how we need to communicate better, and suggestions are made for more modern hymns, livelier services or better vicars. Seldom do we go back to the beginning, to fundamentals, and ask what the gospel is and whether we are keeping faith with it.

Receiving not doing

Most people you speak to inside as well as outside the Church seem to think that Christianity means being good and kind, living a decent life, doing as we would be done by. It's hard to see just how a demand-led ethical system could be construed as good news. Good news after all, whether it's a box of chocolates or a welcome message, is something we receive, not something we do. And what exactly has what we do to do with Jesus Christ? True, we can think of him as a role model, but that will turn out to be bad news when our own efforts result in failure and despair. And what place is here for God if we feel we can meet his standards, on our own, unaided?

Reading St Paul's letter to the Galatians makes us realize that many within the Church have not progressed from faith as a slavish adherence to laws, rules, conduct and commandments, and have yet to hear the gospel that brings us grace and freedom from the law. On what basis are we accepted by God, the epistle asks? Is it, as Paul's opponents claim, by assiduously keeping the law or, as he argues, by faithfully hearing the gospel? There can only be one gospel, Paul argues. There is scope for different expressions of the gospel, to adjust to different contents and people with different backgrounds. But there's an inalienable content that simply can't be compromised, and on that our salvation rests.

Disclosed by God

No one made this clearer than St Paul in his letters. So what is the gospel? St Paul reminds the Corinthian Christians of the gospel: 'I handed on to you as of first importance what I in turn had received: that Christ died for our sins in accordance with the scriptures, and that he was buried, and that he was raised on the third day in accordance with the scriptures, and that he appeared ... also to me.'

The 'facts' of the gospel, what is of 'first importance', are summed up in four verbs: Christ died, he was buried, he was raised, he was seen. The gospel is about 'facts' that are based on argument and evidence. But the claim that Jesus was 'raised from the dead' is not something that anyone can arrive at by argument alone. That's why St Paul says to the Galatians that 'the gospel ... is not of human origin ... I received it through a revelation of Jesus Christ'. Indeed, as Paul himself said, the idea of a crucified Messiah whom God raised from the dead was, and continues to be, dismissed as 'utter foolishness'. It can't be arrived at through reason because of the inherent limits of reason. The resurrection and risen life of Jesus includes but hugely exceeds what we can know from human history and experience. It is God's Spirit who discloses it to us.

The work of Christ

The good news, then, is about God in Christ; it's about his work for us, not our work for him; and it involves a relationship to Jesus Christ.

What is the gospel, the gospel that brings us salvation? It's the acts of Jesus Christ. It is, as we shall say shortly, Christ died, Christ is risen, Christ will come again. It's God's action in Christ that does for us and in us what we could never do for ourselves. It's a gospel of grace. It's only through the corporate memory of the Church, now in Scripture, that we know the gospel. But to make it alive for us, it needs to come as a personal revelation. The gospel isn't merely facts about Jesus, it is the risen and ascended Lord himself, encountering us, revealing himself to us. The gospel isn't only a message, it's a person, the unsubstitutable character of Jesus, the divine Son of God. And it's through revelation that we too know Jesus as Lord and that God raised him from the dead.

Roger Spiller

Suggested hymns

To God be the glory; Tell all the world of Jesus; We have a gospel to proclaim; And can it be, that I should gain.

Presentation of Christ in the Temple (Candlemas)
2 February
Marking the Meaning
Mal. 3.1–5; Ps. 24.[1–6] 7–end; Heb. 2.14–end; **Luke 2.22–40**

Endings and beginnings

Candlemas marks the midway point of winter when we look toward the coming of spring and the lighter half of the year. Traditionally before the days of electricity, when candles were the main source of light in homes, the candles were blessed in church – hence the name 'Candlemas'. Epiphany ends and we turn from the celebrations of Christ's birth and look towards his adult life and ministry and all that it meant. It is a time of endings and beginnings.

As is the story of Simeon and Anna. Simeon is described as a devout man who had been *waiting* for the consolation of Israel. He had been told that God's anointed would be revealed to him before his own death. Anna was an octogenarian prophetess, of the tribe of Asher. The lives of these elderly people were framed by prayer, by God's presence in their daily routine. That day in the Temple both witnessed something remarkable. They realized the time had come. Did they ever expect it to happen in quite such a way – an ordinary and poor couple going about the usual rituals of their faith and culture, a baby in their arms? What must it have meant to Simeon to know the promise had been fulfilled? What did it mean to Anna after all those years of widowhood, of faithful daily prayer, to see at last hope and light in this new life, knowing that her own life would soon end?

Our endings and beginnings

The marking of endings and beginnings is important to our human nature and existence. Endings often involve bereavement, grief, a letting go that needs to be named. Beginnings can be both exciting and daunting. They can be anticipated with both dread and joy. But both need to be marked. We need to take notice of the days, the significance of birth and death, times and seasons. What endings and beginnings are we aware of in our own lives – in the lives of those around us? What difference might it mean for us if we had the time – *made* the time – for marking the changes, reflecting on their significance in a healing and life-giving way, recognizing what they mean for us and for others? What might it mean for us if we changed our priorities, spent time looking for God in our midst, for the light growing among us and between us, watching for the signs of new green shoots of our faith pushing through the fog and brambles of our busy lives?

We live in a culture of targets and pressure to achieve, a world driven by the ever-present clamour of time and money and the limitations of both. Electricity has long taken over from candlelight so we can work 24/7, the natural cycle of night and day no longer being marked or honoured. Many employers have restrictions on attending funerals because it is time lost at work. Time to mark the ending of a life is considered a waste. Grief takes time. Bringing to birth takes time. Neither can be rushed. But we become impatient of waiting, count the cost as wasted time.

Simeon and Anna understood waiting. Both were mindful of the subtle nuances of time and place, the nudges of God in a busy and occupied world. It could be that apart from those four people, two old, two young, meeting in a corner of that vast and crowded Temple, a peasant child between them, no one else noticed anything remarkable at all.

Glimpsing glory

As we turn from the time of Jesus' infancy will we be thinking, *well about time. Christmas was an age away. We're busy people with things to do.* As we turn to look towards Lent, are we aware of full and busy diaries? Or are we preparing for how Lent might change us inwardly?

In the events of human life, birth and death, the changing of seasons in our minds and bodies and the world around us, God is at work, often quietly and without announcement. We could so easily miss the sacred and divine at work in and around us. Candlemas gives us a model for pausing to reflect on endings and beginnings and what they mean for us, an opportunity to prepare ourselves for what lies ahead and what we leave behind; and the gift of a glimpse of God in the ordinary and routine. So may this Candlemas be a reminder that though the winter is not yet over, though the world is rushing past us, though the journey ahead – like Lent – may be challenging, and spring a distance away, the work of transformation deep within us is evidence that God's chosen temple is here, in you and me. A human life in which glory may be glimpsed if we are mindful of it.

Carey Saleh

Suggested hymns

Like a candle flame; Through long years of watchful waiting; Jesus calls us here to meet him; O God, you search me and you know me.

St Joseph of Nazareth   19 March
Who's Cradling Jesus?
2 Sam. 7.4–16; Ps. 89.26–36; Rom. 4.13–18; **Matt. 1.18–end**

As we rightly honour Mary for her remarkable role in the great plan of God, today's Gospel reminds us particularly of Joseph. Joseph too played a significant part in the ordinary human environment within which Jesus was born, and I invite you to imagine with me this morning what the whole experience was like.

Who was Joseph? We know very little about him apart from the fact that he was a carpenter who could trace his ancestry back to the great King David and beyond that to Abraham, the father of the Jewish people. It's probably best if we think of him as a lad in his late teens or early twenties, and Mary as a girl in her early to mid-teens, the point when young women usually became betrothed.

Where did the baby come from?

Betrothal was a more serious business than a modern engagement. The commitment was deeper and could only be broken by divorce. But it wasn't the custom to have sexual intercourse before marriage. So when the moment comes that Mary suddenly starts getting unexplained sickness in the morning and a little bump appears, you can imagine that Joseph is shocked and feels betrayed. He also feels shamed, as well as guilty, because he should have protected Mary from advances, and Mary, for her part, doesn't know what to say. She's found some companionship and understanding from her cousin Elizabeth, but now the moment has come for her to try to explain to Joseph.

We can imagine the conversation running like this: Joseph said, 'So where did this baby come from?' And Mary said, 'As God lives, I don't know!' Anyone who has felt at any time betrayed by a partner will be able to imagine his feelings very readily.

Joseph's wise course of action

Matthew tells us that Joseph was 'righteous'; he tried to obey God according to the laws that had been handed down through the generations from Moses. At that time, a man who'd been cheated like this was expected to shame his wife in public. That course of action, though, seemed to Joseph too drastic – perhaps both for Mary's sake and his own. Another way was allowed: a quiet divorce in the presence of two witnesses. Joseph thought that was the way forward.

The command to marry Mary

When Joseph lay down to sleep that night in a real state, whatever he saw, or heard, he was confronted with a command. One that was so familiar from the well-loved writings of his ancestors: 'Do not be afraid to take Mary as your wife.' Why 'do not be afraid' to marry Mary? Presumably, because of the mocking taunts he could see coming his way. That was the command. The reality which dawned on him through that dream was this: the baby in Mary's womb was the boy through whom God would fulfil all his nation's hopes, through whom God would actually live among them.

Joseph didn't shut his ears to the command or close his eyes to the reality; he opened himself to this new possibility, so different from anything he could have expected for his marriage. He was to be the foster father of God's promised Saviour. And so, Matthew tells us, he acted without delay. The immediate commitment of marriage was the only way to show he took seriously what he had been told.

By marrying Mary he would be her protector. He would bear the public stigma and shame along with her: he had no sex with her until she gave birth to her son. Why not? Joseph and Mary, by staying apart, risked continuing humiliation from people wondering who the real father was. This wasn't just about protecting Joseph's own reputation as one who hadn't broken the betrothal custom. It was about not covering up what God was doing.

Joseph, as father to Jesus

This is nearly the end of Joseph's story in Matthew, but not quite. The last five words of the Gospel reading are very significant. 'He named him Jesus.' By naming the child, Joseph was adopting him into his family. He wasn't only going to be his foster father. He was going to be his legal father by adoption. This meant that Jesus would legally be in that same great line of ancestors, stretching from Abraham through David all the way down to Joseph. Jesus could be seen by his fellow Jews as truly qualified to fulfil his role as the Christ, the Messiah.

But what would this adoption, on top of the marriage, have meant to Joseph? It was a further act of commitment to the child and his well-being. We get glimpses of what that commitment meant a little later when Joseph flees his country, taking Mary and Jesus with him, to escape the violence of the ruler. Later still, Joseph returns when it seems safe to do so, but to a different part of the country where the regime is likely to be less oppressive.

And what about the hidden years of Jesus' boyhood and adolescence, of which we know so little? What was it like for Joseph to bring up not only a child he had not fathered but a child of such unique significance?

There is so much we don't know about Joseph, but we can imagine both the delights and the exasperation of being the adopted father of God's promised Saviour.

Joseph's world and ours

And it's good to imagine them, because this is the world Jesus came into. A world where suspicion easily arises and misunderstandings happen. A world where we are confronted with choices about the best way to treat others, and ourselves. A world, above all, where we are called to cradle Jesus, as it were, as a baby, to protect his identity, to let it shine through; to care for him as a boy and a young man, This world that Joseph experienced, this world that we experience, is the very world into which God has come to be with us, so that we can be involved in his great rescue project.

Stephen Wright

Suggested hymns

Hail to the Lord who comes; O blessed Joseph, how great is your worth; The kingdom of God is justice and joy; Thou didst leave thy throne and thy kingly crown.

The Annunciation of Our Lord to the Blessed Virgin Mary   25 March
The Blessed? Virgin Mary
Isa. 7.10–14; Ps. 40.5–11; Heb. 10.4–10; **Luke 1.26–38**

Missing person

I thought I had everything covered. What could possibly go wrong? With about 60 children expected to attend, all of whom had been asked to come along as a traditional Christmas character, we were bound to get a good mix. Weren't we?

Sure enough, come the day, there was a flock of shepherds, a fleet of angels, enough kings to found a dynasty, a Joseph, an innkeeper or two, even a star. And to cap it all, by prearrangement a young mum had volunteered to place her 6-week-old baby in our make-shift crib. So far so good.

But, animals and children – don't work with them! Spiderman and Tigger were unexpected arrivals. Ah well, at our inn there was room for everyone, including, of course, Mary. You know, Mary who was espoused to Joseph – that Mary. So where was Mary? Nowhere to be seen. All those kids – OK, a lot were boys – but none of the girls turned up as Mary. So, there was Joseph at a singles' club – nothing wrong with that, except that it's hard to properly tableau the nativity without the leading lady. Shame!

Blessed or what?

Despite its disappointment, our Mary-free nativity also had its upside. First, it handed Joseph his moment of glory. All eyes are on the wife. But in our amended version, this faithful and dependable working man literally took centre stage.

Second, the fact that no one chose to be Mary prompted some deeper reflection. I mean, would you want to be Mary – the Blessed Virgin? Well, I wonder if she really was. I have my doubts. I don't mean about the virgin bit. I mean about the blessedness. If you had to endure all that this woman had to put up with, would you want to change places with her?

Simeon's early warning that a sword would pierce Mary's soul was no idle scaremongering. The pain started long before Good Friday. Any mother of a 13-year-old who goes missing for three days is driven to distraction and despair, imagining the worst – and that wedding in Cana of Galilee. 'They have no wine,' reported Mary. 'Woman, what have I to do with you?' Do you suppose Mary felt blessed by that reply? Later on, Jesus is informed that his mother and brothers are outside asking for him. His response? 'Who is my mother?'

But if the sharpness of her son's words hurt, it was nothing compared with the knife-twist of Calvary. Mary's agony is movingly captured by Archbishop Anthony Bloom's description of a seventeenth-century Russian icon of Mary:

> You see a Russian peasant girl. Her eyes are big and she is looking into infinity or into the depths. If you look more you see two hands; two hands that couldn't be where they are simply because anatomy wouldn't allow it. They are not there to be part of a realistic picture. They are hands of anguish. And then, in the corner of the icon, almost invisible, pale yellow on pale yellow background, a little mount and an empty cross. This is the mother contemplating the crucifixion and death of her only begotten son.[32]

Unique

Someone has commented that probably no other person, real or imaginary, features more often in the works of the great artists than the Blessed Virgin Mary. That's also true of the Christian calendar where Mary has four entries. In addition to her festival day of 15 August, there are entries recalling her visit to Elizabeth, about which we've just heard in today's Gospel, her annunciation and her birthday. She has, of course, also been given a place of particular honour in the Roman Catholic Church, which bolsters her position with the doctrines of Mary's immaculate conception and assumption. The other Christian denominations have never signed up to those beliefs. But you don't have to be a Roman Catholic to want to honour this brave woman.

Mary's original response to Gabriel – 'Behold, the handmaid of the Lord; be it unto me according to your word' – went way beyond an indifferent, 'OK, I'll give it a go.' It was a conscious and courageous acceptance of a uniquely demanding vocation that was going to bring heartache and heartbreak. So perhaps it's not surprising then, that in our nativity tableau there were no takers for Mary, blessed or not.

Barrie Overend

Suggested hymns

The angel Gabriel from heaven came; For Mary, mother of our Lord; Tell out my soul, the greatness of the Lord; With Mary let my soul rejoice.

St Mark the Evangelist   26 April (transferred)
Where to Invest Ultimate Trust?
Rev. 15.28–end, *or* Acts 15.35–end; Ps. 119.9–16; Eph. 4.7–16; **Mark 13.5–13**

If I could turn back time, I'd take us to the late 60s of the first century to find St Mark starting work on his Gospel. 'Mark, how's it going?'

'There was a terrible earthquake in AD 61. Three years later, a vicious persecution of Christians. Jerusalem was a hotbed of revolution. In AD 69, four Roman Emperors came and went. Four in a year! Political instability, cumulative and terrifying persecution, and the threat and reality of war. That's how it's going!'

'So, Mark, given that, how will you use your material about Jesus' life to remind your readers of the need to stand firm and be strong?'

'I'm definitely including my recollections of Jesus' words when we were on the Mount of Olives, looking down on the Temple below us. Jesus had just stated that the Temple would be destroyed and we were all alarmed. When would this happen? Jesus painted a picture of a time when people will falsely claim to be God's representative. He spoke of wars and rumours of wars, violence, earthquake and famine – and he called this the beginning of "birth pangs". He talked about coming persecution, of being handed over to councils, hauled before governors and kings, a time when families will betray each other, a time to flee. He urged us not to be alarmed, not to worry. He promised that the Holy Spirit would give us the words to speak. Much more was said and he seemed to be talking both about an immediate situation of struggle and of a greater struggle coming on the horizon of time, when out of darkness and hopelessness, he will come and gather his people to him. Against a backdrop of political, economic and environmental mayhem he was urging us to trust and remain faithful. So that's going into the book! Tell me – what is the backdrop against which you live and how do you think my recollection of Jesus' words that day as he left the Temple might help your age?'

Back in the here and now

There is much persecution in our age. According to the International Society for Human Rights, a secular group with members in 38 states worldwide, 80 per cent of all acts of religious discrimination in the world today are directed at Christians. The most violent anti-Christian pogrom of the early twenty-first century saw as many as 500 Christians hacked to death by machete-wielding radicals in Orissa, India, with thousands more injured and 50,000 made homeless. In Burma, China and Korea, Christians are routinely subjected to imprisonment, torture, forced labour and murder. In North Korea, a quarter of the country's Christians live in forced labour camps after refusing to join the national cult of the state's founder, Kim Il-Sung. Somalia, Syria, Iraq, Iran, Afghanistan, Saudi Arabia, Yemen and the Maldives all feature in the ten worst places to be a Christian. In such mayhem, the faithfulness of these Christians, trusting God in the midst of unimaginable horrors – often poor and displaced – is deeply moving. We are weirdly silent about this persecution in the West, but Mark would have understood.

Where to invest ultimate trust?

Mark's writing asks us to be careful where we put our ultimate trust. We might look at our cathedrals and say 'immovable, unchangeable ...', but religious edifices, whatever their longevity, are not permanent. We might look at our traditions and root our security there. But traditions are not the ultimate source of stability. Like it or not, they change too. We might look at the political instability all around – truth twisted, wars and rumours of wars, hideous persecutions, and be afraid – but Jesus' words urge us to trust in God, whatever the backdrop of our lives. Jesus urges us to steadfast discipleship and faith-filled hope.

'Um,' Mark might say, 'but some of your hearers might be thinking, "OK, easy for you to say. You are not at the sharp end of persecution." Others might comment, "I am not being persecuted for my faith, but my life is falling to pieces. You don't know what I am facing. How am I supposed to maintain faith when everything is falling apart? When the things I thought were stable and solid are crumbling."'

Don't walk alone

Mark again. 'Remind your hearers – whatever they face – that Jesus addressed four disciples on that day on the Temple Mount, not just one, and I wrote my Gospel for lots of people. The "you" is not singular. Alone, we will struggle to hold faith. Together, locally and corporately around the world, the Church of God can and must continue in the Way of Faith.'

Mark is right. Support one another in down-to-earth, practical ways – a listening ear, political support, a shared meal, prayer, a text or tweet, an email, some money. Together. We need to educate ourselves on the needs of the persecuted parts of the Church and stand together with them in prayer, protest and practical action, remembering them and telling their stories. We stand together in faith and in discipleship – attending to God in each other in the present and reminding one another of the ultimate future – held in God's overarching love, embedded in the Advent hope of God meeting us in the final tomorrow. Mark's words point us to the God of all hope. Hang on to him.

Kate Bruce

Suggested hymns

How great is our God; Come, thou fount of every blessing; All hail the power of Jesus' name; Spirit of the living God.

St Philip and St James, Apostles 1 May
Seeing the Father
Isa. 30.15–21; Ps. 119.1–8; Eph. 1.3–10; **John 14.1–14**

We know little about Philip and what we know we know only from St John's Gospel. He asked Jesus a question that people who get into discussion about Christianity often ask, in different forms. So it's an important question.

Philip said to Jesus: 'Show us the Father.' This is the third reference Philip makes to 'seeing' in this Gospel. First, it was Philip who identified Jesus to Nathanael and invited Nathanael to 'Come and see', when Nathanael sniffily replied, 'Can anything good come out of Nazareth?' And then it was Greeks, Gentiles, who sought out Philip, a fellow Greek, and said to him, 'Sir, we wish to see Jesus.'

'Show us the Father'

And now it is Philip who says to Jesus, 'Show us the Father'. Jesus has been talking about knowing and seeing the Father, and he's been giving his disciples a masterclass in the subtleties of 'seeing' and 'perceiving'. But, for all that, the disciples say they still haven't seen the Father. Jesus had expected that the disciples would, by now, have seen the Father in and through him. He replies with the rhetorical question that can be paraphrased, 'Can it be that you do not know me after the long time we have spent together?'

Obscured by false expectations

Philip cuts through the confusion and asks the question. Perhaps he is wanting one of the great appearances, like the theophanies to

Moses and Elijah on Mount Sinai. Or perhaps he's seeking after a mystical vision of God. But these visions and theophanies are at an end now that the Word who is God has become flesh. In seeing Jesus, God is to be seen.

It was, and remains to this day, a daring claim. Two grounds for belief are offered: 'Believe me' and 'Believe (me) because of the works'. Belief in the works as signs acknowledges that they are the work both of the Father and the Son, who are one. Jesus said his words and his deeds are not his own but those of his Father. So they declare that Jesus is intimately related to the Father. If they can't yet believe Jesus when he says he comes from God, maybe the works he performs will convince them. The words and works of Jesus are the credentials for Jesus. They are one in power and action. 'Put your faith in these works so that you may come to know that the Father is in me and I am in the Father,' says Jesus.

Seeing only through Jesus

When people today ask to see God, or ask why he doesn't show up, they ask for a dramatic, miraculous experience that would vindicate the action of God. But for John even the miraculous deeds were only signs, clues, hints, but not compelling enough to remove all questions and doubt. Even if that were possible, it would not reveal God. Only God's Son, Jesus, and he alone can reveal all of the God we can possibly know and grasp in human form. There is, then, no access to the Father independent of Jesus. We can't know the Father in all his fullness except from the life, words and Spirit of his Son.

How could we know the self-giving, vulnerable Father, without the witness of the historic life of Jesus? How could we know that God has embraced and taken upon himself our humanity if it were not for the incarnate Jesus? And how would we know the relationship God has forged with humankind, except for the ascension of 'the Son of Man who came down from heaven'?

Seeing through the cross

Archbishop Michael Ramsey once said, 'God is Christlike, and in him there is no unchristlikeness at all.' This catches a vitally important truth. It can be very easy to see God as a rather stern judge who is distant from us. He can seem like a headmaster who waits to catch us breaking the rules and then gives us detention. Knowing that God is exactly like Jesus helps to correct this view. It can completely revolutionize the way we think of God. The time when Phillip and the other disciples will know Jesus is when he is glorified. So far they can't see him fully because they haven't seen his glory. The glory for John is to be seen most clearly when Jesus is lifted up on the cross. But from this moment, when Christ is glorified, having at last 'seen' him, Philip and the rest *do* know Christ, they *have* seen him; and having seen Christ, they now know God the Father.

We live in a time when the world does not know God, when many people envy and long for the faith of those who do. Those who, through the witness of the Church, contemplate the historic life of Jesus and recognize the divine character – his glory – can attain a knowledge of him which is the real 'vision' of God. The vision is not mediated on abstractions but embodied in a living person. 'If you know me, you will know the Father.' The disciples do know God and have seen him, and we can too.

Roger Spiller

Suggested hymns

O Lord, we long to see your face; Christ is the world's light; Light of the minds that know him; Rejoice in God's saints, today and all days!

St Matthias the Apostle   14 May
Someone Else's Shoes
Isa. 22.15–end; Ps. 15; Acts 1.15–end (*if the Acts reading is used instead of the Old Testament reading, the New Testament reading is* 1 Cor. 4.1–7); **John 15.9–17**

There are many situations in life when we have to follow on in someone else's footsteps, or walk in someone else's shoes. We might step into a new role, take on a new job, be promoted or take on a new level of responsibility. We often have to take on something where others have left off, or continue a project which is not yet complete. Sometimes it's tempting to reflect on the legacy we have been left in a negative way and get drawn into thinking we will sort things out where our predecessors couldn't. The danger of succession planning and replacement strategies are lurking around every corner.

The disciples faced such a challenge when Judas Iscariot, one of the Twelve, after his betrayal of Jesus, orchestrated his own death. The disciples must find another to take his place and Peter stands up among the believers to make plans for finding his replacement. What kind of interview process will there be? What qualifications are needed for the role of apostle? Who would even want to step into his shoes?

Chosen by lot

There are two candidates put forward for the job, Matthias and Joseph called Barsabbas, but who can decide which of them should be elevated to the dignity of apostle? They are both good men, faithful, steadfast and true. But no one present was willing or able to take on the mantle of this decision fully. All the other apostles had been chosen directly by Jesus himself, so the disciples offer the matter to God in prayer. Peter says, 'Lord, you know everyone's heart. Show us which one of these two you have chosen.' So, they cast lots, putting their decision in the hand of God and the lot fell on Matthias.

What must Matthias be thinking? These were intimidating and portentious shoes to fill. The manner of his calling was unusual. Did this make him a second-rate apostle? In the book of Acts, we are told that Matthias was with Jesus from the time of his baptism by John the Baptist, but we know little more about him other than this. We do not know if he witnessed the crucifixion or the resurrection. From relative obscurity, Matthias is raised up into a new calling. From one of many followers of Jesus, he becomes one of the Twelve who will lead the fledging Christian community into the future and build the foundations of the Church of Christ.

Inhabiting the call of Christ

How did Matthias live into his calling? He did nothing other than proclaim the good news of Jesus Christ. He lived out the gospel in word and in deed. He was faithful. Tradition has it that he travelled abroad, sharing the faith with those who had not yet heard the good news and bringing new believers into the life of the church. Perhaps he was chosen not for what he was when the lot fell upon him, but what he was to become?

God saw the potential in Matthias; God saw his heart, and

God set him on a journey that he could never have predicted or expected. God chose him for the job of apostle in the Church and he inhabited that calling as a disciple of Christ.

Perhaps we can all identify with Matthias when we fall into unexpected roles or are given unsought responsibilities. Sometimes we just have to step into our calling and trust in God's purposes for us. There are many situations in life that we do not choose to be in, but sometimes God chooses us for a reason. God sees our hearts and God sees all that we are destined to be. God has faith in us, even if we do not have confidence in ourselves. As Jesus said to his disciples, 'You did not choose me, but I chose you. And I appointed you to go and bear fruit, fruit that will last.'

St Matthias, a good and faithful servant, chosen by lot, became an apostle of the Church and was filled with joy and boldness to preach the gospel. On his foundation we build, as people chosen and sent by God to fulfil his mission to the world.

Victoria Johnson

Suggested hymns

Just as I am; Who are these like stars appearing; It is a thing most wonderful; Have faith in God, my heart.

Visit of the Blessed Virgin Mary to Elizabeth 31 May
Behold – Look Again
Zeph. 3.14–18; Ps. 113; Rom. 12.9–16; **Luke 1.39–49 [50–56]**

Life within

Mary has been so often cast as a meek and obedient girl.

Respectable and respectful. Such respectability was blown clear out of the water by the news of her pregnancy. The people of her town never looked at her in the same way again.

Levitcal law demanded that she be stoned to death. Joseph had decided to divorce her quietly but she would be considered soiled goods.

For a devout Jewish girl, whose only future was to marry, this was a death sentence. Meek? Obedient? A teenager? Newly pregnant? She will have been a hormonal powerhouse!

She rushes off to her kinswoman Elizabeth; the elderly barren woman and the virgin, both finding themselves pregnant, instinctively withdraw from the rest of the critical crowd and turn to each other. Something beyond human knowledge is shared between these two women. The deep intuitive healing and transforming wisdom of the Holy Spirit. Life within us both where life cannot logically have happened. God is at work in us.

We can call it joy and praise. But there was something else in Mary's song. A moment of authenticity, a vast 'at last'.

Finally, God has broken through – and all those stories of her ancestors, about covenant, about promise are to be fulfilled. 'Finally,' she cries, 'God has seen the humiliation of this slave woman and from now on all generations will call me blessed.'

The subversive ways of God

These are the subversive ways of God, lifting up the poor and weak, and bringing down the proud and haughty in their conceit. Filling the hungry with good things and sending the rich away empty. That is the 'at last' of Mary's heart. The Church has missed that subversive text down the centuries, too eager to turn her back into an obedient vessel. Every cell in her body was changed and challenged to accommodate her calling. Her very DNA woven into the mystery imparted to her.

Perhaps Mary remembered another slave girl called Hagar who received an annunciation: 'You shall bear a son and you shall call him Ishmael, for the LORD has *heard your affliction.*'

In Mary's outburst of praise there is a liberation cry. That was the deep understanding of Mary's people – the story they told year after year – how God had heard their anguish and liberated them from slavery, bringing them out into a promised heritage. Now Mary's people are in bondage again to the occupying force of Rome. It is a world where the rich and powerful flourish and make the rules for the poor and downtrodden and rob them of their land, their voice, their freedom. They are burdened by taxation wherever they look, by Rome, by Herod, by the Temple. And across the skyline stand the crosses – a reminder of what happens to those who make trouble for those in power.

There is appropriate anger in Mary's joy, ringing out as a song of vindication.

There is a fierceness there – the new fierceness of a mother for her unborn child. The child that the world could easily have stoned to death while still in the womb. The child that a jealous king will give orders to slaughter – and kill countless baby boys in the process. This young mother cries out against such tyrants and gives praise to the God who cries, 'Let my people go!'

Cry freedom – that is Mary's song.

What stirs in us?

I wonder what God can bring to birth in us that is unexpected, previously hidden away by convention. What intuition might the Holy Spirit cause in us so that we might leap with exaltation of new understanding?

What advent stirs in the unlikely places of realization and raises us to righteous anger? What long unspoken lament will be charged by exultation in the unnoticed corners? The sort of places where the world wouldn't look twice. God has indeed looked twice and regarded the humiliation of this slave woman. 'Regarded' is from the French verb *regardez*, with its sense of 'behold' – to look again.

We have for centuries tried to keep Miriam of Nazareth in that meek, pious, obedient straitjacket. We should look again. There is a reason why Scripture describes God as a mother bear robbed of her cubs, or a mother eagle lifting her young on her own back.

The love that our liberating God has for us.

Who am I, said Hagar, that I might have seen God and live?

Who am I, said Elizabeth, that the mother of my Lord should come to me?

Who am I, said Mary, that this should be?

Who are you? Who are we? And who is God?

We should look again.

For behold, God has done great things in and for and through us; and will go on doing so.

Carey Saleh

Suggested hymns

Tell out my soul; Born in the night; Lord Jesus, at your coming; The angel Gabriel from heaven came.

Day of Thanksgiving for the Institution of
Holy Communion (Corpus Christi)   3 June
What Christians Do

Gen. 14.18–20; Ps. 116.10–17; **1 Cor. 11.23–26**; John 6.51–58

Let me draw your attention to some words from the reading we've just heard. The first is the word 'received'. St Paul writes, 'I received from the Lord what I also handed on to you.' Paul didn't encourage the Corinthian Christians to celebrate the Eucharist because he thought it was a good idea, but because he had received it himself from the Lord. So with us: we do this because we have been given something precious, a holy inheritance that we neither invented nor deserved nor chose for ourselves. This is what Christians do; and we do what we received from the Lord: we do it in memory of him. In churches, hospitals, prisons, schools, homes, in the open air, in concentration camps and detention centres, among migrants and refugees, at weddings and baptisms, this is what we do – because we received it from the Lord.

Hand on what we receive

And, having received it, we are to 'hand it over' to others. The English translation we used today has 'handed on' – 'I received from the Lord what I also handed on to you.' But in the original Greek the same word translated 'handed on' (*paradidōmi*) appears again in the very next line: 'that the Lord Jesus on the night that he was *handed over* [or 'betrayed'] took a loaf of bread ...' So what St Paul is saying is this: you and I have received something precious, something handed over to us by generations of Christians going right back to St Paul and to the first apostles. And we in our turn are commanded to hand it over to those of our own day, not just (and this is why the words matter) out of obedience to those who handed it down to us, but out of a far deeper obedience to Jesus who was himself 'handed over' to be betrayed. So the holy Eucharist is far more than something we have inherited, more even than Jesus' teaching or example – it is the sacrament, the sign, of his willingness to be handed over, betrayed, into the hands of wicked men. Our obedience to his command reflects his obedience to his Father's command: to give himself in love for others, even unto death. Which brings us back to today's reading.

Re-live Christ's sacrifice

St Paul concludes: 'For as often as you eat this bread and drink the cup, you proclaim the Lord's death until he comes.' Jesus was handed over to death, not just for all humanity in a vague kind of way, but for all creatures – including you and me. His death involves you and me. He died to show us how infinitely we are loved: to die for someone is the highest and holiest offering anyone can make. Could you – would you be willing to – die for someone else? Would I? Yet Jesus died for us. And every time we celebrate or are present at the Eucharist, we remember that: in fact we re-present, re-live his sacrifice. And that is an amazing thought. The Eucharist, every time we attend it, should stop us in our tracks – because it reminds us that Christ died for love of us. And not just for love of us. He died for the people of other faiths and of none; for the refugees; for the next-door neighbour who drives you crazy; for creatures that are helpless victims of human cruelty; for the people who betray him, or let him down – which in one way or another is all of us. And that brings us to the most important point of all.

Share table fellowship with all creatures

When we hear of tragedies, or when we just get depressed by the news, we usually feel helpless, as though there is nothing we can do to help. But there is something we can do: we can celebrate this meal together. *It's what we do*, in good times or in bad, when we feel like it and when we don't. And we do it together: celebrating the Eucharist is having a meal, not just with friends and fellow churchgoers, but with all our fellow creatures. The great philosopher Emmanuel Levinas (who was not a Christian) said that 'The authentic Eucharist is actually in the moment when "the other" comes to face me'.[33] Just as Jesus sat at table with the one who would betray him, so every Eucharist is table fellowship with all God's creatures, including those who have hurt us or let us down. It brings us face to face with 'the other', with my neighbour, with everyone and every creature for whom Christ died. And it's to proclaim to them, 'You matter. You are loved. Christ died for you.' And, at least sometimes, it's to say that to ourselves. We 'proclaim the Lord's death', and will go on proclaiming it 'until he comes'. This is what we do. This, and nothing less than this, is good news for the world.

Gordon Mursell

Suggested hymns

God is here! As are his people; We meet as friends at table; And now, O Father, mindful of the love; Now let us from this table rise.

St Barnabas the Apostle   11 June
The Right Man at the Right Time

Job 29.11–16; Ps. 112; Acts 11.19–end (*if the Acts reading is used instead of the Old Testament reading, the New Testament reading is* **Gal. 2.1–10**); John 15.12–17

Barnabas is the saint whose company we'd probably choose to have with us in a tough situation: warm, generous, self-effacing, resourceful. He surely lives up to his name as 'Son of Encouragement'. But he is also a key player at a critical stage in the development and scaling up of the Christian movement. Luke's Acts of the Apostles is an apologia for the spread of Christianity, but we are also directed today to Paul's letter that shows a more down-to-earth, hard-nosed Barnabas that fills out our picture of this significant and underrated saint.

Sponsor

The dispute between Jesus and the Jewish leaders was seen at best as a reform movement within Judaism. The time had come for the gospel to be spread to non-Jews, spearheaded by the apostle to the Gentiles. Paul was in no hurry to meet the leaders of the church in Jerusalem. He was convinced he was called to be an apostle by Jesus Christ and didn't need any other authorization. And he felt that the church leaders did not recognize his commission and were perhaps nervous that Paul was too keen to walk away from his Jewish obligations. So Paul waited some three years after his conversion to meet them. It would be a delicate encounter. He was called by God, not by human leaders and he would travel to Jerusalem of his own choice and not because he was sent for.

Paul needed the support of his friends. So he took Barnabas with him, and also Titus. The choice of Barnabas and Titus was shrewd. Barnabas was a Jew and Titus a Gentile; Barnabas was known and trusted by the 'pillars', Peter and James, in Jerusalem

318

where he was resident. And together they would seek approval for a division of labour in which pillar apostles would minister to Jews, and Paul and Barnabas to the Gentiles. Paul was accepted on the recommendation of Barnabas. But would they have received him if Barnabas had not been there to vouch for him?

Assessor

We read a glowing report of some unnamed missionaries who were achieving great success in their preaching to Jews in Antioch, in one of the greatest cities of antiquity. When they did evangelize non-Jews the response was remarkable. But was this a legitimate extension of the work of Jesus or not? Preaching to Greeks and Gentiles represented a huge sea change which for some was illegitimate, and for others was only permissible subject to conditions; conditions that the Jewish law and rituals were kept. This development exercised the leaders at headquarters, and so they despatched their trusted Barnabas to Antioch to assess and report on the situation and, if necessary, to bring it to an end.

Our default concern for control in the name of decency and order has often led church leaders to deny, suppress or condemn the explosive, exuberant manifestations of the Spirit. Fresh expressions, messy church, pioneer ministry, bread churches, church plants are not to be condemned nor even welcomed simply on the grounds of their novelty, but only when they show evidence of the 'grace of God'. We need a Barnabas to discern the Spirit, and Barnabas does more; he recognizes that new Christians need to be formed. So he seeks out a co-worker, Paul, in order to induct the new Christians in an intensive teaching programme.

Theologian?

In Antioch, a mixed church developed, of Jews and Gentiles, led by Peter for the Jews and by Paul and Barnabas for the Gentiles. Peter the Jew and his Jewish colleagues were prepared to eat with the Gentile Christians in their community. But the authorities in Jerusalem, especially James, got wind of it. He probably hadn't reckoned with the possibility of mixed churches and reacted with horror. So he sent a message to this mixed church along these lines: 'We agreed that Gentiles might be evangelized, and that they might be converted and baptized; we allowed that they did not have to be circumcised, but we never said that they might be permitted to share meals with Jews. They are Christians, but not Christians who can be allowed to share our Eucharist.'[34]

This was followed up by emissaries sent by James to confront the situation in Antioch face to face. But Peter and other Jewish Christians, even Barnabas, hid and separated themselves. Peter and Barnabas, who had participated in shared meals with Gentile Christians, had got cold feet. They feared James in his absence more even than they feared Paul, who was present with them. Paul was horrified. He accused Peter and Barnabas of hypocrisy. How could they who experienced freedom from the law through Christ now turn back into slavery to the law? They would be doing so for no better reason than pressure from headquarters. Were Barnabas and Peter culpable of such a severe charge? Well, they acted out of fear rather than from conviction, and as one scholar says, they 'lacked theology'.[35] Paul and Barnabas won the argument when they visited the pillars in Jerusalem.

We cannot imagine how Paul's ministry would have succeeded if Barnabas had not befriended him and given him a second chance. There is always a place for warmth, generosity and magnanimity within an often harsh and judgemental society.

Roger Spiller

Suggested hymns

The 'Son of Consolation'; Let the round world with songs rejoice; God, whose city's sure foundation; Lord, you give the great commission.

Birth of John the Baptist   24 June
Does History Have a Meaning?
Isa. 40.1–11; Ps. 85.7–end; Acts 13.14b–26, *or* Gal. 3.23–end;
Luke 1.57–66, 80

> All who heard them pondered them and said, 'What then will this child become?' For, indeed, the hand of the Lord was with him. (Luke 1.66)

There can be no doubt that the story of the Tudor monarchy in sixteenth-century England is a fascinating one. Central characters, such as Henry VIII, demand explanation. How could a man who was such a brutal tyrant also be devoutly religious? How could Queen Mary resolve to burn alive hundreds of people who disagreed with her? How did Edward VI, the boy king, impose his Protestant views on the nation? And what about the other players in the drama: Thomas Cromwell, Thomas Cranmer, Anne Boleyn, Jane Grey? What were their real motives? What were they trying to achieve?

Well. To help us make sense of a turbulent and dangerous period in history, great scholars such as Diarmaid MacCulloch and Eamon Duffy have searched through thousands of documents; they have gone back to the primary sources and with enormous skill have created patterns of interpretation so that we can begin to understand what was going on. We owe them a huge debt. They have transformed our understanding of the period.

And alongside these great historians, other people with a different set of skills have also been beavering away; people such as Hilary Mantel with her novels about Thomas Cromwell, and C. J. Sansom, seeing the Tudor world through the eyes of his wary and courageous hero, the lawyer Matthew Shardlake. They have explored the Tudor period by combining real historical scholarship with their novelist's imagination. Again, we owe them a great debt.

What both the academic historians and the novelists are engaged in is an attempt to create pattern. They take the most complex, subtle and often contradictory material and weave it into a picture that helps the rest of us to see more clearly what was going on. The creation of pattern is all.

Pattern in the gospel story

Now, when it comes to the Gospels, we can see the same literary processes at work. The Gospel authors are also trying to create meaningful patterns. But there is one major difference. The Gospel writers are creating their stories with a divine background in mind. They are not writing simple biographies of Jesus; they are interpreting his life in the light of their belief that everything that happened was part of a huge and sweeping divine narrative. The narrative had begun with the creation, had wound its way through the towering figures of Israel's history and was now entering a new and amazing phase.

This sense of the great sweep of divine history is reflected in the episode that Luke offers us about the birth of John the Baptist. He tells a story that involves angels and miracles; it involves the irruption into history of a child who will be the forerunner of the Messiah. His heroes in this story are the priest Zechariah, a priest of Aaron's line who by lot had been selected to burn incense at the Temple altar and there had had an epiphany. Zechariah was astonished by the presence of an angel and was struck dumb. The other hero is Elizabeth, Zechariah's wife, who was past the age of child-bearing but who was promised by God's messenger that she would be the mother of a very special, divinely blessed son.

But then into this extraordinary story Luke drops an all-too-human reaction. When the baby is born, all of Zechariah and Elizabeth's friends and relatives gather at the house. They are delighted for the elderly parents and are cooing over the baby. One of them asks what the baby will be called. Elizabeth replies that the baby is to be called John. A noisy discussion ensues in which members of the family expostulate that no child in their family has ever been called John. The very idea ... preposterous.

Zechariah is asked for his decision. He takes a writing tablet and on it scribes the words 'His name is John'. There is amazement because at the very moment of writing, Zechariah finds his voice. The act of speaking after such a long period of being dumb astounds the extended family. They look again at the tiny baby – and here's the all-too-human bit – they burst into an exclamation that all families use when confronted with the miracle of new life: 'What will this child become?'

What will this child become?

Luke takes a phrase that he has probably heard many times when as a doctor he has attended a birth, and adds a theological dimension to it. The exclamation is not just about the miracle of new life; it is also about this child, this particular child, becoming the forerunner of the Christ in the divine plan; a plan that, astonishingly, is working itself out through a priestly family living in the remote uplands of Judaea.

The family and the relatives were present at that moment when God's plan was revealing itself through the miraculous intervention in the lives of Zechariah and Elizabeth. Can you imagine the kinds of conversations the onlookers might have had when, after all the excitement, they journeyed back to their own homes?

As far as Luke was concerned, this was a turning point in history. Life could never be the same again. His history, his Gospel, was and is about God revealing himself to humanity.

It faces us with a challenge: do we regard Luke's understanding of history to be one with which we can wholeheartedly agree? Or, are we perhaps left as puzzled as the family members were? Do we think that there is an overarching divine plan for our world, or are we inclined to think that everything that happens is simply a series of meaningless events and that it is historians who create and impose the patterns?

Christopher Herbert

Suggested hymns

On Jordan's bank the Baptist's cry; The Church of God a kingdom is; Be still, for the Spirit of the Lord; God is working his purpose out.

SS Peter and Paul, Apostles[36]   29 June
Peter and Paul's Agenda
Gal. 1.13–24[37]

We can be thankful for the compilers of the lectionary, seeking to make meaningful connections between Old and New Testaments. It makes for a stimulating exercise, trying to uncover the rationale of why often-disparate passages are linked. But sometimes their ingenuity defeats us, or the choices are surprising. That's the case today, when the lectionary writers studiously avoid texts that explicitly link Peter and Paul, and instead opt for readings that in the main focus only on Peter, who, like Paul, has his day all to himself. Let's make good their deficit and consider the 15 days that Paul spent with Peter in his home

Authority and experience

After three years, since his conversion and calling, Paul says he went up to Jerusalem to see Peter. Paul's eagerness to communicate with Peter is notable because Paul had already written that he needed no authority other than his own divine commission and made the point that he, therefore, didn't need to go sooner to Jerusalem to seek the authorization of the 'pillars', in particular James and Peter. Paul showed his passionate independence of spirit in handling fierce conflict in the church at Galatia.

Nevertheless, he did care about Peter and the experience he had first hand, as a disciple of Jesus in Galilee. It must have been a spirited and frank meeting. If only we had an eye-witness report! Paul was seeking a new beginning when at length he came to Jerusalem from Damascus. Paul mentions seeing only Peter and James as leaders, but Barnabas was on hand to make the introductions and to assure them that the converted Paul could be trusted. But it's with Peter that Paul spends most of the time.

It's reasonable that Paul would be eager to learn from Peter about the person of Jesus. We cannot know for certain whether Paul had ever encountered Jesus. It isn't impossible, since Paul travelled from Tarsus and studied in Jerusalem during the lifetime of Jesus. But he certainly would not have experienced the ministry of Jesus. Paul's tête à tête with Peter would have included vivid memories of Jesus shared by Peter. After all no one was more qualified than Peter to tell the story of Jesus. But no one was more equipped than Paul to draw out the story and its impact, as he was fresh from his sojourn in Arabia. If Peter was the narrator, Paul was the interpreter and theologian.

Corporate and personal

In coming to Peter, Paul was bringing the private to the public and faith to its origins. Paul knows that the risen Lord spoke to him, and this stays with him as the sole, sufficient persuasion and mandate for his faith. Such experience is personal and can't be spoken except by personal pronouns. Even so, Paul seeks the tradition within which alone his experience occurs. What is deeply private is also clearly public. It needs to be set within a context of history, authority and tradition. If Saul, out of Damascus and Arabia, needed Peter, we are meant to recognize that all inward, personal faith and experience cannot remain private. It needs to be renewed by community. Christians are 'made' through personal discovery but they are 'known' by the recognition of the faith community. In handling the charismatics in his charge, Paul wanted them to realize that there is no spirituality more in danger than the one that believes itself to be exceptional or self-sufficient.

Faith and development

Paul was seeking out the first disciples in Jerusalem, like Peter, who were at the *source* of faith in Christ. But Paul would also be the *developer* of the Christian faith in the Gentile world. Both Peter and Paul would face the enormous revolution by which their Jewishness would meet the Gentile world, and where Jew and non-Jew alike would belong to a race-transcending fellowship across the cultures of the ancient Near East.

Christianity has always undergone extensive development beyond what would be recognized by previous generations, while always striving to be true to its original faith and mandate. There are those who would like to declare that 'nothing changes here', but change is the sign of life and growth and learning. We see in Peter how rigid adherence to past learning, his firm but misleading expectations of what a Messiah would and would not do, became for Peter not a sign of faith but a cause of desertion and denial. How much, too, Paul would have heard from Peter's retelling of Jesus' death that will have shaped his own understanding. Paul's powerful imagery of, for example, dying with Christ, so that we may also live with him, and being raised with Christ, would have drawn on Peter's close experiences with his Lord.

On Peter and Paul the future of the movement of Christianity depended. When Paul stayed with Peter, he knew he had been called to be the apostle to the Gentiles. But for Peter the recognition of an extension of the Christian mission beyond Judaism took time for him to accept. When he accepted that, he vacillated on whether as a Jew he could eat with non-Jewish Christians. This resulted in a showdown in the church at Antioch, described in Paul's letter to the Galatians. Peter's attitude had been that of Shylock: 'I will buy with you, sell with you, talk with you, walk with you ... but I will not eat with you.'[38] Eating with Gentiles was treachery for a Jew, and under the influence of other 'pillars' in Jerusalem, Peter had reverted to a rigid position. In sharp rebuke, Paul told him that he had surrendered his friendship in Christ and returned to slavery under the law. Peter came into line and he and Paul were then able to present a united front as the frontiers for the gospel opened before them. It just might have been a very different story if Paul and Peter had not met and the relationships had not formed. The tensions between them – private experience and public tradition; personal call and church authorization; fidelity to past teaching and a readiness to adapt to new situations – are still there to confront Christ's followers today.

Roger Spiller

Suggested hymns

Hope of our calling: hope through courage won; We have a gospel to proclaim; Go forth and tell; Christ is our cornerstone.

St Thomas the Apostle   3 July
Blessed are Those Who Have Not Seen
Hab. 2.1–4; Ps. 31.1–6; eph. 2.19–end; **John 20.24–29**

A seed of life

There is a legend written of St Thomas the Apostle. In the legend, Thomas is sent by the risen Lord to India to proclaim the gospel, and Thomas brings many people to the Christian faith by powerful acts and words of truth. Among them, Thomas is said to have presided at a royal wedding. At the king's request, the apostle blesses the bridegroom and the bride, saying: 'Lord, give these young people the blessing of your right hand, and sow in their hearts the seed of life.'

Thomas, in this account, is living out the resurrection that at first he found so hard to believe. He understands at last that the resurrection was not just an event without consequence, it was an event that changed everything. He was sent out as a missionary; the word 'apostle' means *one who is sent*, and in the sending he begins to embody the resurrected life of Jesus Christ. He becomes a bearer of the good news of the resurrection. He believes it, he lives it, he breathes it.

Thomas knew that faith was like a seed of life sown in the heart of the believer. He knew that to live in faith was to live in a cycle of being drawn in towards God, and being sent out in his service. Jesus says, 'As the Father has sent me, so I send you.' Thomas was called to follow Jesus, called even to touch his wounds so that he could be sent out to proclaim what he saw and what he believed to be true.

Those who are sent

In every liturgy of the Church, that cycle of being drawn in and sent out by God is very evident. We are invited to the altar, considering every step with all of our faults and fears and doubts, and then we are quite deliberately sent out and away, back down the aisle. We will be dismissed from the church and then leave the building and

326

go out to live the good news we have received. The work of the gospel for each and every one of us begins at the door of the church; our mission begins in worship, but it most definitely moves out of the church into the world outside.

What if those disciples, locked inside with the doors shut, were too afraid to go out into the world and proclaim what they had seen and heard? What if they had not 'stepped out'? What if John had not written down what happened and had not recorded the experiences of the disciples in the Gospel of his name? What if, after that first generation of disciples, those who believed had kept their faith close to their chests, private and personal, and decided to tell no one?

We would not be here today if any of that were true. We were the future that they were sent out to build. Our faith, our church, is only here because generation after generation of believer has passed on their beliefs in faith and without fear, because generation after generation has taken their faith out into the world and with God's grace helped draw in others.

And now it is our turn. The Christian life is one that radiates out beyond ourselves. We are, or should be, constantly in the process of being sent out of the church in the peace of God, to live and work, to his praise and glory. The risen Lord has planted in our hearts the seed of life and that seed will grow best if it's exposed to the elements. For many years the culture of the Church believed that we should do nothing but wait for the world to come in. We should keep our faith private; it was after all a personal thing. We became complacent doubting, what we could do in the name of the Lord.

Open the doors

Now, thankfully, the culture has had to change. We have had to move out of our comfort zones, our safe places; we have had to unlock the doors and look out into the world, and step beyond the threshold as those disciples did, as Thomas the Apostle did, prepared to give a testimony of what we believe and an account of the faith that is in us. The Church is a community that is constantly being sent out into the world to live out and proclaim that living hope that we find in the reality of the resurrection.

Like those disciples, perhaps fearful, doubtful and lacking confidence, we have on this the feast day of St Thomas recalled the greatest miracle ever, and our faith rests on the foundations of that life-changing event two thousand years ago. And though we were not there, we know it to be true, because we see the resurrection permeate the whole world order. Where there is new life, new beginnings, hope coming from sadness, joy from sorrow, peace from hate, and life from death, the resurrection is real.

St Thomas has, through his own doubt and fear, given us God's blessing, for we are those people of whom Jesus said, 'Blessed are those who have not seen, and yet believe.' We are the people to whom Thomas was sent to proclaim the good news of the resurrection. We are the people for whom John wrote his wonderful gospel account.

We are now called to take on the mantle of apostleship. We are to follow the example of Thomas and John, and we are blessed to do this: to go out in God's mission and keep the faith alive so that those who come after us may also believe.

Victoria Johnson

Suggested hymns

Firmly I believe and truly; The Lord is risen indeed; Now the green blade riseth; Colours of day, dawn into the mind.

St Mary Magdalene   22 July
Apostle to the Apostles
S. of Sol. 3.1–4; Ps. 42.1–10; 2 Cor. 5.14–17; **John 20.1–2, 11–18**

What does the name Mary Magdalene bring to mind? Red hair? The oldest profession?

A prostitute?

All four Gospels record her presence at both cross and tomb. John describes her as the first witness to the resurrection – something Paul forgets in his first letter to Corinth. Only Luke mentions Mary earlier in the story, noting that she was among those who accompanied Jesus. Pope Gregory I bears responsibility for associating her with Luke's account of the sinful woman who washed Jesus' feet, making the outrageous assumption that she was a prostitute. Since, according to Gregory, a woman's sin had to equate with sex, Mary must have been a prostitute; indeed, in 591 a papal declaration made this an official teaching of the Church. Why? When Peter said to Jesus, 'Go away from me for I am a sinful man', no one assumed Peter was a pimp.

There is no evidence whatsoever that Mary was the unnamed woman in Luke's Gospel, or that either woman belonged to that oldest profession.

Luke and Mark record that Jesus released Mary of Magdala from seven demons; that too has been wrongly associated with sexual sin. To the Jews, seven was the number of perfection, and thus represented God; whereas humanity was represented by number six, one less than perfection. The fact that Jesus expelled seven demons said to Jewish ears that he made Mary completely whole.

'But,' said Gregory, 'those seven demons represent the seven deadly sins, and this woman had them all – including lust!' Well then, if Jesus freed her from them all, Mary must be the most perfectly cleansed human in history – freed from all that we still struggle with, and fully transformed. Which surely is the calling of Christ for all of us.

Or apostle?

In 1969 the Roman Catholic Church repealed the defamatory teaching as an error. Mary was neither the unnamed sinful woman nor a prostitute. Of course, corrections to error are never as exciting as the accusation; popular culture continued to represent Mary Magdalene as a whore and all else was forgotten.

But the Gospels speak of Mary as a committed disciple of Jesus, who remained so through all challenges. She stayed when most of his other disciples fled; at the foot of the cross, at his burial, and at the tomb before dawn to anoint the body. She was the first to see the risen Jesus. In every Gospel account it is the women who go to the tomb, and to whom Jesus appears, and in John's account it is Mary of Magdala whom Christ instructs, 'Go and tell my brothers ...'

A woman was commissioned to preach the gospel to the men by Christ himself.

Don't keep me to yourself

But women were not seen as reliable witnesses, even though to them on tesurrection morning Jesus entrusted the most important evangelistic outreach of all time! Indeed, the words that are remembered most from John's account are 'Do not touch me' (Latin: *Nolo me tangere*). Many paintings of Mary Magdalene bear this title, emphasizing not her apostolic calling but her apparent unworthiness to touch the risen body of Christ. But Jesus said, 'Do not hold on to me,' surely meaning, 'Don't keep me to yourself, but preach the good news of life for all!'

Yet for two thousand years and more women could not teach or preach, could not be ordained, could not preside at the Eucharist. Thomas Aquinas taught that women were malformed men, and Tertullian called them the devil's gateway. Before the Second World War, far from holding a place on a church council or standing for office of churchwarden, women were not even allowed in the sanctuary when bringing up the offertory, because some deemed it too near the altar for a woman. As recently as 2012 the measure for appointing women bishops failed in General Synod. How completely had we lost sight of Jesus' call to his very first apostle: 'Go and tell my brothers that I am ...'

What a difference it might have made to the Church's witness to the whole world if John's scene in the garden had really been the gospel that was preached; a gospel in which a woman was respected and heard; that did not distort Jesus' treatment of every human being as a unique and valued individual; and in which men such as Constantine and Gregory, Aquinas and Tertullian (among other little foxes in the vineyard), did not have to hide the Apostle to the Apostles behind the legend of a fallen woman with wild red hair, unworthy of any merit. Rather might she have been seen as Christ saw her: renewed, beloved and called by name.

As, indeed, Christ sees each one of us. For that is the gospel of Christ.

Carey Saleh

Suggested hymns

Led like a lamb to the slaughter; Let love be real; Now the green blade riseth; Alleluia, alleluia, raise the gospel; She sits like a bird.

St James the Apostle   25 July
Securing the Best Seats

Jer. 45.1–5; Ps. 126; Acts 11.27—12.2 (*if the Acts reading is used instead of the Old Testament reading, the New Testament reading is* 2 Cor. 4.7–15); **Matt. 20.20–28**

Once I was visiting an ordination candidate in his home to explore his progress on the course of which I was principal. The main concern my colleagues had was that this student seemed to have an over-dependence on his mother. I began to explore this with him over a cup of coffee. I tried to raise this delicate issue as sensitively as I could when a voice came from another room. 'Oh no, he's not!' We continued the exploration but this unidentified voice came to the defence of my student. When I asked to meet her, his mother emerged still fiercely protesting the idea that she had any undue influence over her 26-year-old son.

Who was speaking for whom?

You might think that the mother of James and John was taking matters into her own hand when she asks Jesus to ensure the places of honour in his kingdom go to her two sons. It's not surprising that a mother or any parent would want to put in a word for their children. Perhaps, James and John put their mother up to it, being too shamefaced or fearing the response from their fellow disciples if they made the request themselves.

Some of you will know that in Mark and Luke the request is made by James and John themselves. Their mother plays no part in it. That seems the most likely version. Perhaps Matthew attributed the request to their mother in order to present them in a more favourable light. It won't be the first mother who has been willing to take the rap for their misguided children. The mother of James and John was, of all the parents of the disciples, the one mentioned as being with Jesus. If she was a close follower of Jesus, it might just be credible to think that she would have the relationship with Jesus to want to voice the aspirations of her two sons.

Claiming the best seats

The issue, of course, was seating – who occupies the best seats. You don't have to go to church for long before you realize that who sits where can be a lively and sensitive issue. An unsuspecting newcomer has to tread warily. If they attempt to occupy an empty seat regarded as a personal sinecure by a regular member of the congregation, or the seat reserved for a warden, mayor or patron, they might be in for an awkward exchange or risk eviction. Some special seats already look like thrones, and imitate the superior seating on which James and John had set their sights. The seat of a bishop, notably that in Durham Cathedral, is a throne, 'high and lifted up', whose purpose, if not the mischievous intention of the builders, is to deliver the occupant of the see of Durham breathless and weary to his throne before he opens his mouth.

A false mindset

Whether or not it was James and John or their mother who lay claim to prominent seats, James and John have left their seats in the family fishing business. Shortly before, they heard Jesus promising to those who have left house and father and mother for the sake of the gospel that they will be rewarded. They have done something for Jesus and so they take him at his word and want him to return the favour. They want seats, and they're willing to jostle for position and influence among the Twelve. But they are not alone. The other disciples gang up against them, annoyed not at their self-serving but for unfairly vying for advantage over them. The disciples as a whole are indicted in the struggle for power and service of self.

We might be tempted to view this as a little domestic incident illustrating the congenital drive for ambition and status. But it's much more than that. It's late in the day in the life and work of Jesus. Dark storm clouds are gathering and the countdown to an inevitable conflict between Jesus and his nation was fast moving to its cataclysmic climax.

The clash of the kingdom

Jesus has shown himself to be the man for others, the servant of all, the one who has no concern for himself, who lives in perfect filial obedience of his Father; he won't be deflected from the costly path of self-sacrifice. Jesus has come to serve and to give his life, refusing to save it. He promises that the way of servanthood becomes the way of liberation; the path of renunciation is the path to glory; the life of service and suffering is the way to life. That is the character of the apprenticeship Jesus shared with his disciples for three years. And now, as the dark and demonic forces are poised to eliminate Jesus, the disciples can think of nothing more than securing their own places in the kingdom.

The difficulty we find with the uncompromising demands of Jesus helps us to see that we, too, are like the disciples. The world of hierarchies, pecking orders, insiders and outsiders, vying to secure our goals, benefits, advantages at the expense of others, is so much part of the mechanism of our society that we treat it as normal. The conflict between the aspirations and actions of the disciples and the life and teaching of Jesus presents us with a stark choice. Christ assumes the throne of glory through what he suffered, and that's the way not only for James and John but for all who long for seats close to Jesus in his kingdom.

Roger Spiller

Suggested hymns

From heaven you came; Brother, sister, let me serve you; Beauty for brokenness, hope for despair; For the healing of the nations; In Christ alone, my hope is found.

The Transfiguration of Our Lord   6 August
The Face of Love
Dan. 7.9–10, 13–14; Ps. 97; 2 Peter 1.16–19; **Luke 9.28–36**

The glory

You might not feel you have the energy to be climbing mountains but what about that glory? Don't you long for a glimpse of that?

I wonder what Peter, James and John were expecting as Jesus led them up that mountain. Did they connect this mountain to stories in their own Jewish tradition – the meeting place of God? Or were they just out to enjoy the view and hope that this time someone had packed some sandwiches?

Suddenly the face of their friend Jesus is shining, dazzling, so bright they can hardly look at him. They see Moses and Elijah, from centuries ago. How can this be? What they saw up on that mountain top was *un*created light. The light that was there before God said, 'Let there be light.' They were given a moment of presence – a glimpse of God in glory – the light that brought them, us, the world into being. God's glory reflected in human faces. For the Hebrews in Exodus it was the face of Moses. In Galilee the face of Jesus. Because that is how we can understand God and presence and relationships. Through people. Human faces. For a new baby the distance between the breast at which it feeds and the mother's face is the perfect distance for its new baby eyes to focus. The face of his or her mother is the first face through which the baby understands belonging and love. Or at least that is how it is meant to be. Some carry very deep wounds because that first relationship was either absent or less than secure – perhaps because the mother herself didn't have the security for which she yearned. But seeing love in the faces of others is something we need as we travel through life.

The covering

The radiance is almost too much for those disciples. Here are Moses and Elijah representing the Law and the Prophets, and talking to Jesus who had come to fulfil them. These ordinary men long for protection from such transfiguration. Peter feels the need to do something. He needs to build a shelter – a safe place. Yet it is God who provides the covering. They find themselves immersed in cloud rather than see the glory fade from Jesus' person. It is from that cloud that the voice is heard, the voice of reassurance and hope – 'My beloved. Listen to him. You can trust him. This Jesus you know is me, part of me, with you.'

The voice isn't far away but right here close by amid whatever cloud might be covering your life just now. When it is difficult to see where God might be in all this, know that God is there, here, with you, in the cloud of unknowing, with the assurance that all is known to God.

We may be weighed down with weariness and fatigue, as the disciples were. Perhaps it had been a long climb for them. Your climb may have been a difficult and challenging one this past year. You may have travelled an unexpected and even unwanted road, steeper and more rugged than you had planned. The view from the mountain top may still be covered with cloud, and you have questions that seem unanswered. But from that cloud comes God's voice, an assurance that in the person of Jesus, this known and beloved face, there is the light and presence of God.

334

The promise

Here in this moment, unexpected as it was, you see where heaven and earth have met. The visible and the invisible. The unknowable and the known. And you are held within it, spoken to, reassured that this glimpse of glory is a gift, that there is presence even in the darkness. It is tempting to hold on to the moment, encapsulate it, build it a shelter so that it will always be protected; institutional-ize it and build walls around it. But we cannot capture glory, the Spirit, the sacred meeting place. We cannot structure it to meet our demands. We come down the mountain, return to the ordinary and familiar, and there the questions may still feel unanswered, the road ahead still difficult. Yet we carry the experience of the glory deep within us. The voice that said, 'My beloved'.

I pray that through it all there will be people who can reflect God's love to you – for that is what the body of Christ is about. We are asked to be Christ to one another on life's journey, which can be full of joy and sorrow, wonder and fear. I pray that you will know deep down that God is there with you, in you; that, no matter what road the journey takes, you experience that glimpse that transfigures our understanding and gives us hope; a knowledge that we are not alone. May we experience resurrection that reveals the wonder of transformed lives.

Carey Saleh

Suggested hymns

Shine, Jesus, shine; Lord, enthroned in heavenly splendour; Christ whose glory fills the skies; Glorious things of thee are spoken.

The Blessed Virgin Mary   15 August
Mary's Witness to God's Upheavals
Isa. 61.10–end, *or* Rev. 11.19—12.6, 10; Ps. 45.10–end;
Gal. 4.4–7; **Luke 1.46–55**

Those who are familiar with the services of Matins and Evensong in the Church of England will probably know by heart the canticles sung at those services. The Magnificat is one of three 'hymns', Jewish poetic creations, that Luke collected in the infancy story of his Gospel. The Magnificat, or Song of Mary, is not thought to have been composed by Mary; her Old Testament counterpart, Hannah, had her own song, and Mary needed to have her own song too.

The setting

The song continues the great Jewish theme of God's action in the wider world, but it extends right down to one person, a woman, in a culture where only men were the makers and shakers, to a young woman, and to a poor woman. This poor woman experiences the first fruits of the salvation that had been promised to her people and she commits her life to its cause. She is a focus and role model for us too, one who orchestrates our own praise to God for the grace shown in this remarkable woman to whom so much was entrusted.

In the first two chapters of Luke we learn that both Jesus and John were born in the bosom of a group of poor and pious Jews who lived in anxious hope that God would bring about his promised deliverance to their nation. Mary had been told by the angel to make a visit of some distance to her relative Elizabeth. She had received the incredible news that God had chosen them, a poor priest and a barren woman, to be the parents of the one who was to be the forerunner of the Lord. When the two pregnant women met, Elizabeth, filled with the Holy Spirit, acclaimed 'with a loud cry' her blessing on Mary for believing that God would fulfil the incredible promise made to her. And Mary's response is the canticle we know as the Magnificat.

√[VJ] - confirmation

God's favour on Mary

'My soul magnifies the Lord and my spirit rejoices in God my saviour.' Mary is full of praise to God because God has looked with favour on his lowly servant. As a woman who is also young and poor, she won't find favour from her community or nation. She is humbled in the eyes of the world. Her weak economic position can be inferred from the attack on the rich that follows. It's Mary's socio-economic situation that is foregrounded here. 'Blessed are the poor,' says Luke, not the 'poor in spirit', but the straightforward, actual, economic poor. True, this may also refer to her humble attitude to God, but we must avoid spiritualizing the message and neutering its radical social declaration. An interior disposition, spiritual poverty, is no substitute for remedying the condition of the poor and marginalized. Didn't Luke record Jesus as saying in his so-called 'Galilean manifesto', drawing on the Old Testament prophet Isaiah, that 'The Spirit of the Lord … has anointed me to bring good news to the poor'? But poverty itself can't bring a state of happiness. It can only come as a promise of action made to the poor. Being poor at least left a way open for trust in God for a reversal of fortunes.

Reversal of fortunes for all

Mary says that 'from now on all generations will call me blessed'. The one identified as Mary will be recognized as blessed for all time, as succeeding generations have done, right down to today. Mary then becomes one of the witnesses of God's presence and action, not just in her own life but for her nation too. George Caird, the biblical scholar, wrote, 'Mary sings of her own exaltation from loneliness to greatness as typical of the new order which is to be opened out for the whole people of God through the coming of her son.'[39]

The new order will target two manifestations of the country's division: the proud and powerful will be brought low and the lowly will be exalted; the rich will be sent away empty and the hungry will be fed. That is the revolutionary change long hoped for by a large proportion of the population of Judaea and Jerusalem, who were dependent upon relief and charity, living in a depressed economy. It will be brought about through the coming of the kingdom that Mary's son will inaugurate. But it has already begun. God has scattered the proud, he has brought down the powerful, he has filled the hungry and he has sent the rich away empty. We can revert to the testimony of God's activities throughout the history of Israel. But it has happened to Mary herself, the bearer of God's Son, and those who would bless Mary and follow her son Jesus Christ must share in God's radical reversal of our unjust and divided world.

Roger Spiller

Suggested hymns

With Mary, let my soul rejoice; For Mary, mother of our Lord; Sing we of the blessed mother; Tell out my soul, the greatness of the Lord.

Bartholomew the Apostle   24 August
Legends of Saints

Isa. 43.8–13; Ps. 145.1–7; Acts 5.12–16 (*if the Acts reading is used instead of the Old Testament reading, the New Testament reading is* 1 Cor. 4.9–15); **Luke 22.24–30**

Ah ... the twists and turns of legends about the saints ...

One of my favourite legends about St Bartholomew concerns a tiny island, about 37 square kilometres in size, off the north-east coast of Sicily. The island is called Lipari. It was there, in the fourth century, that the body of St Bartholomew was apparently washed up on the shore. How anyone knew that the corpse was that of Bartholomew is anyone's guess, but one cannot imagine that there was a luggage label attached to the big toe proclaiming whose corpse it was. No matter. The local bishop decided that they could do with one of the 12 disciples as their island's patron saint and soon the relics were ensconced in the island's cathedral. But over the next few centuries the threat from the Saracens intensified and so, in the ninth century, it was decided that at least some of the bones of Bartholomew should be sent for safe keeping to Benevento on the Italian mainland. The bones were placed in the Basilica San Bartolomeo. It was in the tenth century that some of those Benevento relics were taken by the Emperor Otto II and sent to Rome, where they found a home in a church he had founded on an island in the Tiber. The church is called San Bartolomeo alla'Isola (St Bartholomew on the Island). Because that church was built on the site of an ancient place of healing, the Temple of Aesculapius, St Bartholomew became associated with healing – which perhaps (note the word) explains how Bart's Hospital, founded in London in the twelfth century, was given its dedication.

It's a complex, meandering story. There are other stories about St Bartholomew that entirely contradict the Italian version; for instance, that he went on a missionary visit to India and was martyred in Armenia. Be that as it may. All that such stories prove is that we humans love to create stories, whether based on fact or not. And where the stories are about long-dead saints the desire to claim the saint for one's own church is powerful.

From legend to reality

In these kinds of circumstances it would be a waste of time and effort to try to dig beneath the legends to see if there is a kernel of historic truth in them. The task is impossible. However, the creators of the lectionary get around this problem deftly. In Bartholomew's case they don't spend much time on the details in the Gospels about him; after all, those details are very sparse. Instead, and wisely, they redirect our attention to some of the phrases that Jesus used when he talked with his disciples, of whom, of course, Bartholomew was one.

In today's reading our attention is drawn to an argument that the disciples had about which of them was the greatest. It seems a pretty childish thing for them to be doing, doesn't it? Was there jealousy among them? Were some lording it surreptitiously over the others? Did some feel left out of an imagined inner circle?

Such arguments go on, of course, wherever humans congregate. 'It isn't fair' is one of the earliest complaints that primary school children make in the playground. Adults are little better: imagine the under-the-breath comments when top City lawyers receive their annual bonuses: 'He got more than me ... that's not right.' Or bring to mind the sarcastic comments in the armed forces when someone is promoted. And don't imagine that the Church is any different. Among the clergy, mutterings about being overlooked are (sadly) commonplace. If you find that difficult to believe, look at any great church or cathedral procession and there you will see all the subtleties of rank and status on public display.

There is something about us humans that loves status, rank and position. And yet the comments of Jesus are sharp and to be noted: 'The greatest among you must become like the youngest, and the leader like one who serves.'

It is a radical instruction and one that many of the saints tried to put into practice: think of St Francis, for example, and the way in which he embraced poverty. Mind you, it wasn't too long before his followers were disagreeing with one another.

The exercise of power

Perhaps we should reinterpret the words of Jesus by applying them not to issues of rank and status but to the exercise of power. In your own situation, whatever that might be, over whom do you have power? Is that power exercised for the good of the other person or is it to his or her detriment? Does the power you exercise leave the other person feeling diminished or threatened? How can we exercise power justly?

The questions keep coming because they are intensely relevant.

When Jesus ordered the apostles to be servants to each other it was a way of signalling a new form of human community. The fact that it is so difficult to put into practice doesn't mean that we should cease trying, for that way lies the kingdom and that way lies fullness of life.

Christopher Herbert

Suggested hymns

Brother, sister, let me serve you; Come, my way, my truth, my life; Strengthen for service, Lord, the hands; Christians, lift your hearts and voices.

Holy Cross Day   14 September
God So Loved the World
Num. 21.4–9; Ps. 22.23–28; Phil. 2.6–11; **John 3.13–17**

The world

You could say that the clue to understanding Holy Cross Day, and for that matter the Gospel of John as a whole, can be found in just two words in today's reading: in the Greek, *ton kosmon*, 'the world'. The Greek word *kosmos* could perhaps best be translated as 'the created order', not just planet Earth but the whole creation; and it occurs very frequently in the Gospel and Letters of John. It usually carries a negative meaning, as for example in the opening Prologue: 'He [the Word of God] was in the world, and the world was made by him; and the world did not know him,' or, in Jesus' words to his disciples: 'If the world hates you, be aware that it hated me before it hated you.' You could say that in the Gospel of John the term 'the world' means 'all of creation in its brokenness and alienation from its creator', with its damaged ecosystems and unjust political structures as well as its beauty.

Which only makes today's reading all the more extraordinary, with its famous declaration:

340

God so loved the world that he gave his only Son, so that everyone who believes in him may not perish but may have eternal life. Indeed, God did not send the Son into the world to condemn the world, but in order that the world might be saved through him.

Notice that Jesus doesn't say, 'God so loved the Church', or even, 'God so loved the human race', but 'God so loved *the world*'. The object, the scope, of God's love is nothing less than all of creation. And the ultimate goal of its Creator is nothing less than the transfiguration of the entire creation, the 'new heaven and new earth' that John of Patmos writes about in the Bible's closing pages.

God's entry into the world

But for this to happen, the Creator has to enter the creation, enter into 'the world' with all its contradictions – its beauty and its sadness, its good and its evil – and redeem it from within. The cross is the means by which that redemption is achieved. In today's reading, Jesus says that he will be 'lifted up' – the term usually means to be exalted, as you might lift shoulder-high a footballer who scores the winning goal; but here it refers to his being lifted up on the cross. The divine Son of God will not be 'lifted up' like royalty, and sit on a gorgeous throne: his glory will be seen precisely in his humiliation and death. But wait a minute (you might say): why does Christ have to die, and die on a cross, in order to redeem us, and the whole of God's creation? The answer is both simple and profound: to show how much he loved us.

Love to death

Have you noticed the strange fact that in English (and perhaps in other languages too) we use words about death when we're talking about love? We say things like, 'I'm dying to see you', or, 'You're breaking my heart', when we don't really mean that at all. Or, on second thoughts, perhaps we do. For the truth about real love is that it is itself a kind of dying, a dying to self in order to live for someone else. Sometimes that happens literally, when someone lays down their life for someone they love, or for a cause they believe in. So for God to send his only son into the world, and hand him over to death, is to reveal a God whose love for us is so infinitely great that it will require the ultimate sacrifice. God gave all God had to give to show us that nothing can separate us, or all of creation, from the reach of the divine love. When the poet Dante ended his *Divine Comedy* by writing of 'the love that moves the sun and the other stars', he was celebrating Jesus' victory on the cross. And every time we make that love our own, every time we die a little to ourselves and give all we have to give in loving service of our fellow humans and our fellow creatures, we celebrate that victory anew. No one ever put it better than Isaac Watts:

> Were the whole realm of nature mine,
> That were a present far too small;
> Love so amazing, so divine
> Demands my soul, my life, my all.

Gordon Mursell

Suggested hymns

God is love: let heav'n adore him; Name of all majesty; It is a thing most wonderful; When I survey the wondrous cross.

St Matthew, Apostle and Evangelist   21 September
A Memorable Meal
Prov. 3.13–18; Ps. 119.65–72; 2 Cor. 4.1–6; **Matt. 9.9–13**

> Go and learn what this means, 'I desire mercy, not sacrifice.' For I have come to call not the righteous but sinners.

Wealthy Roman citizens must have suffered quite frequently from severe indigestion. Why? Because it was the fashion in the most up-market houses to have a dining room called a triclinium, in which three chaises-longues were grouped in a U-shape around a low table. The food was placed on the table or served directly to the guests by the slaves of the household. The guests did not eat sitting upright but reclined on couches, leaning on their left-hand sides. It must have been distinctly uncomfortable and was not the ideal way to digest food.

An artistic development arising from this strange dining habit was the creation of 'unswept floor' mosaics. These were highly decorated and very skilfully contrived mosaics littered with what appears to be the remains of a meal: bits of fish, nuts, shells and bones. Those things, created with tiny bits of glass and stone, represent the detritus left behind for the slaves to clear up after a feast. Some have claimed that these 'unswept floor' mosaics were not just clever talking-point creations but were meant to be a kind of reminder of death; they were 'memento mori'.

Now, in today's Gospel we are taken into a 'triclinium-type' dining room. In fact, the Greek text specifically says that the guests, including Jesus, were reclining on their couches as they ate. So, the discomfort of indigestion was probably already beginning. But the picture the story conjures up is of a relaxed meal with friends, in which no doubt some of the guests dropped the remains of their food on the floor.

Into this happy meal a note of discord is thrust. The Pharisees pointedly comment to the disciples that their rabbi is eating with sinners and tax-collectors. For the Pharisees it was unacceptable behaviour because the strict cleanness/uncleanness rules were being broken.

A sudden change of mood

Pause the picture for the moment as the household slaves scurry in and out carrying a variety of dishes. The atmosphere, for those with antennae sufficiently subtle to detect it, had suddenly shifted. What had been a relaxed party became a tense religious confrontation. No doubt the slaves averted their eyes and carried on with their allotted tasks, as well-trained servants should, but going back to the kitchen they would have been bound to have gossiped with each other about the ill-mannered guests. What would the response of the chief guest be?

Jesus, with exquisite wit and theological aplomb, turned the conversation around. 'Those who are well have no need of a physician, but those who are sick,' he said. 'Go and learn what this means, "I desire mercy, not sacrifice." For I have come to call not the righteous but sinners.'

It was not simply an adroit social response. It also focused on a text from the prophet Hosea, which Jesus' critics would have known, a quotation that wrong-footed them. Jesus pointed out with rapier-sharp wit that this was a text whose meaning was one that his opponents had yet to grasp. It was a powerful rebuke.

One can imagine a silence descending on the other dining guests. Perhaps some of them, to cover the embarrassment of the social faux pas created by the Pharisees, leant across to the low central table to pluck grapes and eat them, waiting to see how the confrontation would resolve.

A clarion call

But Jesus was not finished with his critics yet. His final parry was to declaim, 'I have come to call not the righteous but sinners.'

It's no wonder that this gem of a story was remembered. It has tension, rhetorical cleverness, and a final line that lodged itself in the memories of those who were there. That final line, for those with enough sense to realize it, implied that he had a supreme authority. This was not a polite dinner-party piece of idle chit-chat, this was a clarion call about his relationship with God.

Goodness knows what the slaves made of it when much later they came to sweep up after the guests had left. Low-born and trafficked immigrants as many of them were, did they class themselves as sinners? Did Jesus have them in mind when he talked about his vocation to 'call' sinners? And were the Pharisees the 'virtuous', or were they also the 'sinners'?

It must have been a troubling and disorientating episode for everyone who had been there. They were all left with a question: who was Jesus?

It is a question that forces all of us to consider very carefully what our answer to it might be: a question that cannot be answered with a quick and easy response, but one that stays with us throughout our lives.

Christopher Herbert

Suggested hymns

Come, dearest Lord, descend and dwell; Come, O thou Traveller unknown; Lord of all hopefulness; We love the place, O God.

St Michael and All Angels   29 September
Revealing the Angels
Gen. 28.10–17; Ps. 103.19–end; **Rev. 12.7–12**, *or* Heb. 1.5–end; John 1.47–end

A coded encouragement

We drop into a scene of a first-century Harry Potter or Chronicles of Narnia produced for an audience who fear for their lives and can see only the evil at work around them. Revelation was a story told in code as an encouragement for persecuted Christians.

The author of Revelation takes his own troubled human political and religious predicament and gives it a cosmic setting. It is a very particular kind of literature, full of codes and symbols depicting supernatural cataclysmic events. It is apocalyptic – which is the Greek word meaning *to reveal*.

It's as though the writer longs to say, 'I know life is tough and you are afraid, wondering how we will survive; you feel alone. Yet if we could lift the veil from our mortal eyes we would see all around us the very powers of heaven working on our behalf!'

When God and goodness seem far away, can we imagine a veil right here in front of our eyes being lifted so we can see present with us the invisible kingdom of God in our midst? The purpose of Revelation was to reveal the beyond in the here and now. In Greek – *apokalupsis*.

The hero of the scene we read today is Archangel Michael, captain of the heavenly host; for today is the feast day of St Michael and All Angels, or, in old English, Michaelmas.

Michael and all his angels fight against the dragon and all his angels. The dragon is the code name for Satan, the devil, Lucifer. Remember, Satan once belonged to the company of heaven but rebelled against God. In Luke's Gospel Jesus talks of seeing Satan fall from heaven. After all, Christ was there in the beginning. Christ knew this angel. Did Christ weep when that angel fell from grace so spectacularly? Is that why Jesus could tell stories so poignantly of the angels rejoicing over one sinner who repents, as a shepherd reunited with his sheep, a father reunited with his son? Might that not reflect God's longing that this fallen angel might be 'found' again?

Michael and Satan

On the outer wall of Coventry Cathedral there is a statue of Michael's victory over Satan.[40] Michael is upright, poised in flight, his great wings rising above him, face turned to the city. Satan, his head beneath Michael's right foot, stares heavenward with bulging eyes.

This cathedral was consecrated in 1962 after the old cathedral was destroyed in the bombing of November 1940. Metaphors of angels and demons battling in the skies above would have seemed very pertinent to residents of cities across Europe during those war years. Within Revelation's metaphorical battle language of victory over evil is the ever-present hope of reconciliation; the forming of right relationship; a recognition that the horrors of evil must be fought with the tools of love and forgiveness.

The building of the new cathedral was a pledge for new relationships, for reconciliation as a Christian witness, based in that cathedral church of St Michael.

The Knife Angel

For a few weeks in 2019 Archangel Michael was accompanied by another angel outside Coventry Cathedral. A statue made from 100,000 knives removed from London's streets in 2019, the *Knife Angel*[41] is 27 feet tall placed on the ground, wings unfurled, hands held out in a gesture of peace. The angel journeyed from city to city through the country – a grieving, angelic, reconciling witness against the evils of knife crime.

For those first readers of Revelation the dragon was indeed in their midst, as though all the evil they could imagine was made manifest in the persecution and horror of their lives. The author's message was – you are not alone. God is here with you; the whole company and power of heaven; angels are here in your midst.

Reconciliation

The power of heaven of course is love. Within Revelation's metaphorical battle language is the ever-present call for reconciliation; the forming of right relationship; a recognition that the horrors of evil must be fought with the tools of love and forgiveness.

Our incarnational faith expresses that, though the dragons of hate, injustice and evil appear throughout history, God is always present with us. When we take physical things of bread and wine and see in them the sacred, Christ present in us; when we acknowledge that with angels and archangels and all the company of heaven we may find a voice to sing God's praise – then we know that heaven is opened and we are not alone, that through all ages we are part of a sacred narrative of reconciling grace.

Carey Saleh

Suggested hymns

We are marching in the light of God; Ye holy angels bright; Lord, we come to ask your healing; We turn to you, O God of every nation.

St Luke the Evangelist   18 October
Carriers of Hope
Isa. 35.3–6, *or* Acts 16.6–12a; Ps. 147.1–7; 2 Tim. 4.5–17;
Luke 10.1–9

Holding the vision

What exciting things are on the horizon for you? Where does your hope lie? Does the future feel rosy for you or are you filled with dread, anxiety or cynicism about what may come? Newspapers warn us that the future is bleak. Our readings today for the feast of St Luke are all about having faith and hope in the future and recognizing that the kingdom of God is breaking in around us. St Luke, the author of the third Gospel and the Acts of the Apostles, witnessed and was part of the birth of Christianity. He recorded for all time what he saw himself and heard from others about Jesus and the earliest Christian communities. His words have shaped the faith and given hope to millions down the centuries. Jump back several hundred years before Luke and hope was in fairly short supply. The Israelites were in exile. Parts of the book of Isaiah are filled with doom and gloom, misery and anxiety. But in chapter 35, a brilliant shaft of light breaks through. The people are far away, powerless to return – Isaiah describes them as blind, deaf, lame and mute – but hope is on the horizon. Weak hands and feeble knees will be made strong, eyes and ears will be opened, new energy and joy will abound. All will be fertile and fresh. New life will come and God will save – says Isaiah. These things are not pipe dreams – not maybes – but sure and certain future events: they will happen. God will come and everything and everyone will be transformed and renewed. It's a vision of beauty and encouragement for people in a bleak place. Isaiah is carrying the hope.

The coming of Jesus

Luke writes powerfully in his Gospel about the effect of the coming of Jesus, the Messiah. His birth is surrounded by miraculous events. Angels play a big part. Women are important. Luke gives them a voice. He is the only one who records the annunciation, the visit of Mary to Elizabeth, the Magnificat, the Hail Mary. The lowly, the oppressed, the sick, the outcast, ordinary people, young and old are all recorded by Luke as being integral to the story of Jesus – God with us. Hope is being realized. The kingdom of God is breaking into ordinary lives and making them extraordinary. This is picked up in today's Gospel reading. Jesus sends out 70 of his followers to go in pairs throughout the towns and settlements that he is going to visit. They are to prepare the ground for the coming of the Messiah. They do this simply. They travel light: no purse, bag or sandals. They deliver messages of peace into people's households. They are commanded to cure the sick – to bring order out of chaos – to tell everyone that the kingdom of God has come near. They carry hope for others. There is urgency about this task. Jesus is the Lord of the harvest of souls – and he needs his followers to prepare that harvest of people so that they recognize him when he comes.

Carriers of hope

Paul writing to Timothy senses that his days are numbered. He's under house arrest in Rome and he speaks like one nearing death. 'I have fought the good fight, I have finished the race, I have kept the faith.' Even in death, he is positive and filled with hope about his future – certain that he will inherit the crown of righteousness. He has experienced Christ standing beside him and giving him strength in adversity. St Luke, the doctor, is with him; perhaps ministering to him, certainly giving support and friendship, keeping hope alive. The ordinary things of life are important – Paul needs his cloak, books and documents – and he retains a concern for his friends and fellow workers, speaking about them by name. Paul has seen the signs of God's kingdom all around him and he has firm and certain hope that the future will be Christ-shaped. Like Isaiah, Luke and Paul, we are called to be carriers of hope for our communities. The future belongs to God who has promised not to let anyone go. Signs of the reign of God in our world are all around us. Where there is love, where there is joy, where there is hope – God is at work. Where there is peace, where there is order, where there is wholeness, where there is new life – God is at work. At every Eucharist we are filled and nurtured with the word of God and the body and blood of Christ. From that experience we are sent out by the Holy Spirit to be the carriers of hope into our world. Wherever you find yourself – whoever you are speaking to, or whatever you are doing – remember that Christ sends you to prepare the ground for him. Are your words and actions filled with peace and hope, love and joy? When people meet you, do they sense that the kingdom of God has come near? Like Isaiah, like Luke, like Paul, can you give hope to others by simply being yourself? Today, this week, every week, watch for the signs of the kingdom, be part of the transformation that Christ brings. Be a carrier of hope for the world.

Catherine Williams

Suggested hymns

All my hope on God is founded; O breath of life, come sweeping through us; For the healing of the nations; Let us build a house.

SS Simon and Jude, Apostles   28 October
Jesus Provokes Key Questions
Isa. 28.14–16; Ps. 119.89–96; Eph. 2.19–end; **John 15.17–end**

Simon and Jude are joined together by the one thing they had in common: little or nothing is known about them with any certainty from Scripture. We know only that they were both disciples of Jesus. But even then, Jude is known as Judas in Luke, but in Mark and Matthew he answers to Thaddaeus, brother of James the Less.

But each of them poses a crucial question that still has the power to resonate with sceptical and unbelieving people.

The use of force

First off the block is Simon, who asks if noble ends can be realized by forceful means. We don't know about Simon's character, we do know about his party affiliations. He is called Simon the Zealot. The word Zealot comes from our words 'zeal' and 'zealous'. It's not a quality much appreciated in the UK. Any zeal that Simon had was not directly to advance the work of the kingdom, at least as

Jesus saw it. Zealot-like Simon saw the only way to overthrow their Roman overlords was through military action leading to armed revolt. Simon was a left-wing extremist, a dangerous man to have around. And yet Jesus enlisted him into his circle as a disciple.

Deliverance by force?

Simon seemed too hot to handle. We can wonder how skilful Jesus needed to be to manage him. Simon believed in at least some sort of kingdom that Jesus was preaching. He was prepared to lay down his life for the revolution. It's not a far-fetched idea. Most of us recognize that, however regrettable, force is sometimes a necessary, if lesser, evil. And it's been suggested that Jesus intended to precipitate a confrontation with the Roman authorities that would force God to act. If, however, Jesus had forsworn the use of violence, why did he enlist Simon? And what of Judas, was he part of an armed group? His name, 'Iscariot', could link him to the Sicarii, or 'Sicarius', an armed group who carried daggers. And what, too, of the sons of thunder, how did Peter and John get their nickname? Almost certainly not for being supine and obsequious.

As with the company he kept, Jesus spent time with publicans, sinners and people driven to the margins of society. So perhaps it's hardly surprising that he chose people with strong views and strong characters to work with him. Simon did seriously misunderstand the nature of the kingdom Jesus was bringing. But so also did the rest of the disciples. How easy it is to deceive ourselves that a worthy cause justifies any means to bring it about. Truth is often obliterated by the force that is deemed necessary to secure it.

Show yourself to the world

But now a second question, and this time it's Jude's turn. Have you asked yourself or been asked, why, if Jesus declined the way of force, did he not provide us with stronger clues to help us to believe in him? In his farewell address to his disciples in John's Gospel, Jesus says the world won't see him any more. And this provokes Jude to make his first and only recorded contribution in the Gospel. Why did Jesus not reveal himself to the world?

What he and non-believers since seem to be asking for is a public, spectacular, decisive appearance that would leave no one in any doubt as to who is boss. Judas has been known as the patron saint of desperate cases and lost causes in the last couple of centuries.

We can wonder why, in the absence of stronger evidence and argument, Jesus did not put himself about more, and throw in more miracles. The faith that he inaugurated might itself be considered by some to be a lost cause, finally to be extinguished by the march of secularism.

Not by might

But this brings us back to Simon and the use of force. If Jesus forswore to resort to miracles for no other purpose than their showy, spectacular character, why would he depend upon them in getting acceptance for his message? If a decisive, unambiguous presentation could convert the world at a stroke, what would be the cost in human freedom and the natural process of maturation? Even some of those who witnessed the resurrection and the ascension did not believe. The reticent, often hidden character of Jesus' ministry on earth gave space and freedom for people to respond as they chose and delayed the prospect of judgement. It may look to the world like a lost cause, but it turns out to be the only cause that will triumph over our force-ridden world.

Roger Spiller

Suggested hymns

Jesus Christ is waiting; Thy kingdom come on bended knee; O Lord, all the world belongs to you; Jesus shall reign, where'er the sun.

All Saints' Day   1 November
Strengthening Our Community with the Dead
Wisd. 3.1–9, *or* Isa. 25.6–9; Ps. 24.1–6; **Rev. 21.1–6a**; John 11.32–44

'Do we believe in life after death?' a leading writer asked recently,[42] noting the reticence of the Church to voice the Easter hope even at a time when the world is convulsed by death and loss through the coronavirus. Many of us are more preoccupied with prolonging life than facing our own mortality. But the real experience of death for us is the death of other people, of the people we love. And, as our Gospel suggests, the bereaved need immediate comfort and not merely the future hope of resurrection. They ask where are their loved ones. Do they live only in our memories, or in reality? Can we hope to sense their presence with us?

Where can the language and ritual to interpret our fleeting, inchoate experiences of loss be found to deliver a credible and satisfying reassurance to support us in our lives and not just in times of desolation? All Saints' Day may give us the clue, so long as we recognize that saints are not exceptional religious celebrities; they are people who display the signs of God's new creation. They comprise what our Apostles' Creed calls 'the communion of saints', a communion in which all followers of Christ living, unborn and dead are included.

Alive in Christ

We on this side of death's divide speak of the living and the dead. But since 'God is God not of the dead, but of the living', Jesus presides over all those who are now alive in him. It's been misleading to speak of them as 'asleep' or lacking consciousness. From the clues in Scripture we can think of them as being in a state of what Tom Wright calls 'restful happiness'.[43] They have been raised by Christ immediately after death but they remain in this blissful state as they await that final consummation with us and with all God's people living and yet to be born. The Revd Professor John Polkinghorne, a distinguished physicist, once began a televised sermon thus: 'Five minutes after your death you'll know the answer to a lot of questions which people ask now, or at least I believe you will.' And he went on to argue for a destiny beyond the end of our life on earth, believing that it is inconceivable that the infinite care and love God has shown to his people will be terminated and snatched from us.

All one in Christ's communion

We share a community of love in which Christ presides. So our closeness to the dead is through Christ. After all, it is Christ alone who has come back to us from the grave and brought us new life. So Christ is the portal through whom we experience our loved ones. 'The closer we come to Christ, the more deeply we enter into community with the dead', so said the theologian Jürgen Moltmann.[44] 'In Christ,' he says, 'we remain indestructibly and unforgettably joined with the dead in love for each other and in a common hope. In him the dead are enduringly with us who are the living.'[45] What does this mean for us in our grief? It means, he says, that we do not only take leave of the dead; 'we also participate in their transformation into that other world of God's'.[46] We keep company with them through grateful remembrance and hope. But through Christ they become a presence with us while letting us go free.

Worship breaches death's divide

We remember the dead, and name them. Many Christians in the West, from different faith traditions, hold services in graveyards on Easter Day. And some people follow the once traditional practice of going to church on Sunday mornings while also visiting the graves of those close to them in the surrounding churchyard. Some churches have poster-sized photos of the saints of their church who are no longer living. These and other innovative rites can bring home the comfort of the community of Christ, the communion of saints.

It can feel that there is a wall of silence between us and the dead. But, at a time of loss, the spontaneous and generous impulse of the human heart must be a guide for drawing us into the communion of saints. We do so through Christ. It's Christ who is our way to the saints. And if through the Spirit we feel the impulse to share our prayer as well as our praises with them, we do so because we know God loves and cares for them and means to draw them and us closer to himself.[47]

The communion of saints is most fully realized in the Holy Communion. We participate 'in the company of all the saints'. They are the cloud of witnesses in whose company we can draw close to those we know and love.[48] We are invited to 'Lift up our hearts' to the Lord in whose communion our loved ones live and praise and rejoice like birds released from their earthly cage. The more our hearts are open to God through Jesus, the more certain we become of God's unconditional, indestructible love for us and for them.

Roger Spiller

Suggested hymns

Sing with all the saints in glory; When on life a darkness falls; Let saints on earth in concert sing; For all the saints who from their labours rest.

All Souls' Day   2 November
Symbols of Hope
Lam. 3.17–26, 31–33, *or* **Wisd. 3.1–9**; Ps. 23, *or* 27.1–6,
16–end; Rom. 5.5–11, *or* 1 Peter 1.3–9; John 5.19–25,
or John 6.37–40

Touching our experience

Each morning when Bill gets up to make his cup of tea, he looks at
the photo on the bedside table and smiles at it. He's been a widower
many years now, but that morning ritual has become as important
to him as the words of 'Good morning' he and Betty exchanged
every day of their married life.

Diane is sitting in a meeting but her mind isn't on it. Her hand
goes to her neck and she plays with the silver chain and cross she
wears constantly. Her mother gave it to her a few days before she
died, and over the past three weeks, through death and funeral
and adjusting back to a working day, Diane often finds her fingers
wrapped around it as her mind fills with memories of her wonderful
mum.

Adam and Lisa stand at the cemetery and look at the new daf-
fodils pushing up through the tiny grave. The teddy-bear headstone
brings only occasional tears to their eyes now, and they stand, hand
in hand, each silently remembering the few short months of joy that
Charlie brought to their lives.

The autumn rains send water pouring through the conservatory
roof and Sheila quickly rolls back the rug and puts out the buckets.
Pete had been going to fix the roof for the past two years, but like
the wonky garage door, like the draughty bathroom window, like
the broken kitchen tiles, like most of his projects in fact, it never
got done. The builder is due next week, but when Pete first died,
Sheila just couldn't bring herself to get it fixed. It seemed too brutal
a reminder that Pete wouldn't be coming back to fix it himself.

Touching our need

We all find unique ways of coping with grief. But common to most
of us are symbols and images. A photograph, a piece of jewellery,
spring flowers, DIY disasters, a special piece of music; we remember
in various and sometimes strange ways, but the symbols and images
are all of them important.

There are times when words are simply not enough. Gestures, images, symbols will sometimes be all that we can manage – and sometimes all that we want. A hug or a held hand might be more comforting than 300 well-meant words. A cross on the wall might speak of more hope than any number of books. A lighted candle might express our prayerful love more powerfully than any inadequate struggle to find the right words.

In our hearts and minds we carry the memories of those we love. We pray for them, because they are and will always be part of our lives. We celebrate them, because they have given us a legacy of love that enriches who we are. And we grieve them, because we're human beings who struggle with the pain of separation.

Touching our faith

But we're also Christian human beings, which means that our sadness is always tempered by the hope Christ promises and by the earth-shattering events of Easter. Death can't be the end of the story because Jesus rose from the dead. Death can't be the end of the story because he has promised that all who see him and believe in him will never be pushed away, but will have eternal life. Death can't be the end of the story because in him we've been born anew into an imperishable and unfading inheritance. No matter how hard it is, grief can't ultimately overwhelm us, because the risen Christ offers his people a share in the eternal life of heaven. And so, as we bring those memories, those griefs and those prayers to our All Souls' Mass, we use words, but we also use symbols.

The candle we're each invited to light and place along the altar rail during the prayers in a few moments is one of those symbols. As the names of those we pray for are carried to the altar and read, our candles will come together to make a wall of prayer, a wall of light. In being united like that, they'll become a bright symbol of the love that conquers death and of the hope that can cast away our darkness.

Each of our individual prayers is gathered and offered to God as part of our collective prayer. Our individual griefs are brought together, shared and eased as we support each other. Our individual candle flame joins many candle flames and the gloom of sadness is dispelled by the dazzling light of God's love: love that embraces us now and holds us firm throughout eternity.

Brett Ward

Ye watchers and ye holy ones; Blest are the pure in heart; Rejoice in God's saints, today and all days; For all the saints, who from their labours rest.

St Andrew the Apostle   30 November
Grace to Follow without Delay
Isa. 52.7–10; Ps. 19.1–6; Rom. 10.12–18; **Matt. 4.18–22**

We often underestimate the magnitude of the disruption that following Christ can cause. The story of the calling of Andrew the Apostle reminds us of both the demand and the cost of responding wholeheartedly to the good news. There is no turning back. Andrew was a Galilean fisherman, an important and respected tradesman, and there he was, standing with his brother Simon at the edge of the lake. They were casting out their nets as part of their daily round. They obviously weren't doing this in an idle moment, they weren't fishing for fun! It was their livelihood, it was their bread and butter, and their success would affect the lives of their family and the life of their wider community. Presumably they weren't looking to drop everything. This wasn't part of their game plan, they weren't looking to escape.

The call of Jesus

Into this picture, almost casually, almost randomly, wades Jesus. He sees the brothers on the shoreline. Perhaps he sees something in them that could be used for the greater purposes of God, or perhaps they were chosen for their very ordinariness. He calls out with a voice that has the authority of the one who made the heavens and the earth, the land and the sea and every living creature with which the waters swarm. 'Follow me,' he says, 'and I will make you fish for people.'

Further along, James and John were sitting on the shore mending their nets. This was not a trivial chore for an idle moment but an urgent task. Perhaps they had already been out fishing that morning and had returned knowing that vital repairs to the nets were needed. Fish were getting away, the catch was being depleted. This could not wait until tomorrow and it required their full attention. So, there they were, sitting in the sunshine as the water lapped around their feet, darning and knotting, a pleasing picture that hides the critical importance of this work. Once again, Jesus calls out and once again, without delay and with immediate effect, James and John rise up and follow him, just like Simon and Andrew did.

The urgency of our calling

Christ often seems to enter into our lives and make his claim upon us unexpectedly, randomly, and sometimes without even an invitation. He wades into the waters of our existence and walks along the shore of our very being. He calls out to us often when we are in the midst of urgent tasks or caught up in the hustle and bustle of daily living. We are interrupted.

There is no ideal time to receive the call; Christ comes when and how he wills and he always causes disruption. 'Follow me' sounds like such a simple command, of course we will follow, but at what cost? What do we have to leave behind and put down? What do we have to leave unfinished?

We know that this following will entail a complete change of heart and mind and a turning away from the old self, towards the one who makes all things new. There is never time to look back when Christ calls us and, whether figuratively or literally, we have to drop everything and immediately rise up and follow; there is no time for prevarication.

Andrew responds to Christ in this way, an example to all of us, and is with him until the very end. He is there when Jesus feeds the five thousand and he is there always pointing to Jesus when others are beginning to respond. He is there at the Last Supper. He is there when Jesus appears in the upper room when the doors were locked.

What miracles he would have witnessed, what teaching he would have received. This life-changing encounter leads Andrew to places he could only have imagined. His calling leads him beyond his comfort zone to embark on missionary endeavours that ultimately lead to his martyrdom, to the cross he himself was called to bear.

As an apostle, his net is cast widely over the sea of this world, gathering in those who hear Christ calling them. Andrew was still a fisherman at heart, but as one who was sent in the name of Christ his catch in the end was, as Jesus said, not fish but people.

Victoria Johnson

Suggested hymns

Will you come and follow me?; *Jesus calls us o'er the tumult*; *Follow me, follow me, leave your homes and family*; *Above the voices of the world around me*.

Harvest Festival
Don't Worry!
Joel 2.21–27; Ps. 126; 1 Tim. 2.1–7, *or* 1 Tim. 6.6–10;
Matt. 6.25–33

Over-anxious

Have you noticed how many television programmes there are at the moment that cater for people who worry about their lives? In an idle moment I went through the TV guide and counted 67 programmes in just one week on terrestrial TV that are about houses, clothing or food. They are programmes that claim to have the answers to our anxiety about ourselves and often stress that if we change the image – the surface things – then all will be well. We love these programmes – we lap them up! There's a real challenge in today's Gospel. It's a challenge from Jesus to stop worrying about things and start trusting God. Don't fret about the way you look, Jesus tells us. Don't worry about what you will eat or drink, don't worry about your body – your health or your self-image. Jesus points us to nature to show us examples of God's creation in all its intricacy, simplicity and beauty. God feeds the birds and clothes the flowers: God will tend us too. The Greek word that's used in this passage for 'worry' is a term that means over-anxious, a state of mind where we are over-concerned about things – where anxiety has begun to take over so that we can no longer be the person God wishes us to be because we're so tense and stressed about life. Frenzied activity is a symptom of this type of anxiety – and that's very prevalent in our society. There's a deep need to work harder and harder, longer and longer hours. The last to leave the office is the hero, not the one who spends the most time with their family. Sometimes we worry so much that we can't sleep at night. Jesus calls us to be free from this type of anxiety – it's a dead end, he says. 'Can any of you by worrying add a single hour to your span of life?' Jesus is tough about this. He links over-anxiety with a lack of faith and trust in God.

358

Priorities

Jesus says that God knows what we need and provides it. Harvest reminds us of that. Everything we have comes from God and belongs to God. We celebrate that fact today by bringing a little of it here to be blessed and given back to God, and then distributed to those in need. By bringing harvest gifts into church first, rather than distributing them directly to our local food banks, care centres or social projects, we are recognizing that everything comes ultimately from God and does not belong to us. It's important too that we don't give just once a year. We should constantly be looking at the hurting and hungry places in our world and communities and helping to provide for them. God provides for all, but the world doesn't always ensure that the sharing out of God's provision is fair or just. Redistribution of resources is a justice issue. Jesus' concern is with priorities. God comes first. We are called to love God, and be committed to finding and doing God's will. God is to come first in our lives and not be crowded out by our material concerns and worries. If we seek God first, and work to establish his kingdom of justice and peace, then, says Jesus, God will take care of the rest. There's a very challenging South African saying that goes: 'It's our job to be faithful; it's God's job to provide.'

God's provision

God promises to provide for our needs. Through the prophet Joel, God tells the earth, the animals and us not to fear. God tells us to rejoice and be glad, to expect God to be good, to celebrate God's goodness shown in the good things that come from the earth. God promises never to put us to shame but to pour out the Holy Spirit so that all people may live life to the full in God's presence. Through our baptism we have a share in that life of the Holy Spirit, and become part of the body of Christ. At the Eucharist we receive together as a body Jesus in our midst feeding and nourishing us. This is God's ultimate provision. But it doesn't stop there. Jesus gives himself for the whole world – God's provision of God's self is for all, and so part of our calling this morning is not only to stop worrying about ourselves but to turn and face outwards – and to hold up to God creation to be blessed and distributed. There are many worriers in our world. People worry about yesterday and tomorrow, next week and next year. People tied up with worrying about the future can miss out on God's gift of today – given in love for all. So, this week as we thank Jesus for God's gifts at harvest time, we need to curb our worrying. We need to let go, relax and enjoy God's goodness and provision. More importantly, we need to go out to others and find loving ways, however small, of stopping them being anxious too. What can you provide this week that will help another not to worry? Ask the Holy Spirit to point you in the direction of someone who needs to experience God's loving provision. Don't worry – God will be with you!

Catherine Williams

Suggested hymns

Come, ye thankful people, come; When I needed a neighbour; All creatures of our God and King; You crown the year (Hillsong).

All-Age Services

Crib Service
Comfort and Calm Continuing ...
Luke 2.1–20

Preparation

Before the talk, ask volunteers to bring forward all of the items for the crib – Mary, Joseph, the crib, Jesus, animals and the wise men. Place the wise men to one side. Make sure you draw attention to items in the scene as you go through the talk, ensuring that Jesus is in the crib for the talk.

Comfort

(*Ask for a volunteer from the congregation (adult or child). Ask the volunteer to create an action for 'comfort', such as giving themselves a hug. Each time you say 'comfort', ask the volunteer to lead the congregation in doing that action.*)

The scene in the stable includes signs of comfort. There is Mary, caring for her newborn son Jesus, and making sure he has everything he needs to bring him comfort, wrapping him up warmly and laying him on soft straw. We can be pretty sure that Joseph would have been doing the same for his beloved Mary, trying to comfort her through the pain of childbirth, and giving her comfort now the baby is safely in the crib. There may have been animals gathered there, no doubt bringing comfort to each other.

But away from the crib there were words of comfort being shared to the shepherds on the hillside. Shocked by a choir of angels in the sky, they were told words of 'comfort and joy' – hope for all people because of that new baby in the crib, Jesus, the Son of God. With those words of comfort in their minds and hearts the shepherds rushed to see Jesus and brought comfort to the scene.

The crib scene reminds us that God sent Jesus to bring comfort to us, and to the world. As the crib scene shows us comfort, so God wants to comfort us whether our lives are great or difficult and challenging. God brings comfort.

Calm

(*Again, ask a volunteer to create an action for 'calm', such as moving their hands downwards. Ask the other volunteer to listen out for 'comfort' as you continue.*)

The crib scene shows comfort, and it shows calm too. The excited shepherds rushed down from the hillside, and when they found Jesus lying in the crib they probably calmed down to avoid disturbing him, and joined the scene of comfort and calm.

Mary knew that Jesus would be special, and as the shepherds left she thought about all that had happened, and could be calm knowing that God was with her through all this, as he had promised to be. And the baby, when fed and sleeping, lay in the crib, cosy and calm.

In the busyness, noise and activity of Christmas it is important that we find time to be calm, and think about that baby in the crib. Now is a good time to stop for a few seconds and think about the busy things in your life where you need calm, and to promise to God who offers us comfort and calm to remember the calm of the stable and crib on Christmas Day.

Continuing

(*First, ask for suggestions as to what 'continuing' means. Then ask a volunteer to do an action, such as rolling hands forward.*)

The crib scene has Mary, Joseph, animals, the crib and Jesus, and later wise men join the scene (*move the wise men into the crib scene at this point*). This is a picture of comfort, and a sign of calm. But that scene is part of a continuing story! God promised to send his son Jesus hundreds of years before Jesus was born, and Mary was told by an angel that she would have a special baby. The story is continuing. Mary and Joseph travelled a long way, and ended up in a stable, putting Jesus in a crib after he was born. Then, later, wise men visited Jesus, Mary and Joseph. And the story is continuing. Jesus grew up, lived, died and rose again. The story is continuing now, from the crib two thousand years ago to us in this church right at this moment. God's story of comfort whatever we face, and calm, whatever takes up our time and energy, is continuing. As the continuing story of

362

God's love is seen in the crib, God calls us all to think about Jesus, to remember Jesus, and most importantly, just like those shepherds, to worship Jesus. For us the story is always continuing.

(*Make sure you thank the volunteers at the end of the talk.*)

Nick Harding

Suggested hymns

Any Christmas carols and songs, except those that include the wise men.

Christingle
Sharing and Shining

Preparation

For this talk you will need a complete Christingle, and one in component parts. Ideally have a different voice read the short Bible passage at the beginning of each section.

> Genesis 1.1: In the beginning when God created the heavens and the earth.

(*Lift up the orange.*) God shared his creation with us. Right at the beginning of what we think is time there was nothing ... but God shared his creativity. Slowly he made the earth as we know it, and he shared it with us people. Out of darkness came light – the light of God that shines on his world. The orange, part of the Christingle, reminds us that God shares it with us. But that's not all, as we all have a responsibility to share the world and the world's resources with each other, all people, and all God's creation.

> Ecclesiastes 3.1: For everything there is a season, and a time for every matter under heaven.

(*Lift up the four sticks with fruit or sweets on.*) As part of God's creativity he made seasons, so that crops could grow, so that time passes, and so that we are given all we need. The sticks remind us that God shares his seasons with us, and shares the things that grow so we can eat. The light shines in the daytime, and the sun shines to encourage fresh and new growth. We can enjoy the sweets/fruit on these sticks, and as we do so we remember the four seasons.

They remind us that God sends light to make good things, and God shares his good things with us.

Philippians 2.8: [Jesus] humbled himself and became obedient to the point of death – even death on a cross.

(*Point out the red band.*) The wonders of God's creation and the seasons that God shares with us are not the only things God offers all people. The red band around the orange as part of the Christingle has a sad meaning – it reminds us that Jesus was shared with us and he died for everyone. He did that so that we can be forgiven and know the love of God not just at Christingle and Christmas, but in every season he shares and every day of our lives. God shared his son Jesus for all of us to be the best ever gift. For a moment, as Jesus died, the whole earth was covered in darkness … but light came shining after it.

John 8.12: 'I am the light of the world. Whoever follows me will never walk in darkness but will have the light of life.'

(*Pick up a candle.*) The light that went out as Jesus died shone even more brightly as he came alive again, and lives on everywhere and in each of us. The candle reminds us that God shares the light of Jesus with us, and that light shines all the time. The light of Jesus shines when we are excited and good things are happening, like at this time of the year. But God also shares the light of Jesus to be with us and help us when bad things happen and we get sick or sad. God shares, and Jesus shines for us and in us.

(*Hold up the complete Christingle.*) The Christingle reminds us of God sharing and shining. He shares the world, the seasons, the food we eat, and his son Jesus with us. The light shines on the world so that things grow, and the light of Jesus shines on us all the time, and takes away the darkness. As you take your Christingle home, remember sharing and shining, and have a think about how you can share the love of God, and be light to shine, helping others. Let's all share and shine!

Nick Harding

Suggested hymns

Christmas songs and carols; Light of the World; This little light of mine; Like a candle flame.

Mothering Sunday

Introductory activity (optional)

Show some photographs (on the screen or passed around). Make sure that some are clear and it is easy to see what is happening and what people are feeling, and some that are not clear at all, maybe faded and old. Discuss with the congregation which pictures are easier to see and relate to than others and why.

Talk

Can you think of something that you have wanted so much that you just cannot stop thinking about it? Perhaps you were hoping for something for Christmas. Perhaps you have desperately wanted your teenager to come home when they have missed their curfew so that you can go to bed and stop worrying. Perhaps you really, really want your parents to give in and get a puppy or a kitten. Perhaps when you wake up on a Monday morning, you really don't want the meeting, presentation or exam you have been dreading to arrive.

Sometimes we can be really obvious about our longings. Maybe we drop subtle hints whenever there is an advert for what we want on the TV. Maybe our grumpy snapping at people might show that we just want to go back to bed and pull the duvet over our head. Sometimes, though, our longings are hidden from everybody, perhaps even from ourselves, because we don't want to admit our pain and disappointment.

It is very easy to look at other people and see something that we want and don't have. Maybe we look at the single person and wish we had the tranquility of their Sunday morning. Maybe we look at the families and wish we had the love and companionship that they seem to share. Maybe we look at other people's children or parents and wish ours were cooler or better behaved like theirs.

The Bible tells us that God knows all of these thoughts and feelings. Jesus describes himself as the Light of the World. It is easy to think that this is just about sunshiny skies and joy, but it is also about light that exposes. Before digital cameras, we used to 'expose' a photograph. (*Consider having pictures of this process on the screen, or linking it to the photos you showed earlier.*) The exposure to the light brought out the true picture. Jesus' light reveals everything. It shows our best bits, the bits that we like and are prepared to put on the wall. It shows our worst bits, the ugly bits that we would prepare to hide, but it also shows our attitudes to things that matter to us.

(*Ask for eight volunteers to come up to the front and line up facing the congregation in height order. If you are concerned this might take a long time, ask some beforehand, selecting a good range of heights.*)

The prophet Samuel was sad that Saul had not turned out to be the king he and the people of Israel had hoped that he would be. God exposed this sadness for what it was, a longing for something that was no longer in God's will, and a fear of what might happen, rather than a hope and obedience to his plan. When he recognized the truth of what God was saying, Samuel set out to Bethlehem to anoint one of Jesse's sons as the new king that God had chosen. We might think that because Samuel was a prophet, a special messenger for God who could hear God speaking to him directly, he would find it easy to make choices that made God happy, but Samuel was just like the rest of us – very good at deciding things about people just because of the way they look.

When Jesse introduced his first son Eliab (*move to the tallest person and pretend to judge their height and strength*), Samuel thought that because he was big and strong he was definitely the king that God had chosen. But God said, 'No. He is not the one. You are looking at his outward appearance, but I look at the heart.'

Jesse introduced his second son, Abinadab (*move to the next tallest person and pretend to judge their height and stature*), but God said, 'No' (*encourage the congregation to join in with the 'No' as you approach and reject the next five volunteers*). Jesse had apparently run out of sons, but then they sent for the youngest, David, who was looking after the sheep and wasn't seen as important enough to meet the prophet. When David arrived, God said, 'Yes, this is the one. Anoint him as the next king' (*place a cardboard crown on your smallest volunteer's head*).

God could see that David's heart was in the right place. He loved God and wanted to do the things that gave God joy and showed other people how amazing he is. Samuel's eyes were open to the possibilities that God is not interested in power or status, or even physical strength or beauty, but what is in their heart – what somebody thinks, says and does (*point to the heart, brain, lips and hands of 'David' as you say this last sentence*).

David wrote lots of poems called psalms about his friendship with God, many of which show that being a friend of God is not always easy, and sometimes we can feel like he doesn't understand our longings and is not listening to our thoughts and feelings. On Mothering Sunday we celebrate the gift of God's parent love for us and the people that he gives us to care for and be cared for by. But for many this is a difficult day, filled with pain and longing for loved ones who are not around for all sorts of reasons. David's Psalm 23 reminds us that we can hold on to the truth of God's light in our lives, even when it feels like we are walking in a dark valley.

(*Read Psalm 23; if you have somebody who can sign, ask them to sign this as you read.*)

Prayer idea

(*Encourage the congregation to join in with the actions as you pray and respond with the refrain, 'Thank you that your light shines in our life'.*)

Heavenly Father,
(*hands on heart*) Thank you that your light shines in our life. Thank you that you know all the thoughts and feelings that we have. Help us to take comfort in the truth that you know the longings of our hearts even when we might feel like we are all alone and unheard.
Thank you that your light shines in our life.
(*hands on head*) Thank you that your light shines in our life. Thank you that your Holy Spirit helps us to know who you are and how much you love us. Help us to think about ways that we can give you joy and show other people how amazing you are.
Thank you that your light shines in our life.
(*hands on lips*) Thank you that your light shines in our life. Thank you that we can say things that help other people to know that they are loved and heard. Help us to speak kindly to each other.
Thank you that your light shines in our life.
(*hands out in front, palm up*) Thank you that your light shines in our life. Thank you that we can do things that bring light into other people's lives. Help us to listen to your prompting, like Samuel, and do things that show how much you love them.
Thank you that your light shines in our life.

Carolyn Edwards

Notes

1 Cited in J. P. Mitchell, *Visually Speaking*, London: T & T Clark, 1999, p. 236, n20.
2 F. Craddock, *Preaching*, Nashville, TN: Abingdon Press, 1985, p. 95.
3 James Jones, in Mitchell, *Visually Speaking*, p. 236, n20.
4 Cited in T. G. Long and E. Farley, *Preaching as a Theological Task: World, Gospel, Scripture*, London: Westminster John Knox Press, 1996, p. 45.
5 Support for biblical scholarship is powerfully argued by John Barton in *The Nature of Biblical Criticism*, London: Westminster John Knox Press, 2007.
6 G. Theissen, *On Having a Critical Faith*, London: SCM Press, 1979, p. 82.
7 See Kate Bruce, *Igniting the Heart*, London: SCM Press, 2015.
8 H. Anderson and E. Foley, *Mighty Stories, Dangerous Rituals*, San Francisco, CA: Jossey-Bass, 2001, p. 48.
9 Walter Wink, *Transforming Bible Study: A Leader's Guide*, Eugene, OR: Wipf & Stock, 2009, p. 110.
10 W. Willimond, *The Intrusive Word*, Grand Rapids, MI: Eerdmans, 1994, p. 68.
11 William O'Malley, cited in David Day, *A Preaching Workbook*, London: Lynx, 1998, p. 3.
12 See 'The Forms that Make Preaching Compelling', in *The Canterbury Preacher's Companion 2020*, London: Canterbury Press, 2019, pp. xix–xxvii.
13 Cf. Craddock, *Preaching*, p. 25.
14 H. D. Gadamer, cited by A. C. Thistleton, 'The New Hermeneutics', in I. H. Marshall (ed.), *New Testament Interpretation*, Exeter: Paternoster Press, 1979, p. 316.
15 Raewynne J. Whiteley, sermon entitled 'Preaching Trouble', available from Anglicans Online, www.anglicansonline.org.
16 W. Willimon, *Undone by Easter*, Nashville, TN: Abingdon Press, 2009, p. 40.
17 R. Williams, *Meeting God in Mark*, London: SPCK, 2014, p. 7.
18 S. S. Montefiore, *Jerusalem*, London: Weidenfeld and Nicolson, 2011, p. 56.

19 M. Oelschlaeger, *Postmodern Environmental Ethics*, New York: State University of New York Press, 1995.

20 Pope Benedict XVI, *Jesus of Nazareth*, London: Catholic Truth Society, 2011, p. 55.

21 See also p. 226, Fifteenth Sunday after Trinity, Principal Service.

22 This was in a programme by two actors, Sylvia Read and William Fry, from Theatre Roundabout, performing at Bradford Cathedral in 1969/70.

23 E. Underhill, *Worship*, 2nd edn, London: Nisbet and Co., 1937, p. 17.

24 A. E. Lewis, *Between Cross and Resurrection*, Grand Rapids, MI: Eerdmans, pp. 261ff.

25 See J. D. G. Dunn, *Jesus and the Spirit*, London: SCM Press, 1975, p. 351.

26 *Gospel of Thomas* in Nag Hammadi library.

27 See B. Hebblethwaite, 'The Problem of Evil', in G. Wainwright (ed.), *Keeping the Faith*, London: SPCK, 1989.

28 I am indebted to Barbara Glasson's book, *I Am Somewhere Else*, London: Darton, Longman & Todd, 2006.

29 It arguably makes more sense if the verses are split differently, sustaining the unity of verses 51–59.

30 E. Peterson, *Subversive Spirituality*, Grand Rapids, MI: Eerdmans, 1997, p. 237.

31 This sermon draws on the words of the centurion at the cross to address today's theme and thus departs from the *Common Worship* lectionary.

32 A. Bloom, *School for Prayer*, London: Darton, Longman and Todd, 1970. Luke 1.26–38.

33 Quoted in J. Robbins (ed.), *Is it Righteous to Be? Interviews with Emmanuel Lévinas*, Redwood City, CA: Stanford University Press, 2001, p. 256.

34 C. K. Barrett, *Freedom and Obligation*, London: SPCK, 1985, pp. 12ff.

35 Barrett, *Freedom*, p. 13, cf. p. 19.

36 I am indebted to Kenneth Cragg's book for inspiration for this sermon: *Peter and Paul, Meeting in Jerusalem*, Abingdon: Bible Reading Fellowship, 1980.

37 This sermon departs from the *Common Worship* lectionary readings in favour of a text that relates to both SS Peter and Paul.

38 W. Shakespeare, *The Merchant of Venice*.

39 G. B. Caird, *Saint Luke*, London: Penguin, 1963, p. 55.

40 St Michael's victory over the devil is portrayed in this statue by Sir Jacob Epstein, mounted on the side of the new Coventry Cathedral in 1958.

41 The 27-foot sculpture is made up of more than 100,000 weapons confiscated from 43 police forces across the country and was created by artist Alfie Bradley at the British Ironwork Centre in Oswestry, Shropshire.

42 Angela Tilby, *Church Times*, 3 April 2020, p. 13.

43 Tom Wright, *Surprised by Hope*, London: SPCK, 2007, p. 183.
44 Jürgen Moltmann, *The Coming of God*, London: SCM Press, 1996, p. 108.
45 Moltmann, *The Coming of God*, p. 106.
46 Moltmann, *The Coming of God*, p. 124f.
47 See Wright, *Surprised by Hope*, p. 184.
48 An example of this is to be found in *The Canterbury Preacher's Companion 2020*, ed. Roger Spiller (London: Canterbury Press, 2019), p. 267.

Acknowledgements of Sources

Permission to use extracts from the following publications is acknowledged with thanks.

Alan Bennett, 'Forty Years On', in *Forty Years On / Getting On / Habeas Corpus / Enjoy*, Faber & Faber, 1996.
R. S. Thomas, 'The Bright Fields', in *Collected Poems: 1945–1990*, Weidenfeld and Nicholson, 2000.
Rainer Maria Rilke, *Rilke's Book of Hours: Love Poems to God*, trans Anita Burrows and Joanna May, Riverhead Books, 1996.
W. H. Vanstone, 'Morning glory, starlit sky', in *Love's Endeavour, Love's Expense*, Darton, Longman & Todd Ltd, 2007.

Index of Names and Subjects

Aaron 239
  the Exodus 93–4
  'Let my people go' 215–17
abiding
  community and 271–2
Abinadab 366
Abram
  God says, 'Go' 79–80
Adam and Eve 73–5, 280
Advent 2–20
Advent Hope (Mursell) 7–8
ageing 258–9
All Saints' Day 351–3
All Souls' Day 354–5
*All the Words that the Lord
  Has Spoken Will Do*
  (Kilworth-Mason) 238–40
ambition 187–9
St Andrew the Apostle
  Feast Day 356–7
  responds to Jesus 356–7
angels
  St Michael and All Angels Day
  344–6
Anna, Simeon and 299–300
Annunciation Day 304–6
'Another King, One Jesus?' (Spiller)
  292–4
St Antony the Great 247
apocalypse 345
Apostle to the Apostles (Saleh)
  328–30
Aquinas, St Thomas 330
Ark of the Covenant 244
As You Like It (Shakespeare) 259
Ascension Day 139–44

Ash Wednesday 69–71
Ask for the Ancient Paths (Bruce)
  161–4
St Augustine of Hippo 264
authority
  good citizenship 177–9
  of Jesus 53–5
The Authority of Jesus
  (Spiller) 53–5

Babylon
  exile in 152–3, 265–6
  Ezekiel's vision in 156–8
Backstairs to Glory (Spiller) 49–51
baptism
  of Jesus 39–44
  mission and 143
St Barnabas the Apostle
  introduces Paul 324
  key player in Christianity 318–20
St Bartholomew the Apostle
  body in Lipari 338
  Feast Day 338–40
  sparse details of 339
Bartimaeus 255–7
'Be Opened!' (Burdon) 222–4
Becket, Thomas 282
Before the Days of Trouble (Spiller)
  258–9
Behold – Look Again (Saleh) 313–15
The Beloved Disciple (Mursell)
  284–6
Benedict, Pope, on creation 61
Bengal, J. A. 262
Bennet, Alan
  Forty Years On 154

Between a Rock and a Hard Place (Spiller) 182–4
birds 265–7
Blake, William 210
blame 34–6
Blessed are Those Who Have Not Seen (Johnson) 326–8
Blessed Reconciliation (Daffern) 219–21
The Blessed Virgin Mary (Overend) 304–6
Bloom, Archbishop Anthony 305
Boasting in Christ (Johnson) 187–9
Bonhoeffer, Dietrich 91, 184
Boxing Day 282
The Bread of Life (Spiller) 203
'The Bright Field' (Thomas) 166
Bruce, Kate
  Ask for the Ancient Paths 161–4
  With God it's Always Bread Week 199–200
  Inconvenient Truths 167–9
  Jesus the Storm Bringer 233–5
  May You Unwrap Hope this Christmas 21–3
  The Thin Black Line of the Horizon 117–19
  What Do You Want Me to Do for You? 255–7
  Where to Invest the Ultimate Trust? 306–9
Buber, Martin
  I and Thou 34
A Bunch of Amateurs (Williams) 149–51
Burdon, Christopher
  'Be Opened!' 222–4
  The King Who is No King 277–9
  A Little Child 231–3
  Living for Ever 208–10
  Salesman or Lover? 246–8
  Speaking in Parables 164–6
Burkett, Christopher
  Clouds of Glory in the Fog 62–5

calm in the stable 362

Cambridge, Duke and Duchess of 136
Cana wedding 49–51
Candlemas 299–301
Carriers of Hope (Williams) 347–9
Catholic Church
  doctrine of justification 295
  place of Mary in 306
The Centrality of Jesus (Williams) 58–60
The Centurion's Confession (Mursell) 274–6
A Challenge to the Nations (Spiller) 96–8
Charles, Prince of Wales 136
Chesterton, G. K. 96
children, wisdom of 231–3
Chocolat (film) 204
Christ on the Cold Stone sculpture 91
Christ the King 277–81
Christianity
  Christians persecuted 306, 307–8
  doctrine of justification 295
  evangelists and hope 347–9
  Jewish and Gentile 318–20, 325
  Prayer for Unity week 294–6
Christingle 363–4
Christmas season 21–39
  Christmas Day 21–9
Church
  as a market 82–3
  as 'mother' 88–9
  restoration of 189–90
Church Cleansing (Spiller) 81–3
citizenship, good 177–9
Clouds of Glory in the Fog (Burkett) 62–5
collaborative preaching
  attention and participation xxiv–xxvi
  dialogue with scripture xxii–xxiii
  engaging with the congregation xviii–xx
  events and issues in scripture xx–xxii
  imagination xxiii–xiv

Comfort and Calm Continuing ...
  (Harding) 361–3
comforting 361–2
community
  caring for the weak 237
  communion of Christ 352–3
  confidence through 85
  with the dead 351–3
  hope in 47–8
  hospitality 236–7
  inclusivity 236
  Jesus in Nazareth 180–2
  mothering 88–9
  mutual abiding 271–2
  reflecting on history 224–6
  social Christianity 147–9
  Trinity as 154–5
  united in worship 131–3
Complete the Story (Spiller) 110–12
confidence
  in Christ 84–5
  in self 83–4
Confidence and Credentials (Spiller)
  83–5
congregations
  attention and participation
    xxiv–xxvi
  collaborative preaching and
    xvii–xx
  traditions 217–19
consumerism 164
continuing 362–3
Conversion of St Paul Feast 297–9
Corpus Christi 316–17
The Cosmic Christ (Spiller) 32–4
Costly Discipleship (Williams)
  282–4
Cotes, Mary
  God's Family Values 159–61
Coventry Cathedral, *Knife Angel*
  346
Craddock, Fred xxi, xxiv–xxv
Cranmer, Thomas 321
creation
  the cosmic Christ 33–4
  God and Christingle 363–4
  our place in 206–8

credentials, displaced 83–4
Crib Service 361–3
Cromwell, Thomas 321

Daffern, Megan I. J.
  Blessed Reconciliation 219–21
  Departures 93–5
  The Future is Bright 46–8
  Living Vocation 125–7
  The Lord Has Judged 9–11
  Love from of Old 122–4
  Whole in Spirit 151–3
Dali, Salvadore 91
Dante Alighieri
  Divine Comedy 342
David, King 366–7
Day of Thanksgiving for the
  Institution of the Holy
  Communion (Corpus Christi)
  316–17
death
  community with 351–3
  facing 196
  love and 341–2
  Paul's closeness to 348
  symbols and hope 354–5
  worship breaches divide 353
Declaring Your Identity (Spiller)
  226–8
Denis, Trevor 199
Departures (Daffern) 93–5
departures, the Exodus and 93–4
despair, ancient paths away from
  161–4
Diana, Princess of Wales 136
disasters, hope and 272–4
disciples
  give up all 247–9
  Mark's Gospel and 241–3
  start as amateurs 149–50
  see also individual disciples
distance, metaphors of 243–5
Does History Have Meaning?
  (Herbert) 320–3
*Does the Snake Speak with Forked
  Tongue?* (Kilworth-Mason) 73–5
Don't Worry! (Williams) 358–60

Doubting Thomas? (Hopkins)
115–17
Dream of Gerontius (Newman) 211
Duffy, Eamon 321
Dyer-Perry, Philip
Learn How to Receive 103–5

Easter
Easter Day 110–15
Vigil of 108–10
Edward VI 321
Edwards, Carolyn
Mothering Sunday 365–7
Egypt
the Exodus from 93–4
Moses and Aaron 215–17
Elgar, Edward
Dream of Gerontius 211
Eli 56–7
Eliab 366
Elijah
fugitive from God 65–8
God's voice 280
sees glory 334
Eliot, T. S. 201, 294
Elizabeth
birth of John the Baptist 322
Mary and 302, 306, 313–15, 336
environment, human responsibility
for 61
Epiphany 34, 39–57, 292–4
eternal life 87
Ethiopian Coptic Church 129–31
Eucharist
bread and 204–5
handing on 316–17
Eve 73–5
exile
in Babylon 113, 152, 156–7
flying and 265–7
reflecting on 224–5
return from 27–9
servant of the Lord in 42–4
*Expectations Reset in the Potter's
Workshop* (Spiller) 2–4
Ezekiel
exile in Babylon 113

new Spirit 151–2
vision of 156–8

The Face of Love (Saleh) 333–5
faith
fear and trust 170–2
renewal of 94–5
restless 165–6
resurrected Jesus and 120–2
St Thomas and 326–8
talking about 227–8
theology and 172–4
without measure 134–6
fear
awe of God 211–12
disciples in boats 242
trust and 170–2
The Fear of Fear (Spiller) 169–72
The Fear of God (Herbert) 210–12
Fiddler on the Roof (musical) 218
food
bread churches 203–4
bread week 199–200
daily bread 127–9
feeding the hungry 194–6
forgiveness 7–8
Forster, E. M. 227
Forty Years On (Bennet) 154
Fowler, James xix–xx
St Francis of Assisi 247
embraces poverty 339
Sister Water and Brother Moon 34
From Christ to Coca-Cola (Kemp)
90
Fullness of Life (Herbert) 134–6
The Future is Bright (Daffern) 46–8

Gadamer, Han-Georg xxvi
Gandhi, Mohandas K. (the
Mahatma) 128, 195
Gethsemane, Garden of 106, 251
giving, receiving and 103–5
Glasson, Barbara 203–4
glory, God's 157–8, 333–5
God
Abram and 79–80
Adam and Eve 74–5
as Christ-like 310–11

covenant with 122–4
creation and 363–4
daily food 127
distance metaphors and 243–5
'gave his only Son' 85–7
gift of land to Israel 248–50
glory of 157–8, 333–5
goodness of 163
hope and 348–9
knowing 145
love of 263–4, 340–1
mercy of 267–9
Moses meets on mountain 239–40
as parent eagle 265
provides 358–60
renewal of people 152–3
returning to 52–3
sacrifices to 192–3
seeing 309–10
servant of the Lord 42–4
sovereignty of 98
stories of 25–6, 31
suffering and 78
the Trinity and 154–6
trust in 170–2
unity of 156
voice of 279–81
wisdom and 202–3
worship of 131–3
God So Loved the World (Mursell)
340–2
'God so loved the world ...' (Spiller)
85–7
*God's Faithfulness and Historical
Evidence* (Spiller) 248–50
God's Family Values (Cotes)
159–61
God's Fugitive (Spiller) 65–8
Goes, Hugo van der 289
good, choosing 163
Good Citizens: Good Neighbours
(Williams) 177–9
Good Friday 106–7
Good News (Spiller) 297–9
gospels
good news 12–13
living 16–18

grace, covenant and 123–4
Gregory I, Pope 328, 330
Growing Up with Jesus (Spiller)
30–2

Hagar 314, 315
Handel, Georg F.
Messiah 198
Harding, Nick
Comfort and Calm Continuing ...
361–3
Sharing and Shining 363–4
Harvest Festival 358–60
Healing and Wholeness (Spiller)
175–7
Heaven's Above (Kilworth-Mason)
156–8
Henry VIII 320–1
Herbert, Christopher
Does History Have Meaning?
320–3
The Fear of God 210–12
Fullness of Life 134–6
Legends of Saints 338–40
Living the Gospel 16–18
A Memorable Meal 342–4
Moving Closer to God 243–5
Out of the Depths 267–9
The Power of Names 289–91
Shaking the Foundations 191–3
The Voice of the Lord 279–81
Who is to Blame? 34–6
Herod
insecure power 287–9
John the Baptist and 185–6
the Temple and 273
Herodias 185–6
Hinduism 281
history, looking forward and 224–6
Holy Cross Day 340–2
The Holy Innocents 287–9
Holy Spirit
nourishing guidance 150–1
the Trinity and 154–6
Holy Week 96–107
hope 46–8
Advent 7–8

Christmas and 21–3
in community 47–8
the kingdom to come 272–4
prophecies 18–20
realistic 47
stories of the past and 224–6
Hope for the World (Johnson)
272–4
Hopkins, Michael
Doubting Thomas? 115–17
Hughes, Gerry 145–6
human beings, falling and rising
60–2

I and Thou (Buber) 34
Inconvenient Truths (Bruce) 167–9
International Society for Human
Rights 307
Into the Wilderness (Spiller) 71–3
Isaiah
context of 4–6
expectations 2
hope and 347
Philip and the Ethopian 129–30
vision of worship 132–3
wine harvest festival 99–101
Israel and Jerusalem
Babylonian exile 265–6
bread and 199–200
cleansing the Temple 81–3
destruction of Temple 182–4, 273,
307
exile 152–3
the golden vine 130
Jericho and 248–50
love song to 27–9
Paul's theological conflict 172–4
revolutionaries 306
Samuel's story of 56
the vine 130

Jairus and daughter 175–6
St James the Apostle (son of
Zebedee)
Feast Day 331–3
glory of Jesus and 333–4
a good seat for 331–3
responds to Jesus 356–7

St James the Apostle (the Just)
gentleness of wisdom 232
Jewish and Gentile Christians
318–20
on judgement 222–3, 224
as 'pillar' 323
Jehoshaphat 9–11
Jenkins, Bishop David 155
Jeremiah
despair and 162
inconvenience and hope of 167–9
new covenant 91
reluctant spokesman 182–4
on the temple 81
Jericho
God and Israel 248–50
Jesse and his sons 366–7
Jesus' Baptism (Spiller) 39–41
Jesus Christ
abiding with 270–2
ambition and 187–9
ascension 139–44
authority of 53–5
baptism of 39–44
at Bethany 101–3, 116
Biblical signposts to 260–2
body and blood of 204–5, 213–15
bread as flesh of 209
building disciples' trust 241–3
centrality of 58–60
the centurion and 274–6
child-like wisdom 231–3
cleansing the temple 81–3
community and discipleship 235–7
confidence in 84
Cosmic Christ 32–4
crucifixion of 91–2, 106–7, 274–6
death and 355
depictions of 90–2
end of story 110–12
the Eucharist 316–17
expectations of 3–4
feeding the hungry 194–6, 199
Galilee and 111–12
given by God 85–7
glory of 333–5
gospel of hope 348–9

healing 175–7, 222, 255–7
'I am the bread of life' 195, 200
identity check 226–8
in Jerusalem 97
Jewish community of 336
judging others 222–4
king and lord 98, 277–9, 292–4
knowing 144–6
light of the world 365–6, 367
'look busy' 189–91
Mary Magdalene and 329–30
as Messiah 76–7, 270–2
naming of 289–91
Palm Sunday 96–8
parables of 164–6
the Paraclete 140–1
peacemaking 220
Peter and 125–7
Pharisees criticize 343–4
political problems 185
prays for unity 295–6
prays for us 256–7
predictions of 307
prophecies of 19–20
purpose and impact of death
   251–3
purposes of the heart 253–5
resurrection of 109–10, 111–12,
   114–22, 253
sacrifice of 193, 252
as salesman 246–8
scandalizes Nazareth 180–2
seeing 44–6
self-giving 104–5
social gospel 147–9
speaking out 159–61
stories of 25–6, 31–2
storm on Lake of Galilee 170–2
taking up the cross 70
Thomas's doubt and faith 115–17,
   326–8
the Trinity and 154–6
voice of 280–1
the wedding at Cana 49–51
in the wilderness 72–3
women at the tomb 118
wounds of 120–2

Jesus on His Terms, Not Ours
   (Spiller) 180–2
Jesus Provokes Key Questions
   (Spiller) 349–51
Jesus the Storm Bringer
   (Bruce) 233–5
Jethro, concern about Moses
   228–30
Jewish people and Judaism
   Christian Jews 318–20, 325
   family of Jesus and 336
   Herod's kingship and 287–8
   king of 292–4
   martyrdom and 252
   Stephen and 282–4
Job
   creation and 206–7
   vindication and 197–8
   wisdom 201, 202
Job's Search for Vindication (Spiller)
   196–8
John of Patmos 341
St John the Apostle and Evangelist
   abides with Jesus 284–6
   Feast of 284–6
   follows Jesus 356–7
   glory of Jesus and 333–4
   mother and brother 331–3
   sorrow of 106
John the Baptist 40
   beheading of 185
   Feast Day 320–3
   Jewish community 336
   violent death of 251
Johnson, Victoria
   *Blessed are Those Who Have Not
      Seen* 326–8
   Boasting in Christ 187–9
   Hope for the World 272–4
   *Looking Back and Looking
      Forward* 224–6
   The Purposes of the Heart 253–5
   Ready to be Judged 14–16
   Seeing Christ 44–6
   The Social Gospel of Christianity
      147–9
   Someone Else's Shoes 311–13

Sorrow and Love Flow Mingling Down 106–7
St Andrew the Apostle 356–7
A Worshipful Company 131–3
Jonah 267–9
Jones, Rt Rev. James xviii
Joseph/Barsabbas 312
St Joseph of Nazareth
  considers divorce 313
  Feast of 301–4
  role in Jesus's life 301–4
  in the stable 361–2
Joshua, Jericho and 248–50
Judas Iscariot 350
  betrayal by 106
  death of 312
  Mary of Bethany and 102
St Jude the Apostle 270–1
  causes and 350–1
  Feast Day of 349–51
St Jude's Question (Mursell) 270–2
judgement
  discrimination and 222–4
  salvation and 86–7
The Jungle Book (film) 73–4
justice theme of prophets 5–6

Kemp, Martin
  From Christ to Coca-Cola 90
The Key to Mark's Gospel (Spiller) 241–3
Kierkegaard, Søren 50, 62
Kilworth-Mason, Wendy
  All the Words that the Lord Has Spoken 238–40
  Does the Snake Speak with Forked Tongue? 73–5
  Heaven's Above 156–8
  Repent (Turn to God) and Do Justice 4–6
  The Royal Wedding 136–8
  The Servant of the Lord 42–4
  A Sinister Song in a Vineyard 99–101
  When God Says Let Go 78–80
The King Who is No King (Burdon) 277–9

kingship 277–9
  Herod's insecurity 292–4
Knowing Jesus (Mursell) 144–6
Kolbe, Maximilian 77–8
Korahites 137

Lange, Ernst xxi
Learn How to Receive (Dyer-Perry) 103–5
Legends of Saints (Herbert) 338–40
Lent 69–95
  Sundays before 58–68
Levinas, Emmanuel 317
Lewis, C. S. 281
life
  dry bones 113–14
  eternal 208–10
  living for today 127–9
light
  creation 58
  in the darkness 56–7
The Light was Still Burning (Saleh) 56–7
The Little Book of Wisdom 201
A Little Child (Burdon) 231–3
Living for Ever (Burdon) 208–10
Living Inside Out (Spiller) 217–19
Living Just for Today (Spiller) 127–9
Living the Gospel (Herbert) 16–18
Living the Trinity (Spiller) 154–6
Living Vocation (Daffern) 125–7
Looking Back and Looking Forward (Johnson) 224–6
The Lord Has Judged (Daffern) 9–11
love
  death and 341–2
  of God 263–4
  God's covenant and 124
  of Jerusalem 27–9
  Jesus and 248
  Mary of Bethany's adoration 102–3
  mutual abiding 271–2
  of neighbours 179, 262–3
Love for God (Spiller) 262–4
Love from of Old (Daffern) 122–4

St Luke the Evangelist
Feast Day 347–9
Lutheran Church 295

MacCulloch, Diarmaid 321
Magi worship the king 293–4
Making Space at Christmas
(Mursell) 23–5
Mantel, Hilary 321
St Mark the Evangelist
Feast of 306–9
writing the Gospel 306–7
Martha of Bethany
service to Jesus 101–2
sorrow of 106
Mary, Blessed Virgin
the annunciation 348
Annunciation Day 304–6
Christmas 23–4, 30–1
comfort and calm in the stable
361–3
Feast Day 335–7
Joseph and 301–3
the Magnificat 335–7
soul-piercing 88
visits Elizabeth 313–15, 336
Mary I, Queen 321
St Mary Magdalene
as apostle 329–30
Feast Day 328–30
prostitute? 328–9, 330
Mary of Bethany
anointment of Jesus 101–3
sorrow of 106
Mary's Witness to God's Upheavals
(Spiller) 335–7
Maslow, Abraham 195
St Matthew, Apostle and Evangelist
Feast Day 342–4
St Matthias the Apostle
Feast of 311–13
steps into role 312–13
Maundy Thursday 103–5
*May You Unwrap Hope this
Christmas* (Bruce) 21–3
A Memorable Meal (Herbert)
342–4

Merton, Thomas 263
Messiah (Handel) 198
St Michael
and All Angels Day 344–6
The Knife Angel 346
Michaelmas 344–6
mission
commissioning 142–4
knowing Jesus 144–6
making disciples 142–3
teaching 143
Moltmann, Jürgen 352
Moses
bronze serpent and 86
the burning bush 211–12
the Exodus 93–4
food supply and 127
glory and 334
Jethro's concern about 228–30
'Let my people go' 215–17
meets God on mountain 239–40
parting the sea 225
the people and covenant 239
preaching to Israelites 122–3
Moses and Aaron: The Plan is Set
(Saleh) 215–17
Mothering Sunday 88–90, 365–7
Moving Closer to God (Herbert)
243–5
Mursell, Gordon
The Advent Hope 7–8
The Beloved Disciple 284–6
The Centurion's Confession
274–6
God So Loved the World 340–2
Knowing Jesus 144–6
Making Space at Christmas 23–5
Restoring the Future 189–91
The Second Pancake 69–71
St Jude's Question 270–2
Two Kinds of Love 101–3
What Christians Do 316–17
A World Turned Upside-down
108–10
music
fear and hope 210–11
the voice 279–81

mystery
  fog and clouds of glory 62–5

names, power of 289–91
Naming and Circumcision of Jesus
  289–91
Nathaneal 44–5, 309
neighbours, love of 179
New Branches (Williams) 129–31
Newman, St John Henry 128
  Dream of Gerontius 211
Nineveh 267–8
Now it's Our Commissioning!
  (Spiller) 142–4

'Ode on Intimations of Immortality'
  (Wordsworth) 64–5
'Only Human?' (Spiller) 60–2
Out of the Depths (Herbert) 267–9
Overend, Barrie
  The Blessed Virgin Mary 304–6

Palm Sunday 96–101
Passiontide 93–5
Passover 93, 97
St Paul the Evangelist
  ambition 188
  Barnabas and 318–20
  bondage to decay 252
  the cosmic Christ 32–3
  credentials 83–4
  discrimination 223
  embodied worship 38
  Feast Day 323–5
  Feast for Conversion of 297–9
  feeling near death 348
  Jewish-Gentile conflict 172–4
  keeping the gospel 298
  name of Jesus 291
  new creation 165
  receiving Eucharist 316
  relationship with God 263–4
  riches and poverty 31
  on secular rulers 178
  seeks out Peter 323–5
  the spirit of adoption 155
  supreme and sufficient Christ 59

walking by faith 165
  wisdom of God 202–3
Pentecost 149–51
  Novena of 144
Perumbalath, John
  *The Practice of Community
    Discipleship* 235–8
Peter and Paul's Agenda (Spiller)
  323–5
St Peter the Apostle
  brother, Andrew and 356–7
  the clean and unclean 223
  confidence of 150
  denies Jesus 106, 108–9, 116
  Feast Day 323–5
  finds vocation 125–7
  following Jesus 285
  glory of Jesus and 333–4
  heading for Jerusalem 63–4, 65
  Jesus as salesman 247
  Jesus washes feet of 104
  Jewish and Gentile Christians
    318–20
  Matthias and 312
  new understanding 118–19
  Paul seeks out 323–5
  suffering of Jesus 76–7
Pharisees
  criticize Jesus 343–4
  the Sabbath and 254
St Philip the Apostle
  Feast of 309–11
  feeding the hungry 194
  'show us the Father' 309–11
  Wilderness Road encounter
    129–31
Phoenician royal wedding 137–8
Pius XI, Pope
  Christ the King feast 277–8
  politics, violent use of 184–6
Polkinghorne, Revd Prof John 352
Pontius Pilate
  Christ the King and 278
poverty
  Mary and 313–15, 336–7
power relations
  the first and last 231–2

The Practice of Community Discipleship (Perumbalath) 235–8
Prayer for Christian Unity, Week of 294–6
preaching
  sermon in the world xxvi–xxvii
Presentation of Christ in the Temple 299–301
Prophecies that Fuel Hope (Spiller) 18–20
purification 14–16
The Purposes of the Heart (Johnson) 253–5

Qoheleth 258–9

Ramsey, Archbishop Michael 205, 310
  keeping time with God 230
Ramsey, Ian, Bishop of Durham 230
Ready to be Judged (Johnson) 14–16
reconciliation 219–21, 275–6
  revelation and 346
Remembrance Sunday 275–6
Repent (Turn to God) and Do Justice (Kilworth-Mason) 4–6
restoration
  of church 189–90
  of the future 190–1
Restoring the Future (Mursell) 189–91
Return to God (Spiller) 51–3
returning
  Easter Day 113–15
  to God 52–3
  remarrying 51–2
Revealing the Angels (Saleh) 344–6
The Right Man at the Right Time (Spiller) 318–20
Rilke, Ranier Maria
  The Book of Hours 266–7
Rome
  AD 69 307
  unswept floors mosaics 342–3

Route Map and Signpost to Jesus (Spiller) 260–2
The Royal Wedding (Kilworth-Mason) 136–8

Sabbath, time for 190
sacrifice
  historical view 192–3
saints
  All Saints' Day 351–3
  communion of 351–3
Saleh, Carey
  Apostle to the Apostles 328–30
  Behold – Look Again 313–15
  The Face of Love 333–5
  The Light was Still Burning 56–7
  Marking the Meaning 299–301
  Moses and Aaron 215–17
  Revealing the Angels 344–6
  Trust Our Heaviness 265–7
  We're Coming Home! 27–9
  You Shall Live! 113–15
Salesman or Lover? (Burdon) 246–8
Salome 186
salvation, judgement and 86–7
Samuel
  Israel and 56–7
  Jesse's sons and 366–7
San Bartolomeo alla'Isola church 338
Sansom, C. J. 321
Satan, Michael and 345
Saul 366
scripture
  dialogue with xxii–xxiii
  events and issues xx–xxii
  narrative imagination xxiii–xxiv
  'texts of terror' xxii
The Second Pancake (Mursell) 69–71
Securing the Best Seats (Spiller) 331–3
Seeing Christ (Johnson) 44–6
Seeing Jesus (Spiller) 90–2
Seeing the Father (Spiller) 309–11
self-discipline 237–8

serpents 73–5
  Moses and bronze 86
The Servant of the Lord
  (Kilworth-Mason) 42–4
Shakespeare, William
  As You Like It 259
Shaking the Foundations (Herbert)
  191–3
Sharing and Shining (Harding)
  363–4
Shaw, Julia 287
Shelter, Festival of 99–101
shepherds, adoration of 289–90
Sign-posting the Messiah (Williams)
  11–13
Simeon, Anna and 299–300
St Simon the Apostle 349–50, 351
  Feast Day of 349–51
sin, original 74–5
A Sinister Song in a Vineyard
  (Kilworth-Mason) 99–101
slavery
  Sojourner Truth speaks 159,
  160–1
social Christianity 147–9
The Social Gospel of Christianity
  (Johnson) 147–9
Soderblom, Nathan, Archbishop of
  Uppsala 229
Someone Else's Shoes (Johnson)
  311–13
*Sorrow and Love Flow Mingling
  Down* (Johnson) 106–7
sorrow, Jesus weeps and 106–7
Soul-piercing (Williams) 88–90
space
  for Jesus 145–6
  making 23–5
Spiller, Roger
  'Another King, One Jesus?' 292–4
  The Authority of Jesus 53–5
  Backstairs to Glory 49–51
  The Bread of Life 203–5
  A Challenge to the Nations 96–8
  Church Cleansing 81–3
  Complete the Story 110–12
  Confidence and Credentials 83–5

The Cosmic Christ 32–4
Before the Days of Trouble 258–9
Declaring Your Identity 226–8
*Expectations Reset in the Potter's
  Workshop* 2–4
The Fear of Fear 169–72
Feed the Hungry 194–6
'God so loved the world …' 85–7
*God's Faithfulness and Historical
  Evidence* 248–50
God's Fugitive 65–8
Good News 297–9
Growing Up with Jesus 30–2
Healing and Wholeness 175–7
Jesus' Baptism 39–41
Jesus on His Terms, Not Ours
  180–2
Jesus Provokes Key Questions
  349–51
Job's Search for Vindication
  196–8
The Key to Mark's Gospel 241–3
Living Inside Out 217–19
Living Just for Today 127–9
Living the Trinity 154–6
Love for God 262–4
The Management of Love 228–30
Mary's Witness to God's Upheavals
  335–7
Now it's Our Commissioning!
  142–4
'Only Human?' 60–2
Peter and Paul's Agenda 323–5
Prophecies that Fuel Hope 18–20
Return to God 51–3
The Right Man at the Right Time
  318–20
Between a Rock and a Hard Place
  182–4
Route Map and Signpost to Jesus
  260–2
Securing the Best Seats 331–3
Seeing Jesus 90–2
Seeing the Father 309–11
*Strengthening Our Community
  with the Dead* 351–3
Suffering to End Suffering? 76–8

384

'Those who eat my flesh ...'
213–15
When Going is Also a Coming
139–41
When People Get in Our Way
185–7
When Theology and Experience
Clash 172–4
Who Do You Want to Murder?
287–9
Why Did Jesus Die? 251–3
Into the Wilderness 71–3
Wisdom 201–3
Worship: A Living Sacrifice 37–9
spirituality, the wilderness and 71–3
St Andrew the Apostle (Johnson)
356–7
St Stephen's Feast 282–4
stories
  endings 111–12
  God's 31
  Jesus's 31–2
Stories (Williams) 25–7
storms, Jesus and 233–5
Strengthening Our Community with
  the Dead (Spiller) 351–3
suffering
  Job 197–8
  voluntary and involuntary 69–71
Suffering to End Suffering? (Spiller)
76–8
Symbols of Hope (Ward) 354–5

Tanner, Mary
  The Unity for Which Jesus Prays
  294–6
Temple, William 194
Tennyson, Alfred, Lord 245
St Teresa 263
Tertullian 330
The Book of Hours: Love Poems to
  God (Rilke) 266–7
theology
  logic and belief 172–4
The Thin Black Line of the Horizon
  (Bruce) 117–19
Thistleton, Tony xxvi

Thomas, R. S.
  'The Bright Field' 166
St Thomas the Apostle
  doubt and faith 115–17, 326–8
  Feast Day 326–8
Thoreau, Henry David 188
Thorneycroft, Lord 2
'Those who eat my flesh ...' (Spiller)
  213–15
time
  beginnings and endings 299–301
  history of clocks 191–2
  living forever 208–10
  words for 209–10
Timothy
  Paul and civil authority 178
Titus, Barnabas and 318
traditions
  challenging and respecting 217–19
The Transfiguration of Our Lord
  333–5
The Trinity
  commissioning and 143–4
  as community 154–5
  unity of God 156
Trinity season 154–259
trust, disciples and 241–3
Trust Our Heaviness (Saleh) 265–7
Truth, Sojourner 159, 161
Two Kinds of Love (Mursell) 101–3

Underhill, Evelyn 103
The Unity for Which Jesus Prays
  (Tanner) 294–6

Vanstone, Bill 279
violence, power and 184–6
Visit of the Blessed Virgin Mary to
  Elizabeth 313–15
vocation 182–4
Vocation Sunday 125–7
The Voice of the Lord (Herbert)
  279–81

Ward, Brett
  Symbols of Hope 354–5
  Wounded Resurrection 120–2

wars
  reconciliation and 275–6
Watts, Isaac 342
weddings
  at Cana 49–51
weddings, royal 136–8
We're Coming Home! (Saleh) 27–9
What Christians Do (Mursell)
  316–17
*What Do You Want Me to Do for
  You?* (Bruce) 255–7
When God Says Let Go
  (Kilworth-Mason) 78–80
When Going is Also a Coming
  (Spiller) 139–41
When People Get in Our Way
  (Spiller) 185–7
*When Theology and Experience
  Clash* (Spiller) 172–4
Where to Invest the Ultimate Trust?
  (Bruce) 306–9
Whit Sunday 149–51
Who Do You Want to Murder
  (Spiller) 287–9
Who is to Blame? (Herbert) 34–6
Whole in Spirit (Daffern) 151–3
Who's Cradling Jesus? (Wright)
  301–4
Why Did Jesus Die? (Spiller) 251–3
wilderness 71–3
  becalmed sea and 128
  Moses and Aaron 216
Williams, Catherine
  The Big Picture 206–8
  A Bunch of Amateurs 149–51
  Carriers of Hope 347–9
  The Centrality of Jesus 58–60
  Costly Discipleship 282–4
  Don't Worry! 358–60
  *Good Citizens: Good
    Neighbours* 177–9
  New Branches 129–31
  Sign-posting the Messiah 11–13

Soul-piercing 88–90
Stories 25–7
Williams, Archbishop Rowan
  good news 7
  praying 294
Willimon, Revd William xxvii
wine and vineyards
  harvest festival 99–101
  new branches 130–1
Wink, Walter
  connecting with scripture xxiii
wisdom
  of a child 231–3
  God and 202–3
  searching for 201–2
With God it's Always Bread Week
  (Bruce) 199–200
the Word
  Jesus and 58–9
Wordsworth, William
  'Ode on Intimations of
    Immortality' 64–5
work, management of 228–30
world 340–1
A World Turned Upside-down
  (Mursell) 108–10
worry 358–60
worship
  breaching death's divide and 353
  in company 131–3
  sacrifice to God 37–9
Worship: a Living Sacrifice (Spiller)
  37–9
Wounded Resurrection (Ward)
  120–2
Wright, Stephen
  Who's Cradling Jesus? 301–4
Wright, Tom 352

You Shall Live! (Saleh) 113–14

Zechariah 322

  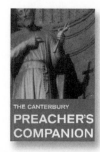

Advance order for the 2022 editions *(available May 2021)*

quantity

Prices are subject to confirmation and may be changed without notice

CANTERBURY CHURCH BOOK & DESK DIARY 2022 *Hardback*   **£19.99** + p&p* ....

CANTERBURY CHURCH BOOK & DESK DIARY 2022 *Personal Organiser* (A5)   **£19.99** + p&p* ....

CANTERBURY PREACHER'S COMPANION 2022 *Paperback*   **£19.99** + p&p* ....

For details of special discounted prices for purchasing the above in any combinations
or in bulk, please contact the publisher's Norwich office as shown below.

Order additional copies of the 2021 editions

Subject to stock availability

Hardback Diary **£19.99***..............

Preacher's Companion **£19.99*** ....   A5 Personal Organiser **£19.99*** ....

Ask for details of discounted prices for bulk orders of 6+ copies of any individual title when ordered direct from the Publisher.

Sub-total £................

*Plus **£2.50** per order to cover post and packing (UK only): £................

All orders over £50 are sent POST FREE to any UK address.
Contact the Publishers office for details of overseas carriage.

TOTAL AMOUNT TO PAY: £................

I wish to pay by ...

... **CHEQUE** for £ .... made payable to **Hymns Ancient and Modern Ltd**

... **CREDIT CARD** All leading credit and debit cards accepted (*not American Express or Diners Club*)
Your credit card will not be debited until the books are despatched.

Card number: ....   Expiry: ____ /____

Issue No: ____ Valid from: ____ /____

Switch or Maestro only

Signature of
cardholder: ....   Security code:_____

Last three digits on signature panel

Please PRINT all details below.

Title: ....   Name: ....

Delivery address: ....

....

....

.... Post Code: ....

Telephone or e-mail: .... Date: ....

Please ensure you have ordered the edition you require for the correct year. No liability will be accepted for incorrect orders

Return this order form or a photocopy – with details of payment – to

Norwich Books and Music, 13A Hellesdon Park Road, Norwich NR6 5DR

Telephone: 01603 785900   Fax: 01603 785915   Website: www.canterburypress.co.uk